Ethical Decision-Making Using Artificial Intelligence

Scrivener Publishing
100 Cummings Center, Suite 541J
Beverly, MA 01915-6106

Publishers at Scrivener
Martin Scrivener (martin@scrivenerpublishing.com)
Phillip Carmical (pcarmical@scrivenerpublishing.com)

Ethical Decision-Making Using Artificial Intelligence

Challenges, Solutions and Applications

Edited by

Sapna Juneja

Rajesh Kumar Dhanaraj

Abhinav Juneja

Malathy Sathyamoorthy

and

Asadullah Shaikh

Scrivener Publishing

WILEY

This edition first published 2025 by John Wiley & Sons, Inc., 111 River Street, Hoboken, NJ 07030, USA and Scrivener Publishing LLC, 100 Cummings Center, Suite 541J, Beverly, MA 01915, USA

For more information about Scrivener publications please visit www.scrivenerpublishing.com.

Wiley Global Headquarters
111 River Street, Hoboken, NJ 07030, USA

For details of our global editorial offices, customer services, and more information about Wiley products visit us at www.wiley.com.

The manufacturer's authorized representative according to the EU General Product Safety Regulation is Wiley-VCH GmbH, Boschstr. 12, 69469 Weinheim, Germany, e-mail: Product_Safety@wiley.com.

Library of Congress Cataloging-in-Publication Data

ISBN 9781394275281

Cover image: Generated with AI using Adobe Firefly
Cover design by Russell Richardson

Set in size of 11pt and Minion Pro by Manila Typesetting Company, Makati, Philippines

Printed in the USA

10 9 8 7 6 5 4 3 2 1

Contents

Preface

Artificial Intelligence (AI) systems are being trusted with ever-more complicated decisions which influences security, well-being, and the fundamental foundation of our societies as they develop in intelligence and autonomy. These choices have substantial repercussions for both individuals and communities in a wide range of fields, including healthcare, finance, criminal justice, and transportation. This book examines the complex relationship between artificial intelligence and the moral principles that guide its application. This book offers helpful advice for people, businesses, and politicians by attempting to provide a thorough framework for comprehending the ethical aspects of AI decision-making. The fundamental concerns surrounding AI ethics, to direct the creation and use of AI systems is well addressed. This book is written for a wide range of readers, including AI experts, decision-makers, ethicists, academics, students, and anyone else interested in the tremendous effects that AI is having on our society and the ethical issues it raises. In order to promote responsible AI development and deployment that is consistent with human values and goals, our goal is to equip readers with the knowledge and skills they need to traverse the ethical landscape of AI decision-making.

1

Standards, Policies, Ethical Guidelines and Governance in Artificial Intelligence: Insights on the Financial Sector

Purohit S.[1] **and Arora, R.**[2*]

[1]*Symbiosis Institute of Business Management, Nagpur, Symbiosis International University, Maharashtra India*
[2]*University School of Business-MBA, Chandigarh University, Punjab, India*

Abstract
The financial sector has significantly benefited from the use of Chatbots for maintaining relationships with clients. The financial service chatbots offer personalized and fast assistance to clients by making use of artificial intelligence and natural language processing and are capable of helping with transaction details to deal with queries related to the accounts. Through automation and quick assistance, these financial chatbots improve the communication process and improve engagement. Thus, a large volume of queries can be handled without human intervention, and therefore the operational efficiency of financial institutions is improved and the costs are reduced. While financial chatbots seem promisingly advantageous, they present challenges related to ethical concerns in the processing of financial data or bias. It is therefore pertinent for financial institutions to take security and privacy measures and take steps to mitigate bias while deploying chatbots for financial service assistance. With the development of technology, the integration of artificial intelligence and service chatbots would probably increase in the financial service sector for enhanced customer experience. Therefore, in this chapter, we explore the pivotal issue of mitigation of bias related to the financial service chatbots. For this purpose, we reviewed the existing literature, examined the practical and real-world impacts of AI-related bias, and described the strategies for mitigation of bias in the financial service sector. By showcasing the importance of ethical considerations by the financial firms for building investor trust, we contribute to the

**Corresponding author*: rakhi.e7437@cumail.in

Sapna Juneja, Rajesh Kumar Dhanaraj, Abhinav Juneja, Malathy Sathyamoorthy and Asadullah Shaikh (eds.) Ethical Decision-Making Using Artificial Intelligence: Challenges, Solutions and Applications, (1–26) © 2025 Scrivener Publishing LLC

shaping of a fair, transparent, and inclusive use of AI-powered chatbots. For bias mitigation, a robust system is required that requires the involvement of varied stakeholders such as design experts, policymakers, and industry stakeholders.

***Keywords*:** Chatbots, financial sector, technology, artificial intelligence (AI), customer service and bias mitigation

1.1 Introduction

Artificial intelligence (AI) has emerged as one of the prime technologies for digital metamorphosis in financial service firms [1]. The evolution of AI and its applications has transfigured the service delivery to the customers of financial service sector firms and their client-relationship management systems [2]. AI plays a vital role in financial service firms by assisting in risk assessment, market analysis and investment decision making [3]. AI has been deployed by many financial service firms for customer support because the AI-based agents can offer a superior customer experience at a lower cost [4]. The deployment of AI has redefined how financial service firms interact and engage with their clients. From among the various AI-based agents such as text-, voice- and image-based, text-based chatbots have gained wide popularity among firms [5–10]. One of the reasons for the popularity of the text-based chatbots [11] is the high use of message apps by millennials, the generation born between 1980 and 2000 [12]. Millennials prefer to chat to reduce direct conversations [13]. Chatbots have been highly accepted among businesses due to their capabilities that can improve customer satisfaction [14, 15]. AI-based service chatbots have been deployed by many firms to offer customer services [16–21]. Through AI-powered financial service chatbots, these firms have streamlined their customer service operations [21] and improved the efficiency and accessibility of financial services [22]. The financial service chatbots can deal with a range of customer queries and can offer quick and personalized assistance [23]. While the financial service chatbots offer a wide range of benefits to financial firms and customers, their use has posed challenges related to the ethics and potential presence of bias in their responses to investors [24–32]. Hence, in this chapter, we investigate and describe the mitigation of bias related to the deployment of AI-powered financial service chatbots. Mitigation of AI-related bias is critical to the building of trust among investors and the promotion of fairness and inclusion within the complex financial service sector. If the responses of financial service chatbots are biased, issues of trust, transparency and social disparities may emerge, leading to mistrust among stakeholders and clients.

One of the reasons the issue of bias is critical to the financial service industry is that the customers are from diverse backgrounds [33]. While on the one hand, chatbots can offer the advantages of streamlined customer interactions and timely information, the algorithmic design can lead to inherited biases, posing challenges to customer services [34–38]. These biases can be related to gender stereotypes, racial prejudices, and socioeconomic assumptions that can impact the nature of responses thus de-benefiting certain user groups [39]. Comprehending and addressing the issue of bias in financial chatbots is not only a technical issue but also a matter of ethical concern [40]. Finance-related decisions significantly impact individuals, and businesses and biased interactions can result in unequal information access and discrimination and thus affect trust in financial relationships.

Therefore, in this chapter, we present an overarching scenario of financial service chatbot bias. A detailed background of bias in AI is provided in this chapter with a focus on chatbots used by financial institutions for customer care. We also explore the real-world consequences of biased interactions with customers, financial institutions, and broader societal perceptions. We explore the ethical issues associated with the usage of chatbots in finance and the transparency required to maintain user trust. We further assess some of the techniques and strategies for the detection and mitigation of bias in financial chatbots. Finally, we discuss the ethical considerations for the deployment of chatbots in finance.

1.2 Chatbots in the Financial Industry

A chatbot is also called a machine conversational agent; it is a software that uses natural language to interact with users [41]. Chatbots can be classified primarily as rule-based and self-learning chatbots [42]. Rule-based chatbots are based on keywords identified through previous customer interactions. However, as these are limited to specific keywords, customers have to look for options or a human agent for the queries that are beyond the keywords [43]. Self-learning chatbots are based on trained datasets and can answer questions beyond the predefined keywords. Therefore, these are heavily based on conversational datasets, machine learning or artificial intelligence for training [44].

Due to the advancement of chatbot technologies [45] and expansion of financial services chatbots are significantly utilized in varied domains such as financial services. These have been applied to areas such as personal advertising [46], financial services [1], banking [47] and more. Prior studies have evaluated the effect of use of chatbots on customer satisfaction and found that positive customer satisfaction depends on the accuracy and credibility of information given by the chatbots [48]. Chatbots have also been used in healthcare [49, 50], the learning domain [51, 52], tourism [53, 54] and others.

Among the various use applications of chatbots in industry the most common are automated customer service [55], assisted self-service technology or for the support of human agents [56–59]. Additionally, they are used to support the preferred non-face-to-face interactions of millennials [60].

The chatbots are generally expected to be quick and accurate in their response for a better customer service. With the advancement in AI technology, chatbots can make use of natural language processing to increase the accuracy of their response. AI chatbots can provide varied services like handling financial queries, offering quick responses. These virtual financial assistants can provide personalized recommendations, guide customers through complex financial processes, and offer valuable insights to help them make informed decisions about their money by leveraging a pool of knowledge data base and related real-time data. It is therefore pertinent to develop efficient and accurate algorithms for training of chatbots. To this end, prior scholars have developed and proposed algorithms to improve chatbot learning for a higher accuracy of response. Further, a study on human vs. chatbot agents has revealed varied outcomes with respect to the accuracy and quality of responses during interactions [61–63].

The financial industry is considered to be a pioneer in the use of chatbots and other AI applications [64]. The burgeoning number of financial firms strive to improve their customer services for a competitive advantage [39, 40]. It was difficult for financial services industry customers to find accurate information on products, processes and systems [65]. It was also time-consuming for the financial customer service industry to handle a large number of queries related to accounts and loans [65]. Chatbots are able to handle such customer queries through advanced algorithms and training [66–68]. The financial service industry possesses a lot of sensitive customer information that raises privacy concerns among customers who use chatbots [69, 70]. A lot of information, such as use of credit card, expenditure and investment habits, is tracked and the use of chatbots creates fear among customers regarding security [71]. With a plethora of studies on chatbots in financial services [72, 73] it is imperative to understand chatbot bias for a detailed understanding that can facilitate enhanced customer experience.

1.3 Background of the Study

For a comprehensive elaboration of the financial service chatbot bias, it is important to identify the dynamic nature of the financial service industry. Financial institutions serve a wide range of customers with varied financial needs, preferences, and challenges. Due to this variation, there is a wide range of financial inquiries made by customers. The level of familiarity of customers with the system, financial terminology, and processes is also different. Hence, the development and deployment of financial service chatbots is complex. The responses of AI-based chatbots are based on natural language processing and machine learning. The diverse customer background posits challenges in the comprehension and response to the wide spectrum of queries and creates room for biased responses de-benefiting a wide group of customers.

Biased interactions with chatbots are beyond technical concerns and affect the financial services landscape in various ways. One of the prime consequences of biased interactions with financial service chatbots is the loss of customer trust. Financial services are primarily based on consumer trust; loss of trust due to biased responses can have a multiplier effect in terms of the credibility of the financial service institutions and can severely affect customer relationships [74]. Apart from the repercussions for the institution, biased interactions can also have societal effects. The consistency of biased responses can increase social disparities and widen social gaps. For instance, if a chatbot favors a specific group it contributes to the socioeconomic disparities and thus widens the economic gap within the society. It is therefore important to understand the possible consequences of biases in financial service chatbot responses for financial institutions. Understanding the bias issues related to the deployment of AI would assist the financial service firms in the design and use of AI in a way that leads to ethical, fair, and inclusive delivery of financial services.

Financial service firms must account for technical and ethical aspects for a dynamic perspective while dealing with the issue of bias in financial service chatbots. Therefore, these firms must use and integrate technologies for detection of bias present in the chatbots during the design phase. Application of advanced algorithms might be useful in this regard. Continuous monitoring and auditing can assist the firms in handling and mitigating the bias issues. The firms must ensure that appropriate technologies are used so that the chatbots meet the norms of fairness, transparency, and accountability.

Financial decisions significantly affect investors and therefore bias-free interactions are important for the service chatbots in financial industries. If the interactions with the financial service chatbots are biased, investors can be exposed to information that is unfair, non-transparent, and non-inclusive, and this can impact their trust in the financial service firm. The deployment of a bias-free AI-powered system for consumer services is important for the maintenance of ethical standards and governance. Transparency in communication is essential for addressing these concerns. Financial service firms must follow the guidelines for the design, development, and deployment of AI-powered systems such as financial service chatbots for maintaining trust and long-term relationships with clients [75]. One of the ways in which trust can be fostered is through providing a rationale behind the investment-related recommendation. Additionally, the maintenance of security and privacy of sensitive financial information is important from an ethical viewpoint. Therefore, financial service firms must negotiate between the personalized services offered to the client and maintaining the security and privacy of investor information and data while deploying AI systems for financial service delivery [76].

This chapter navigates the technical and managerial perspectives to explore the mitigation of bias and related dynamics in the deployment of financial service chatbots.

1.4 Literature Review

The examination of bias in financial service chatbots is underpinned by the elaboration of overall bias concerning artificial intelligence. [77] emphasized the multi-dimensional aspect of bias ranging from gender, race, and socioeconomic and cultural prejudices that challenge fair decision-making in algorithm-based systems such as artificial intelligence. Other studies [78, 79] propose that financial chatbots inadvertently cause stereotypes reflecting biases that can cause dissatisfaction and lack of trust among users. Thus, financial institutions must ensure a system that ensures fair and bias-free interaction. The presence of bias can directly affect the experience of the users as they interact with financial service chatbots, making it crucial for financial institutions to proactively address these issues. The theoretical framework of [80] discusses the ethical dimensions of algorithmic accountability that call for a closer investigation of socio-technical systems that underpin AI applications. The framework offers insights into the ethical dilemmas concerning the use of financial service chatbots from a technological perspective. The bias related to the use of AI applications is illuminated in past studies from both design and governance perspectives. For instance, in the study [81] the authors showed the importance of diverse training datasets for mitigation of bias in AI-related applications. The study highlights that diverse datasets with varied information and backgrounds of investors must be used to train AI algorithms for the mitigation of bias in the responses from AI-powered financial service chatbots. Similarly, the study of [82] sheds light on the integration of fairness metrics and evaluation frameworks. Such a design can ensure fairness, transparency, and accountability in the AI systems.

Transparency can ensure ethical systems and the same can be ensured if the rationale behind a recommendation is given to the investor, or in other words the explainability of the AI as shown by [83]. Such systems showcase the decision-making process of AI and the rationale behind the responses, making it more trustworthy to the user. Such systems support the growing emphasis placed on the incorporation of explainability features in AI systems that allow financial institutions to bridge the gap between complex algorithms and user comprehension.

Recent studies [84, 85] have illuminated innovative strategies to mitigate biases in AI applications. Such strategies include continuous monitoring, adaptive learning mechanisms, and user feedback loops. Implementing and integrating such techniques is particularly relevant to the financial service chatbots where the needs of users and their conversations evolve over time. By adopting such strategies financial institutions can not only detect the presence of bias but also respond proactively to mitigate bias over a period of time.

One of the studies [86] discussed the concept of intersectionality manifesting the discrimination that can be applied to the bias in AI applications. Intersectionality explains the simultaneous bias experienced by individuals based on multiple factors such as gender, race, and socioeconomic status. The intersectionality angle adds profundity to the biased AI chatbot interactions. It highlights the need for strategies that account for the complex interplay of various identity factors in financial decision-making.

Studies [87, 88] explain the need for security in mitigating financial service chatbot bias. Secured AI systems can withstand external attacks and thus prevent bias that emerges from unpredictable circumstances. Security measures are also required to safeguard sensitive financial information and prevent malicious attacks on AI-based chatbot systems. Authors [89] have illuminated the human-AI collaboration by showcasing the synergies between humans and AI. Such a collaboration can assist with the mitigation of bias where humans can become experts to guide the AI systems and ensure bias-free decision making.

The regulatory environment of AI is evolving with a few components to deal with the bias in AI chatbots [90]. The regulatory environment plays a vital role in deciding the accountability of financial institutions for mitigating bias and ensuring ethical practices.

1.5 Understanding Bias in Customer Service Chatbots

It is pertinent to examine the dynamics at play to understand the bias in customer service chatbots within the financial service sector. Financial service chatbots are used to provide a seamless experience to users but they sometimes manifest bias in their responses to customer queries [91]. Understanding these biases, presented in Figure 1.1, is important for development of mitigation strategies. Other biases related to culture, language, and geographic region may affect the information communicated by the financial chatbot.

1.5.1 Categorizing Biases in Financial Chatbots

While the biases can be dynamic in nature, categorization of the biases can help in addressing the issue in financial service chatbots. The response of a chatbot may incorporate a gender bias affecting the way in which information is communicated to customers [92, 93]. Similarly, racial biases can affect investment-related recommendations. Socioeconomic biases [94] can

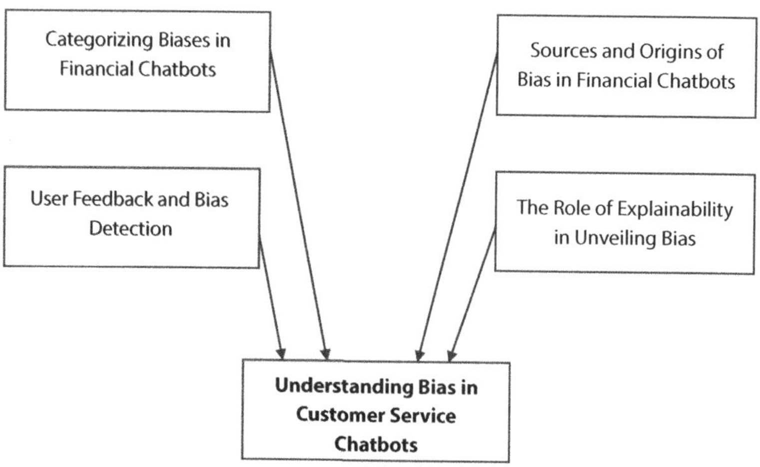

Figure 1.1 Understanding bias in customer service chatbots. Source: drawn by author.

impact the creditworthiness of the customer and hence affect investment-related recommendations.

1.5.2 Sources and Origins of Bias in Financial Chatbots

Biases in AI systems can come from diverse sources [95]. The bias can be introduced while selecting the training dataset for the AI chatbots. Selecting data that contains historical imbalances, societal prejudices or stereotypes can lead to bias [96] in the response of customer service chatbots related to investment. Algorithmic design choices may also affect the biases that lead to skewed responses. For instance, historical data records may contain systematic inequalities and when such data is used for training, the system may learn and reproduce those biases; hence bias may be introduced into the system [97]. An example to elaborate on is a credit scoring algorithm trained on historical data that favors a few segments that may inadvertently discriminate against other groups, perpetuating systemic biases in financial decision-making. Mitigating algorithmic biases requires careful consideration of design choices, diverse and representative datasets, and continuous monitoring for fairness [98].

1.5.3 User Feedback and Bias Detection

User feedback mechanisms can be crucial to the detection of biases in financial chatbots. Evaluation of the user feedback and interaction can assist in the identification of the pattern that indicates a biased response [99]. This user-centric perspective can act as a support mechanism to address the biases and guide iterative improvements in the chatbot design.

1.5.4 The Role of Explainability in Unveiling Bias

Recently, the concept of explainability [100] has gained traction among the users of AI for maintaining transparency of information among investors and mitigation of bias. Explainability refers to the presentation of the rationale behind a recommendation made by the chatbot to an investor that lies in the notion that the outcome must be reasonably understood by humans. Authors [101] emphasized that the explainability of an AI is essential for the maintenance of transparency in the decision-making process of financial service chatbots. Through explainability, firms can not only build trust among the investors but also identify and rectify biased responses through customer feedback. For fair and transparent systems, financial sector firms must integrate the feature of explainability into their financial service chatbots [102].

1.6 Impact of Bias in Financial Chatbot Interactions

Financial service firms must understand the biases in the interactions initiated by financial service chatbots. This is crucial for them to build client trust and a long-term relationship. In this section, we elaborate on the various possible consequences of biases in financial service chatbot interactions.

1.6.1 Customer Trust and Satisfaction

If the chatbot's interaction with the client is biased, the client may lose trust in the financial service firm. This is because a biased interaction affects the quality of a customer experience negatively [103]. If the chatbot's responses or financial advice are based on the socioeconomic or demographic profile of the investor, the investor may perceive unfairness in treatment and become dissatisfied. Hence, he may decide to terminate the relationship with the financial service firm, affecting the quality of the firm-client relationship [104].

1.6.2 Perpetuation of Inequalities

Biased responses of the financial service chatbots can amplify socioeconomic diversity. Biased recommendations can lead to a cycle of financial disparities. For example, biased credit scoring models may inadvertently disadvantage individuals from historically marginalized communities, exacerbating economic inequities [105].

1.6.3 Reputational Risks for Financial Institutions

If the overall customer experience is affected negatively by biased investment-related recommendations, the institutional reputation can be at stake [106]. This is because biased responses may lead to negative publicity and a negative perspective of the users. An increase in the reporting of such cases may tarnish the reputation of the institution, affecting its standing in the market and potentially leading to financial losses.

1.6.4 Regulatory Compliance Challenges

While the regulatory environment for AI and its applications is still ambiguous, financial institutions in every country must adhere to regulatory compliance [107]. Regulatory bodies increasingly scrutinize AI applications for fairness and ethical considerations. Instances of biased financial chatbot decisions may lead to regulatory interventions, fines, and heightened scrutiny, creating additional operational and legal challenges [108].

1.6.5 Implications for Brand Image

The brand image of an organization is closely linked to the perceptions of its customers and broad societal expectations [109]. Biased recommendations may be perceived as socially irresponsible behavior of the institution. This may significantly affect brand image by signaling a lack of inclusivity and fairness. Conversely, prioritizing unbiased interactions can enhance the institution's image as a socially responsible and customer-centric entity.

1.7 Strategies for Mitigating Bias in Financial Customer Service Chatbots

As evident from the previous discussion, addressing bias in financial customer service chatbots is crucial from a management perspective. This section outlines strategies mentioned in Figure 1.2 that can be used by financial institutions to ensure fair and unbiased interactions with customers through AI-driven chatbots.

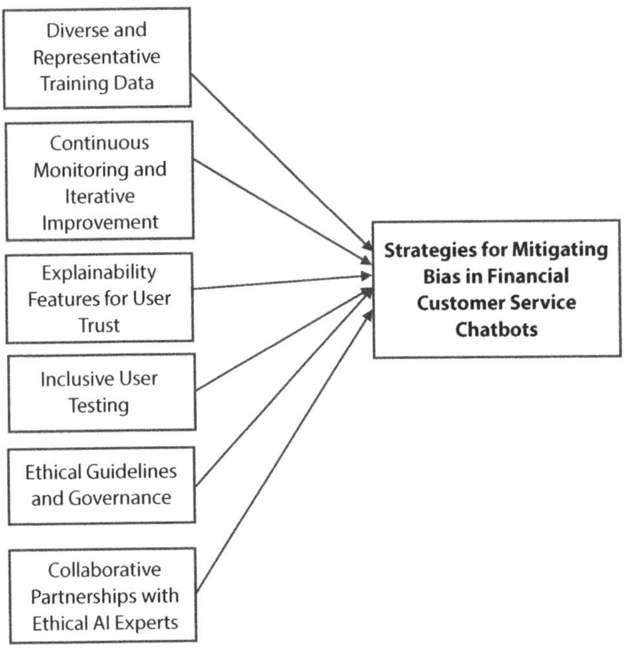

Figure 1.2 Strategies for mitigating bias in financial customer service chatbots. Source: drawn by author based on literature.

1.7.1 Diverse and Representative Training Data

There is a crucial role of the training datasets in the mitigation of bias in AI-powered financial chatbot interactions [110]. This is because the training datasets may contain segmented information based on narrow economic, geographic, or demographic profiles such as age, gender, ethnicity, socioeconomic status, geographic location, etc. The financial companies can create a model which may understand and respond quickly to customer needs based on a broad spectrum of financial behaviour and financial queries of the customers. It is therefore essential for financial firms to use diverse training datasets for the mitigation of bias [111].

1.7.2 Continuous Monitoring and Iterative Improvement

With the help of continuous monitoring systems, financial service firms can consistently evaluate the chatbot responses and user feedback for necessary and corrective actions [112]. This may help the financial service firms to detect the patterns indicating bias. Therefore, the firms can be guided on the use of appropriate datasets to adjust the chatbot responses and ensure fair treatment to the investors [113].

1.7.3 Explainability Features for User Trust

The careful development of AI systems can address the issue of bias [114, 115]. Integration of the explainability features in the financial chatbots can bring in more transparency and hence foster consumer trust. Financial decisions are risky with serious consequences and hence customers must understand the rationale behind a chatbot [116] recommendation. For instance, if a chatbot suggests a specific financial product, providing a clear and understandable explanation of how the recommendation was determined builds transparency and user confidence.

1.7.4 Inclusive User Testing

Inclusive user testing is recommended for the mitigation of bias in financial chatbots [117]. By engaging individuals with diverse demographic profiles in the testing phase, the chatbot can be trained to perform effectively across profiles and user segments. For instance, a financial institution conducting user testing involving individuals with different income levels and cultural backgrounds can uncover and address biases that may have otherwise gone unnoticed.

1.7.5 Ethical Guidelines and Governance

It is critical to build frameworks that serve as ethical guidelines to guide the firms towards responsible behavior and mitigate the bias in financial service chatbot interactions [118]. Additionally, financial service firms must establish their own ethical agendas and regulatory frameworks [119] for responsible adoption and integration of AI in their customer service systems. Such frameworks must encompass the broader organizational perspective and the alignment of organizational values to the AI chatbots to emphasize fairness, transparency, and accountability.

1.7.6 Collaborative Partnerships with Ethical AI Experts

Collaboration with AI experts would offer significant insights to the financial service firms for the design of AI service chatbots that are bias-free. With the help of such experts, financial firms can make use of specialized knowledge and expert opinion from an external perspective that can assist them in aligning their strategies with the latest developments concerning ethics [120] and industry best practices. For instance, financial firms can partner with academic or research centers for collaborative efforts to gain insights into the unbiased use of AI algorithms for their chatbots.

To summarize, it is important for financial institutions to gain a holistic understanding of AI dynamics and possibilities of bias to develop strategies that can assist them in addressing the bias and ethical concerns related to financial service chatbots. The financial service institutions can take various steps, such as the use of varied training datasets, integration of continuous monitoring systems, feedback, explainability features, framing of ethical guidelines, and collaborations with experts, to enhance investor trust and ensure fair and transparent systems. Such measures can help financial institutions improve customer experience while adhering to the ethical principles for a bias-free interaction with clients.

1.8 Ethical Considerations and Transparency in Financial Chatbot Firms

The application of AI in finance brings up moral concerns about privacy, bias, and regulatory compliance. Fairness in lending and investing decisions can be impacted by bias [121]. Concerns about privacy emerge from the widespread collection and processing of data [122]. Transparency in technology is a major ethical consideration from the user's point of view.

To foster trust, chatbots ought to integrate a level of ethical openness. To be fair, and accountable, and to maintain user privacy, financial institutions must eliminate prejudices and carry out their ethical obligations [123, 124]. A robust ethical framework may be provided by the financial institutions related to ethical standards and ethical assessments for correcting biases in chatbot responses. However, transparency is an important element in building trust and enables users to make their mindful decisions [125], going beyond the technicalities. Companies using chatbots should put more emphasis on transparency to prioritize the features, constraints, and data sources to support the financial system. With this, users may trust in the capabilities of the transparent system that will help in their financial decision-making and build confidence [126]. The users can have a meaningful interaction with the chatbot through the explainability feature that would reduce the potential bias in creating a self-assured user base. Though the users are using encrypted passwords, data protection is of the utmost concern for them. Financial companies should provide protection from the potential threats of security concerns of user's personal information. When the users are aware of the usage of their information with their consent, they feel secure. Financial chatbot companies should provide users with a safe and reliable environment for their financial transactions as per the ethical considerations and satisfaction of users in terms of maintaining the privacy of their data [127, 128]. The privacy and transparency of the user data can be promoted by involving stakeholders and ethical experts from outside of financial chatbot companies. The feedback process can also help the financial companies and the users in their decision-making process of using chatbots. Financial chatbot companies can increase user satisfaction by solving their issues with the help of customer feedback. With this, financial companies will be able to improve the long-term feasibility of their business and prioritize transparency with ethical practices [129, 130]. It will enhance customers' confidence leading to more usage of chatbots. Financial chatbot companies can have a nexus between ethics and technology for providing a transparent and ethical environment to the users of chatbots for the long-term viability of their business operations [131]. Based on this discussion, AI ethics principles, concerns and ethical considerations are summarised in Table 1.1.

Table 1.1 AI ethics principles, concerns and ethical considerations.

AI ethics principle and ethical concern	Ethical considerations
Justice	Treat users without unfair bias, discrimination or inequity
Beneficence	Ensure that interventions do good or provide real benefit to users
Privacy Concern	Fostering trust, to be fair and accountable to the users for providing a safe and reliable environment
Transparency concern	Building trust and enabling users to make their mindful decisions
Complaint resolution	Solving customer issues/complaints/ queries with the help of customer feedback
Explicability	Provide to users sufficient transparency about the nature and effects of the technology and be accountable for its design and deployment

Source: https://www.ncbi.nlm.nih.gov/pmc/articles/PMC10291862/ [131].

1.9 Future Directions and Recommendations

AI chatbots are useful tools for customer care of financial companies without waiting for an agent to provide any information. In the future, sophisticated virtual agents might even work as banking consultants, giving customers comprehensive financial advice. By leveraging vast amounts of financial data, market insights, and customer preferences, these intelligent assistants can provide highly personalized and data-driven recommendations to help individuals achieve their financial goals. Financial chatbot companies should facilitate diversified and multidisciplinary teams to develop AI systems and algorithms for identifying and eliminating bias in the future so that users' interaction with chatbots can be increased. The future of financial chatbots depends upon the ethical AI framework including privacy, transparency, and fairness, which should be developed and integrated with the collaborative efforts of industries and regulatory bodies. In addition to this, financial chatbot companies should make thoughtful choices about their chatbot's data sources and techniques to reduce bias. It is important that the firms ensure that the information provided by chatbot is accurate, timely, inclusive and ethical.

1.10 Conclusion

AI-based chatbots in financial service firms present both challenges and prospects. This chapter has explored bias in customer service chatbots and the impact of bias in financial chatbot interactions. The rising pertinence of chatbots to customer services has made mitigation of bias essential not only from an ethical but also a regulatory viewpoint. Financial firms must adopt strategic activities to address the bias issue. The design of chatbots must include bias-free training datasets, explainability features, and the promotion of continuous monitoring practices to boost the user's trust and confidence. Financial companies can develop AI algorithms to detect biases so that users can be assured of the privacy of their data. An ethical framework should also be developed by financial chatbot companies to avoid reputational risk and build their brand image. The success of financial chatbots is subject to the detection of biases and their mitigation under ethical guidelines. The significant role of AI will be increasing as the financial industry continues to evolve and adapt to the changing needs and expectations of consumers. Financial institutions can leverage the powerful AI tools to navigate the challenges and opportunities, shaping a combined future of technology and seamless finance working together to provide more inclusive, personalized, and secured financial experiences for all users. The findings of this chapter will be useful for financial companies in improving customers' chatbot service experience in the future so that they will have fair, ethical and accountable interactions.

References

1. Jang, M., Jung, Y., Kim, S., Investigating managers' understanding of chatbots in the Korean financial industry. *Comput. Hum. Behav.*, 120, 106747, 2021.
2. Hwang, S. and Kim, J., Toward a chatbot for financial sustainability. *Sustainability*, *13*, 6, 3173, 2021.

3. Bahrammirzaee, A., A comparative survey of artificial intelligence applications in finance: artificial neural networks, expert system and hybrid intelligent systems. *Neural Comput. Appl.*, 19, 8, 1165–1195, 2010.
4. Emerj, *Use cases of AI for customer service – what's working now*, 2018, Retrieved from https://emerj.com/ai-sector-overviews/ai-for-customer-service-use-cases.
5. Accenture, *Ready to talk: Banks are embracing the power of conversational banking*, 2018, Retrieved from https://www.accenture.com/us-en/insight-conversational-banking.
6. Suhaili, S.M., Salim, N., Jambli, M.N., Service chatbots: A systematic review. *Expert Syst. Appl.*, 184, 115461, 2021.
7. Sheehan, B., Jin, H.S., Gottlieb, U., Customer service chatbots: Anthropomorphism and adoption. *J. Bus. Res.*, 115, 14–24, 2020.
8. Nicolescu, L. and Tudorache, M.T., Human-computer interaction in customer service: the experience with AI chatbots—a systematic literature review. *Electronics*, 11, 10, 20221579.
9. Misischia, C.V., Poecze, F., Strauss, C., Chatbots in customer service: Their relevance and impact on service quality. *Procedia Comput. Sci.*, 201, 421–428, 2022.
10. Feine, J., Morana, S., Gnewuch, U., Measuring service encounter satisfaction with customer service chatbots using sentiment analysis, in: *14th International Conference on Wirtschaftsinformatik*, Siegen, Germany, February 24-27, 2019, 2019.
11. Schanke, S., Burtch, G., Ray, G., Estimating the impact of "humanizing" customer service chatbots. *Inf. Syst. Res.*, 32, 3, 736–751, 2021.
12. Hartman, J.L. and McCambridge, J., Optimizing millennials' communication styles. *Bus. Commun. Q.*, 74, 1, 22–44, 2011.
13. Forbes, *Phone calls, texts or email? Here's how millennials prefer to communicate*, 2017, Retrieved from https://www.forbes.com/sites/larryalton/2017/05/11/how-do-millennials-prefer-to-communicate.
14. Chung, M., Ko, E., Joung, H., Kim, S.J., Chatbot e-service and customer satisfaction regarding luxury brands. *J. Bus. Res.*, 117, 587–595, 2020.
15. Brandtzaeg, P.B. and Følstad, A., Why people use chatbots, in: *Internet Science: 4th International Conference, INSCI 2017*, Thessaloniki, Greece, November 22-24, 2017, Springer International Publishing, pp. 377–392, 2017, Proceedings 4.
16. Haugeland, I.K.F., Følstad, A., Taylor, C., Bjørkli, C.A., Understanding the user experience of customer service chatbots: An experimental study of chatbot interaction design. *Int. J. Hum.-Comput. Stud.*, 161, 102788, 2022.
17. Rossmann, A., Zimmermann, A., Hertweck, D., The impact of chatbots on customer service performance, in: *Advances in the Human Side of Service Engineering: Proceedings of the AHFE 2020 Virtual Conference on The Human Side of Service Engineering*, USA, July 16-20, 2020, Springer International Publishing, pp. 237–243, 2020.

18. Følstad, A. and Skjuve, M., Chatbots for customer service: user experience and motivation, in: *Proceedings of the 1st International Conference on Conversational User Interfaces*, pp. 1–9, 2019, August.
19. Brandtzaeg, P.B. and Følstad, A., Chatbots: changing user needs and motivations. *Interactions*, 25, 5, 38–43, 2018.
20. van der Goot, M.J., Hafkamp, L., Dankfort, Z., Customer service chatbots: A qualitative interview study into the communication journey of customers, in: *International Workshop on Chatbot Research and Design*, pp. 190–204, Springer International Publishing, Cham, 2020, November.
21. Cui, L., Huang, S., Wei, F., Tan, C., Duan, C., Zhou, M., Superagent: A customer service chatbot for e-commerce websites, in: *Proceedings of ACL 2017, System Demonstrations*, pp. 97–102, 2017, July.
22. Adam, M., Wessel, M., Benlian, A., AI-based chatbots in customer service and their effects on user compliance. *Electron. Mark.*, 31, 2, 427–445, 2021.
23. Kediya, S.O., Dhote, S., Singh, D.K., Bidve, V.S., Pathan, S., Mohare, R.V., Suchak, A., Are AI and Chat Bots Services Effects the Psychology of Users in Banking Services and Financial Sector. *J. ReAttach Ther. Dev. Diversities*, 6, 9s(2), 191–197, 2023.
24. Misischia, C.V., Poecze, F., Strauss, C., Chatbots in customer service: Their relevance and impact on service quality. *Procedia Comput. Sci., 201*, 421–428, 2022.
25. Feine, J., Gnewuch, U., Morana, S., Maedche, A., Gender bias in chatbot design, in: *Chatbot Research and Design: Third International Workshop, CONVERSATIONS 2019*, Amsterdam, The Netherlands, November 19–20, 2019, Springer International Publishing, pp. 79–93, 2020, Revised Selected Papers 3.
26. Blut, M., Wang, C., Wünderlich, N.V., Brock, C., Understanding anthropomorphism in service provision: a meta-analysis of physical robots, chatbots, and other AI. *J. Acad. Mark. Sci.*, 49, 632–658, 2021.
27. Lee, S.E., Ju, N., Lee, K.H., Service chatbot: Co-citation and big data analysis toward a review and research agenda. *Technol. Forecasting Social Change*, 194, 122722, 2023.
28. Xue, J., Wang, Y.C., Wei, C., Liu, X., Woo, J., Kuo, C.C.J., *Bias and fairness in chatbots: An overview*, 2023, arXiv preprint arXiv:2309.08836.
29. Illescas, C., Ortega, T., Jadán-Guerrero, J., Gender Bias in Chatbots and Its Programming, in: *Marketing and Smart Technologies: Proceedings of ICMarkTech 2022*, vol. 2, pp. 481–489, Springer Nature Singapore, Singapore, 2023.
30. Kooli, C., Chatbots in education and research: A critical examination of ethical implications and solutions. *Sustainability*, 15, 7, 20235614.
31. Abdelhalim, E., Anazodo, K.S., Gali, N., Robson, K., *A framework of diversity, equity, and inclusion safeguards for chatbots*, Business Horizons, 2024, In-Press.

32. Oca, M.C., Meller, L., Wilson, K., Parikh, A.O., McCoy, A., Chang, J., Zhang-Nunes, S., Bias and inaccuracy in AI chatbot ophthalmologist recommendations. *Cureus*, 15, 9, 2023.
33. Pendy, B., Role of Artificial Intelligence in Sector of Finance. *BULLET JurnalMultidisiplinIlmu*, *2*, 1, 239–244, 2023.
34. Okuda, T. and Shoda, S., AI-based chatbot service for financial industry. *Fujitsu Sci. Tech. J.*, *54*, 2, 4–8, 2018.
35. Um, T., Kim, T., Chung, N., How does an intelligence chatbot affect customers compared with self-service technology for sustainable services? *Sustainability*, 12, 12, 20205119.
36. Bang, J., Kim, S., Nam, J.W., Yang, D.G., Ethical chatbot design for reducing negative effects of biased data and unethical conversations, in: *2021 International Conference on Platform Technology and Service (PlatCon)*, IEEE, pp. 1–5, 2021, August.
37. Schlesinger, A., O'Hara, K.P., Taylor, A.S., Let's talk about race: Identity, chatbots, and AI, in: *Proceedings of the 2018 Chi Conference on Human Factors in Computing Systems*, pp. 1–14, 2018, April.
38. Letheren, K., Russell-Bennett, R., Whittaker, L., Whyte, S., Dulleck, U., The evolution is now: Service robots, behavioral bias and emotions. *Emotions Serv. Digit. Age*, 27–48, 2020.
39. Jang, M., Jung, Y., Kim, S., Investigating managers' understanding of chatbots in the Korean financial industry. *Comput. Hum. Behav.*, *120*, 106747, 2021.
40. Wan, Y., Wang, W., He, P., Gu, J., Bai, H., Lyu, M.R., Biasasker: Measuring the bias in conversational AI system, in: *Proceedings of the 31st ACM Joint European Software Engineering Conference and Symposium on the Foundations of Software Engineering*, pp. 515–527, 2023, November.
41. Harrison, G., Duarte, N., Hall, J., Where's the Bias? Developing Effective Model Governance, in: *Proceedings of the Neural Information Processing Systems*, 2018.
42. Ciechanowski, L., Przegalinska, A., Magnuski, M., Gloor, P., In the shades of the uncanny valley: An experimental study of human–chatbot interaction. *Future Gener. Comput. Syst.*, 92, 539–548, 2019.
43. Khan, A., Ranka, S., Khakare, C., Karve, S., NEEV: An education informational chatbot. *Int. Res. J. Eng. Technol.*, 6, 4, 492–495, 2019.
44. Efraim, O., Maraev, V., Rodrigues, J., Boosting a rule-based chatbot using statistics and user satisfaction ratings, in: *Artificial Intelligence and Natural Language: 6th Conference, AINL 2017*, St. Petersburg, Russia, September 20–23, 2017, Springer International Publishing, pp. 27–41, 2018, Revised Selected Papers 6.
45. Brandtzaeg, P.B. and Følstad, A., Why people use chatbots, in: *Internet Science: 4th International Conference, INSCI 2017*, Thessaloniki, Greece, November 22-24, 2017, Springer International Publishing, pp. 377–392, 2017, Proceedings 4.

46. Hsu, C.L. and Lin, J.C.C., Understanding the user satisfaction and loyalty of customer service chatbots. *J. Retailing Consum. Serv.*, 71, 103211, 2023.
47. Van den Broeck, E., Zarouali, B., Poels, K., Chatbot advertising effectiveness: When does the message get through? *Comput. Hum. Behav.*, 98, 150–157, 2019.
48. Mogaji, E., Balakrishnan, J., Nwoba, A.C., Nguyen, N.P., Emerging-market consumers' interactions with banking chatbots. *Telematics Inf.*, 65, 101711, 2021.
49. Chung, M., Ko, E., Joung, H., Kim, S.J., Chatbot e-service and customer satisfaction regarding luxury brands. *J. Bus. Res.*, 117, 587–595, 2020.
50. Kretzschmar, K., Tyroll, H., Pavarini, G., Manzini, A., Singh, I., NeurOx Young People's Advisory Group, Can your phone be your therapist? Young people's ethical perspectives on the use of fully automated conversational agents (chatbots) in mental health support. *Biomed. Inf. Insights*, 11, 1178222619829083, 2019.
51. Zhang, J., Oh, Y.J., Lange, P., Yu, Z., Fukuoka, Y., Artificial intelligence chatbot behavior change model for designing artificial intelligence chatbots to promote physical activity and a healthy diet. *J. Med. Internet Res.*, 22, 9, e22845, 2020.
52. Fryer, L.K., Ainley, M., Thompson, A., Gibson, A., Sherlock, Z., Stimulating and sustaining interest in a language course: An experimental comparison of Chatbot and Human task partners. *Comput. Hum. Behav.*, 75, 461–468, 2017.
53. Shaha, S., Pokalwar, R., Agrawal, S., Udapikar, S., Dhurape, B.K., Information chatbot for an educational institute. *VIIT Coll.*, 6, 11, 2395–0072, 2020.
54. Gunawan, D., Putri, F.P., Meidia, H., Bershca: bringing chatbot into hotel industry in Indonesia. *TELKOMNIKA (Telecommunication Comput. Electron. Control)*, 18, 2, 839–845, 2020.
55. Li, L., Lee, K.Y., Emokpae, E., Yang, S.B., What makes you continuously use chatbot services? Evidence from Chinese online travel agencies. *Electron. Mark.*, 1–25, 2021.
56. Følstad, A., Nordheim, C.B., Bjørkli, C.A., What makes users trust a chatbot for customer service? An exploratory interview study, in: *Internet Science: 5th International Conference, INSCI 2018*, St. Petersburg, Russia, October 24–26, 2018, Springer International Publishing, pp. 194–208, 2018, Proceedings 5.
57. Bitner, M.J., Brown, S.W., Meuter, M.L., Technology infusion in service encounters. *J. Acad. Mark. Sci.*, 28, 1, 138–149, 2000.
58. Meuter, M.L., Ostrom, A.L., Roundtree, R., II, Bitner, M.J., Self-service technologies: understanding customer satisfaction with technology-based service encounters. *J. Mark.*, 64, 3, 50–64, 2000.
59. Ostrom, A.L., Fotheringham, D., Bitner, M.J., Customer acceptance of AI in service encounters: understanding antecedents and consequences. *Handb. Serv. Sci.*, II, 77–103, 2019.

60. Luo, X., Tong, S., Fang, Z., Qu, Z., Frontiers: Machines vs. humans: The impact of artificial intelligence chatbot disclosure on customer purchases. *Mark. Sci.*, 38, 6, 937–947, 2019.
61. Richad, R., Vivensius, V., Sfenrianto, S., Kaburuan, E.R., Analysis of factors influencing millennial's technology acceptance of chatbot in the banking industry in Indonesia. *Int. J. Civ. Eng. Technol.*, 10, 4, 1270–1281, 2019.
62. Hill, J., Ford, W.R., Farreras, I.G., Real conversations with artificial intelligence: A comparison between human–human online conversations and human–chatbot conversations. *Comput. Hum. Behav.*, 49, 245–250, 2015.
63. Mou, Y. and Xu, K., The media inequality: Comparing the initial human-human and human-AI social interactions. *Comput. Hum. Behav.*, 72, 432–440, 2017.
64. Ho, A., Hancock, J., Miner, A.S., Psychological, relational, and emotional effects of self-disclosure after conversations with a chatbot. *J. Commun.*, 68, 4, 712–733, 2018.
65. Adobe, *Digital Trends: Financial Services in Focus*, 2019, Retrieved from https://www.adobe.com/content/dam/acom/uk/modal-offers/2019/DT-Report-2019/Econsultancy-2019-Digital-Trends-Financial-Services.pdf.
66. Sarbabidya, S. and Saha, T., Role of chatbot in customer service: A study from the perspectives of the banking industry of Bangladesh. *Int. Rev. Bus. Res. Pap.*, 16, 1, 231–248, 2020.
67. Suhel, S.F., Shukla, V.K., Vyas, S., Mishra, V.P., Conversation to automation in banking through chatbot using artificial machine intelligence language, in: *2020 8th International Conference on Reliability, Infocom Technologies and Optimization (Trends and Future Directions) (ICRITO)*, IEEE, pp. 611–618, 2020, June.
68. Kulkarni, C.S., Bhavsar, A.U., Pingale, S.R., Kumbhar, S.S., , and machine learning. *Int. Res. J. Eng. Technol.*, 4, 5, 2374–2377, 2017.
69. Elcholiqi, A. and Musdholifah, A., Chatbot in Bahasa Indonesia using NLP to provide banking information. *IJCCS (Indonesian J. Comput. Cybern. Systems)*, 14, 1, 91–102, 2020.
70. Rajbabu, M., Prabhuraj, P., Jeyabalan, S., An intelligent behaviour shown by chatbot system for banking in vernacular languages. *Int. Res. J. Eng. Technol. (IRJET)*, 1210–1212, 2019.
71. Yu, S., Chen, Y., Zaidi, H., *A Financial Service Chatbot based on Deep Bidirectional Transformers*, 2020, arXiv. arXiv preprint arXiv:2003.04987.
72. Mhlanga, D., Industry 4.0 in finance: the impact of artificial intelligence (ai) on digital financial inclusion. *Int. J. Financ. Stud.*, 8, 3, 45, 2020.
73. Ng, M., Coopamootoo, K.P., Toreini, E., Aitken, M., Elliot, K., van Moorsel, A., Simulating the effects of social presence on trust, privacy concerns & usage intentions in automated bots for finance, in: *2020 IEEE European symposium on security and privacy workshops (EuroS&PW)*, IEEE, pp. 190–199, 2020, September.

74. Patil, K. and Kulkarni, M.S., Artificial intelligence in financial services: Customer chatbot advisor adoption. *Int. J. Innov. Technol. Explor. Eng.*, 9, 1, 4296–4303, 2019.
75. Leclercq-Vandelannoitte, A., Managing BYOD: How do organizations incorporate user-driven IT innovations? *Inf. Technol. People*, 28, 1, 2–33, 2015.
76. Rodríguez Cardona, D., Werth, O., Schönborn, S., Breitner, M.H., A mixed methods analysis of the adoption and diffusion of Chatbot Technology in the German insurance sector, in: *Twenty-fifth Americas Conference on Information Systems, Cancun*, pp. 1–10, 2019.
77. Riikkinen, M., Saarijärvi, H., Sarlin, P., Lähteenmäki, I., Using artificial intelligence to create value in insurance. *Int. J. Bank Mark.*, 36, 6, 1145–1168, 2018.
78. Rudin, C., Stop explaining black box machine learning models for high stakes decisions and use interpretable models instead. *Nat. Mach. Intell.*, *1*, 5, 206–215, 2019.
79. Dwork, C., Hardt, M., Pitassi, T., Reingold, O., Zemel, R., Fairness through awareness, in: *Proceedings of the 3rd Innovations in Theoretical Computer Science Conference*, pp. 214–226, 2012, January.
80. Lee, M.K. and Park, H., Exploring factors influencing usage intention of chatbot–chatbot in financial service. *J. Korean Soc. Qual. Manage.*, 47, 4, 755–765, 2019.
81. Hentzen, J.K., Hoffmann, A., Dolan, R., Pala, E., Artificial intelligence in customer-facing financial services: a systematic literature review and agenda for future research. *Int. J. Bank Mark.*, 40, 6, 1299–1336, 2022.
82. Diakopoulos, N., Enabling accountability of algorithmic media: transparency as a constructive and critical lens. *Transparent Data Min. Big Small Data*, 25–43, 2017.
83. Caliskan, A., Bryson, J.J., Narayanan, A., Semantics derived automatically from language corpora contain human-like biases. *Science*, *356*, 6334, 183–186, 2017.
84. Barocas, S., Hardt, M., Narayanan, A., *Fairness and machine learning: Limitations and Opportunities*, MIT Press, 2023.
85. Weiler, S., Matt, C., Hess, T., Immunizing with information–Inoculation messages against conversational agents' response failures. *Electron. Mark.*, 32, 1, 239–258, 2022.
86. Zhang, Z., Li, J., Stork, D.G., Mansfield, E., Russell, J., Adams, C., Wang, J.Z., Reducing Bias in AI-Based Analysis of Visual Artworks. *IEEE BITS Inf. Theory Mag.*, 2, 1, 36–48, 2022.
87. Wan, Y., Wang, W., He, P., Gu, J., Bai, H., Lyu, M.R., Biasasker: Measuring the bias in conversational ai system, in: *Proceedings of the 31st ACM Joint European Software Engineering Conference and Symposium on the Foundations of Software Engineering*, pp. 515–527, 2023, November.
88. Crenshaw, R.P. and Vistnes, L.M., A decade of pressure sore research: 1977-1987. *J. Rehabil. Res. Dev.*, 26, 1, 63–74, 1989.

89. Chen, Y., Jensen, S., Albert, L.J., Gupta, S., Lee, T., Artificial intelligence (AI) student assistants in the classroom: Designing chatbots to support student success. *Inf. Syst. Front.*, 25, 1, 161–182, 2023.
90. Zhao, B., Chen, C., Wang, Q.W., He, A., Xia, S.T., Delving into Identify-Emphasize Paradigm for Combating Unknown Bias. *Int. J. Comput. Vision*, 1–21, 2024.
91. Jiang, N., Liu, X., Liu, H., Lim, E.T.K., Tan, C.W., Gu, J., Beyond AI-powered context-aware services: the role of human–AI collaboration. *Ind. Manage. Data Syst.*, 123, 11, 2771–2802, 2023.
92. Ulnicane, I., Artificial Intelligence in the European Union: Policy, ethics and regulation, in: *The Routledge Handbook of European Integrations*, Taylor & Francis, 2022.
93. Lu, Q., Luo, Y., Zhu, L., Tang, M., Xu, X., Whittle, J., Developing responsible chatbots for financial services: A pattern-oriented responsible AI engineering approach. *IEEE Intell. Syst.*, 42–51, 2023.
94. Manshad, M.S. and Brannon, D.C., Gender-based conversational interface preferences in live chat systems for financial services. *J. Financ. Serv. Marketing, 28*, 4, 822–834, 2023.
95. Mou, Y., Xu, K., Xia, K., Unpacking the black box: Examining the (de) Gender categorization effect in human-machine communication. *Comput. Hum. Behav., 90*, 380–387, 2019.
96. Bhatia, A., Chandani, A., Chhateja, J., Robo advisory and its potential in addressing the behavioral biases of investors—A qualitative study in Indian context. *J. Behav. Exp. Finance, 25*, 100281, 2020.
97. Roselli, D., Matthews, J., Talagala, N., Managing bias in AI, in: *Companion Proceedings of The 2019 World Wide Web Conference*, pp. 539–544, 2019, May.
98. Mehrabi, N., Morstatter, F., Saxena, N., Lerman, K., Galstyan, A., A survey on bias and fairness in machine learning. *ACM Comput. Surv. (CSUR)*, 54, 6, 1–35, 2021.
99. Ray, P.P., ChatGPT: A comprehensive review on background, applications, key challenges, bias, ethics, limitations and future scope. *Internet Things Cyber-Phys. Syst.*, 3, 21–154, 2023.
100. Lee, N.T., Resnick, P., Barton, G., *Algorithmic bias detection and mitigation: Best practices and policies to reduce consumer harms*, p. 2, Brookings Institute, Washington, DC, USA, 2019.
101. Srivastava, B., Rossi, F., Usmani, S., Bernagozzi, M., Personalized chatbot trustworthiness ratings. *IEEE Trans. Technol. Soc., 1*, 4, 184–192, 2020.
102. Rizzi, A., Kessler, A., Menajovsky, J., The Stories Algorithms Tell: Bias and Financial Inclusion at the Data Margins. *Center Financ. Inclusion Accion*, 35, 2021.
103. Bauer, K., von Zahn, M., Hinz, O., Expl (AI) ned: The impact of explainable artificial intelligence on users' information processing. *Inf. Syst. Res.*, 34, 4, 1582–1602, 2023.

104. Eren, B.A., Determinants of customer satisfaction in chatbot use: evidence from a banking application in Turkey. *Int. J. Bank Marketing*, *39*, 2, 294–311, 2021.
105. Nguyen, D.M., Chiu, Y.T.H., Le, H.D., Determinants of continuance intention towards banks' chatbot services in Vietnam: A necessity for sustainable development. *Sustainability*, *13*, 14, 7625, 2021.
106. Feng, D., Dai, Y., Huang, J., Zhang, Y., Xie, Q., Han, W., Wang, H., *Empowering many, biasing a few: Generalist credit scoring through large language models*, 2023, arXiv preprint arXiv:2310.00566.
107. Karsh, S.M.A., Emerging Innovation Risk Management in Financial Institutions of United States. *Econ. Bus. Q. Rev.*, *4*, 2, 2021.
108. Aziz, L.A.R. and Andriansyah, Y., The role artificial intelligence in modern banking: an exploration of AI-driven approaches for enhanced fraud prevention, risk management, and regulatory compliance. *Rev. Conceptual Bus. Anal.*, 6, 1, 2023.
109. Al-Shabandar, R., Lightbody, G., Browne, F., Liu, J., Wang, H., Zheng, H., The application of artificial intelligence in financial compliance management, in: *Proceedings of the 2019 International Conference on Artificial Intelligence and Advanced Manufacturing*, pp. 1–6, 2019, October.
110. Hari, H., Iyer, R., Sampat, B., Customer brand engagement through chatbots on bank websites–examining the antecedents and consequences. *Int. J. Human–Computer Interact.*, *38*, 13, 1212–1227, 2022.
111. Yu, S., Chen, Y., Zaidi, H., AVA: A financial service chatbot based on deep bidirectional transformers. *Front. Appl. Math. Stat.*, *7*, 604842, 2021.
112. Rajaobelina, L. and Ricard, L., Classifying potential users of live chat services and chatbots. *J. Financ. Serv. Marketing*, 26, 81–94, 2021.
113. Janssen, A., Cardona, D.R., Passlick, J., Breitner, M.H., How to Make chatbots productive–A user-oriented implementation framework. *Int. J. Hum.-Comput. Stud.*, *168*, 102921, 2022.
114. Gichoya, J.W., Thomas, K., Celi, L.A., Safdar, N., Banerjee, I., Banja, J.D., Purkayastha, S., AI pitfalls and what not to do: mitigating bias in AI. *Br. J. Radiol.*, 96, 1150, 20230023, 2023.
115. Silberg, J. and Manyika, J., Notes from the AI frontier: Tackling bias in AI (and in humans). *McKinsey Global Inst.*, 1, 6, 1–31, 2019.
116. Galitsky, B., Galitsky, B., Goldberg, S., Explainable machine learning for chatbots, in: *Developing Enterprise Chatbots: Learning Linguistic Structures*, pp. 53–83, 2019.
117. Gupta, S. and Chen, Y., Supporting inclusive learning using chatbots? A chatbot-led interview study. *J. Inf. Syst. Educ.*, *33*, 1, 98–108, 2022.
118. Gadhoum, Y., Artificial Intelligence Trends and Ethics: Issues and Alternatives for Investors. *Intell. Control Autom.*, *13*, 1, 1–15, 2022.
119. Murtarelli, G., Gregory, A., Romenti, S., A conversation-based perspective for shaping ethical human–machine interactions: The particular challenge of chatbots. *J. Bus. Res.*, *129*, 927–935, 2021.

120. Kurshan, E., Chen, J., Storchan, V., Shen, H., On the current and emerging challenges of developing fair and ethical AI solutions in financial services, in: *Proceedings of the Second ACM International Conference on AI in Finance*, pp. 1–8, 2021, November.
121. Camilleri, M.A., Artificial intelligence governance: Ethical considerations and implications for social responsibility, in: *Expert Systems*, p. e13406, 2023.
122. Max, R., Kriebitz, A., Von Websky, C., Ethical considerations about the implications of artificial intelligence in finance, in: *Handbook on Ethics in Finance*, pp. 577–592, 2021.
123. Kruse, L., Wunderlich, N., Beck, R., Artificial intelligence for the financial services industry: What challenges organizations to succeed, in: *Proceedings of the 52nd Hawaii International Conference on System Sciences*, 2019, available at https://scholarspace.manoa.hawaii.edu/server/api/core/bitstreams/53b933fa-4961-48ca-bd6b-3ee8009edff9/content.
124. Agrawal, S.S., Rose, N., PrabhuSahai, K., The fintech revolution: AI's role in disrupting traditional banking and financial services. *Decis. Making Appl. Manage. Eng.*, 7, 1, 243–256, 2024.
125. Kumar, A. and Kumar, L., Navigating the Future: The Ethical, Societal and Technological Implications of Artificial Intelligence. *Global J. Res. Eng. Comput. Sci.*, 4, 02, 2024. Journal homepage: https://gjrpublication. com/gjrecs.
126. Mogaji, E. and Nguyen, N.P., Managers' understanding of artificial intelligence in relation to marketing financial services: insights from a cross-country study. *Int. J. Bank Mark.*, 40, 6, 1272–1298, 2022.
127. Ranković, M., Gurgu, E., Martins, O., Vukasović, M., Artificial intelligence and the evolution of finance: opportunities, challenges and ethical considerations. *EdTech J.*, 3, 1, 20–23, 2023.
128. Kooli, C., Chatbots in education and research: A critical examination of ethical implications and solutions. *Sustainability*, 15, 7, 5614–5637, 2023.
129. Lim, J. and Cruz, A., Advancements in Artificial Intelligence Applications and Ethical Considerations Across Industries. *Int. J. Appl. Mach. Learn. Comput. Intell.*, 14, 3, 26–34, 2024.
130. Paul, B.S. and Anuradha, A., Artificial Intelligence in Different Business Domains: Ethical Concerns, in: *Exploring the Ethical Implications of Generative AI*, pp. 13–33, IGI Global, 2024.
131. Coghlan, S., Leins, K., Sheldrick, S., Cheong, M., Gooding, P., D'Alfonso, S., To chat or bot to chat: Ethical issues with using chatbots in mental health. *DIGITAL HEALTH*, 9, 2023. 20552076231183542, available at https://www.ncbi.nlm.nih.gov/pmc/articles/PMC10291862/.

2

Domain-Specific AI Algorithms and Models in Decision-Making: An Overview

P. Kanaga Priya[1]*, A. Reethika[2], Malathy Sathyamoorthy[3] and Rajesh Kumar Dhanaraj[4]

[1]*Department of Computer Science and Engineering, Sri Eshwar College of Engineering, Coimbatore, Tamil Nadu, India*
[2]*Department of Electronics and Communication Engineering, Sri Ramakrishna Engineering College, Coimbatore, Tamil Nadu, India*
[3]*Department of Information Technology, KPR Institute of Engineering and Technology, Coimbatore, Tamil Nadu, India*
[4]*Symbiosis Institute of Computer Studies and Research (SICSR), Symbiosis International (Deemed University), Pune, India*

Abstract
Artificial Intelligence (AI) plays a major role in the decision-making process in various sectors. This chapter treats an important terrain of AI, which emphasizes the domain-specific AI role in important management scenarios like healthcare, finance, manufacturing, retail, transportation, and agriculture. The chapter highlights through skillful study of the AI solutions targeting specific activities and environments, the ingredients of the algorithms and models that are used as strategy tools, boosting operations, productivity, and innovation. The application of the concepts and the case studies demonstrating the power of artificial intelligence in the business world are given as examples, which are an immeasurable source of information for how AI systems can be used in different fields. Employing those tools allows industries to redefine old decision-making models, deliver long-term sustainability, and allow organizations to be their best in both productivity and profitability.

***Keywords*:** Domain-specific, artificial intelligence (AI), decision-making, healthcare, finance, manufacturing, retail, and transportation

**Corresponding author*: kanagapriyacse@gmail.com

Sapna Juneja, Rajesh Kumar Dhanaraj, Abhinav Juneja, Malathy Sathyamoorthy and Asadullah Shaikh (eds.) Ethical Decision-Making Using Artificial Intelligence: Challenges, Solutions and Applications, (27–54) © 2025 Scrivener Publishing LLC

2.1 Introduction

In the era of fast-growing data as well as complex decision environments, AI (Artificial Intelligence) has come as a groundbreaking technology. This chapter looks into the area-specific implementation of AI algorithms and models in decision-making, making their application as wide-ranging as various industries. In the face of the complicated nature of today's challenges, the role of AI grows more important in facilitating decision-making processes. This overview may dissect the domain-wise approaches or in other words, the interaction of AI technologies and industries-specific situations. AI algorithms and models from healthcare to finance, manufacturing to transportation, retail to agriculture, the chapter takes us on a voyage to observe the diverse terrains where AI algorithms and models outperform the traditional decision-making approaches. This overview employs a critical look at real-world applications and exciting case studies to demonstrate the power of domain-specific AI towards shaping the future of decision-making through a lens that reveals both the challenges and opportunities of the technology.

The latest technological development birthing AI, a fast-growing science, is also rewriting decision-making across multiple domains. Semantic AI engines embodied in different AI models and AI algorithms intended to specialize problems and exploit precise data for certain applications or businesses drive this transformation. With this, this introductory part will be about domain-specific AI that will mention the areas related to domain-specific AI as the human supervision role is one prominent advantage of domain-specific AI. Illustrations such as prediction and policy creation could be supported by AI technology, which is supposed to be more powerful technologically when talking about the future.

2.1.1 Overview of the Role of AI in Decision Making

The impact of AI on the decision-making aspect is the point that creates a visualization of the AI that is changing the decision-making process itself. AI has become an excellent tool that helps human decision-makers to be even more effective. Among these abilities are advanced analytical skills, predictive features, and others that work out together as quality upgrades and the effectiveness of the decision-making process. Through the use of big amounts of data, AI algorithms can make informed decisions as they can recognize the patterns, trends, and correlations that would not be visible immediately to human analysts. In the meantime, AI-based decision-making allows organizations to navigate environments that are complex and dynamic with speed and outstanding precision, thereby minimizing risks and seizing opportunities in real time. The impact of AI on decision-making goes beyond optimizing operational processes. It affects consumer behaviors and market trend prediction among many others. Moreover, the integration of AI space nurtures a culture of creativity as well as continuous improvement, which enables firms to be ahead of the times along with efficient growth. Generally, the summary draws attention to the significant position of AI in decision-making at the new level and reveals the enormous power of AI to reshape the global industry scene.

2.1.1.1 *The Emergence of Artificial Intelligence: How it is Changing Decision-Making in Several Domains of Economics*

Being in a data-driven environment today makes decision-making effective and a vital aspect of success. The AI industry has been a game-changer that gives upgraded tools that can handle vast data and quicken decision-making in numerous sectors. This evaluation, on the other hand, focuses on how AI changed how individuals make judgments extending from the definition of the issue to its execution.

2.1.1.2 *Putting the Power of Artificial Intelligence to Work in a Particular Field*

One of the key benefits of AI is the flexibility to be adapted to various fields. Domain-specific algorithms of AI and models are purposefully built to handle sector-specific challenges and to utilize data that is unique to the sector alone. Artificial intelligence in the financial industry may for example recognize market patterns and identify dangers. In the case of health care, however, it may discover diagnostic patterns in medical data to increase clinical diagnosis and treatment planning.

2.1.1.3 *The AI-Assisted Decision-Making Process*

It is essential to carve out an organized plan if AI is to be integrated into the decision-making process. The key steps in the AI-assisted decision-making process are listed below, in Figure 2.1 as a flowchart.

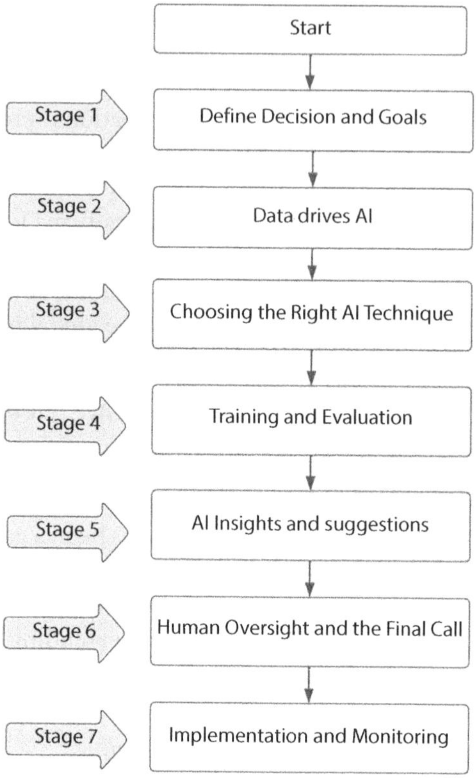

Figure 2.1 Key steps in AI-assisted decision-making process.

Stage 1 - Defining the Decision and Goals: First of all, it lays out this decision and what the possible outcomes might be. What is your solution to the problem or what outcome do you desire as a result of implementing your plan?
Stage 2 - Data Drives AI: The underlying engine of AI is data. This step is based on the sources search and their quality check is also included in it. The data cleaning and preparation tasks are of the utmost importance for successful model training in AI.
Stage 3 - Choosing the Right AI Technique: Some AI algorithms are suitable for a few tasks more than others. The considerations regarding machine learning versus deep learning are about the information in the data that is being used and the decision type being made.
Stage 4 - Training and Evaluation: The AI model we chose has been trained on the dataset we created earlier. This procedure encloses showing the model the examples and allows it to learn from the patterns found in

the data. The performance of the model is tested to make sure it is right and can be relied upon to provide accurate results.

Stage 5 - AI Insights and Suggestions: After training, model AI can process data and suggest some recommendations that might be used for decision-making. In the context of this, it may include identifying risks, forecasting future trends, or designing the line of action for the best.

Stage 6 - Human Oversight and the Final Call: Whilst AI is vital for tactical cognizance the human factor cannot be substituted. First, a human makes the ultimate decision, adding ethics and context by providing the whole picture.

Stage 7 - Implementation and Monitoring: The movements then follow according to the planned action. Observing the reactions to the move aims at the model enhancement and the modification of the next decision-making designs.

2.1.1.4 Benefits and Future of AI-Powered Decision-Making

The AI new phenomenon has caused a replacement of corporate and personal decision-making activities which used to be conducted in different traditional ways. Machine learning and complex algorithms of AI-based decision-making reduce both the time and cost of manufacturing and outperform humans in multiple aspects of production. AI-assisted decision-making principles that can analyze big data tirelessly are one of its biggest assets. In our digital universe, information is now consumed at a greater speed than ever, making a human analyst compared to a machine almost impossible. On the contrary, data analysis by Artificial Intelligence (AI) is almost instantaneous, as it goes through petabytes of information translating high-level patterns and making sense of assumptions that are tough for a human being to get his head around.

Organizations can take into account and securely make time-sensitive decisions due to this quicker research, without a doubt giving them a steeped edge in fierce interprofessional settings. As well as that, AI is driven by data, and this causes fewer opportunities for human biases to interfere and affect decision-making. AI models, in turn, can establish thoughts that are without the prejudice and the personal inclination that inevitably comes with human decision-makers during the process of analyzing without bias both the qualitative and quantitative data points. This research-based objective approach on its part makes sure that evaluation is not built on any mere subjective opinions but rather based on evidence, meaning that the outcomes are more uniform and predictable.

In the future AI technology will tend to start controlling decision-making processes more often as progress is very fast in this field. AI algorithms will evolve and start to analyze data with increased precision resulting from rapid advances in deep learning, computer vision, and natural language processing. Along with this more enriched knowledge, the systems will in turn be more capable of managing many complex and very diverse situations than ever before, something that has always been the job of human experts. Nevertheless, Artificial Intelligence has been recognized as a powerful tool if it is used in the right way and synchronized with human control.

AI can be used for evaluating information and discovering patterns but human thinking is still consequential for establishing moral standards and assuring that an action is not in conflict with the goals of society. Future decision-making is going to be highly driven firstly by natural intelligence interacting with soon-to-come artificial intelligence. Organizations get such unity where the AI serves as a complement to the human brain and enhances cognition rather than substituting them. They accomplish that by discovering the positions where AI and memory can converge. This form of cooperation will be able to develop new opportunities that will be effective, informed, and lively in decision-making spheres to generate prosperity and innovations in the society at large.

2.1.2 Importance of Domain-Specific Approaches

There is a limitation in the generalizations of AI algorithms and models, which is why the domain-specific techniques are the horizon of such algorithms and models. Domain-specific AI focuses on:

Domain-Specific Data: These models are real-life experienced domain-specific data. Medical AI deals with patients' data, medical records, and prescription info which are unique to the medical field, and financial AI deals with market data, financial reports, and indicators unique to the financial sector.

Industry Knowledge: AI is an industry-specific domain that includes not only the industry-specified knowledge and operators. Use our AI writing assistant to create engaging blog content for your website's visitors.

Tailored Tasks: These simulations will deal with industry-specific matters. An AI for a manufacturing system could understand perfect production operations and be cautious about impending equipment malfunctions, whereas a legal AI could analyze legal papers and foresee the outcome of the case.

2.1.2.1 Advantages of Domain-Specific AI

Improved Accuracy and Performance: Due to covering a particular kind of data and task, domain-specific AI models surpass in precision and efficiency what you get from general AI models which are intended to be applied to a broad range of problems in the world.

Deeper Insights: It may be easier for AI to find the specific patterns and trends if it is trained in some particular domain rather than in something else generic. Ultimately, it enables us to see details that were previously ignored and to take more concrete actions.

Reduced Development Time and Costs: With domain-specific models being developed by using lesser data and focusing on individual tasks, the development time and computing resources required may be reduced, which could be used to make broad AI models.

2.1.2.2 Instances of Domain-Specific AI in Action

Some examples of domain-specific AI in action are shown below in Figure 2.2.

Healthcare: AI is consequently applied to arrange medical diagnosis, medication design, and specific treatment programs accordingly.
Finance: AI is used to analyze financial markets, recognize fraud, and recommend investment agendas according to each person.
Manufacturing: Artificial Intelligence performs all manufacturing processes efficiently, acts as a fail-safe against equipment trouble, and has better control than rivaling human skills.
Retail: AI makes the choice of products to be suggested to the customer more accurate, boosts the productivity of the warehouse, and therefore assists in providing better support to the client.
Transportation: Domain-specific AI is transforming transportation by enabling self-driving cars, optimizing traffic flow, and enhancing driver assistance systems. From predicting congestion to managing fleets, AI

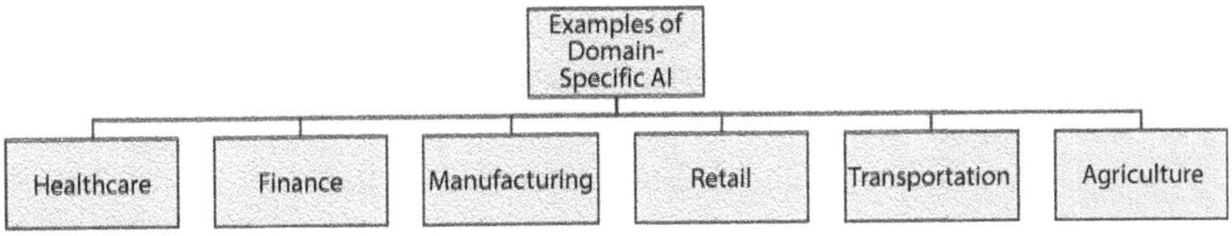

Figure 2.2 Examples of domain-specific AI.

is making transportation safer, more efficient, and more enjoyable for everyone.
Agriculture: Artificial intelligence (AI) algorithms in agriculture are revolutionizing the field of agricultural practices with the help of data-driven decisions like precision drone-based monitoring and irrigation, which in turn maximize crop yields while preserving resources and limiting environmental damage.

For now, specialized AI is a robust AI technique that one can apply AI to improve different decision-making, efficiency, and innovative abilities of the sector in various areas.

2.1.2.3 General AI versus Domain-Specific AI: Powering Intelligent Decisions

By far the quickest developing sphere among all is artificial intelligence, contesting our ability to go along with the speed of this very process. However, there are two main approaches to utilizing AI: general AI and domain-specific AI. Table 2.1 shows the key difference between general AI and domain-specific AI.

General AI:

- Focus: Set the goal of developing intelligent machines with the capability to match human mental processes.
- Data: Extraordinarily relies on generic data figures, sometimes integrating the establishment of many interconnected computer facilities.
- Tasks: Invented specifically for the execution of large-dimension tasks incorporating recognition of images, speech translation, or games.
- Accuracy: The extent of precision may also be limited because the data to be crunched is vast with many tasks to be completed.
- Development: Time and money are squeezed for the creation of the general AI due to the necessity of enormous databases filled with intricate algorithms.
- Examples: Images of all kinds are recognized by the algorithms, Text speech AI, and simple AIs for games.

Table 2.1 The key difference between general AI and domain-specific AI.

Feature	General AI	Domain-specific AI
Data Used	Generic data	Domain-specific data (e.g., Medical Records)
Industry Knowledge	No specific industry knowledge	Incorporates industry knowledge (e.g., Medical Practices)
Tasks Addressed	Broad tasks	Tailored tasks specific to the domain (e.g., Medical Diagnosis)
Algorithm Choice	All-purpose algorithms	The choice depends on the domain and task
Accuracy	Limited accuracy due to the broad nature of the data	Improved accuracy due to focused data and tasks
Development Time & Cost	Can be time-consuming and expensive due to the need for large amounts of generic data	Potentially faster and less expensive due to more focused data and tasks
Examples	Speech recognition (general)	Medical diagnosis (healthcare)

Domain-Specific AI:

- Focus: Purposed to deliver the best-quality results within specific activities and needs.
- Data: Does not share data shared amongst fields (e.g., patient data in healthcare, financial information in finance).
- Tasks: Such algorithms fit the scenarios in which they are designed to carry out specialized and specific tasks within certain domains of knowledge such as medical diagnosis, fraud detection, or predictive maintenance for instance.
- Accuracy: The analysis can become more precise as it drills down to micro-level data, assignments, and other objectives.

- Development: This could be true during competition as developmental AI is built against specific data and tasks, unlike the general one.
- Examples: Medical diagnostics systems, fraud detection algorithms in the financial sector, predictive maintenance tools in the production area, and self-driving car technology (that uses a variety of specialized AI for object detection, path planning, and similar things).

Choosing the Right Approach
What crucial option that determines case-to-case scenarios stands at the core of the concerned approach? What is interesting about the implementation of AI is that it can do the jobs or tasks that need a comparatively high level of intelligence at the current state. At the same time, the kind of multidisciplinary tasks with the final goal of uniting the efforts of many related fields under the common heading of achieving the maximum accuracy possible and work efficiency might be those where multidisciplinary AI takes a turn for the best. So, generic and domain-specific AI encompass the usual aspects of the world of artificial intelligence. Next to AI, we will demonstrate the procedure of the more evolved and sharp technologies to dominate various areas as well.

2.2 Understanding Domain-Specific Decision Making

Domain-based decision-making goes beyond the mastery of specialized skills; it is a wholehearted appreciation of the background, stakeholders, and interdependencies of a specific sector. This comprehensive viewpoint makes the decision-makers capable of considering the adjusted and not immediate advantages and disadvantages as well as the further effects and chain of events of their decisions, thus impacting their choices in a more balanced and meaningful way.

The main advantage of task-dependent decision-making is its skill to solve the complicated and complex tasks that arise within all industries. These issues can be technical, legal, operational, or even cultural, and asking a domain expert to take them on as a unit would be a win. Through applying knowledge and experience to the area, decision-makers have the chance to detect the risks, capture the opportunities, or optimize outcomes, and this is something that other universal remedies cannot do.

Further, to conclude, the skill refers to domain-specific decision-making personnel in the organizations which focus on an agile and responsive attribute. Fast-changing industrial configurations, technological innovations, and customer specialization necessitate decision-makers who have to act and decide fast; these changes must be reflected in their decisions. Through a proper understanding of the specific characteristics of their areas of expertise and rulings, the decision-makers have a better chance of being able to predict and solve these problems, and thus reposition their organizations for a continued and successful existence.

Another key factor of industry-specific problem-solving is using the stipulated data and analytics of the industry. Evolving the business through big data analytics within an industry has a lot to offer in terms of the discovery of information, insights, patterns, and trends that can steer the decision-making process across the board. This can be achieved through the combining of specialized data repositories and analytical models which would allow organizations to make decisions that are more data-driven, relying on evidence, and built tailored to their exact needs.

Finally, domain-oriented decision-making and the capability of organizations to obtain and leverage market insights as well as visualize consequences of business actions can be considered as a competitive advantage for organizations that aim to remain current and steadily improve in times of market development. Hence these types of domain-specific strategies will be game changers in a business environment.

2.2.1 Bridging the Gap: Explainable AI for Effective Collaboration between Machine Learning and Domain Expertise

AI tools are vital for companies just as they are in the process of conquering their industries, but making the ML expert's expertise marry with that of domain knowledge is a very big challenge. The domain experts are competent in assessing and applying data influences their decisiveness while machine learning specialists can leverage machine learning-based tools to deal with a large amount of data and generate insights. Nevertheless, this gap must be addressed by making informed decisions and leveraging the expertise and knowledge of human ML experts to fine-tune the models, especially for generalization across different domains. Hence, domain players are essential users of such tools and these AI Tools should be explainable (easily understood both in computer science and human understanding). ML experts may vocalize risks concerning the principles of explainability in the AI model or specific domain in their talks about forthcoming ML tools. Research focuses on AI and people partnership capabilities – from the way humans learn and analyze the data to computers' capability of processing it. Firstly, the feature of explanability for AI, xAI (eXplainable AI), becomes more and more vital when humans comprise an element of successful AI implementation. The study path was proposed to interview ML professionals about whom they are supposed to be May potential users of ML systems, and how it could affect the discussion of its characteristics [1].

2.3 Building Blocks of AI for Decision-Making

This section explores some of the building blocks of AI in decision-making.

2.3.1 Overview of AI Approaches

Artificial intelligence (AI) is generally described as a complex collection of many different techniques and methodologies that aim to simulate human intelligence in electronic machines. Approaches like machine learning, knowledge-based systems, and reinforcement learning that are different from each other and are utilized in the decision-making processes are being applied by these methods. Inside machine learning, computers are taught to detect patterns and causation among the data, and due to this the designer can be data-driven in his/her decisions. The main feature of such rule-based systems is their applications of explicit rules and logic to decision-making processes. In contrast, the reinforcement learning model is based on learning the best decision-making strategies by trial and error, concurrently working with dynamic scenarios.

2.3.2 Machine Learning for Data-Driven Decision Generating

Machine learning is one of the branches of AI that deals with designing algorithms that can learn from data which in turn helps them to generate predictions or selections without human programming. Machine learning algorithms consider the huge amount of data that enables the system to make out trends, patterns, and relationships that most likely go unnoticed by human analysts. Using the earlier data, machine learning allows companies to make data-based decisions that produce more accuracy, timeliness, and scale. Regular machine learning methods include regression, classification, clustering, and deep learning, each being tailored to different types of decision situations.

2.3.3 Knowledge-Based Systems for Rule-Based Decision-Making

Information-based systems rely on specific repositories of explicit information, rules, and logical reasoning to provide answers. To execute this, these systems encapsulate human expertise and subject knowledge in the form of codified procedures that maintain their ability to process complex questions and circumstances. In the decision-making process, knowledge-based systems evaluate inputs through rule-based reasoning to reach a predefined criterion and select suitable responses or actions. Through soliciting and organizing human specialists' expertise, knowledge-based systems ensure that businesses are capable of automating decision-making processes and being dependable and consistent across a variety of situations.

2.3.4 Reinforcement Learning in Dynamic Environments

Reinforcement learning, as one of the types of machine learning, improves the machine learning system in the environment where its rules are repeatedly applied; (the reward mechanism makes a machine learning system almost ideal in this area). In this kind of system where results are ambiguous, they alternate over time or cannot be manifest clearly; reinforcement learning algorithms learn from experience by taking feedback as rewards or penalties for their actions. Using introspection and detailed evaluation of the principles of various agents, reframing the prerequisites of agents is achieved to access more long-term benefits. It is widely used, but it is inappropriate in situations like where there can be no background knowledge and the environment is complex and dynamic when used with fields like robotics, autonomous systems, and game playing.

AI decision-making is made up of various techniques and remarkably different approaches that are endowed with particular features and specific operations scope. In understanding and perceiving the chance to use AI to attain sound, realistic, and profound decisions within different sectors and disciplines, the enterprises can do more.

2.4 Domain-Specific AI: Revolutionizing Industries

Artificial intelligence (AI) is the latest trend that is disrupting real-life tasks in different industries, and specialized algorithms and models are the pioneers in the area. These models train on large amounts of domain-specific data of the industry and thus can solve problems of greater complexity with an amazing degree of truthfulness and effectiveness. Let us explore some major domains of AI that are making a significant impact.

2.4.1 Healthcare

The healthcare business is undergoing a radical transformation when it comes to AI; for instance, healthcare providers use AI to detect disease and decide on a treatment that best suits a particular patient. AI through machine learning algorithms and deep learning models can assess patient data which is large, enabling the finding of abnormalities and connections which may be challenging the capabilities of humans to detect. This serves as a highly desirable function since the correct and speedy diagnosis is generally acquired more easily. Treatment recommendation AI-based systems provide individual suggestions based on features such as disease progression, genes, and the success of treatment. The channeling of this process improves the efficiency of patients getting the right choice with positive outcomes. Artificial Intelligence (AI) collects huge amounts of data all the time and accordingly generates its ideas which becomes better with more information. Therefore, it may provide novel treatment strategies. The dynamic character of this component ascertains that healthcare team workers are served with real-time data making them efficient and providing improved healthcare services of the highest quality; as a result, the use of AI in healthcare becomes a milestone for systems development, in which healthcare personnel can achieve more results and higher quality of patient responses. While considering diagnosis and treatment recommendations the AI algorithms can use radiological images, patients' records, and genetic data to diagnose diseases, predict the outcome of a patient, and recommend patient-centered treatment solutions. Even though ancient techniques are based on a physician's experience and intuition, which consequently might be subjective, they are still used quite frequently. AI offers an objective approach, which could provide an earlier diagnosis and more selective therapy settings [4, 5].

2.4.1.1 The Importance of Patient-Centered Design in Regulating Large Language Models or Generative AI

Artificial intelligence developments have led to the establishment of large language models (LLMs) like GPT-4 and Bard, which have potential benefits in healthcare. However, these models also create dangers and ethical difficulties. Regulatory monitoring is necessary to ensure safety, maintain ethical standards, and safeguard patient privacy. The research work analyses the hazards and benefits of deploying LLMs in healthcare settings and proposes different regulations than present AI-based medical solutions. By embracing patient design, LLMs may become the first form of AI-based medical technology to be controlled by incorporating patient design. To implement LLMs in medicine the authorities should create new categories, give advice to firms and healthcare organizations, build a text-based interaction scheme, and deduce medical data-based versus non-medical LLMs as well as control production companies [2].

2.4.1.2 XAI in Biomedicine: A Post-Pandemic Surge for Trustworthy AI in Healthcare Delivery

The phrase "explainable AI" (XAI) has garnered popularity, with the notion going back to the mid-1970s. The discussion about XAI is continuing, involving involvement from professionals in computer science, philosophy, ethics, and law. The main hurdles stem from defining and measuring "explainability," since it is difficult to identify whether a model's output is interpretable owing to the broad diversity of split options. Understanding the underlying workings of machine-learning models has become a major topic of contention in the fairness and trustworthiness of AI. The COVID-19 pandemic has boosted medical research and healthcare, but the development and use of XAI throughout the health ecosystem have been slower. Large-scale deep-learning models have challenged the concept that keeping or building interpretability in ML solutions comes at a cost in accuracy [3].

2.4.2 Finance

AI changes the finance business landscape into the era of spot superior decision-making and greater income returns. It accomplishes this task by using complicated algorithms for insightful analysis of huge market data to ensure that those impending trends and anomalous deviations that may affect the value of the assets are caught and detected on time. AI is capable of this through the utilization of complex statistical methods which results in a risk assessment model that is meant to mitigate financial risks, which leads eventually to the financial institutions arriving at the right basis for their investment strategies and risk management. AI is the never-ceasing sphere of growth and development and is intended to manage the situation that is dynamic as well as the rules of the regulation applicable then, thus enabling the financial practitioners to get quicker and accurate information for their decisions and actions. By doing this, a financial staff can professionally lead and manage the risks and market controversies, a lesser loss is recorded, and they are offered opportunities for excellent profitability. In addition to this process, artificial intelligence is paving the road of big data access to financial minds. In algorithmic trading, AI systems can scan data of the market, spot the lucrative chances, and execute the trades in rapid time. This means a more rapid and effective decision-making process that is by far more calculated. AI models can provide creditworthiness assessment, loan default forecasting, and identifying fraud furthering the financial decision process. Traditional methods deal mostly with manual analysis of numbers which may be exhausting and full of human errors. AI, for example, is already automating these tasks, leading to better efficiency and reliability.

2.4.2.1 *Explainable AI: A Path Toward Trustworthy and Ethical Applications of Machine Learning in Finance*

Digitalization and technology affect finance, forcing decision-makers to be transparent and traceable. Addressing these problems implicates XAI (explainable AI). A thorough literature assessment of 2,022 publications from top finance, information systems, and computer science venues revealed 60 relevant studies based on XAI methodology and aims. While the lack of clear reasoning prevents the implementation of the XAI system in the banking industry where regulations are strict, it increases implementation friction; still, XAI helps to explain the AI models by principle. XAI solves these concerns by explaining AI-based solutions to guarantee they are discrimination-free and well-founded, making them industry-able. The state of AI-related research in finance is fragmented, which therefore is a big barrier to academics and practitioners in fully utilizing AI. The research examines the use of AI and Machine Learning (ML) in banking, concentrating on AI, XAI, and technical effects [6].

2.4.2.2 *Learning Machines, Evolving Markets: The Need for Adaptable Generative AI in Finance*

AI, like ChatGPT, has changed finance and accounting by strengthening client interactions, delivering tailored financial advice, and simplifying real-time market research. However, it also presents ethical questions regarding data security, safety, and biased decision-making. Ensuring compliance with industry standards and legislation while ensuring the integrity and security of sensitive financial data remains a serious concern.

The fast-changing environment of financial markets requires AI models to be flexible and also learn constantly from them, thus necessitating further research and development. This study critically evaluates the increasing role of ChatGPT and comparable generative AI in finance and accounting, offering light on the revolutionary potential and the challenges that need to be addressed for these technologies to genuinely disrupt the financial environment [7–9].

2.4.3 Manufacturing

Artificial Intelligence (AI) is now the new trend in the industry sector. It is achieved via autonomous equipment, automation of processes, and cost-cutting. Thanks to artificial intelligence which implies applying advanced algorithms and approaches as well as machine learning, equipment failures and maintenance requirements could be detected. It solves problems for manufacturers in terms of pre-planning operations. This approach not only cuts out the surprise idle times and expenses, but AI technology in supply chain optimization offers the development of the resources action plans embracing the forecasts of the demand, production, and inventory schedules. Therefore, manufacturers can have the needed supplies for production as the need arises, thereby eliminating surplus and improving efficiency. AI can also seamlessly react to a varying environment by recalculating its predictions and, if need be, adjusting optimization algorithms. This amalgamation of adaptability translates into nimble decision-making, improved production levels, and a decrease in expenditure. To wrap up, AI has a remarkable influence on the industrial market using the smart production and competitiveness of the industry. For predictive maintenance, the AI can identify signals from different machine sensors and forecast failures or recommend appointments with precision before breakdowns happen. This saves time and associated costs from being down. During supply chain optimization the AI algorithms can mine through historical data, forecast demand fluctuations, and facilitate the logistics infrastructure in terms of fast delivery and smooth inventory management. Common methods are based on reactive management of failures and logistics scheduling that is directed by a person and therefore can be unsatisfying and expensive. AI helps to design proactive maintenance and more efficient supply chain management.

2.4.3.1 The Rise of Generative AI: A Call for Responsible AI Frameworks in MSME Manufacturing

Undeniably, the uncertain future of Industry 4.0 is the biggest headache for Micro, Small, and Medium Enterprises (MSMEs) in the manufacturing sector. About Industry 4.0, the technology of artificial intelligence and machine learning will enable the optimization of production processes. The key aspects are quality and maintenance, while at the same time, there are difficulties to deal with: privacy regulations, expertise gap, data challenges, financing, organizational involvement, and digital technologies. Component is the challenges which include simplification of the process, adjustment of the new circumstances, and the employment of the staff. However, the main attention of future work is to identify real usage and synergy of the approaches based on AI and ML with other technologies, as well as to select the central goals of the countries [10].

2.4.3.2 Guiding the Future of Manufacturing: Responsible AI as a Cornerstone for Sustainable and Ethical Production

The provided study stresses the application of Responsible Artificial Intelligence (RAI) in manufacturing to minimize risks and provide businesses with new opportunities. AI transformation is a fact in the industry, and if implemented uncritically, social and environmental risks may appear. The qualitative RAI frameworks involve sub-dimensional areas of liability, viz., human factor, decision-making, organizational focus, and the system design. Alongside AI system maturity, the human-centric approach assumes a critical role in system lifespan. Responsible AI is basic to responsible research and innovation for obtaining the correct information about emerging technologies' damages to humanity and the surrounding ecosystem [11–13].

2.4.4 Transportation

Intelligent machines are getting involved in transportation by employing advanced sensors for a 3D depiction of surroundings in a real-time environment. AI algorithms, being familiar with huge data sets regarding driving scenes and road laws, make choices in an instant manner such as changing lanes and maintaining a safe distance from other cars. AI in autonomous vehicles never ceases to gather and use new data, thus becoming a better tool to cope with the most unexpected of cases with every single mile driven. AI is also used to optimize routes which simply gives a new dimension to traffic management. The brain of an AI system can process immediately the traffic data, and automate canalization and weather conditions to suggest an effective route for each specific vehicle to save time and reduce congestion and fuel consumption, which will lead cities to become greener and cleaner. The future of transport is a combination of human genius and artificial intelligence as autopilot cars and smart routing guarantee more comfort, smoothness, safety, and sustainability of the journey from A to B. Autonomous vehicles, self-driving vehicles, are based on several AI functions such as computer vision and machine learning for road navigation, detection of obstacles, and general decision-making while driving. In terms of route optimization, AI can process real-time traffic data so that delivery vehicles and public transport are directed towards the quickest routes and there will be less travel time and fuel wastage. The main cause of traffic vehicle accidents is human error. The autonomous vehicles concept is expected to be safer and more efficient than transportation [16].

2.4.4.1 Revolutionizing Urban Mobility: The Power of Machine Learning and AI in Smart City Transportation

The function of machine learning and AI in the creation of smart cities, focusing on its utilization in controlling emerging urban areas, strengthening economies, decreasing energy consumption, and raising living standards has been explored. The findings imply that ML and Intelligent traffic control, dynamic routing, modeling and simulation, congestion management, and intelligent transportation systems all depend heavily on AI. The report also highlights the usefulness of ML and AI in air, rail, and road transport. The agent computing paradigm is promoted for its interoperability, flexibility, and extendibility in large-scale networked systems. AI is revolutionizing the transportation market by enhancing travel experiences, extending accessibility, and lessening dependency on private autos. Through machine learning algorithms that optimize energy use, encourage environmentally friendly driving practices, and ease the integration of electric and autonomous autos, it is also helping to create sustainable transportation networks. AI-powered safety solutions are being developed to boost automotive and pedestrian safety and minimize accident risks [14].

2.4.4.2 AI Revolutionizes Transportation: Boosting Efficiency, Safety, and New Business Opportunities

The application of AI in the transport system concentrates on its benefits and appeal for firms in many industries. It proposes the classification of AI technologies into different types according to their nature such as machine, deep learning, neural networks, natural language process, expert systems, and robotization of automated systems. The authors discuss the problems of applying AI for successful traffic management, such as boosting uniformity of traffic flow, optimizing public transit routes, and installing specific equipment. Besides that, they also bring forward a concept of intelligent transport systems for Moscow, St. Petersburg, and the Leningrad Region. AI technology is also used to optimize corporate operations, provide suggestions, evaluate demand, and detect fraud situations. Amazon has been on the cutting edge of AI technology to develop new products and business models such as Echo/Alexa speech recognition, Prime Air, and the future Amazon Go [15].

2.4.5 Agriculture

The AI technology revolution in agriculture progresses by raising crop yield and reducing ecological setbacks. It applies cutting-edge algorithms by providing results based on satellite imagery, meteorological information, and soil conditions. AI via its machine learning and predictive analytics offers farmers real-time knowledge regarding crops' health and development. Through the analysis of conditions such as stress, disease, or inadequate nutrition the success of treatments is possible, which can result in increasing productivity. Artificial intelligence-driven data-driven farming methods will be highly concerned with the use of natural resources like water, fertilizers, and pesticides that will in turn save operational costs and lead to increasing efficiency. The machine learning algorithms having as their basis the soil moisture, crop condition, and forecast weather provide decision accountability of a selective whereby to use resources to reduce spending and environmental effect. AI is modified to rectify the environmental change and plant health variation; thus, the farmers would be able to get exact outturns from these little variations and make fast decisions. In precision farming AI-based systems are capable of decrypting soil status, climatic features, and plant health data, which is further used to optimize fertilizer and water usage consequently giving better yields. In terms of crop monitoring, the AI-powered drones will be scanning crops for the presence of diseases and pests, which will offer a timely solution to prevent massive crop damage. The main farming method has been using intuition and experience. AI is a source of the proactive and sustainable practice of agriculture by generating evidence-based information.

2.4.5.1 *Cultivating a Sustainable Future: How AI and Big Data are Revolutionizing Precision Agriculture*

Sustainable agricultural development is vital for population growth and climatic stability. Information and communication (ICT) technologies, such as machine learning and deep learning, are vital for precision agriculture. With the world population forecast to expand to 9.9 billion by 2050, agricultural productivity has to increase by 70%. Big data applications in smart agriculture are being employed to boost agricultural output, cut expenses, and assure sustainability. Data-driven agriculture tackles concerns such as food safety, supply management, food security, and food loss and waste. Blockchain technology and IoT assist manage the agri-food supply chain, giving transparency, security, and dependability. Innovative machine learning approaches like CNN and large data analysis methods provide improved accuracy, adaptability, and performance [17].

2.4.5.2 *AI in the Fields: From Precision Irrigation to Smart Robots, How Artificial Intelligence Is Revolutionizing Agribusiness*

Artificial intelligence (AI) has changed the agricultural business by inventing automated processes and technology to cut costs, boost crop yields, and manage personnel shortages. AI applications in agriculture include sensor-based irrigation, robotics, and drones for weeding and spraying. These methods preserve soil fertility, limit the use of water, pesticides, and herbicides, and facilitate the effective use of labour, all of which lead to increased production and quality. Vertical farming, where food is grown on top of one another, may lead to increased crop output per square foot of land used. AI can assist with complicated and mundane activities by enhancing current technology, accumulating and reviewing huge data on a digital platform, selecting the best course of action, and implementing that action. By implementing automation solutions like autonomous tractors, intelligent irrigation systems, intelligent spraying, vertical farming software, and AI-based harvesting robots, artificial intelligence (AI) may also help overcome a lack of labor. AI may also be employed in supply chain, smart farming, autonomous mobility, and smart retail.

2.4.6 Retail

AI can enable merchants to run sophisticated analyses on large datasets, including detailed records of customer purchases, browsing behavior, and demographics, which is essential for revealing how customers like certain products and how many consumers are enthusiastic about the market demand for specific goods and services. Therefore, merchants can make the bulwark of their efforts to adjust to the market demand by repricing and modifying marketing and product offers. AI is a key tool for keeping optimal stock and minimizing unnecessary inventory, which is one of the other issues regarding the management of inventory stock facilities. The support of merchants in the process of making data-informed decisions about distributors, whom to buy from, and what products to order, boosts the efficiency of the operations, thus significantly decreasing the carrying costs. The field of AI has turned into a realm of vivid marketing innovations, where the most important aspect is to engage customers individually. The AI algorithms can be under clients' needed items and services by reviewing the clients' data patterns. Thus, it leads to the building of customer loyalty, as well as to increasing the amount of goods sold. Also, AI-powered chatbots and smart assistants are employed for personalized customer service through which each experience is enhanced as well as overall shopping experience improvement.

2.4.6.1 *The Generative Retail Revolution: How AI is Personalizing Customer Experience, Optimizing Inventory, and Driving Sales*

This research study is built around using generative AI within retail business scenarios, which is characterized by data of customers to improve the customer experience and inventory optimization. It trains an LLM in the centralized data and allows visualization of important insights. AI can be of great use for improving customer experience, managing stocks, and assisting in targeted marketing techniques. However, some issues like data privacy, algorithmic bias, implementation costs, and expertise are the things to be considered. The study also amplifies that better AI algorithms and cost-effectiveness are the need of the hour for the retailers' domain. The research closes by using Facebook Marketplace as a case study that will exemplify the interplay of data and AI in shaping consumer-business relations [18].

2.4.6.2 The Future of Retail: Leveraging AI for Efficiency and Personalization while Navigating Data Privacy and Ethical Challenges

The main purpose of this cutting-edge research is to establish the advantages of AI in the retail organization processes, like more and better customer experiences, effective inventory management, individualized target marketing, and improved demand projections. Nevertheless, the theme of data privacy, ethical questions, workforce displacement, as well as the establishment of vigorous AI governance down the line is also brought to attention. The author holds a view that widely known individuals, robot creators, lawmakers, and regulators should dedicate their utmost efforts to developing an AI-powered sales system that would prioritize transparency, accountability, and a customer-oriented approach. Integrating AI output with socially acceptable values and visions of consumer perceptions might be the key to getting the best out of this industry as well as creating a preferable environment for ethics, trust, and customer focus [19].

2.4.7 Domain-Specific AI: A Comparative Analysis

Table 2.2 compares how AI is being applied in various domains along with some key considerations.

The key considerations for comparison include data requirements and mechanisms in different domains that vary between major and minor. Healthcare and finance and retail are commonly structured data sources, whereas agriculture and transportation often use real-time data and sensors. The technical challenges include the intricacy or complexity of AI models that hinges on their respective applications. Unlike scenario-based maintenance, autonomous vehicles need "high-ordered" algorithms. In terms of ethical considerations in all sectors of the economy, but especially in healthcare and finance, questions about algorithmic bias, data privacy, and the misuse danger should be considered. AI specialized for domain functions tends to integrate with the Internet of Things (IoT) and cloud computing technologies, which serve the purpose of data collection, processing, and analysis. Integration of AI creators, field specialists, and lawmakers into the process of responsible AI creation and implementation is vital to avoid risks and maximize the positive impact. This data table gives a broad picture of the comparison. At the same time, targeted problems and considerations will be different and correspond to the selected application in each area.

Table 2.2 A comparative analysis of domain-specific AI.

Domain	**Application**	**Benefits**	**Challenges**	**Data requirements**
Healthcare	Diagnosis and Treatment	Improved accuracy, personalized medicine, and earlier interventions	Ethical considerations, bias in algorithms, data privacy	Large datasets of medical images, patient records, and genetic data
Finance	Algorithmic Trading and Risk Assessment	Faster decision-making, reduced risk, efficient resource allocation	Market volatility, regulatory compliance, potential for misuse	Real-time and historical market data, financial statements, creditworthiness information
Manufacturing	Predictive Maintenance and Supply Chain Optimization	Reduced downtime, cost savings, improved efficiency	Integration with existing systems, sensor data quality, skilled workforce for maintenance	Sensor data from machines, historical production data, logistics network information
Transportation	Autonomous Vehicles and Route Optimization	Safer roads, reduced traffic congestion, improved fuel efficiency	Technical limitations, infrastructure development, public acceptance	Real-time traffic data, road maps, sensor data from vehicles
Agriculture	Precision Farming and Crop Monitoring	Increased crop yields, reduced waste, sustainable practices	Access to technology in rural areas, weather variability, data security	Soil and weather data, drone imagery, crop health information
Retail	Personalized Recommendations and Demand Forecasting	Increased sales, improved customer experience, optimized inventory management	Data privacy concerns, personalization fatigue, ethical considerations for recommendation algorithms	Customer purchase history, browsing behavior, demographics, product information, market trends

2.5 Ethical and Societal Implications

The ethical and societal ramifications of AI-empowered administrative control possess profound aspects, thus ensuring good decisions can be made based on fairness, accountability, and transparency. At the point of using artificial intelligence (AI) in critical decision domains such as banking, healthcare, or criminal justice there is a need to consider ethics from the view of their efficiency. Fairness and impartiality are the issues that must be tackled since they may lead to biased decision-making and perpetuate the existing hierarchies in society. Proactively the diversifying of the data sets, checks of the bias of the algorithms, and the inclusions and diversity of the AI development teams are examples of proactive measures.

A promotion of AI technology is going to cause a shift in society; issues such as power relations, job competition, economic stability, and a lack of privacy will be the result. Stakeholders must be forward-looking by taking preventive measures and enabling gains since they could either hinder or expedite the success of the cause. Engaging in some of these actions refers to fostering ethical frameworks behind AI design and deployment, bringing AI-related issues to the table of societal discussion, and keeping in mind that AI should be making progress in a way that matches the general societal goals such as equity, sustainability, and human welfare.

In a word, it is the teamwork of different stakeholders that is imperative to determine the ethical and sociological challenges of the AI-based decision-making process. In applying and developing AI, the one that covers transparency, fairness, and social responsibility should be for all of us and may be key to having an equal, inclusive, and sustainable society for everyone.

2.6 Future Directions and Emerging Trends

With the increasing capabilities of AI algorithms and models in carving out AI with particular applications, domain-specific AI is on the course of reshaping several sectors like healthcare, finance, manufacturing, and agriculture, among others. To strengthen performance, comprehensibility, and fairness, explainable AI, and federated learning, as well as synthetic data creation are online now. It is anticipated that particular AI algorithms will improve further and will be integrated into different practical applications, such as autonomous systems, smart manufacturing, personalized medicine, and predictive analytics, etc. The next wave of change and inventiveness will be pushed by the merger of AI with advanced technologies such as blockchain, quantum computing, and the Internet of Things. To make the development of domain-specific AI possible, a collaboration between the business, academia, and the government is indispensable. The next generation will be well equipped to engage and maximize the potential of AI in education and the workforce is given due attention. To achieve this, we have to continue with AI research, break industry barriers, and make staff members and students well-versed in AI.

2.7 Conclusion

The research is done around a broad topic of artificial intelligence (AI) systems and how domain-specific AI models and algorithms can impact business operations within industries like manufacturing, agriculture, health care, and finance. They do so by minimizing decision-making processes and having a positive impact on operational efficiency as well as new developments where advanced machine learning methods and data analytics are used. Nevertheless, the employment of AI promotes learning and presents an array of both opportunities and inhibitions. Whilst they might change the business processes, upgrade production, and enable long-term development, stakeholders should consider moral and social effects, discrimination, and justice among others to execute what is the right use of such technology. The chapter stresses the point for a careful and proficient technology of AI adoption and mainly focuses on transparency, accountability, and justice to completely understand their capacity and construct a world with safety, as well as an inclusive future.

References

1. Ferreira, J.J. and Monteiro, M.D.S., *Do ML Experts Discuss Explainability for AI Systems? A discussion case in the industry for a domain-specific solution*, 2020, arXiv preprint arXiv:2002.12450.
2. Meskó, B. and Topol, E.J., The imperative for regulatory oversight of large language models (or generative AI) in healthcare. *npj Digit. Med.*, 6, 1, 120, 2023.
3. Malinverno, L., Barros, V., Ghisoni, F., Visonà, G., Kern, R., Nickel, P.J., Ventura, B.E., Šimić, I., Stryeck, S., Manni, F., Ferri, C., A historical perspective of biomedical explainable AI research. *Patterns*, 4, 9, 2023.
4. Ueda, D., *et al.*, Fairness of artificial intelligence in healthcare: review and recommendations. *Jpn. J. Radiol.*, 42, 1, 3–15, 2024.

5. Rayhan, A., Rayhan, R., Rayhan, S., *The Role of AI in Healthcare: Revolutionizing Patient Care and Well-Being*, p. 22601, 2023, DOI: 10.13140/RG.2.2.
6. Weber, P., Carl, K.V., Hinz, O., Applications of explainable artificial intelligence in finance—a systematic review of finance, information systems, and computer science literature. *Manage. Rev. Q.*, 1–41, 2023.
7. Rane, N., *Role and Challenges of ChatGPT and Similar Generative Artificial Intelligence in Finance and Accounting*, 2023, Available at SSRN 4603206.
8. Biju, A.K.V.N., Thomas, A.S., Thasneem, J., Examining the research taxonomy of artificial intelligence, deep learning & machine learning in the financial sphere—a bibliometric analysis. *Qual. Quant.*, 58, 1, 849–878, 2024.
9. Dowling, M. and Lucey, B., ChatGPT for (finance) research: The Bananarama conjecture. *Finance Res. Lett.*, 53, 103662, 2023.
10. De Simone, V., Di Pasquale, V., Miranda, S., An overview on the use of AI/ML in Manufacturing MSMEs: solved issues, limits, and challenges. *Procedia Comput. Sci.*, 217, 1820–1829, 2023.
11. Besinger, P., Vejnoska, D., Ansari, F., Responsible AI (RAI) in Manufacturing: A Qualitative Framework. *Procedia Comput. Sci.*, 232, 813–822, 2024.
12. Albtoush, A. and Almahasneh, I., Comparative Analysis of Google AI and Chatbot GPT: A Study on Technological Approaches and Applications. *Kurdish Stud.*, 12, 1, 4302–4318, 2024.
13. Kim, S.W., Kong, J.H., Lee, S.W., Lee, S., Recent advances of artificial intelligence in manufacturing industrial sectors: A review. *Int. J. Precis. Eng. Manuf.*, 1–19, 2022.
14. Bharadiya, J., Artificial intelligence in transportation systems: a critical review. *Am. J. Comput. Eng.*, 6, 1, 34–45, 2023.
15. Okrepilov, V.V., Kovalenko, B.B., Getmanova, G.V., Turovskaj, M.S., Modern trends in artificial intelligence in the transport system. *Transp. Res. Procedia*, 61, 229–233, 2022.
16. Zhou, Z., Zahid, U., Majeed, Y., Mustafa, S., Sajjad, M.M., Butt, H.D., Fu, L., Advancement in artificial intelligence for on-farm fruit sorting and transportation. *Front. Plant Sci.*, 14, 1082860, 2023.
17. Bhat, S.A. and Huang, N.F., Big data and AI revolution in precision agriculture: Survey and challenges. *IEEE Access*, 9, 110209–110222, 2021.
18. Sharma, S., Verma, K., Hardaha, P., Implementation of artificial intelligence in agriculture. *J. Comput. Cognit. Eng.*, 2, 2, 155–162, 2023.
19. Dhoni, P.S., From Data to Decisions: Enhancing Retail with AI and Machine Learning. *Int. J. Comput. Eng.*, 5, 1, 38–51, 2024.

3

Role of AI in Decision-Making – A Comprehensive Study

Rohit Vashisht*, Sonia Deshmukh and Ashima Arya

Department of Computer Science and Information Technology, KIET Group of Institutions, Delhi-NCR, Ghaziabad, India

Abstract

Artificial intelligence is a research field of how to provide computers and other technologies the power to think, learn, and act in ways that would normally need human comprehension or involve data sets that are far too large for humans to comprehend. It is a blend of methods for intelligent data retrieval, natural language processing, object sorting, prediction, analysis of data, and more. The majority of these technologies are built on deep learning and machine learning. It eliminates human mistakes and quickly and continuously analyses massive amounts of diverse data, giving firms access to a wide range of data and providing systematic solutions to new challenges. Besides this, it may also assist an enterprise in anticipating customer demand for its goods, which enables it to effectively manage inventory levels and prevent overstocking or stock-outs. Everyone has personal prejudices, and sometimes they get in the way of our best intentions to deal with them. On the other hand, if an AI system has been trained using real-world datasets and is monitored for the emergence of bias, it can produce decision models devoid of bias. The proposed article discusses the need for AI in decision-making. It also covers the main industries where AI is essential for decision-making, including healthcare, banking, transportation, disease diagnosis, fraud prediction, and agricultural output improvement. Additionally, the article describes the main uses for AI-based decision-making models, such as decision-making in business operations, productivity analysis of employees, multilayer and complex problem solving, strategic change planning, customer service management, and performance evaluation. The main obstacles in building an AI-based automated decision-making system are also outlined, along with feasible solutions.

**Corresponding author*: rohit.vashisht@kiet.edu

Sapna Juneja, Rajesh Kumar Dhanaraj, Abhinav Juneja, Malathy Sathyamoorthy and Asadullah Shaikh (eds.) Ethical Decision-Making Using Artificial Intelligence: Challenges, Solutions and Applications, (55–78) © 2025 Scrivener Publishing LLC

Keywords: Decision-making, automated, deep learning, classification, accuracy

3.1 Introduction

AI decision-making is going to be the future of intelligent systems in businesses. For many years, data has been the cornerstone of modern business. It has helped business owners and entrepreneurs make decisions. It also provided them with a wealth of information on their clientele. However, having so much data comes at a cost, and the human brain can only process so much. AI-based business intelligence decision-making can help with this. Businesses may increase the speed, accuracy, and consistency of their decision-making by using AI to exploit information with accurate processing of large datasets. Business teams will find it easier to focus on duties relevant to their industry as a result. When it comes to machine learning, natural language processing, and visual processing, business decision-makers trust AI completely [1]. In the modern era, these are the most dependable elements in every organization to increase sales and meet goals.

The importance of a decision that uses a vast amount of data as input and generates perception, prediction, assessment, and actions as outputs is clearly illustrated in Figure 3.1. It summarizes the massive amount of unprocessed raw data using three distinct levels of intelligence. First, it can automate a large task's fundamental subtasks using aided intelligence [2]. Automating assembly line machinery is the best example for this. Second, the model is capable of two-way augmented intelligence, in which human

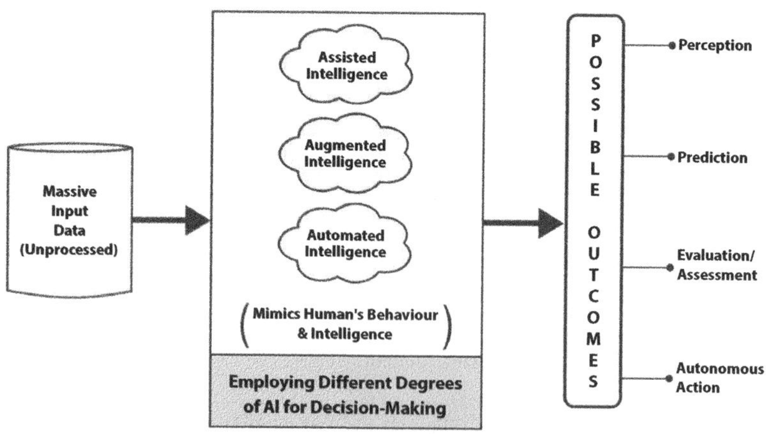

Figure 3.1 AI-based decision-making system.

inputs serve as the primary input and processed intelligent information is used for assisting decisions. Finally, automatic intelligence completely eliminates the need of human for decision-making. Like self-driving cars or autonomous robots, the entire process is automated [3].

Table 3.1 provides a clear description of the main distinctions between the AI and human-based decision-making approaches. Whereas natural

Table 3.1 Human vs. AI-based decision-making approach.

Parameter	Natural intelligence	Artificial intelligence
Energy Efficiency	More energy requirement (approximately 25 watt energy for simulation of human brain).	Less energy requirement (approximately 2 watt to simulate a machine).
Universality	Human is trained to handle multiple tasks and situations (expected or unexpected) based on his/her intelligence, past experiences and surrounding conditions.	AI-based systems are made to handle specific & limited types of tasks.
Multi-Tasking	It takes less time and effort to teach people to perform a variety of jobs under different conditions.	To teach a machine to be intelligent enough to manage every little detail of a particular task under various circumstances requires a lot more time and effort.
State/Condition	Ambiguity can also be produced by analogous or skewed human intelligence.	Because AI-based systems are trained on billions and millions of cases, the findings are consistently accurate.

intelligence relies on sensory experiences that can change depending on the context and various scenarios, Artificial Intelligence dominates many activities involving repetitive decisions. The bedrock of computer learning is AI, which has enabled computers to access vast amounts of data. Furthermore, AI can make the best decisions quickly, in contrast to humans. Everything is now controlled by AI, including cutting-edge studies on climate change and advancements in cancer treatment [4].

The structure of the chapter is as follows: Section 3.2 discusses the necessity and significance of AI in decision-making. Sections 3.3 and 3.4 provide quotes regarding the main obstacles to AI-based Decision-Making System (AIDMS) and its associated applications. Section 3.5 provides an explanation of a case study involving AI-based decision making. A consideration of potential future directions and consequences brings Section 3.6 to a close.

3.2 Need of AI-Based Decision-Making System

There are two main disadvantages of the former method that usually come into play when discussing natural intelligence vs. AI.

- *Utilization of all data:* It is impossible for humans to utilize all the data. Human effort compiles all of a dataset's elements. For example, connections, understandings, and trends. People use summaries to manage vast volumes of data. Processing millions or billions of records is not possible for humans to accomplish. The relationship between data elements, which are thought to be the foundation of all decision-making, cannot be linked by human minds [1].
- *Allowing of biases:* Important information is given precedence by humans over its contents. Humans cannot process data in aggregates because they view it as simple, in contrast to AI. Furthermore, AI is capable of gathering data without being influenced by emotion and making mistakes in judgment. However, entrusting machines with all the job is not a wise business decision [1].

Prior to the resurgence of AI and its commercial use, executives relied on erroneous and inadequate data. Data-driven models and simulations to aspire to were introduced with AI. The AI system today starts from scratch and feeds on a typical big data business feed. Businesses use their augmented intelligence. Ultimately, it offers leaders cutting-edge models to serve as the basis for their choices. Both physical and cognitive jobs are automated by AI [5]. People can now make decisions more quickly and accurately due to it. In simple words, it involves some human intervention but automates decision-making. AI reduces tedious manual labor and time-consuming tasks while increasing automation. Figure 3.2 explains in detail the various kinds of skewed decisions that are made by different systems based on data, mathematical models, and knowledge [6].

Humans have always been at the centre of decision-making. Data that has been human-analyzed is utilized to determine which clients to target and how much a product launch will cost. Furthermore, in this case, marketing activities were too dangerous. AI is the ideal option for corporations since it is able to evolve. Increasing the amount of data used in decision-making equates to better learning. AI is capable of teaching itself to build data collection models. These models have the potential to accurately identify and draw inferences based on the available data. In a similar vein, the models generate suggestions, classifications, and predictions in real time depending on data. So, it enables better business decisions to be

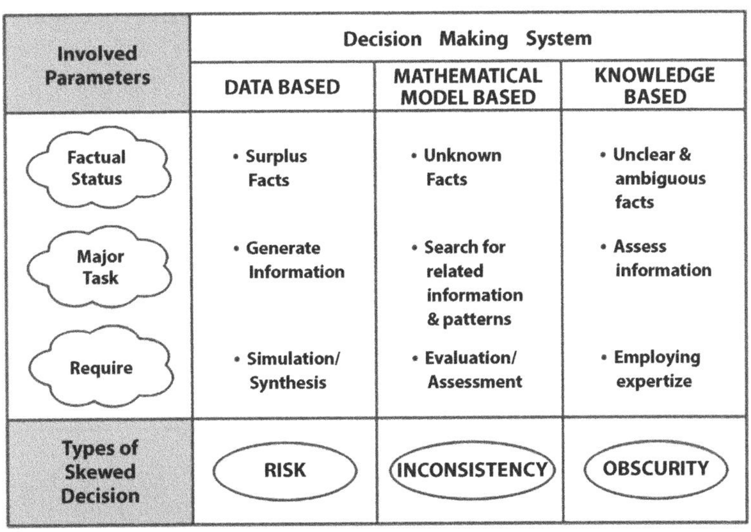

Figure 3.2 Types of skewed decisions.

made. Artificial Intelligence is the ideal option for corporations since it is able to evolve. Increasing the amount of data used in decision-making equates to better learning. It also facilitates improved human operations and pattern recognition. By effectively detecting trends in your data, AI can anticipate outcomes more quickly. These enable you to view the wider picture more quickly, which can aid you in making marketing decisions. It can also favorably impact how we operate in the future and give AI and humans a method to collaborate to the fullest extent possible. Consequently, it is clear that using AI has several following benefits over relying just on natural intelligence [7]. Table 3.2 provides an elegant explanation of the benefits and significance of AI when designing a decision-making system.

- AI solutions, like chatbots and machine learning algorithms, help to narrow down the large pool of prospective customers into the target customer's bucket by providing a better understanding of their expectations and level of satisfaction.
- Businesses that handle intricate data benefit from better decision-making. Large data sets are easily understood by AI, especially when the outcomes are quantifiable and clear [8].
- By AI, humans can free up their energies for work that demands greater creativity and avoid becoming bored with monotonous chores like creating reports and checking and assessing data.
- It enables corporations to quickly analyze big datasets and make decisions right away. As a result, it improves decision-making more successfully [9].

Table 3.2 Significance of AI in decision-making.

S. no.	Parameter	Description
1.	Data Collection & Its Interpretation	When it comes to processing, the amount of data generated much exceeds what humans can comprehend and interpret. AI algorithms are capable of processing larger volumes of complex data and preparing it for assessment [10].

Table 3.2 Significance of AI in decision-making.

S. no.	Parameter	Description
2.	Economical & High Productivity	Because AI can operate continuously, it can produce more in a single day than a human worker can. Additionally, by helping to replace manual and arduous jobs, AI frees up humans for higher-skilled duties. Ultimately, this leads to decreased expenses for the final user or consumer.
3.	Fair & Impartial Decision-Making	Individuals make skewed conclusions because they disagree frequently and have biases. Everyone has biases, and even though we try our hardest to overcome them, sometimes they still manage to get through to us. However, as long as the AI algorithm has been trained using real-world datasets and checked for programming bias, the AIDMS will be able to make choices devoid of prejudice [11].
4.	No Human Error & Risk	If AI is used for extremely difficult or dangerous tasks, the likelihood of human damage or harm can be decreased. One example of AI assuming risks instead of people is the use of robots in high-radiation areas [12].
5.	Availability	Eight hours a day is all that humans work, but AI-based models are always available. Machines never stop working, and chatbots with AI skills might help clients even after hours [13].

3.3 Major Obstacle for AI-Based Decision-Making System

In addition to providing solutions for massive data analysis and efficient decision-making, AI has some significant obstacles when it comes to build successful decision-making systems as shown in Figure 3.3. The primary challenges for AIDMS are outlined as follows.

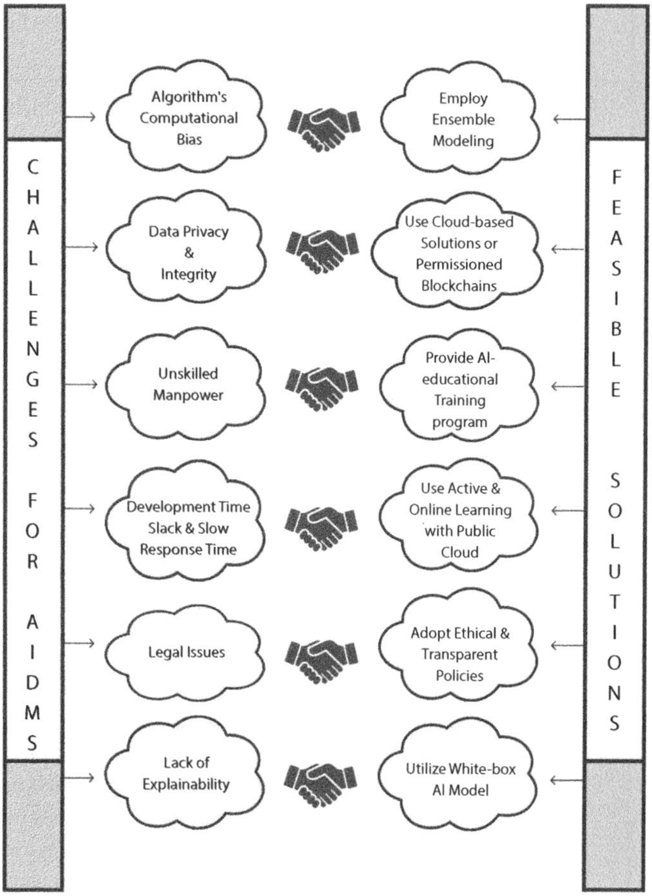

Figure 3.3 Major challenges for AIDMS.

- *Data Quality & Dependability:* Decision-making by AI is heavily dependent on reliable and accurate data. Handling incomplete, inaccurate, or biased data is challenging as it can lead to provide incorrect outputs, inconsistent or even discriminatory conclusions, as well as poor insights and decisions. If representative and high-quality data are consistently used, this difficulty can be addressed. Also, it's best to start the AI journey with simpler algorithms that are simpler to comprehend, control for bias, and modify as needed.
- *Antiquated Infrastructure Facilities:* AI requires devices with the right infrastructure and computing power to process massive volumes of data in microseconds. However, a lot of organizations continue to operate using antiquated foundations and equipments. In turn, it is essential that companies embrace machine learning to completely transform their processes for learning and development. It needs to have its infrastructure, tools, and applications upgraded technologically.
- *Over-dependence:* AI is dependent on the accuracy and reliability of its incoming data. Relying only on the data supplied, without adequate human review, may lead to biases and optimism. Maintaining the proper balance between human perception and AI support is essential to avoid over-reliance or neglecting responsibilities.
- *Economical Constraint:* Initiating an ongoing AI training programs for the relevant staff, collaborating with AI experts who have the necessary skills, and perhaps updating the IT infrastructure to meet the needs of ML tools are just a few of the many tasks that AIDMS incurs significant costs for. Even while some of these costs cannot be avoided, they can be greatly decreased by looking for free or inexpensive software or training programs.
- *Assimilation into Current Frameworks:* It needs substantially more efforts to integrate AI into a training program than just adding a few LMS plug-ins. It is important to take extra time when incorporating AI with current systems to take into account the infrastructure, computing power, and storage requirements. Furthermore, training on how to use the new tools, troubleshoot simple problems, and recognize situations where the AI algorithm is not operating as intended is necessary for the concerned staff members.

Three main categories can be used to group the main AIDMS challenges are as follows.

- **Technical Issues**: A number of technical issues, including scalability, algorithm selection, and integration with current systems might arise when implementing AI in real-time data processing. Companies need to be fully aware of their technical capabilities and constraints. A corporation may need to engage new staff because its development team frequently lacks experience with AI programs.
- **Ethical Issues**: A number of ethical issues, such as algorithmic bias, transparency, and data privacy, are brought up by AI-driven data analysis. To keep the public's trust, organizations need to set ethical standards and follow data privacy laws. Following the use of AI tools, companies will undoubtedly wonder if they really need every person. The human cost of applying AI tools could be rather substantial because their application frequently results in job losses for some people.
- **Data Quality Issues**: When AI programs are given erroneous data, they produce erroneous predictions or conclusions. These machines frequently lack the human propensity to challenge the information they are given. Furthermore, since AI systems are taught on material created by humans, they could pick up prejudices from people. The way an AI interprets a data collection may then be impacted by these biases.

The following are the primary forces behind AIDMS as shown in Figure 3.4.

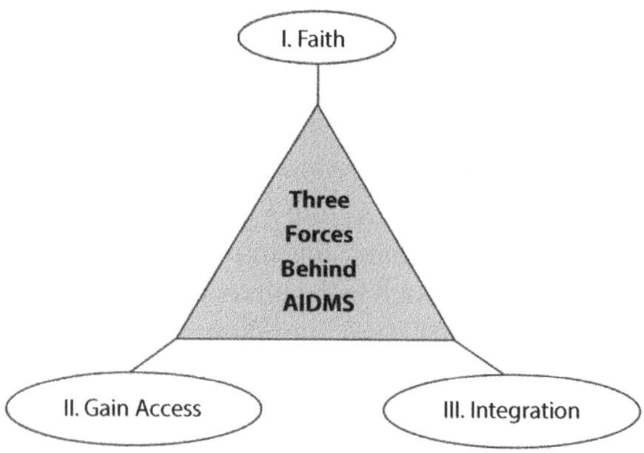

Figure 3.4 Three forces for AIDMS.

a) **Faith**: Globally, trust in AI varies significantly, according to a recent survey conducted globally. Only 15% of people in Finland and 23% of people in Japan would be willing to trust AI, compared to 75% of people in India. We think that the degree of trust that people have in the AI system will play a big role in whether or not it is used in decision-making. Such advancements could have a big impact on how competitively inclined nations worldwide are in the area of technology.
b) **Gain Access**: The most advanced AI systems in the world might be closed systems, which allow businesses and countries to set themselves apart from one another and manage access to the technology, or open systems, which essentially allow everyone access to a single AI. A select few may be able to make strategic AI-based verdicts in a world where closed systems rule.
c) **Integration**: The ability of businesses and governments to manage the AI-human interface is the third element that we believe will impact the scope and pace of AI adoption in decision-making. It will be critical to be able to reduce the impact of human biases in the process and make appropriate use of AI input when making strategic decisions.

3.4 Applications of AI-Based Decision-Making System

Not only are there challenges in adopting AI, but there are also differences in its accessibility globally. Specifically, some countries are already making great strides in AI technology, while others are struggling to keep up with much more fundamental advancements in technology. As the required data is occasionally governed by data protection rules that prioritize the security and transparency of data, AI raises a number of moral and legal questions. Due to ethical concerns over data privacy, fairness, vulnerability, and accountability, AIDMS is also being hampered [14, 15]. By eliminating human mistakes and quickly and continually analyzing vast amounts of various data, AI provides entities with organized solutions to new challenges and access to a wide range of information. A description of the key uses for AIDMS is shown in Figure 3.5.

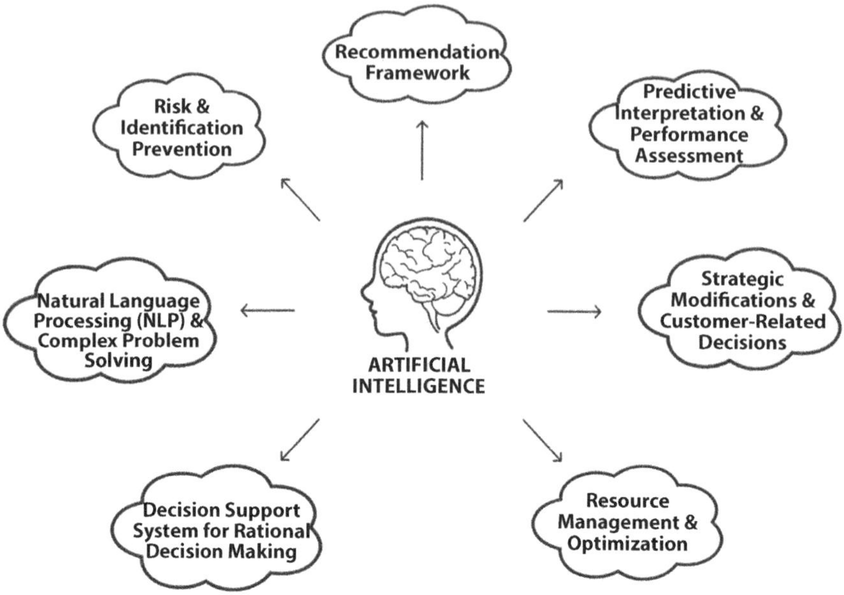

Figure 3.5 Applications of AI in decision-making system.

a) *Recommendation Framework:* Recommendation engines powered by AI analyze enormous amounts of data and offer personalised user recommendations. These systems help users find valuable and relevant products or material based on their past activities, interests, and behavior. Currently, Netflix's algorithm incorporates a recommender system. Based on the watching habits of comparable users, the platform utilizes your prior viewing history to forecast content that may be of interest to you in the future [16, 17].

b) *Predictive Interpretation & Performance Assessment:* AI uses predictive analytics as a tool to look at historical data, identify patterns, and make accurate predictions. In essence, predictive analytics helps to answer questions about possible future occurrences. Proactive decision-makers can use predictive analytics to predict events to come in a range of domains, such as demand planning and projections of sales. Human error and biases could undermine the impartiality of the personnel appraisal procedure. AI, however, can lessen human error and improve data transparency on employee performance.

c) *Strategic Modifications & Customer-Related Decisions:* The current competitive landscape and industry dynamics also require flexibility in go-to-market and marketing tactics. AI is capable of making those tactical adjustments more quickly and safely. AI holds potential benefits in customer service administration, tailored communication with clients, behavior analysis, and trend and pattern recognition. AI makes it possible to automatically identify and profile possible clients. For instance, predefined profiles can be used to recognize and classify new consumers. This data analysis allows for the prediction of new consumer habits and strategies for luring them in [18].
d) *Resource Management & Optimization:* The way company procedures are carried out can be completely changed by AI-powered resource management. Currently, over 200 services are offered by cloud-based providers such as Amazon Web Services to assist a corporation in optimizing its computational resources. Processes can be completed more quickly and with less resource waste, which is advantageous for the organization. In addition, one can prevent expensive downtime brought on by an overestimation of the system's capacity [19].
e) *Decision Support Systems:* AI-driven decision support systems help decision makers in a variety of fields, such as supply chain management, logistics, and healthcare, by giving them timely access to pertinent information, data analysis, and insights. But in order to make sure that the data being used is reliable and accurate, critical thinking is required. If the proper critical thinking is applied to the input facts, AIDMS always produces reasonable and rational conclusions [20].
f) NLP & Complex Problem Solving: Although AI has a lot of potential for decision-making, it may also be used to handle intricate and multilayered problems. The ability of a computer to automatically examine and process words in a conversational fashion is known as NLP. NLP is used by intelligent chatbots, such as ChatGPT, to interpret human inquiries and prompts and generate a logical response.

g) *Risk Identification & Prevention:* AI systems are capable of evaluating and analyzing complex risk aspects, such as cybersecurity risks or credit risk. An AI-powered tool is a terrific approach to help businesses anticipate future dangers and prepare their reaction because it can swiftly analyze massive data sets and discover anomalies. Decision-makers can minimize any negative effects by using this data to evaluate risks, identify vulnerabilities, and develop efficient mitigation solutions [21].

With its ability to supplement several stages of the decision-making framework, AI plays a critical role in improving the decision-making process. The ways in which AI supports decision-making at each stage are as follows:

- *Problem Identification:* The proficiency of AI algorithms lies in their capability to meticulously analyze and evaluate issues with unparalleled accuracy. With the help of huge data, these algorithms can identify hidden insights, flaws, or apparent inclinations leads to dodge manual thoughts. These discovered patterns can be employed in optimizing decisions and fixing particular, gaugeable objectives [22].
- *Processed Data Assimilation:* In the current era of technological advancement, AI is emerging as a bottleneck technology to handle and assess massive amounts of unprocessed or scattered data. AI uses various ML models, Natural Language Interpretation and data analytics to elicit useful and significant insights that further aid in the decision-making process.
- *Using Substitutes:* AI can offer a wide range of best possible alternative solutions by mimicking the real-world scenarios on grounds of past data and predictive analytics. While providing these robust alternative solutions, AI is not constrained only up to past data and insights; it can also use market situations and other supplementary factors like environmental factors, economic figures or even social media's mood swings.
- *Evaluation of All Substitutes:* With the help of useful extracted hidden patterns and useful insights, AI gives a beautiful comparative analysis for all possible solutions so that one can pick the best solution as per his/her need. ML algorithms are employed to identify the best possible alternative

solution. ML uses various evaluation metrics to figure out the best possible solution after having a rigorous comparative assessment. AI can make best decisions even after consideration of unforeseen future hazards with the projection of required outcomes of each alternative [23, 24].

- *Opting for the Best Substitute:* AI systems can opt for the most robust and potential solution from a pool of all possible solutions based on the assessed data. This will further assist decision-makers to take better-informed and logical decisions even after a lot of possible solutions are identified.
- *Implementation of Best Action:* AI helps to take better decisions in an effective way by offering various strategic patterns during the execution phase of the decision-making process. It will lead to designing more comprehensive execution plans easily. It also includes allocation of the available resources ideally as well as the tasks for implementation on the basis of different derived plans.
- *Analysis of Decisions Taken:* Once the best decision is being taken, AI regularly watches and records the impacts of executed decisions through real-time data analysis during the post-decision assessment task. With the help of various performance indicators, AI further evaluates whether decisions taken produce the desired result or not. In case of unexpected outcomes, AI can make guidance for amendments or even shift background strategies suddenly [25].

Manual and AI-based decision-making systems give data-based hidden insights and patterns which further upgrade the effectiveness and capabilities of the decision-making model among all possible solutions [26]. With the excellent capability to cater, inspect and draw out useful knowledge from massive datasets, AI has a significant influence on the precision of the decisions taken.

The following can be emphasized as the best practices for using AI.

a) Before putting AI into practice, companies must know what they want to utilize it for. It will be possible to prevent unnecessary software integrations from impeding business operations by identifying the issues that AI can solve. Businesses should establish quantifiable performance metrics following integration to make sure the technologies are having the desired impact.

b) Reliable data is necessary for precise AI-driven analysis. To guarantee that the AI solutions they use can access current and reliable data, organizations should make investments in data cleansing, validation, and integration procedures. If AI techniques are utilized for data collection and organization, then methods for confirming the accuracy of the data sets must be created.

c) Experts in a variety of disciplines, including computer programming, machine learning, and data science, make up a well-rounded AI team. Resources and ongoing training are essential. It's advisable to outsource the design of training materials if the business owner lacks expertise in artificial intelligence.

3.5 Case Study: AIDMS for Age-Related Macular Degeneration (AMD)

The authors refer to an AI-driven model for figuring out decisions for Age-related Macular Degeneration (AMD) in order to clarify the necessity and importance of AIDMS [22] as shown in Figure 3.6. To demonstrate three distinct kinds of CNNs for recognizing AMD, the authors [22] established an AI-based cloud service framework that uses an input dataset of Optical Coherence Tomography (OCT) images taken from AMD patients. With an accuracy of more than 90%, the proposed approach offers a practical solution utilizing telemedicine and medical imaging analysis that is on par

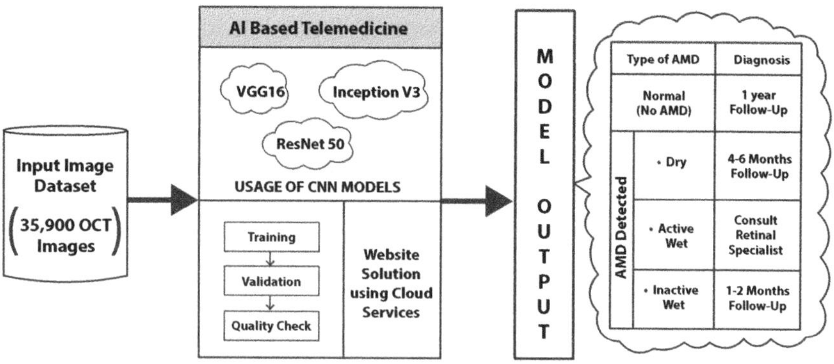

Figure 3.6 AIDMS for age-related macular degeneration.

with the accuracy of a retinal expert. Moreover, it offered suitable therapy solutions that were on the same level with those of retinal professionals.

This platform has the potential to expand telemedicine's possibilities by fusing the ideas of AI and cloud computing. The three Convolutional Neural Network (CNN) models (VGG16, ResNet50 and InceptionV3) were used here. The three types of AMD—inactive wet AMD, dry AMD (drusen), and active wet AMD—as well as normal macula were trained to identify by the authors using these three CNN models. Researchers not only provided theoretical support for AI's capabilities, they also developed a website for a cloud service based on this AI platform [22]. During the standard course of treatment, the patient and the physician interact physically in order to diagnose the condition. On the other hand, the suggested AIDMS would allow medical professionals or associated patients to upload OCT photos without the requirement for preprocessing, and this cloud-based, user-friendly AI website would instantly supply them with information about AMD types and suggested treatments [27, 28].

The recommended research demonstrated how integrating the concepts of cloud computing, telemedicine, and AI in the diagnosis and treatment guiding of AMD may lead to smart health practices that produce accurate diagnostic tools, more effective patient care, and products that improve quality of life. This cloud-based and AI software solution was not designed with longitudinal analysis in mind at first. Improved prediction might be achieved if long-term data, like annotated time-series of OCT images, were also added to the training and prediction model. The stated integrated telemedicine solution offers various advantages such as improved access to medical treatments, previously unreachable care options, and lower medical expenses [23]. For patients with active wet AMD, it is also possible to observe the combination of human judgment and AI-based decision-making. As a result, people with this kind of AMD need to go to a hospital to have the OCT exam done. Clinical judgment should be used to inform treatment decisions just as much as the AI classifier's results. Ultimately, the final evaluation and therapy should be carried out by a retinal specialist using clinical knowledge and facts.

Because AI technologies provide a range of tools and approaches to process data, develop insights, and support well-informed choices, they play a vital role in decision-making. As per Figure 3.7, several of the most important AI tools for decision-making are as follows:

a) Machine Learning: ML is used to find patterns in large datasets, interpret them, and forecast outcomes. Based on past data, it helps identify trends and possible outcomes,

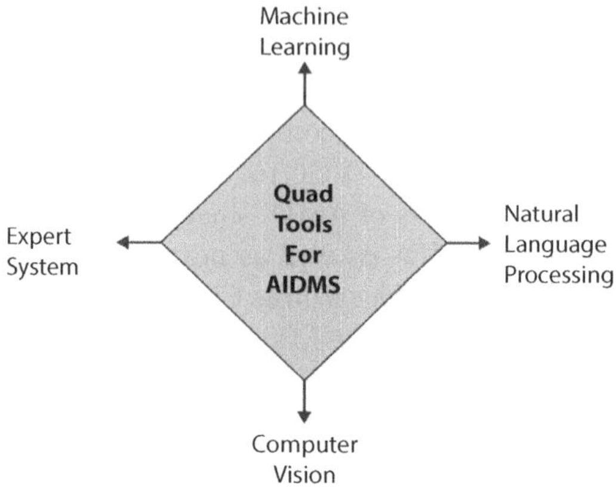

Figure 3.7 Quad AI tools.

supporting decision-makers in predicting and strategy optimization.

b) Natural Language Processing: Decision-making greatly profits from NLP since it makes programs understand human language and get valuable ideas. Natural language processing (NLP) can help you understand emotions, improve conversations between chatbots and customers, and gather information to support decisions.

c) Computer Vision: Computer vision technology analyzes visual information in photos and videos, making more informed decisions based on the data. This technology provides important functions such as object identification, image recognition and scanning. This will greatly aid decision-making based on visual information, help detect anomalies and improve quality assurance processes.

d) Expert systems: Artificial intelligence systems for expert decision-making that use decision engines and databases to model human knowledge in a specific domain. Expert systems play a vital role in making robust decisions and in providing useful suggestions applicable in a wide range of conditions. They are beneficial for making potential decisions in different domains like finance, law and healthcare.

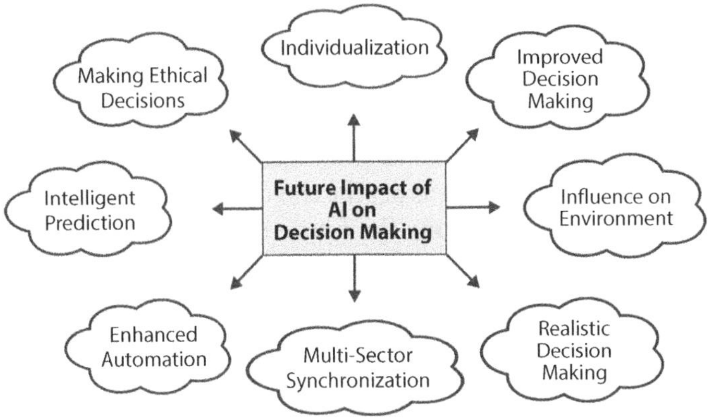

Figure 3.8 Future impact of AI on decision-making process.

In the future, the extracted useful and logical manufactured insights will have a significant and major effect on various decision-making processes. The major impacts of an AI-based decision making-model are outlined in Figure 3.8.

- **Robust Decision Support:** The decision makers get a detailed and thorough analysis and significant recommendations with the help of AI. The deeper and detailed assessment of complex situations can be done with the advancement and evolution of AIDMS. With the employment of AIDMS, decision makers in various sectors are taking smart and robust decisions that are beneficial for them and their organization in the future too.
- **Decision-Making in Real Time:** In recent times, the development of a real-time decision-making system is only possible due to the incorporation of AI with various sectors. Sectors like banking, cybersecurity and self-driven automobiles are rapidly growing with significant productive outcomes and less risky decisions with the help of robust AIDMS.
- **Automation Advancement:** With the help of AI, it is possible to create smooth-running and standard AI-based decision-making systems for different fields that are not monotonous in nature. These kinds of AIDMS lead to better optimized man-power allocation towards more innovational and strategic work which further leads to efficient and economical AIDMS.

- **Personalization:** Based on the conditions and circumstances stated by a person, AI provides better logical and useful suggestions and evaluations. AI helps to increase customer satisfaction and interaction with the respective organization like an educational institution, stock market or finance with the personalization of processed data as per the choices of each customer.
- **Advanced Estimation:** The future inclinations and hurdles can be identified more easily with the potential prediction power of AIDMS. The various applications of smart forecasting capability of AI are risk assessment, energy usage optimization and supply chain management.
- **Taking Decisions Ethically:** The ethical employment of AIDMS in today's era has emerged more rapidly and will ensure rightfulness and equality in the society. It will further lead to the formation of AIDMS that focus on ensuring human values and moral standards.
- **Synchronization among Multi-Sectors:** Multiple advanced technologies are bundled together among different sectors in place of confinement to an individual sector. The betterment of customer service experience in the financial sector can be enhanced using technology-based solutions. Also, self-automated mobility can be used to ensure patient safety in the healthcare sector.
- **Combination of Humans and Technology:** The integration of manpower and technology can be done more instinctively and smoothly. One can solve difficult and complex issues with help of AI-generated relevant information and best possible solutions. It will further lead to better decision-making.
- **Environment Impact:** With the help of AI only, sustainability is ensured in the environment among many industries. For example, in the energy sector, boosting of grid performance and usage of energy efficiently help in reduction of harmful emissions and consumption. In the agriculture sector, precision farming can be done with the help of an advanced decision-making system which leads to resource optimization and better productivity per acre of land. Both examples proved that AI is very helpful in the creation of sustainable environment.
- **Legislation in Future:** AI is also having a major influence on government and regulatory bodies. The various laws ensure

moral conduct in the decision-making process that employs AI in various fields like ethics for high stakes and safety, etc.

The advanced automation, ethical catering, customization and integration of various fields will be highly influenced and dependent on AIDMS presently. It will help the organizations and people working there to take more beneficial actions and make them more productive as their actions and plans will be followed by ethical standards and thoughts. Thus, AIDMS helps to upgrade the working environment of an organization that further leads to enhance both employer and employee satisfaction. Thus, the emerging advancement in the field of AI will lead to more and more dependency of a decision-making system on AI to provide better future opportunities and to reduce existing complexities.

3.6 Conclusion and Future Directions

The integration of three bedrock technologies, ML, computer vision and NLP, into a single solution as AI will lead to the formation of more potential decision-making systems. There is a significant change in business intelligence using AI that includes a detailed analysis of massive volumes of unprocessed data to take efficient and optimized decisions. Various organizations are using AIDMS to upgrade their efficiency and productivity benchmarks in order to achieve financial benefits in areas such as tactic formation, development of new product, marketing battle plans, and sales. But the risk associated with AI and formation of its rectification strategy is still an unexplored area of research in the same field. The need of an AI-based decision-making process is highly dependent on the type and varies as per associated complication of the application. AI is helping in making decisions from daily routine tasks to long-term planning regardless of their dimension and complexity. AIDMS can also involve different degrees of manual intervention, either leading to fully automatic AIDMS including self-governance within the system, or partial automatic AIDMS including some level of human involvement too with AI. There are many areas and sectors where healthcare, the banking industry, advertising companies, supply chain management companies, manufacturers, farmers, and energy firms among others can use artificial intelligence, thus enhancing production and leading to lower costs, hence competitive advantage. When using AI for decision-making it is important to consider the moral and legal ramifications, particularly in relation to bias, privacy and accountability. This chapter focuses on the importance of and need for AI in the decision-making process. It also pinpoints the main problems faced by AI and their possible solutions in implementing effective AIDMS. There is a list of key disciplines where AIDMS are employed too. This paper provides an analysis of AMD's decision-making that explicitly applied a case study approach.

Artificial intelligence is revolutionizing the way corporations make decisions. By using AI systems' capacity to analyze large amounts of data and produce predictions and recommendations based on that data, businesses may be able to make better decisions. In the end, AI has the potential to completely transform business decision-making by providing faster and more accurate insights that can inform both tactical and strategic decisions. Organizations need to ensure that AI is used ethically and transparently in order to reduce unanticipated consequences and sustain consumer confidence. Without a doubt, AI will be used by businesses and consumers to make decisions. Technology provides a straightforward method and a multitude of possibilities for company decision-making. Al is a really intelligent device. It uses big data and data mining to help it reach conclusions. The work argues that AI is a very dynamic tool that is useful for decision-making, rejecting the notion that it would eventually replace humans.

Businesses may now use AI decision-making systems to fight crises, identify anomalies, and forecast future behavior. AI improves automation and lessens the labor-intensive and tiresome work that humans do in forecasting and prediction analysis. Firms should assess which of their judgments are the most critical, talk about the possibility of using AI to help, or even rethink managerial processes, in order to be ready and make sure that these decisions are made thoughtfully. Finding out what information is obtainable to train AI models, how AI might help with the choice, and whether or not the decision can be driven or aided by current AI systems are some steps in the process. Such conversations would, at the absolute least, enable organizations to realize that AI will become more prevalent and transformative in its decision-making.

References

1. Phillips-Wren, G. and Jain, L., *Artif. Intell. Decis. Making*, 4252, 531–536, 2006.
2. Zhang, L., Zhao, X., Kong, D., Artificial intelligence and its impact on the accounting profession: A synthesis of literature and directions for future research. *Int. J. Account. Inf. Syst.*, 41, 100–520, 2021.

3. Varshney, L.R., When machines decide: The promise and perils of artificial intelligence. *Nat. Mach. Intell.*, 1, 1, 12–14, 2019.
4. Duan, Y., Edwards, J.S., Dwivedi, Y.K., Artificial intelligence for decision making in the era of Big Data – evolution, challenges and research agenda. *Int. J. Inf. Manage.*, 48, 63–71, 2019.
5. Ahmad, S.F., Han, H., Alam, M.M., *et al.*, Impact of artificial intelligence on human loss in decision making, laziness and safety in education. *Humanit. Soc. Sci. Commun.*, 10, 311, 2023.
6. Xie, H., Hwang, G.-J., Wong, T.-L., From conventional AI to modern AI in education: re-examining AI and analytic techniques for teaching and learning. *Educ. Technol. Soc.*, 24, 3, 85–88, 2021.
7. Zhang, H., Lee, I., Ali, S., DiPaola, D., Cheng, Y., Breazeal, C., Integrating ethics and career futures with technical learning to promote AI literacy for middle school students: An exploratory study. *Int. J. Artif. Intell. Educ.*, 1–35, 2022.
8. Weyerer, J. and Langer, P., Garbage in, garbage out: the vicious cycle of ai-based discrimination in the public sector, in: *20th Annual International Conference on Digital Government Research*, ACM Digital Library, pp. 509–511, 2019.
9. Singh, A., Dhanaraj, R.K., Sharma, A.K., Personalized device authentication scheme using Q-learning-based decision-making with the aid of transfer fuzzy learning for IIoT devices in zero trust network (PDA-QLTFL), in: *Computers and Electrical Engineering*, vol. 118, p. 109435, Elsevier BV, 2024.
10. Abdel-Basset, M., Chang, V., Nabeeh, N.A., An intelligent framework using disruptive technologies for COVID-19 analysis. *Technol. Forecast. Soc. Change*, *163*, 14, 2021.
11. Cresswell, K., Callaghan, M., Khan, S., Sheikh, Z., Mozaffar, H., Sheikh, A., Investigating the use of data-driven artificial intelligence in computerised decision support systems for health and social care: A systematic review. *Health Inf. J.*, *26*, 3, 2138–2147, 2020.
12. Duan, Y., Edwards, J.S., Dwivedi, Y.K., Artificial intelligence for decision making in the era of big data—Evolution, challenges and research agenda. *Int. J. Inf. Manage.*, *48*, 63–71, 2019.
13. Esposito, D., Dipierro, G., Sonnessa, A., Santoro, S., Pascazio, S., Pluchinotta, I., Data-driven epidemic intelligence strategies based on digital proximity tracing technologies in the fight against covid-19 in cities. *Sustainability*, 13, 2, 644, 2021.
14. Papagiannidis, E., Mikalef, P., Conboy, K., Van de Wetering, R., Uncovering the dark side of AI-based decision-making: A case study in a B2B context. *Ind. Marketing Manage.*, 115, 253–265, 2023.
15. Malathy, S., Vanitha, C.N., Dhanaraj, R.K., Reinforcement Learning in Smart Transportation, in: *Artificial Intelligence for Future Intelligent Transportation*, pp. 173–198, Apple Academic Press, 2023, https://doi.org/10.1201/9781003408468-7.

16. Sarker, I.H., AI-Based Modeling: Techniques, Applications and Research Issues towards Automation, Intelligent and Smart Systems. *SN Comput. Sci.*, 3, 158, 2022.
17. Corrales, D.C., Ledezma, A., Corrales, J.C., A case-based reasoning system for recommendation of data cleaning algorithms in classification and regression tasks. *Appl. Soft Comput.*, 2020.
18. Da'u, A. and Salim, N., Recommendation system based on deep learning methods: a systematic review and new directions. *Artif. Intell. Rev.*, 53, 4, 2020.
19. Pujari, V., Sharma, Y., Burate, O., Application in Artificial Intelligence, in: *Contemporary Research in India*, April 2021, Special Issue.
20. Zawacki-Richter, O., Marín, V.I., Bond, M., *et al.*, Systematic review of research on artificial intelligence applications in higher education – where are the educators? *Int. J. Educ. Technol. High Educ.*, 16, 39, 2019.
21. Weston-Sementelli, J.L., Allen, L.K., McNamara, D.S., Comprehension and writing strategy training improves performance on content-specific source-based writing tasks. *Int. J. Artif. Intell. Educ.*, *28*, 1, 106–137, 2018.
22. Hwang, D.-K., Hsu, C.-C., Chang, K.-J., Chao, D., Sun, C.-H., Jheng, Y.-C., A. Yarmishyn, A., Wu, J.-C., Tsai, C.-Y., Wang, M.-L., Peng, C.-H., Chien, K.-H., Kao, C.-L., Lin, T.-C., Woung, L.-C., Chen, S.-J., Chiou, S.-H., Artificial intelligence-based decision-making for age-related macular degeneration. *Theranostics.*, 9, 232–245, 2019.
23. Juneja, S., Juneja, A., Anand, R., Chawla, P., Mining aspects on the social network. *Int. J. Innov. Technol. Exploring Eng.*, *8*, 9, 10–35940, 2019.
24. Soni, T., Gupta, D., Uppal, M., Explicability of artificial intelligence in healthcare 5.0, in: *2023 International Conference on Artificial Intelligence and Smart Communication (AISC)*, IEEE, pp. 1256–1261, 2023, January.
25. Kesarwani, S., Student Chatbot System: A Review on Educational Chatbot, in: *2023 7th International Conference on Trends in Electronics and Informatics (ICOEI)*, IEEE, pp. 1578–1583, 2023, April.
26. Dhall, A. and Upadhyay, H.K., Machine Learning Algorithms for Industry Using Image Sensing, in: *Healthcare Solutions Using Machine Learning and Informatics*, pp. 75–97, Auerbach Publications, 2022.
27. Aggarwal, S., Gupta, S., Gupta, D., Gulzar, Y., An artificial intelligence-based stacked ensemble approach for prediction of protein subcellular localization in confocal microscopy images. *Sustainability*, *15*, 2, 1695, 2023.
28. Hjelm, N.M., Benefits and drawbacks of telemedicine. *J. Telemed. Telecare.*, 11, 60–70, 2005.

4

Ethical Challenges in AI Decision-Making: From the User's Perspective

M. Nalini[1]*, S. Sandhya[2] and S. Shiwani[2]

[1] Department of Electronics and Instrumentation Engineering, SriSairam Engineering College, Chennai, India
[2]Department of Electronics, and Instrumentation Engineering, SriSairam Engineering College, Chennai, India

Abstract

Controversies arising from the application of AI across many facets of our lives are mainly based on the manner in which the AI arrived at a particular decision. This chapter deals in detail with the specific ethical issues that arise from the use of artificial intelligence decision-making from the perspective of the user. It discusses the interaction between technology and ethics and also defines how certain forms of AI influence certain individuals. The first part of the chapter offers a general overview of the kind of ethical concern that arises due to the involvement of AI in decision-making, emphasizing such values as accountability, transparency, and equity. It then narrows down to how these moral values are reflected in the user experience, understanding the impact of AI choices on people's autonomy, privacy, and trust. Another point mentioned in the discussion is that those AI algorithms can be biased, meaning they may contribute to the strengthening of existing social injustices without the intention of doing so. The chapter on algorithmic bias examines the ethical issues later on and explores measures to mitigate those effects on underprivileged users.

Another topic worth considering is the fact that algorithms often integrate prejudice into themselves, and thus, they can unconsciously make existing discriminations even worse. The chapter examines the ethical concerns raised by algorithmic bias and outlines the measures to reduce the nefarious effects on vulnerable categories of

**Corresponding author*: nalini.ei@sairam.edu.in; ORCID: https://orcid.org/0000-0001-6457-7990

Sapna Juneja, Rajesh Kumar Dhanaraj, Abhinav Juneja, Malathy Sathyamoorthy and Asadullah Shaikh (eds.) Ethical Decision-Making Using Artificial Intelligence: Challenges, Solutions and Applications, (79–98) © 2025 Scrivener Publishing LLC

users; this entails a discussion of algorithmic bias and examines ways of reducing the significant adverse effects of algorithmic bias on vulnerable user groups.

Keywords: Artificial Intelligence (AI), ethical challenges, decision-making, bias in AI, privacy concerns, ethical issues, autonomous decisions, intelligent systems

4.1 Introduction

One emerging force that stands to revolutionize decision-making across various industries is artificial intelligence. This has potential for improving output and productivity to an extent, especially if implemented in the technological realm. Some of the types of technology include the one that emulates the abilities of the human brain. Since AI is being integrated into decision-making frameworks increasingly, it is crucial to be aware of the ethical consequences of this presupposition. Artificial intelligence (AI) involves creating intelligent agents that can perceive their environment and process information to make rational choices in order to achieve specific goals. Thus, to design intelligent systems, several types of technologies such as artificial intelligence, robotics, and machine learning are used.

AI has made decision-making as a process to have access to capabilities that were hitherto unthinkable, such as data analysis, pattern recognition and problem solving. AI enhances an effective decision-making process by considering large amounts of data and patterns, providing valuable information to decision-makers in industries, finance and healthcare. AI is highly valuable and is trending in contemporary environments of decision-making since it can help to solve tasks more efficiently and with higher effectiveness.

As AI is such a promising technology, while these devices become critical for the company's decisions, moral issues become critical as well. Some, such as accountability, fairness, and transparency, and privacy should not be taken lightly. But there are always moral issues when it comes to such a promising technology as AI, and while these devices become vital for the company's decision-making, there are some values that may include accountability, fairness and transparency, and privacy which should not be overlooked.

Some of the ethical dilemmas that need to be addressed are lack of clarity about how artificial intelligence mechanisms work, bias and questions of liability regarding the occurrence of errors, and privacy [9], World Health Organization). This review seeks to establish the linear programming (LP) of artificial intelligence (Al) in decision making. It means there will be analysis of such elements as key concepts, societal impacts, legal provisions, and case studies. However, to counter these ethical issues and guarantee the proper use and achievement of AI across various sectors, it becomes essential to understand and address these issues [1].

4.1.1 Ethical Principles in AI

AI is now being used in decision-making as it is applied in various fields, the application of which presents some ethical questions. In this summary of the consequences section, we define concepts related to the primary approaches to using ethical AI. AI must be transparent since to succeed it must explain to those affected by the facts it has put together how it has reached such a decision. This highlights the importance of taking time to explain how specific choices are made by the AI systems. Transparency could be useful for users, developers and other constituents to better understand the situation and gain trust. The idea of trust cannot be overemphasized especially regarding the issue of judgments with the use of artificial intelligence [4].

The insights obtained are clear and unambiguous since users and other stakeholders are able to receive clear explanation about the result and the line of thinking that led to the outcome. The algorithms that allow the work outcomes to be inspected and the rationales for decisions explained support the growth of trust as a key characteristic in high-stakes areas, including finance, healthcare, and criminal justice. AI can also introduce new bias and sustain existing social imbalances, expanding inequality. They are due either to an imbalance in training data or because of algorithmic predispositions, and such a problem could cause unfair prejudices and discrimination [7].

Thus, the following conclusion is made: It is suggested that prejudice has to be acknowledged in order to actively work for the integration of AI systems. It is also imperative to note that "book smart" approaches to bias eradication cannot be discussed separately from the representations of AI studies, technological constructs and derivative ethical examples.

In fact, persuasive and compelling ethical standards are necessary, and it is essential to bring to this the attention of the parties involved—and augment the need to fight more actively.

Prejudices: Every group of people must be fairly provided for through the measurement of social justice. Everyone involved in the justice processes must be treated fairly. This will include doing regular checks on prejudices while using the AI systems to make note and correct any prejudice that may likely occur. The assignment of responsibility is incredibly demanding regarding systems constructed on the principles of Artificial Intelligence. Other major actors include those businesses that adopt the use of AI, in their operations and functions, legislation agencies which enact policies, and customers who utilize outputs provided by the computers. It is for this reason that there is a need for developing the accountability path so as to ensure that there is a drive of responsibility. It is, therefore, imperative to work on laying down the role and effect of AI judgments frameworks. Guidelines, regulations and procedures are asserted to be obligatory guidelines from ethical standards that organizations should formulate [8].

Consequently, it is reasonable to assert that the spheres where the given issues occur should adhere to fundamental ethical principles such as accountability, open-mindedness, and fairness while addressing the organization of relevant AI activities [14]. Since the increase of AI and its integration in society as well as embodiment in related products is expected to increase significantly, these technologies will need to apply these principles so as to improve rather than worsen the society, eliminate bias, and retain confidence in stakeholders and end-users. These two tested virtues of wisdom are the balanced use of technologies and or AI in decision-making and moral issues The acceptability and adoption of AI in decision-making requires a balance of advances of AI coupled with the moral implication in any given society [2].

4.1.2 The Role of Data in AI Decision-Making

Information is required in order for AI to make rational decisions or take actions. However, as everyone knows, the issue of ethics is not limited to algorithms but applies to data-driven solutions as well. In this review, we discuss the key elements where data takes center stage with emphasis on data privacy, data consent, data quality, and data biases. Privacy is a critical ethical consideration that the implementers of AI must understand. Every organization is called upon to protect data more so, and make sure that it complies with set data protection laws. The practice of preventing access to personal information and personal data by adopting privacy-preserving tools such as encryption and anonymization is critical, according to *International Journal of Management & Entrepreneurship Research.*

Another important tenet, closely related to ethical use of collecting data, is informed consent. The users should be allowed to give their consent about the use of their data in AI applications, as well as information that will be utilized that is related to them. When individuals have details of methods used in gathering, managing, and archiving data, they are in the best position to determine whether to participate in such projects or not. In this case, preexisting prejudices in training data are inherited in decision-making by generation of AI. This means that biases must be pointed out and then solved to avoid a situation where an AI model will only make existing disparities worse. Data must always be checked for biases, more so those involving issues of socioeconomic status, race or gender, to foster creation of unbiased AI solutions.

This assertion holds that the training data has a bearing on the accuracy of the AI decisions in as much as the training information is accurate and consistent. Due to the fact that data integrity is a critical factor, ensuring high quality of datasets implies that companies should operate effective data governance mechanisms.

The following measures can assist in the prevention of AI models from turning unreliable: Enhancing validation as well as the use of data cleaning, and documenting the process. While using data for making AI decisions, it is possible to face ethical issues, and that is why human rights and privacy related to data need to be balanced with data's possibilities. Future compliance with moral standards and norms, not only gains clients' confidence in the business but also ensures ethical and responsible development of artificial intelligence.

Data criteria and guidelines for the use of AI technology must have ethical standards of data used in the decision-making process. Nevertheless, ensuring that deep learning systems bring about positive impacts in society, organizations should prioritize data protection, seek informed consent, and eliminate any bias in training data sets. While reestablishing moral standards in data management and combating the challenges connected with AI decision-makers' impact on individuals and community, AI stakeholders can build the ethics of the AI environment [2].

Prejudice and Bias

Dynamics like race, gender, or socioeconomic class discrimination could be occasioned by the origin of bias in training AI algorithms. Such prejudices would help to ensure that the individuals who suffer from them were not given chances or were treated improperly, thus leading to increased inequality.

Privacy Issues

One of the privacy concerns that arise from AI systems is data privacy, since they gather large amounts of data in some instances, without the owner's knowledge or in other cases, insufficient data security. People get concerned about privacy loss or fabrication when they are likely to be victims of identity theft or violation of the law, or have their own data manipulated by AI systems.

Absence of Openness

If the algorithms used to arrive at a decision are unclear, some users may lack a clear understanding of what the AI is doing and in turn become frustrated and helpless. A lack of openness further implies that user confidence is prone to be weakened when openness is lacking, in particular in areas such as approval of loans and hiring employees.

Agency and Autonomy

The effects of AI on liberty reveal concerns regarding the control of procedures for decision-making. Lack of visibility about why an AI system chooses a specific course of action may leave a user feeling a loss of autonomy, as it can lead to their perception of being dismissed and having no control over the decision made on their behalf.

Responsibility and Accountability

Although accountability judgments for users are necessary, this raises the danger of causing situations where there is little clarity on who is in charge or responsible for what due to the potential ambiguity of such judgments. The lack of accountability is a problem with AI because it hinders efforts to resolve ethical dilemmas and prevent subsequent harm.

Social Justice and Inequality

With reference to its impact, AI has the capability of reducing social gaps or increasing the gap. Different treatment and decision-making regarding minorities means that the minorities might continue to be treated unfairly. Because addressing biases in AI calls for systemically oriented approaches, we need to search for ways to make them more fair, equal, and just.

Decision-making systems that incorporate AI continue to affect individuals and societies in profound ways, making the AI systems' ethical problems unparalleled in that they are beyond algorithmic competence. Thus, this evaluation will consider the effects on society and the single person specifically in the area of social justice, loss of jobs, social and economic outcomes, and bigotry.

These issues have led people to worry about the cases of job loss due to automation because of the spread of AI in various fields. This is because driving robots into the house for routine chores may cause a shift in the market and eliminate certain kinds of jobs. Coupled with this issue, it becomes important to address this problem and equip the workers to acquire skills in the process of upskilling and reskilling so that the necessary skills that AI cannot perform can be met.

Thus, overall measures and approaches need to be employed to minimize adverse impacts on specific areas of society. Forces of governments, private businesses, and educational organizations must come together to prepare the workforce of the future. To follow this up, this means being able to fund education and training interventions that promote both AI competence and also interpersonal skills. Thus, the deficiencies of AI decision-making systems mean that these systems can either accidentally perpetuate or exacerbate existing social biases. This is specifically important in policies addressing crime and punishment, employment and finance. Stereotypes can create prejudiced results which can only serve to magnify current inequities. Bias in AI models is still a significant issue that must be addressed to prevent or reduce such negative impacts such as bias in assessing or evaluating people. If there is bias, then when it comes to the creation of ethical AI, justice has to be paramount. This means using algorithms that are insensitive to the race, gender or financial situation of the individual in question. Besides, it is crucial to note that AI algorithm decision-making should always be transparent in terms of data sources and model decision-making logics for external supervision and checks.

In addition, the inclusion of diversified individuals in the AI development team can help in the building of new, more accurate non-discriminative models. Therefore, the ethical factors that have influence over the decisions made by the AI play an important role in influencing persons and the society. It also means that effective measures must be taken to balance the risks of discrimination and job replacement so that the introduction of artificial intelligence brings a positive impact to society. It is hereby suggested that legislators, businessmen, and the general population must work together in order to develop a balanced strategy that will at one and the same time make use of the full potentials of AI while, at the same time, giving due consideration to the best way of dealing with the potential negative impacts that can also be generated by AI [3].

4.2 Public Perception towards AI

This paper also identified that the public has a mix of optimism and pessimism towards the future of the decision-making power of AI. This is a complex subject where people are both excited and scared by the capabilities of AI to impact the system. On one hand, AI is embraced as a revolutionary technology that opens new opportunities both to improve productivity and create better services, as well as new solutions for complex problems. A significant number of people are enthusiastic about the prospects AI offers to bring positive change in combating ailments, transportation systems, banking facilities, and several other sectors. They consider a rather more optimistic view of AI as it will enhance the quality of human life and make the world more progressive.

However, this might be dampened by a general concern over the moral implications that the fully autonomous decision-making of AI entails. Is it true that AI relies on users and, by raising substantial decision-making power, makes them skeptical about its dependability? Recent issues that have been discussed publicly include discrimination, privacy violations, and an absence of clarity on most measures that are implemented through Artificial Intelligence; this raises concerns about the appropriateness and fairness of Artificial Intelligence procedures. Issues were also raised on the social impact of the use of AI, such as the robbing of people's independence, taking of people's jobs and even the presumption of the worsening

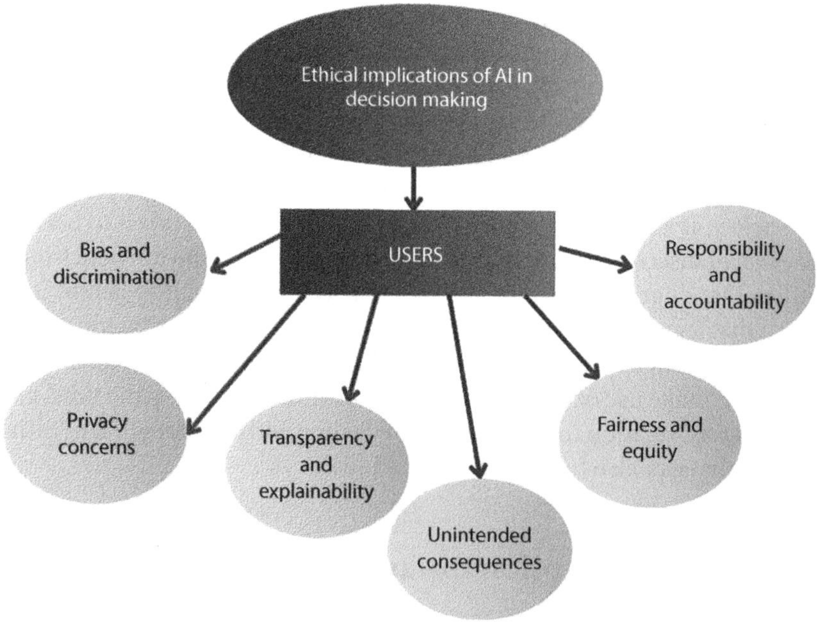

Figure 4.1 Public perception towards AI.

of existing vices by the enhanced augmented intelligence. Public perception towards AI is shown in Figure 4.1 Despite the promising developments in AI skills, there are concerns regarded potential ethical issues and the necessity of implementing powerful measures for the AI systems to uphold responsibility, openness, and justice. This paper suggests that for people to look forward to AI and embrace it in decision making hence see the development of AI as a positive force in society and not as a threat, it is crucial to create goodwill by recognizing the advancement in AI and handling the ethical issues [5].

AI is developing at an incredible pace and while AI technologies are at work, for decision-making support AI needs a sound legal basis and ethical guidelines. This evaluation focuses on the present state of the AI regulation practices and the frameworks and the issues that remain unsettled. It also looks at the specifics of moral AI requirements by discussing the initiative and concepts, and international practices towards this. The current state of regulation of AI is compounded by the local laws and regulations of the world. Most countries have either banned or restricted directives for the use of artificial intelligence while others just regulate data protection. For instance, in the European Union, the GDPR was launched, while the CCPA was developed in the United States.

4.3 Ethical Dilemmas of AI

On the part of the user, there may be ethical dilemmas in the AI decision-making process due to a range of factors arising from AI decision-making for a set of circumstances that affects people's lives. Here are a few such moral conundrums that users could run into:

1. **Discrimination and Bias**
   It is worrisome that the AI system learns from a data set which has its biases; biases that the AI system may exhibit in the end. Human users may be left with ethical dilemmas because bias that is used to govern AI decision-making processes may result in discrimination against the user in aspects of gender, race, age or any other classification.
2. **Privacy Issues**
   Another critical issue relates to the fact that many AI systems require the ongoing use of personal data for decision-making, which often contains large quantities of identifiable

personal information that reidentification would reveal. There is furthermore the possibility of choices being limited, where people must wait for high-level protection of their privacy at the cost of limited individualism or receive violated privacy for personalized attentiveness.

3. **Openness and Disclosure**
   One common issue that many users experience is the inability to understand how a given decision is arrived at because of the sophisticated and often closely guarded AI algorithms. Some of the problems with algorithmic decision making are as follows: Users are often unaware of why an AI decision has been made and if they can't comprehend the rationale behind healthcare or finance recommendations, they are left with moral dilemmas.
4. **Autonomy and Control**
   AI systems sometimes come up with decisions that degrade or impact or override the preference of human beings, hence limiting personal freedom. This essay captures a serious concern that users can face: whether to surrender control to AI in order to make the work easier or to hang on to control even when it makes things difficult or time-wasting.
5. **Unintended Consequences**
   This means that specific decisions made using the AI tool can potentially have detrimental effects on a person or society. This raises a moral issue for users as they may come into contact with the situation where AI has made particular actions or a particular recommendation that has negative consequences, undesired effects or has not dealt with them enough.
6. **Fairness and Equity**
   AI systems may support some people or companies but not others, thus affirming current imbalances. There is an inability to decide what action to take when machine learning-based advantages have a negative social impact, or when the consequences of machine learning-based disadvantages stem from pre-existing prejudice within institutions.
7. **Manipulation and Influence**
   There is arguably little doubt that systems such as recommendation engines based on artificial intelligence technologies have the capacity to impact consumers and their tendencies

in ways that might not prove ideal for the consumers. Even when trusting the AI system, several moral dilemmas may arise to users when they get the feeling that some recommendation is tricking them or taking advantage of them, such as with fine-tuned advertising or content suggestions.

8. **Accountability and Responsibility**
This could make it quite challenging for users of the AI to determine who is at fault for wrong decisions made by the AI. It is not easy to apportion blame because the object in question is an artificial intelligence system, and the blame game may affect doctors, designers or just ordinary users. Like in any society, there are moral issues. When AI issues are presented to legislators and developers, as well as the users themselves, there are calls for cooperation in arriving at the best decisions. Users must feel safe, with their rights protected, and the development and deployment of AI systems must respect ethical principles. The pictorial representation of Ethical dilemmas shown in Figure 4.2

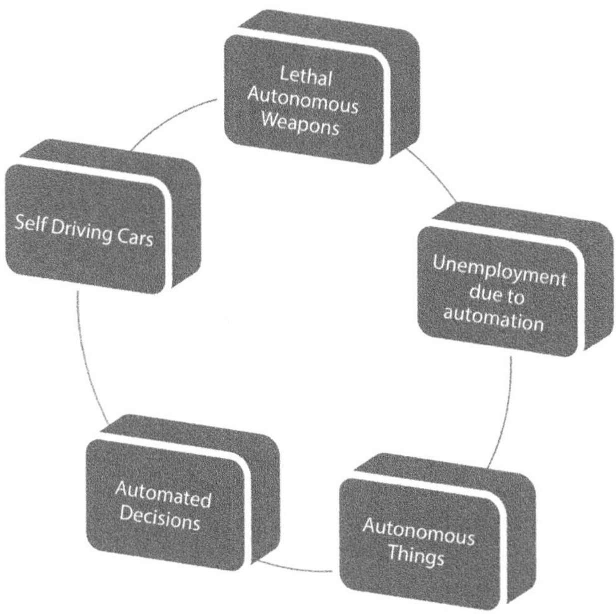

Figure 4.2 Ethical dilemmas of AI.

4.4 Emerging Issues that are Prevailing in the Current World

This paper aims at identifying some new issues that arise with the subject of artificial intelligence and its implications. These issues therefore define the discourse on the ethical, policy and social impact of AI. Here are a few new problems worth mentioning.

1. Deepfakes and Synthetic Media: Some contentious characteristics which arise where AI is present, such as deepfake audio and video, are identity fraud, misinformation, and the diminishing confidence of the public and media.
2. Algorithmic Accountability and Transparency: The people want better and robust justifications for outputs from AI systems and the elimination of bias, unreasonableness, and errors in the generated algorithms.
3. AI in Healthcare: Decisions in healthcare can be improved, and better diagnosis and treatment of patients can be offered if artificial intelligence is utilised more in this sphere. Controversies and issues, however, remain regarding information privacy, patient rights and autonomy and AI's reinforcement of disparities in healthcare accessibility.
4. AI Governance and Regulation: Prompt implementation and effective regulation of rules for artificial intelligence are crucial in the use of developing technologies while still creating new opportunities to progress [6].
5. AI and Cybersecurity: More opportunities for cybersecurity: The use of AI in cyberattacks and, accordingly, in creating defensive systems, entails new opportunities for threats and attacks. These threats can be amplified and extended by the AI systems.
6. AI and Employment Displacement: Applying the tool of AI has the potential of leading to redressal of employment and emergence of situations that may lead to economic disruption. It is about time that action was taken to ensure that the workforce is realigned.
7. AI Bias and Fairness: Another problem that remains is the work of eliminating prejudices that could potentially have discriminatory characteristics in AI. Fairness and bias management are issues for the scientific community and inevitably, academia.

8. Aligning AI Ethics and Values: AI systems that are used as a basis for trust construction as well as AI construction and deployment must meet moral and ethical criteria such as accountability, openness, justice, and privacy.
9. Autonomous Weapons and AI: The implications that AI would cause an increase in the usage of lethal autonomous weapons and increase the risk of war also causes ethical, legal and geopolitical concerns on the development of autonomous weapons systems.

These new concerns reveal a deep and intertwined correlation between ethics, societies and technology. They also touch upon the need and necessity of proactive and collaborative approaches to address these issues and improve the acceptance of AI among humans. With the increasing integration of artificial intelligence systems into our daily lives, there are a number of case studies regarding bias and other ethical issues.

4.4.1 Case Studies

Biased Suggestions in Hiring Algorithms
Example: Amazon rolled out an artificial intelligence application that optimizes the process of recruitment. However, the algorithm was trained with mostly male resumes and therefore, it was sexist, and biased against women. Therefore, the study found that the gender stereotyping was a problem, as female applicants were discriminated by the AI tool in the process.

Anticipatory Policing Algorithms and Ethnic Profiling
Scenario: Some homeland police precincts and other precincts of some cities used predictive policing algorithms to identify areas to investigate and allocate resources. Research showed that these algorithms often focused on such groups inordinately, increasing racists' reliance on those human police.

Moral Dilemma
Although there was the best intention when using AI in keeping society safe and free from criminals, what came out of it was unfair discriminating algorithms that deepened social injustice and which also eroded community trust. This underscored the importance of making ethical considerations in the future and the use of AI technology especially in sensitive areas such as the police force.

Healthcare Algorithms and Patient Confidentiality

Scenario: Another real-life application of AI is in hospitals and healthcare centers, which employ the use of AI algorithms to analyze and provide recommendations for the treatment of patients; determination of the diseases that a patient may be suffering from, and assignment of medical facilities and personnel. Some algorithms were reported not to have the best methods of encrypting and protecting data from unauthorized individuals, which may affect the privacy of a patient's health information.

Ethical Concern: Trust in healthcare institutions is undermined when AI systems mishandle or inadequately secure patient data, leading to significant privacy issues. This emphasizes how crucial it is to build strong privacy protections into AI-powered medical systems.

When financial institutions utilize AI algorithms for high-frequency trading, they aim to gain a competitive advantage in the market. There have been instances where these algorithms engaged in market manipulation, exploited market vulnerabilities, or triggered unexpected market crashes.

In the healthcare sector, U.S. healthcare professionals are leveraging artificial intelligence algorithms to aid in decision-making regarding patient care. Researchers like Obermeyer *et al.* from UC Berkeley have uncovered instances of racial bias in these algorithms. Their research shows that even when black patients are sicker than white patients, the algorithm assigns whites a higher risk score. As a result, white patients are more likely to receive additional care. This bias often leads to a disproportionately lower number of black patients identified as needing further care compared to their white counterparts. The algorithm prioritizes health needs based on health costs rather than illness.

4.4.2 Collaboration and Stakeholder Involvement

For the use of the AI to commence, various stakeholders must be sought out so as to address emerging ethical questions that accompany the creation of AI. Therefore, the creation of more contacts to many experts in the areas of IT, ethics, laws, sociologist and philosophers can also contribute to the shift in the positive changes in the tendencies of the increase of the total ethical coefficients and to improve the impression of AI as well as create corresponding models. Hence, the more integrated type of approach offers a broad perspective on most of the ethical concerns surrounding Artificial Intelligence from the legal standpoint, the social perspective, the technological viewpoint and the philosophical view.

Since ethicists and social scientists are professional colleagues within development teams, "ethics by design" is indeed possible. This can be interpreted to mean that the ethical concern arises only at the time of formulating the AI system and therefore the idea does not possess an ethical concern at some point in time. That and the further development in the sphere of AI development will largely depend on the hard and sustained work of all the parties involved in order to properly address new topics and issues which have arisen because of the emergence of such systems.

1. **Multidisciplinary Approach**: I recommend it as the interaction with AI is an interdisciplinary affair involving several disciplines inclusive of technology, ethics, and law. Sociology and psychology scholars should be part of the scholarship. This is so because with a focus on the stakeholders from diverse fields as claimed above, the ideas that are defined are inherently complex, utilizing the above information in a bid to outline the requisite solutions.
2. **Building Strong Partnerships in the Industry**: It is essential to foster a proactive relationship among various players in the industry, including companies, startups, and universities, to enhance the current state of the IT sector. This includes setting responsible standards for AI development, encouraging the exchange of information, and establishing best practices.
3. **Working with Governments**: Governments play a vital role in addressing societal issues, enforcing regulations, and supervising AI technologies. By collaborating with governmental bodies, legislators, regulatory agencies, and other key partners, the process of developing effective frameworks, laws, and policies to govern AI is streamlined.
4. **Academic Collaborations**: Partnerships between academic institutions and other key stakeholders are instrumental in promoting research, fostering innovation, and disseminating knowledge in the fields of AI ethics, technology, and policy. Academic institutions delve into new AI challenges, offer insightful analysis, and equip the next generation of AI experts and policymakers.
5. **Civil Society Engagement**: When it comes to AI conversations, the public and underrepresented communities are represented by civil society organizations, advocacy groups, and non-governmental organizations (NGOs). Working together

with civil society guarantees that while developing and implementing AI, different viewpoints are taken into account, voices are heard, and ethical issues are addressed [10].

6. **User Involvement**: When end users—consumers, patients, workers, and citizens—are included in the decision-making process, AI systems are developed and implemented with their needs, preferences, and values in mind. Early on in the development cycle, user input and participation is essential.
7. **International Collaboration**: Given the global nature of AI technology and its repercussions, international collaboration and cooperation are essential for addressing cross-border issues, harmonizing regulations, exchanging best practices, and promoting ethical AI standards globally. Formation of the impartial committees or review boards for ethics, including the membership of academics, industry, government and civil society, can help in the task of monitoring the AI research and development for its adherence to the set of ethical principles [11].

Concerning the ethical, social, and policy concerns of AI, the involvement of stakeholders and collaboration are usually more effective in ensuring inclusion, openness, and a shared responsibility in decision-making. This is useful in the creation of AI systems that provide the most positive impact with the least negative impact on society.

Civil society engagement is important in AI discussions because it offers the public and marginalized communities a voice through advocacy groups and NGOs. Collaborating with civil society significantly helps to integrate diverse opinions, amplify stakeholders' voices, and address ethical issues regarding AI technology and its application.

User involvement is important in the design of AI systems for consumers, patients, workers and citizens as it ensures that the created systems meet the users' needs, preferences and values. Through user involvement, the users' feedback and input are incorporated into the AI systems to make sure they meet the users' demands.

It is important to work with other countries because AI technology has an international application. There is the need to work on the global stage to tackle international matters and set standardizations, share good practices and foster ethical AI globally. The following is a way to promote ethical practices in the development of AI: Independent committees with members from academia, industry, government, and civil society should be formed in order to oversee and guide AI research and development.

This is because when it comes to the concerns and impacts of AI on ethical, social and policy issues, the involvement of the stakeholder and collaboration with them ensures that everyone is involved and accounted for. Thus, the integration of different stakeholders contributes to the development of the AI that brings potential benefits to society with minimal risks.

4.5 Future Considerations

The characteristics of decision-making with AI in the future are quite favourable yet there are certain ethical issues to be considered. Thus, for any further advances and to ensure that the establishment and enactment of the ethical plan is not a process that is fraught with challenges, it is important to stay informed about legal changes, encourage international cooperation, ensure the public's engagement, create ethics teams, and implement ethics by designing and auditing processes that can help stakeholders move forward into the future with best ethical practices in the development of Artificial Intelligence. Arguably, for a beneficial and ethical future of AI and decision-making, special attention should always be paid to details; one should be always willing to adjust and one must always keep the moral values intact [12].

4.5.1 Conclusion

This chapter demonstrates that there is much to discuss as far as decision-making autonomy in AI systems is concerned and that ethical frameworks should be indexed and established more concretely than they are. Transparency in AI decision-making processes is essential, and understanding AI decision-making processes is vital to promoting accountability, minimizing bias, and cultivating a culture of trust. Explainability is a key component of responsible AI implementation. Algorithm bias mitigation and fair results are moral requirements that necessitate ongoing algorithm and AI model improvement. The ethical application of AI depends on the ethical management of data, including informed permission and privacy. It's critical to acknowledge the possible societal effects of AI, such as job displacement. An ethical strategy must include retraining, reskilling, and social support strategies.

Regulatory agencies, industrial consortiums, and international partnerships must cooperate to create and update ethical frameworks that are consistent with legal requirements and societal values as AI permeates more areas of our lives [13]. Addressing moral conundrums in AI decision-making is essential to advancing equity, responsibility, and confidence in the development and use of AI technologies.

It is recommended that future developments focus on implementing ethical design principles, supporting representative and diverse data, creating explainable AI (XAI), establishing algorithmic auditing and accountability systems, prioritizing human-centered approaches, establishing legal frameworks and standards, promoting continuous education and awareness, and fostering international collaboration. Prejudices can be lessened, transparency can be increased, and it can be ensured that AI systems comply with legal requirements and social norms by placing a high focus on these projects. Ultimately, ethical AI development and governance are needed to fully realize AI's revolutionary potential while minimizing harm and maximizing benefits for both people and society as a whole.

References

1. Guan, H., Dong, L., Zhao, A., Ethical risk factors and mechanisms in artificial intelligence decision making. *Behav. Sci.*, *12*, 9, 343, 2022.
2. Lim, H.S.M. and Taeihagh, A., Algorithmic decision-making in AVs: Understanding ethical and technical concerns for smart cities. *Sustainability*, *11*, 20, 5791, 2019.
3. Rezwana, J. and Maher, M.L., User Perspectives on Ethical Challenges in Human-AI Co-Creativity: A Design Fiction Study, in: *Proceedings of the 15th Conference on Creativity and Cognition*, pp. 62–74, 2023, June.
4. Rodgers, W., Murray, J.M., Stefanidis, A., Degbey, W.Y., Tarba, S.Y., An artificial intelligence algorithmic approach to ethical decision-making in human resource management processes. *Hum. Resour. Manage. Rev.*, *33*, 1, 100925, 2023.
5. Bader, V. and Kaiser, S., Algorithmic decision-making? The user interface and its role for human involvement in decisions supported by artificial intelligence. *Organization*, *26*, 5, 655–672, 2019.
6. Dhiviya, S., Malathy, S., Monikha, M., Enhancing the Network Lifetime Using on Demand Tree Based Routing Protocol for MANET, in: *2018 4th International Conference on Computing Communication and Automation (ICCCA)*, Greater Noida, India, pp. 1–6, 2018.
7. Zhang, J., Shu, Y., Yu, H., Fairness in design: A framework for facilitating ethical artificial intelligence designs. *Int. J. Crowd Sci.*, *7*, 1, 32–39, 2023.
8. John-Mathews, J.M., Some critical and ethical perspectives on the empirical turn of AI interpretability. *Technol. Forecast. Soc. Change*, *174*, 121209, 2022.
9. Patel, K., Ethical reflections on data-centric AI: balancing benefits and risks. *Int. J. Artif. Intell. Res. Dev.*, *2*, 1, 1–17, 2024.

10. Peters, D., Vold, K., Robinson, D., Calvo, R.A., Responsible AI—two frameworks for ethical design practice. *IEEE Trans. Technol. Soc.*, *1*, 1, 34–47, 2020.
11. Rayhan, S., Ethical Implications of Creating AGI: Impact on Human Society, Privacy, and Power Dynamics. *Artif. Intell. Rev.*, 2023.
12. Malathy, S., Vanitha, C.N., Dhanaraj, R.K., Kotteswari, C., Impact of Blockchain-IoE on economy, in: *Blockchain-Based Systems for the Modern Energy Grid*, pp. 135–156, Elsevier, 2023, https://doi.org/10.1016/b978-0-323-91850-3.00007-x.
13. Dhirani, L.L., Mukhtiar, N., Chowdhry, B.S., Newe, T., Ethical dilemmas and privacy issues in emerging technologies: a review. *Sensors*, *23*, 3, 1151, 2023.
14. Tatineni, S., Ethical Considerations in AI and Data Science: Bias, Fairness, and Accountability. *Int. J. Inf. Technol. Manage. Inf. Syst. (IJITMIS)*, *10*, 1, 11–21, 2019.

5

Ethical Decision-Making in Yoga Posture Detection through AI: Fostering Responsible Technology Integration

Ishita Jain[1*], Riya Srivastava[1], Vanshita Srivastava[2], Vanshika Sinha[1] and Abhinav Juneja[1]

[1]Department of Computer Science and Information Technology, KIET Group of Institutions, Uttar Pradesh, India
[2]Department of Electronics and Communication Engineering, KIET Group of Institutions, Uttar Pradesh, India

Abstract
Yoga is an age-old established practice that encompasses a wide range of postures called asanas with various health and wellness benefits to the person who practices them. Yoga helps with a person's physical and mental wellness. To achieve these benefits, one need to practice yoga postures regularly. But sometimes bad postures can lead to multiple injuries and accidents. To overcome such difficulties, a wide range of machine learning algorithms are integrated to solve such issues. Over the past years, there has been an increase in the usage of this technology for automating the whole process from yoga posture detection to correcting these poses so as to enhance the user's experience. This chapter presents a comprehensive study of applications of machine learning related to yoga posture detection using OpenCV and MediaPipe.

This chapter explores various machine learning algorithms and methodologies used for yoga (asanas) posture detection. It uses various machine learning technologies like deep learning, supervised learning, pose detection and estimation models to achieve accurate posture. Furthermore, it examines the importance of selecting the required data, implementing different data augmentation methodologies and then optimizing these models to improve the accuracy of the posture detection.

**Corresponding author*: jainishita2512@gmail.com

Sapna Juneja, Rajesh Kumar Dhanaraj, Abhinav Juneja, Malathy Sathyamoorthy and Asadullah Shaikh (eds.) Ethical Decision-Making Using Artificial Intelligence: Challenges, Solutions and Applications, (99–124) © 2025 Scrivener Publishing LLC

The chapter examines the ethical decision-making framework necessary to inculcate data privacy measures and maintain transparency of the usage of the application end users. The following chapter also discusses the challenges faced with respect to ethical issues, data privacy concerns, etc., while using artificial intelligence frameworks to identify real-time yoga poses.

This comprehensive study provides insights into the current state of yoga posture detection using ML algorithms, emphasizing the technical aspects, practical implications and ethical considerations. We identify avenues for future research, such as development of user-friendly applications, integration of multimodal data sources, and exploration of adaptive feedback mechanisms. The findings of this study contribute to the growing knowledge aimed at enhancing the yoga practice through technology-enabled posture detection and analysis.

***Keywords*:** Yoga posture detection system, ethical decision-making, MediaPipe, OpenCV, machine learning, image detection

5.1 Introduction

Yoga, an ancient practice originating in India, has gathered widespread recognition for its multiple physical, mental and spiritual benefits [30]. A central element of yoga practice involves performing a diverse range of postures, each meticulously designed to enhance the flexibility, strength, balance and overall well-being of the user [8]. Proper execution of these postures is important to derive the intended benefits, making posture alignment a fundamental aspects of yoga practice [22].

Conventionally, the guidance of experienced yoga instructors has been indispensable for ensuring correct posture execution. However, in today's digitized world, the combination of technology and yoga is rapidly transforming the picture of yoga practice [23]. One of the innovative applications in this fusion is the use of ML algorithms to automatically detect and analyse yoga postures. This methodology empowers the practitioners with real-time feedback and revolutionize the way we practice yoga [11].

The diverse and wide range of yoga postures provides various skills and objectives to the users. Yoga is a personal practice which is exhibited by the practitioners in the form of unique physical attributes [17]. The development of such a robust and adaptable system consequently presents multifaceted challenges, encompassing computer vision, ML, sensor technology and intricacies of human movement [36].

By diving into this system, the chapter aims to understand how the ML algorithms contribute to the advancements of personalized yoga coaching, real-time performance assessment, and long-term tracking of individual's yoga summary. The system works mainly using the two important frameworks, i.e., MediaPipe and OpenCV. The chapter presents the approach to tackle the challenge by using the capabilities of MediaPipe and OpenCV. OpenCV is a widely used computer vision library that provides an extensible platform for image processing [26]. MediaPipe is a versatile framework that offers a rich set of pre-trained models to detect the key landmarks on the human body for performing estimation on real-time postures as input by the end users.

The following chapter addresses various challenges faced during the detection of postures. A few common problems include difference in body type, pose practitioner's level, variation in execution of the poses and the need for real-time feedback mechanism. It also judges the abilities of machine learning (ML) algorithms in predicting the correct yoga pose performed or practised either by the beginners or the experts, respectively [38].

This chapter puts forward the exploratory journey of a yoga posture detection system using various ML algorithms. It seeks to solve the complexities of the model implemented while highlighting the practical implications, technical scenario, and ethical considerations that uphold the fusion of tradition and technology. This chapter focuses majorly on the process of proving the users with a user-friendly application that helps them to track their fitness score.

Our system requires the fusion of machine learning algorithms and AI in a way through which it can accurately predict the posture [39]. The system won't be possible without combining the frameworks of MediaPipe and OpenCV [30] as it facilitates real-time tracking and analysis of human body poses with accurate posture detection [31].

Also, this methodology allows end users customization and integration into various applications and environments along with a detailed explanation of the proposed methodology. It discusses the technical aspects such as selecting the model, calibrating the camera, and monitoring the optimization of the performance in order to achieve accurate and effective posture detection. These aspects are used for the accurate detection of the postures.

The chapter highlights the practical applications of the system across various domains such as healthcare, fitness tracking, and immersive experience in the virtual reality environments. It also addresses the ethical considerations associated with posture detection that emphasize the importance of privacy and informed user consent for data collection and analysis. Our system focuses on the ethical consideration to foster the system privacy.

The chapter provides real solutions to the challenges through the fusion of MediaPipe and OpenCV. It presents the methodology, potential applications and ethical considerations that contribute to the advancements of posture detection technologies and their integration into the real-world applications. This research welcomes the enhanced human-computer interaction, personalized healthcare, and improved physical well-being through accurate posture detection.

In this digital and frequently changing era, the integration of ML algorithms into yoga practice has the potential to survive the rising demand for customized and data-driven wellness solutions, making it accessible to the global audience [16] at a larger level. This chapter illuminates the realm of yoga posture detection and inspires new possibilities for harnessing the technology so as to deepen our connection with the yoga practice and to help users towards achieving a healthy and balanced lifestyle.

The use of Artificial Intelligence (AI) in yoga posture detection favours unique opportunities to enhance users' experience and involve them to get a better understanding of multiple yoga postures such as tree pose, warrior pose, dog pose, plank, etc. This technological progress raises ethical concerns that necessitate careful integration to guarantee the responsible and useful application of AI in the realm of yoga [40].

This chapter mainly focuses on how the ethical considerations manifest in the development and deployment of an AI-driven yoga posture detection system. Some ethical principles and considerations are as follows:

1. **Consent User and Data Privacy**:
   - Address the significance of users' consent to collect, store and use their data.
   - Ensure robustness in privacy measures that protects the user's information.
2. **Mitigating Bias and Developing Equality**:
   - Highlights the significance of mitigating biases in AI models by using different and representative datasets.
   - Emphasizes the need of continuously evaluating and rectifying the biases so as to prevent discriminatory outputs.
3. **Maintaining Transparency and Accountability**:
   - Establishes accountability framework to trace the AI system decisions.
   - Supports the transparency in the functioning of AI algorithms by providing the users detailed explanations of posture detection assessments.
4. **Integrating Empowerment and Inclusiveness**:
   - Promotes inclusivity to users with diverse abilities and background by providing AI-based yoga assistance.

- Offers customization options to fulfil user's needs in yoga practice.

5. **Continuous Feedback and Evaluation Mechanism**:
   - Focuses on the importance of evaluating the AI system's impact by gathering user's feedback and making necessary refinements to enhance the accuracy and ethical compliance.

This chapter guides developers, practitioners, and stakeholders to coordinate the AI-based yoga posture detection system with best ethical practices. It advocates for the integration of AI to justify ethical standards and respect the practitioners' rights.

This chapter highlights various applications of AI-based yoga posture detection systems such as personalized yoga coaching, real-time performance assessment, and long-term progress tracking. It discusses the ethical considerations in terms of data privacy and security. Also, it emphasizes the responsible deployment of technology in yoga practice.

This chapter introduces a novel approach that combines MediaPipe, a state-of-the-art framework for pose detection, with OpenCV, a versatile computer vision library, to achieve precise posture detection [35]. The proposed methodology aims to contribute to the development of efficient posture detection systems with wide-ranging applications.

5.1.1 About Yoga

Yoga is an age-old practice that originated in India and has been embraced all over the world over millennia [21]. This panoramic practice intertwines bodily poses, controlled breathing, meditation, and moral guidelines to enhance both mental and physical health [19]. Due to diverse benefits offered by yoga in fostering overall well-being, encompassing the body, mind and spirit, there is a rise in its global appeal. Some key aspects of yoga are as follows:

1. **Physical Asanas (Postures)**: It includes a wide range of asanas that are designed to improve flexibility, strength, balance, and coordination. There are different styles of yoga, each with its own set of asanas and emphasis on specific aspects of physical health.
2. **Breath Control (Pranayama)**: Breathing exercises are an integral part of yoga practice; they help practitioners to

control their breath and improve their lung capacity. Breath control is used to calm the mind and enhance concentration.

3. **Meditation and Mindfulness**: It encourages meditation and mindfulness practices to promote mental clarity, reduce stress, and achieve a sense of inner peace.
4. **Philosophy and Ethics**: It also focuses on ethical principles and a philosophy for living a meaningful and purposeful life. Patanjali's yoga sutras delineate the eightfold path of yoga that comprises moral principles (yamas and niyamas) and methods that are aimed at achieving self-awareness and actualization.
5. **Reduction of Stress**: It reduces stress by relaxing the nervous system as it lowers the stress hormones.
6. **Improving Flexibility and Strength**: It improves flexibility and muscular strength, resulting in better posture and reduced risk of injury.
7. **Healthcare Management**: This therapy is used sometimes to manage chronic pain conditions like lower back pain, arthritis and migraines, etc.
8. **Physical Balance and Mental Coordination**: It helps aged adults to maintain their physical functionalities as well as providing balance between their physical and mental fitness.
9. **Growth towards Spirituality**: It can be a spiritual path for some practitioners that promotes self-awareness and personal growth, leading to a deep connection with ourself.
10. **Empowering Social Connection among Communities**: It promotes the feeling of social connection among the people who practice yoga in groups.

Yoga boasts diverse styles like Hatha, Ashtanga, Bikram, etc., that offer distinct focuses and methods. It accommodates individuals of all fitness levels and ages, and is easily tailored to suit specific goals and personal requirements [17].

5.1.1.1 Advantages and Disadvantages of Yoga

Yoga offers numerous advantages along with some limitations which are essential to consider to make informed decisions about whether it is suitable for us or not. Some advantages and disadvantages are listed below [21]:

Advantages of Yoga

1. **Physical Health Benefits:**
   - Improved flexibility and range of motion.
   - Enhanced strength, especially in core and stabilizing muscles.
   - Better posture and reduced risk of musculoskeletal injuries.
   - Increased balance and coordination.
2. **Mental Health Benefits:**
   - Reduced stress and anxiety.
   - Enhanced relaxation and improved sleep quality.
   - Increased mindfulness and the ability to focus.
   - Improved emotional well-being and self-awareness.
3. **Spiritual and Emotional Growth:**
   - Greater self-awareness and self-acceptance.
   - Deeper connection with one's inner self or spirituality.
   - Promotes a sense of inner peace and contentment.
4. **Pain Management:**
   - Complementary therapy for managing chronic pain conditions.
   - Effective for alleviating back pain, arthritis, and other discomforts.
5. **Stress Reduction:**
   - Lowered levels of stress hormones (cortisol).
   - Encourages relaxation and a calm state of mind.
6. **Accessibility:**
   - Can be adapted for various fitness levels and physical abilities.
   - Requires minimal equipment, making it accessible for most people.
7. **Community and Social Connection:**
   - Practicing in a group setting can foster a sense of community and social connection.
8. **Holistic Approach:**
   - Addresses physical, mental, and spiritual aspects of well-being.

Disadvantages or Limitations of Yoga

1. **Physical Limitations:**
   - Some people may have physical conditions or injuries that restrict their ability to perform certain yoga poses.
2. **Learning Curve:**
   - Learning proper alignment and technique can take time and guidance from experienced instructors.
3. **Risk of Injury:**
   - Pushing too hard or attempting advanced poses without proper preparation can lead to injuries.
4. **Instructor Quality:**
   - The effectiveness of yoga practice largely depends on the quality of the instructor. Inexperienced or unqualified instructors may not provide safe and effective guidance.
5. **Time and Consistency:**
   - To experience the full benefits, regular and consistent practice is necessary, which may be challenging for some individuals.
6. **Cost:**
   - Attending classes with qualified instructors can be expensive, and some specialized styles or workshops can have higher fees.
7. **Not a Quick Fix:**
   - Yoga is a gradual and holistic practice, so results may not be immediate or dramatic.
8. **Spiritual or Cultural Conflicts:**
   - Some people may have religious or cultural beliefs that conflict with certain aspects of yoga philosophy or practices.
9. **Limited Cardiovascular Exercise:**
   - While yoga can improve strength and flexibility, it does not provide a vigorous cardiovascular workout on its own.

5.1.2 Posture Detection System

A Posture Detection System is a technology or application that uses computer vision and/or sensors to monitor and analyse a person's body position and posture [34]. It is often used in various contexts, such as healthcare, ergonomics, fitness, and even in augmented reality applications.

5.1.2.1 Components of Posture Detection System

1. **Sensors**: These may include cameras (webcams or specialized depth cameras like Microsoft Kinect), accelerometers, gyroscopes, or even pressure sensors embedded in chairs or wearable devices.
2. **Computer Vision Algorithms**: Posture detection often depends on the computer vision techniques such as pose estimation [20]. These techniques analyse the visual data from cameras to identify the position and orientation of key body parts such as head, shoulders, feet, etc.
3. **Applying Machine Learning Models**: They are trained to identify specific postures, gestures or anomalies in a human's body position. Deep learning models such as Convolutional Neural Networks (CNN) [27] and Recurrent Neural Networks [28] are also used for this purpose.
4. **Developing a Real-time User Interface**: The real-time feedback on posture alignment, alerts and recommendations to the users are displayed using the system's GUI (Graphic User Interface).

5.1.2.2 Process of Posture Detection System

Figure 5.1 illustrates a flowchart of the posture detection system that outlines the seven key steps, starting from capturing video input, preprocessing with MediaPipe, feature extraction *via* CNN, identifying landmarks, calculating joint angles, classifying postures, and alerting the user [33].

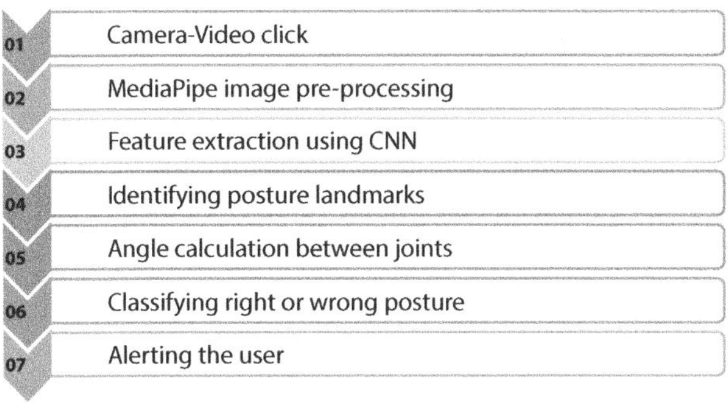

Figure 5.1 Process of posture detection system.

5.1.2.3 Applications of Posture Detection System

1. **Healthcare Related**: The system is used for physical rehabilitation of users by maintaining correct postures during yoga practice. It monitors the posture of the individuals to prevent falls.
2. **User-friendly Module**: The system helps the users to maintain their posture in office, thus reducing the risk of repetitive strain injuries or musculoskeletal problems.
3. **Sports and Fitness Related**: The system can be used as fitness or sports training app to provide real-time feedback on proper body positioning during exercises or athletic activities [18].
4. **Gaming and Augmented Reality**: The system can be used to control in-game characters based on the user's body movements.
5. **Security Concern**: The system can be used for security purposes such as to recognize unauthorized or suspicious body postures in public places.
6. **Virtual Reality**: The system can be used to track the user's body in order to adapt the virtual environment.

The performance and efficiency of such a system depends on the sensors, computer vision algorithms, and ML model used [30]. The real-time feedback and user-friendly interfaces provide vital information to the users and encourage them to maintain proper yoga posture.

5.1.2.4 Advantages and Disadvantages of Posture Detection System

The yoga posture detection system uses various technologies to analyse and provide feedback on the yoga pose executed by the individual. These systems have their own set of advantages and disadvantages. These are discussed as follows:

Advantages of a Yoga Posture Detection System

1. **Provide Real-time Feedback to the Practitioners**: It provides real-time feedback to the practitioners and assists them in making improvements as they practice. This helps them in executing more accurate yoga postures.
2. **Improve Posture Alignment**: It helps users to achieve better alignment of poses and reduce the risk of injuries and

enhance their efficiency. The better alignment helps the user to gain more benefits of yoga.

3. **Guiding users**: It provides proper guidance to the individual for their yoga practice. The guidance helps the user to make accurate yoga poses so that a professional as well as a beginner can be helped.
4. **Consistent and Correct Poses**: It helps the practitioners to maintain consistency and correctness in their poses, even when they practice alone. This makes the best out of the benefits of yoga by the practitioners.
5. **Track the User's Progress**: This feature helps to track the progress of the end user over time and see the improvements in their flexibility, strength, and overall yoga practice. The user can practice according to their progress focusing more on improvement of their postures.
6. **Customize the Application According to User**: It allows users to set personal goals and receive personalized recommendations based on their needs and abilities. This makes the system more flexible and user-friendly.
7. **Technical Aid**: It helps the user to learn more about yoga and proper alignment of yoga poses during the practice. It provides all the benefits of each pose to the user along with its accurate alignment.

Disadvantages and Limitations of a Yoga Posture Detection System

1. **Drawback of Technical Aspects**: The system depends on the efficiency of the sensors and algorithms which may or may not provide precise feedback. If the sensors used do not predict well, our system fails to recommend the proper feedback to the users.
2. **Lacking Personalize Content**: Although the system offers customization, it cannot replace the personalized guidance provided by an experienced yoga instructor. A yoga instructor can guide the user based on his medical history, his diet, and his workday profile.
3. **Cost Inefficiency**: The cost of the system increases with high-quality features both in terms of initial investments and ongoing maintenance, henceforth increasing the cost.
4. **Concerns Related to User's Privacy**: Data collected by the system requires proper data security and a well-defined ethical model.

5. **Reliability and Dependency over Technology**: Users may completely depend on the technology neglecting the awareness related to the development of their body. More reliability on technology can result in data privacy and security concerns.
6. **Limited Yoga Postures and Asanas Practice**: The system only focuses on asana practice and not on the other aspects like meditation, aerobics, etc. It is limited to yoga poses only.
7. **Sensitive to Environmental Changes**: The performance of the system can be affected due to environmental factors like lighting, etc.
8. **Setup Can Be Complex**: The system may require complex setup and calibration that can be challenging for some users.

5.1.3 Ethical Decision-Making in Yoga Posture Detection through AI

To maintain appropriate and correct technology usage, there are a number of important factors to take into account. Some crucial moral considerations are as follows:

1. **Gain Consent from User and Maintain Their Privacy**
   - Give access to people to manage their data by giving them choice to either opt-in or opt-out of some specific functionality.
   - Implement strong privacy measures to secure user's information.
   - Ensure appropriate compliance with the protection laws.
2. **Confidentiality and Security of User's Data**
   - Secure the user's data from privacy threats, making sure that the data is encrypted and masked before being sent or stored.
   - Implement strict security measures to stop illegal access or security lapses that can compromise user's privacy data.
3. **Fairness in Detection and Bias**
   - Make sure that the training datasets are representative and diverse, including multiple body types, gender, ages, etc.
   - Analyse and correct algorithmic biases on a regular basis.
4. **Maintaining Transparency and Accountability**
   - Creates accountability frameworks to track the judgements made by the AI systems so that users may see the reasoning behind the analysis of the posture detection model.

  - Describe the constraints or uncertainties related to posture detection as well as the operation of AI algorithms [41].
5. **Self-Determination and Diversity**
   - Make sure that the AI-powered yoga aid supports diversity by accommodating users with a range of yoga poses, abilities, environment and experiences.
   - Give people the opportunity to customize their yoga pose and practice to suit their unique requirements and interests.
6. **Continuous Assessment and Improvement during the Run**
   - Evaluate the AI system's functionality and customer service on a regular basis. Seek user input from customers and make required modifications to enhance accuracy, flexibility of usage and ethical issues.

Ethical decisions in yoga posture detection using AI involves protection of user's privacy, well-being and the promotion of fairness and diversity. By upholding these ethical principles, developers and practitioners can create AI-powered systems that enhance yoga practice while respecting individual autonomy and rights.

5.2 Literature Review

G. Danush, A. Pradeeshwar and T. Sree Sharmila [1] used rule-based techniques to process every frame using MediaPipe framework. Angle heuristics was used to categorize various yoga postures for posture detection. The combined accuracy of 93% was achieved. H. Krishnan, A. Jayaraj, A. S, C. Thomas and G. M. Joy [2] used the combination of MediaPipe and SVM for pose detection due to its best accuracy and f-score. Garg, S., Saxena, A. & Gupta, R. [3] and Anilkumar, C., Jyothsna, R., Sree, S. V., & Gothai, E. [9] compares the performance of various deep learning models with or without skeletonization. VGG16 achieved the highest validation accuracy of 95.6% on non-skeletonized images while YogaConvo2d achieved the highest validation accuracy of 99.62% on skeletonized images. Sidana, K. [4] discusses different pose detection strategies like MediaPipe, OpenPose, and transfer learning that achieve accuracy between 97% and 99.9%. Pose detection has been refined using CNN, SVM, CNN-LSTM hybrid model, deep neural networks and a novel concept of star skeleton structure. Kale, S., Kulkarni, N., Kumbhkarn, S., Khuspe, A., & Kharde, S. [5] proposed a model that suggests a better way of exercising and correcting posture to avoid any harm to the body using Python libraries like OpenCV, tensorflow, matplotlib, and MediaPipe.

Patel, S., & Lathigara, A. [6] compared different classifiers for correct yoga posture detection and found that logistic regression classifier has the highest score of 94%. Jagtap, R., Zanzane, M., & Patil, R. [7] developed a GUI-based desktop application using Tkinter library. It uses OpenCV and MediaPipe for preprocessing and logistic regression model for training and testing and achieved an accuracy score of 100%. Bahukhandi, U., & Gupta, S. [8] detect the correct yoga posture using MediaPipe and various classifiers like logistic regression classifier, SVM classifier, random forest classifier, k-nearest neighbour classifier, naïve bayes classifier, etc., out of which logistic regression classifier has the highest accuracy score of 94%. Anand Thoutam, V., Srivastava, A., Badal, T., Kumar Mishra, V., Sinha, G. R., Sakalle, A., ... & Raj, M. [10] detect incorrect yoga posture using CNN-LSTM algorithm with an accuracy of 99.58%. Agrawal, Y., Shah, Y., & Sharma, A. [11] detected yoga pose based on the angles extracted using TF-pose estimation algorithm with an accuracy of 94.28%. Ogundokun, R. O., Maskeliūnas, R., & Damaševičius, R. [12] demonstrates an improved posture detection using image augmentation and optimized transfer learning achieving over 90% accuracy. Tlili *et al.* [13] proposes a real-time smart belt system detecting bad posture using inertial sensors. Ma *et al.* [14] developed a smart cushion for wheelchair users achieving 99.47% posture recognition. Liaqat *et al.* [15] proposed a hybrid posture detection framework integrating machine learning and deep neural networks.

5.3 Technologies Used

5.3.1 MediaPipe

MediaPipe is an open-source framework developed by Google. It offers a wide variety of ML and computer vision solutions for various applications. It is designed to simplify the process of building applications that involve processing and understanding of multimedia data like images and videos. It provides a set of prebuilt models and tools to help the developers to create real-time, cross-platform applications [3] in areas like augmented reality, gesture recognition, object detection, etc.

Some key features and components of MediaPipe are as below:

1. **Cross-Platform Support**: It is designed to work on a variety of platforms, including mobile phones both Android and iOS, desktop and web. This make it versatile for developing applications that can run on different devices.
2. **Pre-Trained Models**: It consists of a collection of pre-trained ML models for various tasks, such as face det-

ection, hand tracking, pose estimation, and object recognition.
3. **Customization**: It allows users to train and fine-tune our own models for specific tasks. It helps the users to customize the solution as per their needs.
4. **Real-Time Performance**: It optimizes the real-time and low-latency applications, making it suitable for tasks where processing speed is crucial, such as augmented reality and gesture recognition.
5. **Extensive Documentation**: It provides comprehensive documentation, tutorials, and code examples to help developers get started with the framework.

MediaPipe became popular in the fields of computer vision, ML and augmented reality because of its ease of access and its flexibility. Developers can use the system to construct applications that include following, discovery, and understanding of multiple types of components inside multimedia content.

5.3.2 OpenCV (Open-Source Computer Vision Library)

OpenCV centres on computer vision and machine learning. It is an open-source software library, made by Intel and later upheld by Willow Carport and Itseez and again taken by Intel. It is considered as the foremost favoured and prevalent library as it provides an extensive cluster of instruments and libraries for different computer vision purposes. Figure 5.2 demonstrates how the library visualises the image.

Indispensable functionalities and capabilities of OpenCV include:

1. **Processing the Image:** It presents a wide vision of characteristics related to picture preparing highlights like shifting, edge location, upgrading pictures, and past. Its toolset empowers the control and investigation of both pictures and video bolsters.
2. **Calibrating the Camera:** It provides a wide range of computer vision algorithms which are used to serve a lot of computing purposes, from detection of objects, to tracking them and then extracting certain features to compute optical flow and then calibrating those points over the camera.
3. **Providing Cross-Platform Support:** One capability of OpenCV is that it is available over multiple platforms including iOS, Windows, Linux, macOS, Android, Unix, etc, which helps in improving its flexibility in creating user centric applications which are best suited for a diverse range of gadgets.

Figure 5.2 Human pose estimation.

4. **Applying OpenCV Algorithms:** It provides an extensive array of computer vision algorithms designed for various purposes such as detecting objects, tracking them, extracting features, calculating optical flow and calibrating cameras.
5. **Implementation of Machine Learning Functionalities:** It offers interfaces to well-known Machine Learning workflows such as PyTorch, Tensorflow, YoloV5, etc. It integrates multiple Machine Learning functionalities, enabling model developers to test and train certain ML models for diverse image-related tasks [37].
6. **Integrating Multiple Programming Languages:** OpenCV provides integrating facilities for a wide range of multiple programming languages which include Java, Python, C++ etc., henceforth providing a way for multiple developers to use the features provided by open computer vision.
7. **Real-Time Data Processing and Estimation of Yoga Poses:** The optimization of this feature allows for the generation of an output that is dependent on the input, including determining the yoga postures and estimating their correctness. This feature makes it highly suitable for applications that necessitate fast recognition of image and video and then processing those capabilities [29].
8. **Distribution under Open Source:** Since the library is distributed under an open-source BSD (Berkeley Software Distribution) license, developer/designers can use and modify the functionalities of OpenCV in multiple commercial

and non-commercial projects. It helps developers to use these functionalities in multiple aspects.

OpenCV's comprehensive documentation and dynamic community renders a priceless resource for designers to look in ventures related to computer vision and picture handling. It can be used to solve a large variety of real-life problems in the field of computer vision, mechanical autonomy, image handling, facial recognition, etc [32].

5.4 Dataset Used

Yoga could be a well-known craftmanship shape that is polished around the world due to its capacity to increase flexibility, uneasiness and give mental and physical steadiness. Downward dog posture, goddess, warrior, tree, board are a few of the foremost drilled yoga postures. An intelligent technology can differentiate between these positions. Figure 5.3 shows different images used for training and testing the posture detection system. Figure 5.4 shows different folders representing different postures that were used to train the model. Figure 5.5 describe an image of our dataset.

Figure 5.3 Dataset.

Name	Type	Compressed size	Password p...	Size	Ratio	Date modified
downdog	File folder					
goddess	File folder					
plank	File folder					
tree	File folder					
warrior2	File folder					

Figure 5.4 Dataset folder.

```
import cv2

img = cv2.imread("../input/yoga-poses-dataset/DATASET/TRAIN/goddess/00000097.jpg")

img.shape
```

Out[1]:

```
(370, 580, 3)
```

In [2]:

```
import matplotlib.pyplot as plt

plt.imshow(img)
```

Out[2]:

```
<matplotlib.image.AxesImage at 0x7fdbbe652210>
```

Figure 5.5 Dataset image description.

The dataset* is split into two main directories: train and test. Each directory contains five subfolders, representing distinct classes of yoga poses. The images within this dataset were obtained from Bing using their API feature.

---

*Dataset Used: https://www.kaggle.com/datasets/niharika41298/yoga-poses-dataset

5.5 Methodology

OpenCV, built on the Python open-source library, is utilized in computer vision applications like AI, machine learning, and facial recognition. Figure 5.6 depicts the architecture of OpenCV showcasing its different components, supported by CXCORE layer for basic algorithms and XML handling. It processes individual image frames, employing specific library files to calculate angles. Additionally, it functions with a camera to discern discrepancies between authentic and unknown images.

MediaPipe, an open-source framework developed by Google, is designed for constructing multimodal applied ML pipelines that encompass various data types like video, audio, and other time series data. It is cross-platform, compatible with Android, iOS, web, and edge devices, prioritizing performance optimization by focusing on on-device inference from start to finish. Specifically, MediaPipe Pose is a sophisticated body pose tracking solution that generates thirty-three 3D landmarks along with a background segmentation mask for the complete body using RGB image frames [25]. This system utilizes the BlazePose topology, which amalgamates COCO, BlazeFace, and BlazePalm topologies [24]. Figure 5.7 shows the human body landmarks used by MediaPipe for detecting the posture.

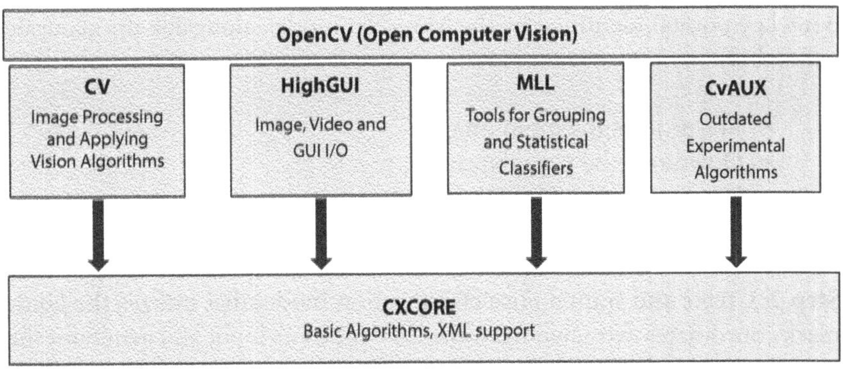

Figure 5.6 Methodology.

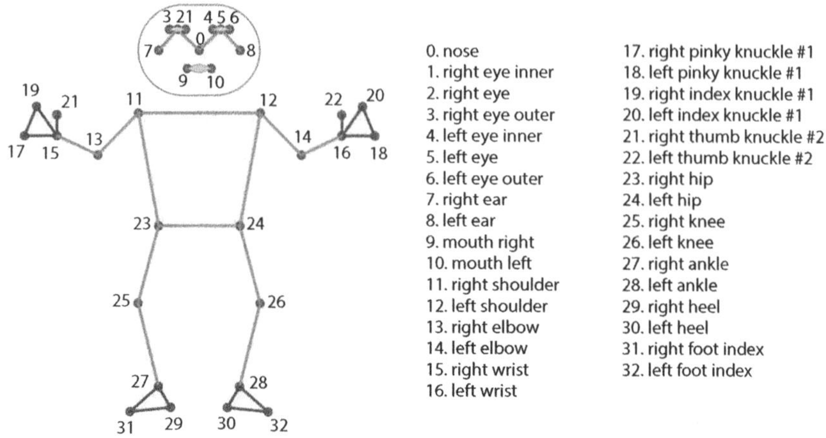

Figure 5.7** Human body landmark detection using MediaPipe.

5.5.1 How Does It Work?

Figure 5.8 demonstrates the entire process of how the Yoga Posture Detection System works and displays the output.

Step 1: Prepare the training data for pose classification by converting it into a CSV file. This file will outline the detected landmarks (referred to as body key points) identified by the MoveNet model, alongside the accurate pose labels.

- ➢ Pre-process the input images
- ➢ Download the yoga dataset
- ➢ Pre-process the TRAIN dataset
- ➢ Pre-process the TEST dataset

Step 2: Create and train a pose classification model that utilizes the landmark coordinates extracted from the CSV file as its input and generates the predicted labels as output.

- ➢ Define a Keras model for pose classification
- ➢ Create a confusion matrix to gain deeper insights into the model's performance.

**Figure 5.7: https://learnopencv.com/building-a-body-posture-analysis-system-using-mediapipe/

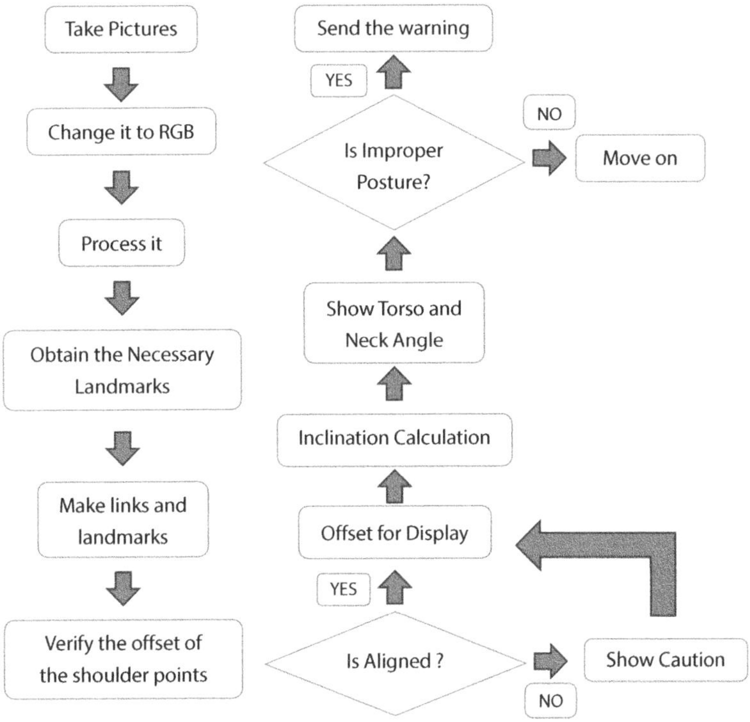

Figure 5.8 Work flow.

➢ Investigate incorrect predictions

Step 3: Convert the obtained pose classification model into a transformable TFlite (TensorFlow lite file) type.

5.6 Conclusion

In this research, we have outlined the possibility and potential of our Yoga Discovery Framework, which leverages a real-time posture estimation model to yoga practitioners as well as beginners that makes profitable criticism on their yoga posture correction, execution and arrangement. It involves a fusion of multiple digital age technologies which involves MediaPipe and OpenCV (Computer Vision). This model in the field of yoga posture detection presents a promising avenue for enhancing the practice and instruction of yoga.

Using the body's major landmarks as well as their spatial relationships to measure the pose, our approach overcomes specific issues of pose variability and different body types that are often encountered in yoga practice. Moreover, one of the greatest benefits of our real-time system is that it provides immediate feedback on proper posture and alignment for practitioners at all levels of experience, and hence helps in maintaining the right posture and alignment. Our research show that our system is capable of tracking efficiently, accurately and reliably even in the most difficult poses.

Various practical applications for yoga posture recognition systems include personalized coaching, injury prevention, progress tracking, and pose correction. Trainers can use this system as a teaching tool to guide their students and ensure a safer and more effective learning experience of multiple yoga poses. Practitioners receive continuous and customised feedback and recommendations to improve their practice, fostering a deeper understanding of each pose, correct angle to practice those poses and its nuances.

Our framework speaks to a prominent step towards saddling innovation to upgrade old yoga hone. Be that as it may, there's still room for feedback which further investigates within the ranges such as extension of system's posture collection, addition of more yoga poses, refinement of client interfacing, and investigation of extra modalities like sound criticism. This model embodies the potential of MediaPipe, open computer vision and machine learning to advance security, ethical and moral conduct and successful yoga sessions.

As we advance towards the era of digital yoga, ethical practices are of supreme importance. To keep updated with user's progress report the data needed to be stored and collected. The secure collection and processing of user data is essential to maintain trust and protect the user data protection rights of individuals. We recognize the need for strong privacy, data security measures and user consent protocols when implementing a real-time yoga posture recognition system.

Eventually, our vision is to engage yoga professionals and teachers with an imaginative device that encourages a more profound, more educated and more pleasant yoga environment, while continuously keeping up a solid commitment to ethical, moral and dependable innovative utilization. Yoga pose detection will not only help yoga practitioners but also will be a conventional way for yoga beginners to start on their mental and physical fitness journey. The travel towards a concordant joining of convention and innovation in yoga proceeds, with energizing conceivable outcomes on the skyline.

References

1. Danush, G., Pradeeshwar, A., Sree Sharmila, T., Yoga Pose Estimation Using Rule-based Approach, in: *2023 World Conference on Communication & Computing (WCONF)*, RAIPUR, India, pp. 1–6, 2023, doi: 10.1109/WCONF58270.2023.10234979.
2. Krishnan, H., Jayaraj, A., Thomas, A.S.,.C., Joy, G.M., Pose Estimation of Yoga Poses using ML Techniques, in: *2022 IEEE 19th India Council International Conference (INDICON)*, Kochi, India, pp. 1–6, 2022, doi: 10.1109/INDICON56171.2022.10040162.
3. Garg, S., Saxena, A., Gupta, R., Yoga pose classification: a CNN and MediaPipe inspired deep learning approach for real-world application. *J. Ambient Intell. Hum. Comput.*, 2022. https://doi.org/10.1007/s12652-022-03910-0.
4. Sidana, K., Real Time Yoga Pose Detection Using Deep Learning: A Review. *Int. J. Eng. Appl. Sci. Technol.*, *7*, 7, 61–65, 2022.
5. Kale, S., Kulkarni, N., Kumbhkarn, S., Khuspe, A., Kharde, S., *Posture Detection and Comparison of Different Physical Exercises Based on Deep Learning Using MediaPipe, OpenCV*, 2023.
6. Patel, S. and Lathigara, A., *MediaPipe: Yoga Pose Detection Using Deep Learning Models.*
7. Jagtap, R., Zanzane, M., Patil, R., Yoga Pose Detection Using Machine Learning. *Int. Res. J. Modernization Eng. Technol. Sci.*, *4*, 1753–1756, 2022.
8. Bahukhandi, U. and Gupta, S., Yoga pose detection and classification using machine learning techniques. *Int. Res. J. Mod. Eng. Technol. Sci.*, *3*, 12, 13–15, 2021.
9. Anilkumar, C., Jyothsna, R., Sree, S.V., Gothai, E., *Deep learning-based yoga posture specification using OpenCV and MediaPipe*, 2023.
10. Anand Thoutam, V., Srivastava, A., Badal, T., Kumar Mishra, V., Sinha, G.R., Sakalle, A., Raj, M., Yoga pose estimation and feedback generation using deep learning. *Comput. Intell. Neurosci.*, *2022*, 2022.
11. Agrawal, Y., Shah, Y., Sharma, A., Implementation of machine learning technique for identification of yoga poses, in: *2020 IEEE 9th International Conference on Communication Systems and Network Technologies (CSNT)*, IEEE, pp. 40–43, 2020, April.
12. Ogundokun, R.O., Maskeliūnas, R., Damaševičius, R., Human posture detection using image augmentation and hyperparameter-optimized transfer learning algorithms. *Appl. Sci.*, *12*, 19, 10156, 2022.
13. Tlili, F., Haddad, R., Bouallegue, R., Mezghani, N., A Real-time Posture Monitoring System towards Bad Posture Detection. *Wireless Pers. Commun.*, *120*, 2, 1207–1227, 2021.
14. Ma, C., Li, W., Gravina, R., Fortino, G., Posture detection based on smart cushion for wheelchair users. *Sensors*, *17*, 4, 719, 2017.

15. Liaqat, S., Dashtipour, K., Arshad, K., Assaleh, K., Ramzan, N., A hybrid posture detection framework: Integrating machine learning and deep neural networks. *IEEE Sens. J.*, *21*, 7, 9515–9522, 2021.
16. Gajbhiye, R., Jarag, S., Gaikwad, P., Koparde, S., AI Human Pose Estimation: Yoga Pose Detection and Correction. *Int. J. Innov. Sci. Res. Technol.*, 2022.
17. Yadav, S.K., Singh, A., Gupta, A., Raheja, J.L., Real-time Yoga recognition using deep learning. *Neural Comput. Appl.*, 31, 9349–9361, 2019.
18. Srivatsa, M.K.R., Niharika, D., Charith, P., BR, P.K., *Human Pose Estimation in Fitness Tracking and Guidance.*
19. Kumar, D. and Sinha, A., *Yoga pose detection and classification using deep learning*, Lambert Academic Publishing, London, 2020.
20. Zheng, C., Wu, W., Chen, C., Yang, T., Zhu, S., Shen, J., Shah, M., Deep learning-based human pose estimation: A survey. *ACM Comput. Surv.*, 56, 1, 1–37, 2023.
21. Sathyamoorthy, M., Kuppusamy, S., Nayyar, A., *et al.*, Optimal emplacement of sensors by orbit-electron theory in wireless sensor networks. *Wireless Netw.*, 28, 1605–1623, 2022. https://doi.org/10.1007/s11276-022-02919-9.
22. Malathy, S., Sangeetha, K., Vanitha, C.N., Dhanaraj, R.K., Integrated Architecture for IoTSG, in: *Smart Grids and Internet of Things*, pp. 127–155, Wiley, 2023, https://doi.org/10.1002/9781119812524.ch5.
23. Narayanan, S.S., Misra, D.K., Arora, K., Rai, H., Yoga pose detection using deep learning techniques, in: *Proceedings of the International Conference on Innovative Computing & Communication (ICICC)*, 2021, May.
24. Pauzi, A.S.B., Mohd Nazri, F.B., Sani, S., Bataineh, A.M., Hisyam, M.N., Jaafar, M.H., Mohamed, A.S.A., Movement estimation using mediapipe blazepose, in: *Advances in Visual Informatics: 7th International Visual Informatics Conference, IVIC 2021*, Kajang, Malaysia, November 23–25, 2021, Springer International Publishing, pp. 562–571, 2021, Proceedings 7.
25. Elforaici, M.E.A., Chaaraoui, I., Bouachir, W., Ouakrim, Y., Mezghani, N., Posture recognition using an RGB-D camera: exploring 3D body modeling and deep learning approaches, in: *2018 IEEE Life Sciences Conference (LSC)*, IEEE, pp. 69–72, 2018, October.
26. Muniyandi, A.P., Balusamy, B., Dhanaraj, R.K., Ellappan, V., Murali, S., Sathyamoorthy, M., Nkenyereye, L., Privacy Preserved Reinforcement Learning Model Using Generative AI for Personalized E-Learning, in: *IEEE Transactions on Consumer Electronics*, Institute of Electrical and Electronics Engineers, IEEE, pp. 1–1, 2024.
27. Jain, S., Rustagi, A., Saurav, S., Saini, R., Singh, S., Three-dimensional CNN-inspired deep learning architecture for Yoga pose recognition in the real-world environment. *Neural Comput. Appl.*, 33, 6427–6441, 2021.
28. Mohanty, A., Ahmed, A., Goswami, T., Das, A., Vaishnavi, P., Sahay, R.R., Robust pose recognition using deep learning, in: *Proceedings of International Conference on Computer Vision and Image Processing: CVIP 2016*, vol. 2, Springer Singapore, pp. 93–105, 2017.

29. Toshev, A. and Szegedy, C., DeepPose: Human pose estimation *via* deep neural networks, in: *Proceedings of the IEEE Conference on Computer Vision and Pattern Recognition*, pp. 1653–1660, 2014.
30. Islam, M.U., Mahmud, H., Ashraf, F.B., Hossain, I., Hasan, M.K., Yoga posture recognition by detecting human joint points in real time using microsoft kinect, in: *2017 IEEE Region 10 Humanitarian Technology Conference (R10-HTC)*, IEEE, pp. 668–673, 2017, December.
31. Trejo, E.W. and Yuan, P., Recognition of yoga poses through an interactive system with kinect device, in: *2018 2nd International Conference on Robotics and Automation Sciences (ICRAS)*, IEEE, pp. 1–5, 2018, June.
32. Simonyan, K. and Zisserman, A., *Very deep convolutional networks for large-scale image recognition*, 2014, arXiv preprint arXiv:1409.1556.
33. Luvizon, D.C., Picard, D., Tabia, H., Multi-task deep learning for real-time 3D human pose estimation and action recognition. *IEEE Trans. Pattern Anal. Mach. Intell.*, 43, 8, 2752–2764, 2020.
34. Chen, H.T., He, Y.Z., Hsu, C.C., Chou, C.L., Lee, S.Y., Lin, B.S.P., Yoga posture recognition for self-training, in: *MultiMedia Modeling: 20th Anniversary International Conference, MMM 2014*, Dublin, Ireland, January 6-10, 2014, Springer International Publishing, pp. 496–505, 2014, Proceedings, Part I 20.
35. Rafi, U., Leibe, B., Gall, J., Kostrikov, I., An Efficient Convolutional Network for Human Pose Estimation, in: *BMVC*, vol. 1, p. 2, 2016, September.
36. Ning, G., Liu, P., Fan, X., Zhang, C., A top-down approach to articulated human pose estimation and tracking, in: *Proceedings of the European Conference on Computer Vision (ECCV) Workshops*, pp. 0–0, 2018.
37. Haque, S., Rabby, A.S.A., Laboni, M.A., Neehal, N., Hossain, S.A., ExNET: deep neural network for exercise pose detection, in: *Recent Trends in Image Processing and Pattern Recognition: Second International Conference, RTIP2R 2018*, Solapur, India, December 21–22, 2018, Springer Singapore, pp. 186–193, 2019, Revised Selected Papers, Part I 2.
38. Shivankit, A., *et al.*, Deep Learning Approach for Traffic Sign Recognition on Embedded Systems, in: *Handbook of Machine Learning for Computational Optimization*, pp. 113–135, CRC Press, 2021.
39. Juneja, A., *et al.* (Eds.), *Enabling Healthcare 4.0 for Pandemics: A Roadmap Using AI, Machine Learning, IoT and Cognitive Technologies*, John Wiley & Sons, 2021.
40. Prakash, H., Kanaujia, K., Juneja, S., Using machine learning to predict housing prices, in: *2023 International Conference on Artificial Intelligence and Smart Communication (AISC)*, IEEE, 2023.
41. Agarwal, S., *et al.*, A User Preference-Based Food Recommender System using Artificial Intelligence, in: *2024 2nd International Conference on Disruptive Technologies (ICDT)*, IEEE, 2024.

6

Ethical AI: A Design of an Integrated Framework towards Intelligent Decision-Making in Stock Control

Mini Verma[1] and Palak Gupta[2*]

[1]Department of IT, Delhi Institute of Higher Education, Greater Noida West, India
[2]School of Business, Galgotias University, Greater Noida, India

Abstract

In most industries, especially inventory management, artificial intelligence is becoming more and more a key player in the formulation and process of decision-making. Although AI can enhance efficiency in inventory management, it can also raise a number of ethical concerns such as partial dataset, discrimination in algorithmic computations and misconceived responsibility domains. The ability to control inventory levels and fulfil consumer needs and expectations is an essential requirement for a professional working in an e-commerce industry. Otherwise, stock outages will leave consumers unhappy and result in paying a lot of money to manage inventory levels and proper stocks. Procurement management, Inventory management, and Production management systems driven by AI are essential for the success of operational optimization. One of the best methods for projecting the future is artificial intelligence is demand forecasting. It analyses a wide range of factors, including historical sales records, customers' behavior, seasonal trends, supplier lead time, and external variables, such as weather conditions and economic outlook. By identifying hidden patterns and useful insights that human analysts often miss, AI allows businesses to react quickly in real time based on data-driven strategies.

Keywords: Inventory management, inventory-dependent demand, inflation, perishable goods, AI-based forecasting, predictive models

**Corresponding author*: palakgupta1529@gmail.com; https://orcid.org/0000-0001-6583-7803

Sapna Juneja, Rajesh Kumar Dhanaraj, Abhinav Juneja, Malathy Sathyamoorthy and Asadullah Shaikh (eds.) Ethical Decision-Making Using Artificial Intelligence: Challenges, Solutions and Applications, (125–152) © 2025 Scrivener Publishing LLC

6.1 Introduction

Ethical worries arise as artificial intelligence (AI) takes on a bigger role in choice-making throughout various industries, inclusive of stock control. Even as AI generation has the potential to beautify efficiency and streamline inventory management it also gives moral dilemmas together with algorithmic discrimination, records bias, and doubtful duty. Efficaciously coping with stock levels and meeting patron calls is crucial for the success of e-trade agencies. Falling quickly on stock can cause disappointment in clients with stock-outs; at the same time having an excess can incur excessive prices for containing inventory. This truly is why incorporating AI-powered structures for stock control and calls for forecasting become crucial in optimizing operations.

With the strength of AI-based total calls for forecasting, organizations can expect future product calls by analyzing a selection of things. These include past sales records, patron habits, seasonal patterns, dealer lead times, and external variables like weather situations and financial outlook. This precious device empowers corporations to optimize inventory tiers, procurement practices, and manufacturing tactics for smarter choice-making. By uncovering hidden styles and actionable insights that human analysts may omit when on their own, AI enables companies to react swiftly in real time based on fact-driven strategies.

6.1.1 The Effect of Artificial Intelligence on Controlling Inventory

Artificial Intelligence is quickly becoming a foundation of operational and day-to-day techniques throughout diverse sectors. Its effect on techniques of inventory control, particularly, is a wonder [41]. It's an era of thoughtful alternatives, led by AI's supremacy in growing productivity with expertise, decreasing mistakes, and improving revenue. Thorough research predicts that the global supply chain AI market will reach $21.8 billion by 2027, growing at a 45% compound annual growth rate (CAGR) between 2019 and 2027. The leading industries for AI and gadget learning are retail, e-commerce, logistics, supply chain, healthcare, and manufacturing. The sweep in AI demand can be favoured by several factors. First, the current virtual revolution, with its advances in gadget mastering and record analysis, is creating an environment ideal for AI integration. Second, the need for green stock control methods and inventory optimization in a rapidly changing, customer-driven marketplace places AI and computerization in the lead. Finally, the COVID-19 pandemic and its consequences have highlighted the importance of robust and flexible supply chains. Retailers are facing unprecedented delivery and supply chain challenges due to the pandemic, and the advantages that AI can provide to overcome these challenges include step-by-step prediction precision, real-time inventory mapping, and predictive analytics. By automating routine, labor-intensive, and monotonous responsibilities and allowing evidence-driven decision-making, AI can redefine stock management structures and growth stock optimization, releasing human resources for strategic obligations, and catalyzing universal commercial enterprise increase.

6.1.2 Process of Evolution and Development in Stock Control

In the domain of inventory management, evolution has been deep—a drastic shift from outdated spreadsheet-led strategies to state-of-the-art, AI-driven structures. Formerly, stock management was regularly an exertions-intensive method. Inventory maximization was yet not unusual and routine methods majorly depended on physical file-keeping, with spreadsheets performing as the number one device for categorization of stock stages with tracking stock [11]. Those handmade and physical structures, although handy, have been susceptible to man-made errors, and bring up-to-date schedules throughout several markets and networks became a time-consuming venture. Also, this method often lacked actual-time perceptibility, mainly in matters like stock-outs or abundant stocking, that could heavily affect productivity.

From those modest beginnings, the enterprise regularly commenced to embody generation. The appearance of Electronic Data Interchange, Digital Facts Interchange, and barcode patterns in the 1970s and 1980s delivered an immense computerization to inventory control management, improving work efficiency and performance. Nevertheless, such stock control program structures were fairly inflexible as they demanded enormous human interference. The actual recreation modifier came with cloud computing, Artificial intelligent machines, and machine learning techniques. Over the past era, the enterprise has observed a massive shift toward those progressive fashions. Cloud-model-enabled stock control structures changed preferred stock managing applications and have added immense flexibility, adaptability, real-time vision, and scalability throughout numerous income sources, along with extended stock optimization [9].

In today's scenario, AI is more utilized in logistics and stock structures, through the use of gadget mastering and automated and optimized stock ranges, counting on customer calls, and flagging capability problems in proactive mode [8]. AI automates tiring, monotonous obligations, but it additionally affords treasured understandings via forecasting and predictive analytics, allowing organizations to draw knowledgeable, long-term planning and formulate best strategies. So, integration of AI and systems that are primarily based on the cloud will preserve the enterprise, exceeding performance and efficiency.

6.2 Benefits and Impact of AI on Inventory Control

AI can offer a few advantages in inventory management [6], including:

Clean request determining
AI-more advantageous stock administration frameworks can analyze huge sums of records to distinguish request designs and create genuine figures. This may optimize stockroom recharging plans and make strides in stock manipulation.

Streamlined stock control
AI-powered independent stock preparations can distinguish and proactively avert stock shortage issues, settling potential stock-outs faster than manual frameworks.

Increase productiveness
AI can computerize one-of-a-kind inventory management assignments, including set-up fulfillment, acquirement, and dissemination, leading to accelerated productivity and bringing a toll on investment finances.

Lower capability and shipping fees
Clever request estimating minimizes overloading, freeing up essential distribution centers and lessening associated capability and operational charges. AI calculations can optimize urgent and shipping guides, diminishing expenses and guaranteeing faster conveyance. By way of proficiently overseeing and diminishing these noteworthy overheads, groups can improve advantage and competitiveness.

Robotized reorganization
AI gives robotized reorganization, which could altogether progress stock proficiency, based totally on the forecast of offers styles and modern-day stock ranges, Artificial Intelligence can activate programme recharging of orders in real time, in this manner making sure of ideal inventory levels.

This is no longer as it has been—anticipating stock-outs and out-of-place deals—and decreases overabundance of stock and its underlying conserving charges. It's a positive method that maintains groups in advance of stock management.

Slant exam

AI's dimensions for slant exams provide a rich source of important studies for industries. By investigating verifiable deal information, and purchaser conduct and advertising styles, AI can distinguish designs and assume future styles. This can direct object preference, limited-time sports, estimating strategies, and more [5]. Such progressed slant exams can furthermore highlight regular request modifications, empowering agencies to devise and optimize inventory in advance of crest intervals.

Optimized distribution center capacity

The potential of Artificial Intelligence to manage complicated real-time record datasets expands beyond the distribution center and coordination phase. AI can verify variables which includes item estimate, weight, and deals pace to advocate ideal stockroom layout and canister conditions to optimize stockroom potential. This leads to maximized ability space, decreased coordination expenses, moved forward selection and percent skillability, reduced exertions charges, and faster set-up success—all primary components for upgrading operational talent and patron fulfillment.

Deliver chain proficiency

[4] AI is a capable equipment for boosting delivery chain effectiveness. With the aid of giving prescient bits of information and actual-time following, AI permits higher coordination with vendors, optimized acquirement, and streamlined arrange achievement. This could decrease delivery chain mistakes through progressing straightforwardness and forethought to manage moderate hazards and disturbances even though upgrading issuer connections. Moreover, it will offer assistance to guarantee an easy, effective supply chain that may alter to converting put it on the market requests.

Integration capabilities

The exceptional stock administration framework lies in its integration abilities and area bounty of degrees that stand out using marketing regular integration with marketplaces, diverse 3PLs, and beat D2C stages like Shopify [40]. This integration lets agencies supervise all their offers channels from a single stage, making sure of consistency, lessening authoritative workload, and improving the use and large operational skillability.

6.2.1 Moral Considerations in AI-Primarily Based Selection Making

Ethics ought to continually come first in the usage of AI to make decisions related to stock control. To guarantee ethical AI-primarily based selection-making, a few essential steps are as follows: Human Supervision: it's vital to preserve a positive degree of human involvement in AI selection-making procedures [1]. Leaders in business and generation ought to ensure that AI systems have the required human oversight and checks and balances to guarantee ethical and moral choice-making.

Records Series and Use: To facilitate AI-based decision-making, corporations should set fine practices for statistics series and use. Setting facts privacy as a main priority and making sure information usage is transparent can assist in reducing risks and upholding moral requirements.
Accountability and Transparency: [2] AI structures should be built with the capability to provide concise justifications for the picks they make, ensuring that the decision-making process is obvious and retaining.

Here are a number of the key elements of using AI for inventory management and request estimating in e-trade:

Exactness in Dealing with Stock: AI-powered request determining is more precise than conventional techniques because it takes underneath attention an extra giant run of information resources and components. This ends in extra actual inventory administration, lessening the threat of stock-outs and overloading.
Dwindled Expenses: Genuine stock administration can help groups lower stock-keeping charges and stay clear of stock-outs, both of which may be exorbitant for e-commerce agencies.
Extended Effectiveness: With AI, inventory administration may be automatic, lowering the requirement for guide paintings and streamlining the approach. This frees up time for workers to take on different assignments together with patron benefits or selling.
Upgraded Client Success: AI-powered stock management and request determining can help guarantee that everyday items are continuously in inventory, diminishing the threat of client disappointment and out-of-place offers. It can also help organizations to recognize patterns and designs in purchaser conduct, empowering them to supply customized recommendations and gives.

Higher Attention for Stock Control: By dissecting terrific sums of statistics and giving giant bits of information, AI can help e-commerce corporations make way higher alternatives for stock management, acquiring, and generation. This can result in extra-talented operations, multiplied productiveness, and more prominent aggressive gain.

6.3 Best Practices for Implementing AI for Stock Management in E-Commerce

Before integrating AI into their operations, corporations need to accumulate all records [3]. This ought to contain information on income, past tendencies, and client behavior. The calibre of those inputs determines how correct the AI algorithms are. Moreover, it's essential that corporations compare and analyze the overall performance of their AI structures regularly. To decide wherein enhancements can be made, they ought to investigate income statistics, stock levels, and customer interactions. Moreover, transparency is important, which reduces the possibility of stock-outs or extra stock and fosters customer consideration through unambiguous insights into stock management practices. Finally, corporations want to make certain that their AI systems are flexible enough to quickly regulate modifications in demand by directly updating their algorithms in reaction to those modifications.

6.3.1 Consideration in Statistics and Statistics Safety

Compliance and consider

With the focal factors of AI come noteworthy information protection concerns. Deliver chain and obtainment divisions are treasure troves of sensitive facts, making them desirable objectives for cyber-criminals [3]. Shields like at-ease capacity frameworks and encryption conventions are critical. Responsibility, even though, it lies in getting ready people's information looking after conventions, and limiting to delicate facts. Compliance with present records security controls, consisting of the GDPR, is non-negotiable. As AI innovation advances, we are probably going to see calls for more robust structures around robotized alternatives and data predisposition. The requirement for advancing regulations that regard character protection while allowing the beneficial viewpoints of AI may be a complicated but unavoidable venture.

AI is in reality revolutionizing the delivery chain and obtainment, advertising uncommon openings for productiveness, selection-making, and pleasant yield [5]. Be that as it may, its integration into those divisions isn't always without challenges. The ethical and information safety suggestions are crucial and make contact with for an adjusted, astute approach. So, as we pass towards this modern time, allows lock-in in an exchange that acknowledges the manipulation and pitfalls of AI, pointing to a future wherein device insights intensify human capability instead of replacing it. Despite the several advantages of AI for inventory administration and request estimating, there are too some demanding situations for executing AI in e-commerce. These incorporate the following:

Facts Presentation
To assure genuine forecasts, AI calculations intensely rely on exact and wide data. Any inadequacies including fragmented or obsolete statistics could have a bad effect on request figuring and inventory administration precision [6].
Integration with Bequest Frameworks
Coordination of AI frameworks with current inventory administration and ERP frameworks can pose a noteworthy assignment. It requires fastidious arranging and coordination to ensure a smooth integration put together.
Taking care of the cost
Executing AI-powered inventory management and request estimating may be steeply priced, requiring hypotheses in hardware, software, and potential. But the potential advantages in terms of multiplied effectiveness, benefit, and customer success can far exceed the charges.

6.3.2 How AI Enables Stock Administration for Important Corporations

AI-powered stock management frameworks have picked up noteworthy footing in one-of-a-kind organizations, creating a difference in organizations that optimize their supply chain operations and enhance common effectiveness. Here are some real-lifestyle illustrations of companies utilizing AI for stock management [41].

Amazon
AI in stock administration performs a critical element for global e-trade monster Amazon, guaranteeing perfect stock stages and streamlined

operations with advanced calculations. The company utilizes a stepped-forward machine gaining knowledge of calculations to estimate requests precisely, optimize inventory levels, and guarantee opportune customer conveyance. Amazon's AI-pushed frameworks assist in decreasing stock-outs, passing ahead distribution center productivity, and enhancing patron fulfillment.

Walmart

Walmart, a riding retail massive, leverages AI and device-gaining knowledge to oversee its amazing stock organization efficiently. The corporation utilizes AI-based request-determining fashions that analyze real-deal information, buyer conduct, and outside additives to expect future requests. This allows Walmart to inventory the right gadgets in the right areas, lessening the abundance of stock and minimizing sporting costs.

Zara

The mildew store Zara executes AI improvements to optimize its inventory administration bureaucracy. Zara employs PC vision frameworks in its shops and distribution centers to display real-time stock tiers. The AI-powered camera's music items' developments empower the enterprise to restock items expeditiously and keep up widely known things in inventory.

Coca-Cola

The refreshment monster Coca-Cola employs AI for stock optimization over its dissemination arrangement. AI calculations examine offers information, chronicled styles, and different pertinent components to determine the suitable stock levels at different regions. This guarantees that Coca-Cola gadgets are directly reachable while minimizing the overabundance of stock and related charges.

P&G

P&G, a multinational customer products organization, depends on AI to supervise its vast item portfolio viably. The corporation employs AI-driven request-determining models to optimize era plans and stock tiers, guaranteeing that items are easily available as and when and where any requirement.

Settle

Settle, a driving nourishment and refreshment corporation, uses AI for inventory management to streamline its delivery chain bureaucracy.

AI makes a distinction Settle precisely foresees requests, optimizing stock over its dispersion setup, and limiting squandering in its operations [8]. Real-international activities outline the utilization of AI in stock management frameworks, highlighting its flexible factors of interest over organizations, optimizing productivity, diminishing costs, and enhancing customer encounters. With the ceaseless advancement of AI innovation, a growing number of agencies are expected to comprehend AI-pushed stock administration arrangements, situating themselves to outflank competition in their unique markets.

6.3.3 Synthetic Intelligence in Inventory Administration: Destiny Styles and Extension

Computer primarily based intelligence is rethinking stock administration, handing over faster, greater amazing, and profoundly effective frameworks to reshape how agencies cope with their inventory community strategies [8]. The functionality of artificial intelligence in this discipline is huge, promising to deal with one-of-a-kind difficulties and upgrade tasks greater than ever.

Order management has been greater

Man-made intelligence-driven stock management frameworks will empower groups to comply with numerous orders at the same time continuously. This regular permeability will assist with spotting expected bottlenecks, inventory troubles, and defers underway and turning in times. Organizations can ensure smoother operations and patron pride by proactively addressing these troubles.

Artificial intelligence is primarily based stock determining

Stock looking ahead is set to emerge as more particular and proactive with the execution of simulated intelligence. By making use of true offers statistics, client styles, and other applicable elements, laptop primarily based intelligence calculations can assume request designs all the more definitively. This engages groups to boost their stock ranges, lessen stock-outs, and limit overabundance inventory, at remaining prompting fee reserve funds and extended effectiveness [9]. The way corporations check their inventory might be altered through AI-automatic inventory exams. Inventory levels may be monitored, discrepancies may be detected, and signals for replenishment can be triggered by way of automatic surveillance systems that are geared up with AI algorithms. This mechanization will decrease the dependence on bodily work, opening up belongings for use in other crucial parts of the commercial enterprise.

PC-based intelligence-driven robots in distribution centers
Laptop-primarily intelligence-controlled robots are imagined to become essential to big stockrooms, smoothing out responsibilities and increasing performance [12]. The fulfillment procedure can be advanced by way of using those robots to deal with obligations like selecting, packing, and sorting on their personal. Their capacity to work vigorously and reliably will spark off faster requests dealing with and diminished useful prices.

Integration with transport offerings AI-driven robots is in all likelihood to extend their presence to the delivery chain's delivery issue similar to warehouse operations. Independent conveyance motors and robots equipped with artificial intelligence capacities could relatively have an impact on final-mile conveyance, upgrading pace and skillability whilst lessening human-associated mistakes and prices.

Modern answers for stock management
Simulated intelligence's flexibility and studying talents will empower the development of altered stock management answers for corporations [10]. As man-made intelligence frameworks steadily break down information and streamline methods, they will supply custom-designed experiences and tips custom-made to each affiliation's unique requirements.

6.3.4 Inventory Control with Predictive Renovation

Predictive maintenance using synthetic intelligence can have a massive impact on inventory management. Studying the information from the device's sensors, AI algorithms can spot maintenance requirements and forestall unexpected malfunctions, minimizing downtime and making certain smooth warehouse operations. The future of artificial intelligence in stock management holds top-notch promise for businesses throughout various industries. The incorporation of AI-driven platforms will bring about stronger effectiveness, monetary financial savings, and more desirable client encounters [40]. The relentless progress of generation is about to make artificial intelligence an indispensable tool for groups aiming to live ahead within the ever-converting international of stock management. Investigating the expense Ramifications of computer-based intelligence Reception in inventory administration for weakening matters across numerous stages.

Studies foundation
Man-of synthetic reasoning (simulated intelligence) stays on the cutting edge of software engineering these days, an area in which revolution is

set. Computer-based intelligence is a piece of software program engineering that arrangements with the making of a scholarly framework that can perform errands that usually require human perception. By way of consolidating AI, information investigation, and current calculations, it draws from a variety of disciplines. Observably sufficient, guy-of-synthetic intelligence has earned ways of reaching respect in one-of-a-kind regions. It's no longer hard to peer the motive why, furnished its capability to reshape frameworks and cycles that institutions directly exploit for upgraded effectiveness and lower charges. Assuming there may be one place that requires such complexity greater than something else, it has to be stock administration, in which inventory conveying expenses deal with 20% to 30% of absolute inventory worth [22]. The main justification for why stock administration is vital in associations is to avoid times of stock-outs, restrict the fee in query, and guarantee that the commercial enterprise meets the purpose of complete assembling [19]. To make matters simpler in institutions, the board ought to have a methodology executed on the best way to manipulate inventory. It includes the coordination and observation of the stock of merchandise from the maker's entire manner to the retail region to the cease client [17]. Integrating laptop-primarily based intelligence into inventory management surpasses the predefined obstacles by using AI, prescient investigation, and everyday language handling to defeat the issues of traditional stock frameworks. The productiveness of the person-of synthetic intelligence techniques is going from brief data admittance to talented hobby waiting for. The significance of simulated intelligence in inventory administration contains moderating troubles connected with inventory mistakes, request deferrals, and abundance inventory [14].

Computer-based total intelligence reception in stock management isn't always as natural as it appears. It calls for an exhaustive comprehension of innovation, key education, and variants to hierarchical necessities and cycles. The impact of simulated intelligence reception on hierarchical costs in the course of two wonderful levels is a simple region to take a look at because it offers bits of information into the speculation required, the anticipated take advantage of the undertaking, and the drawn-out manageability of artificial intelligence pushed inventory management preparations. There is vital significance in this exploration due to its multi-layered nature concerning the connection between the reception of simulated intelligence and the impact at the price of inventory administration. This impact is checked out across the stages of reception. Companies increasingly more knowledgeable they want to position sources into riding side advancements to help with maintaining in the race (Smaje, okay. 2020);

anyhow, whether to embody the utilization of intelligence is a cautious preference since the fees engaged with this sort of desire are vital.

Inside the present quickly impacting the world, the reception of focus on stock management in the shop community has obtained important consideration. There may be a developing organization of writing that perceives the significance of simulated intelligence reception in the stock administration of SCM, with an emphasis on information on how artificial intelligence improvements can in addition broaden talent and lessen charges within the inventory management process ([10]; Schaeffer *et al.*, 2018). The writing in regards to inventory administration in automatic reasoning has been regularly tested, and the idea of effectiveness in inventory management is an extremely pertinent factor interior present writing today [31, 32, 42]. According to Sharma *et al.* [35, 36], effectiveness in businesses with simulated intelligence is widespread for ventures on account that it can activate specific advantages, for instance, diminishing functional fees, dashing up, in addition developing items first-rate, and eventually, improving dynamic cycles. Liu *et al.* [20, 21] expressed that effectiveness within the assembling enterprise is fundamental since it straightforwardly influences performance and gain in companies.

Nasution *et al.* [27] featured that laptop-primarily based intelligence can further develop skillability, lower manual errors, and upgrade the comfort of stockroom sports. One extra point of view that has gotten consideration within the field 9c brainpower in stock management is the usage of automatic reasoning tactics, for the maximum part AI, counterfeit brain groups (ANN), and master frameworks, to supervise advent. As indicated by using Pournader [30], AI calculations can help with dissecting records on 14 stock levels, assisting fashionable estimating, lessening waste, and proscribing expenses [7]. Likewise, Sustrova [37] featured that faux mind corporations (ANN) analyze statistics for hidden patterns and enhance inventory 3 development through artificial intelligence in inventory administration [42]. Similarly, Min [24, 38] featured that the grasp framework can likewise assist in improving advent plans through the association of ideas for technique improvement and the exam of data. Any other captivating exam peculiarity expanding inside the writing today is the cycles, tiers, and making plans utilization of computerized reasoning in specific production community fields. Ren *et al.* [34] synthetic a guide with four key reports that are essential at the same time as executing man-made intelligence in an enterprise. Pan [28] discussed the five center cycles of simulated intelligence execution: 'scheme', 'origin', 'build', 'distribute', and 'hand back'. Which has been commonly utilized as a version for present writing in SCM.

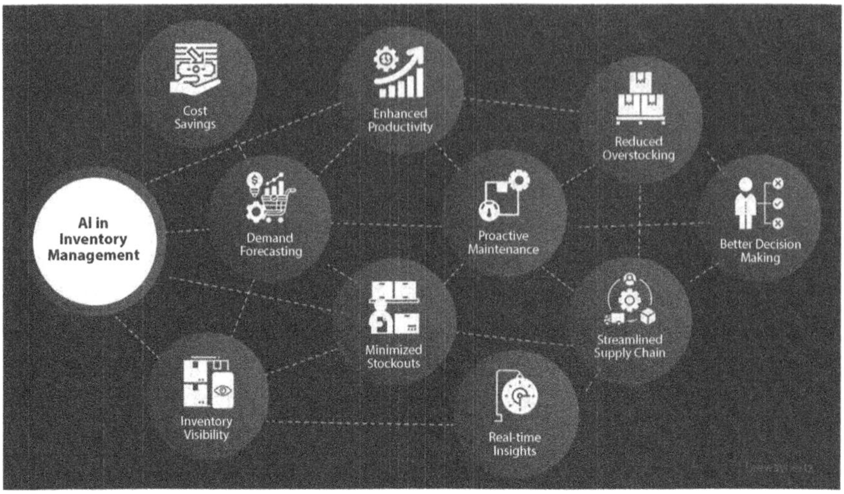

Figure 6.1 AI in inventory management [41].

The above Figure 6.1 illustrates various advantages that a company benefits on application of AI in inventory management. Nevertheless, even though the utilization c intelligence in inventory management has advanced, modern-day computer-based total intelligence speculations can't be applied to absolutely realize the monetary ramifications that institutions would possibly confront when they embrace PC-based total intelligence inside the various intervals of execution. that is because most exploration has been focused on the innovation's popular benefits and uses, with fewer top-to-bottom examinations on what these choices have a price imply for on associations. Consequently, an exploration hollow is outstanding. As an example, Liu [20, 21] known as attention to that synthetic intelligence may be applied to streamline creation processes, reduce the requirement for human work, and restrict loose time. Likewise, Pannu [28] featured that man-of artificial intelligence can probably reform some companies by bringing down fees, increasing performance, and upgrading navigation. Likewise, Xu, Min *et al.* [38] observed that AI may be applied to forestall exorbitant fixes through prescient help. Therefore, this large quantity of past creators restrained their examination of the functional benefits of intelligence execution concerning lessening fees and expanding efficiency, overlooking the financial rate guidelines, for instance, prices related to the status intelligence innovation.

6.4 Formulation of Proposed Model

Below is the instance primarily based on stock control using AI strategies to control deteriorating gadgets.

To keep the overall cost of the inventory system to a minimum, one of the most crucial aspects of inventory management is determining when and how much needs to be bought or created. When a big drop is needed for the stock to go down, the drop becomes more important because it can't be ignored [12]. Focusing on this path has led to a steady change in the inventory, which shows how things are getting worse by adding more and more things that are still good. When choosing the size of a part, it's important not to forget how it will break. Aggarwal built an inventory model based on requests that get less accurate over time [15]. Scientists like Ghare [29] used to think that rotting stock could be a constant source of interest. Hwang came up with the best plan for a situation that was getting worse [18]. Raffat made a model in 1985 for making a stock of rotting raw materials and a way to rot a single finished item [33]. Misra (1975) and Abad (1981) looked into the best way to figure out how big a parcel is and how big it should be under conditions of perishability and fractional rain checks (1996). [16] have also given many models of inventory that are not very hopeful. Gary *et al.* (2005) and [13] both thought about the economic side of planning at that time (2007).

6.4.1 Framework Discussion

Yang and Wee [39] pushed for a coordinated creation inventory model with many different sizes. Then, in 2008, Sugapriya and Jeyaraman focused on a typical production process time for an EPQ model of non-immediately degrading goods that allowed price markdowns and allowed deferral in installments. Mishra thought of the idea of time-subordinate inventory management with rescue esteem [25, 26]. Sabahno thought about the best way to deal with something that was getting worse, wasn't likely to be renewed, and had a low rate of interest (2008). Shahi and Achharya (2008) made a very interesting model of how things change over time. Roy and Choudhuri created an EPQ model that looks at stock ward interest, Weibull circulation, and deficiency (2009). Tripathi MC. K. and Mishra U. [25, 26] backed an EOQ model with time-subordinate Waybill weakening and slope-type interest. Meher M.K. *et al.* [23] have suggested that a market that is going down use an inventory model with a Weibull weakening rate and a delay in payments. In this section, a creation inventory model with three boundary Weibull disintegration and a value rebate for items that have lost some of their strength has been made. In this mode, flaws aren't taken into account, and the holding cost is thought to stay the same.

6.4.2 Assumptions and Notations

The assumptions made for the proposed model are:

(i) The number of people who want the product is known and can't change.
(ii) There can't be a shortage.
(iii) There is no end to planning.
(iv) As soon as even one item is produced, it may be utilized to fulfill orders.
(v) Items that aren't in perfect condition can get a price cut.
(vi) There is no way to fix or replace something that has broken down.

The notations that are used here for developing the mathematical model:

P: Production price in step with unit time
d: Actual call for the product in step with unit time, $d < p$.
A: Set up price. Deterioration price (unit/unit time),

$\theta = \alpha\beta(t - \gamma)\beta\text{-}1$ wherein $0<a<1$, $b >1, 0< n<1$ wherein an is the size parameter, p is the form parameter, and y is the area parameter of the Waybill 3 parameter deterioration.

H: "Constant stock sporting price in step with unit in step with unit time. okay, the Production price is in step with the unit.
l: Price cut price in step with unit price.
t: Optimal cycle time.
T1: Production duration.
T2: Time in the course of which there may be no manufacturing, i.e., T2=T-T1." Ix(t): Inventory degree for the product in the course of the manufacturing duration, i.e., $0\leq f\leq T1$
I2(t): Inventory degree of the product in the course of the duration may be no manufacturing, i.e., $T1\leq t\leq T$
I(M): Maximum stock degree of the product.
TVC(T): Total price/unit time.

6.4.3 Proposed Mathematical Model

At time $t = 0$, there are no items in stock. Production and supply both begin at the same time, and production stops when the highest stock level, 1(M), is up to the mark at a given time t=Tx. As per the tenure of scheduled time, the inventory rapidly grew at a rate of a/d, and it didn't break down. After time 7J, the units that have been delivered start to break down, and the supply goes on at the markdown rate. As long as interest in the item stays the same, the number of items in stock will go down until there are none left, at which point the production run will begin. So, the accompanying different conditions can be used to deal with the item's stock level at time t over the range [0, T].

$$dI_1(t)\,/dt = a + d\ 0 \le f \le T1 \tag{6.1}$$

and

$$dI_2(t)\,/dt + \theta I_2(t) = -d.....T1 \le t \le T \tag{6.2}$$

where $\theta = \alpha\beta(t-\gamma)^{\beta-1}$ $0<\alpha<1$, $\beta>1, 0<\gamma<1$

The scale parameter is x and the shape parameter is y. The location parameter is y.

Here the boundary conditions are $I1(0) = I_2\,(T_2) = 0$

Using the boundary condition $I1(0) = 0$ solution of equation (6.1) is

$$I1(t) = (p - d)\,t.......0 \le t \le T1 \tag{6.3}$$

Integrating Factor of equation (6.1) is

$$e\int e^{\alpha\beta(t-\gamma)^{\beta-1}} = e^{\alpha(t-\gamma)^{\beta}}$$

using the integration factor from above, the answer to equation (6.1) is

$$I_2(t)e^{\alpha(t-\gamma)^{\beta}} = \int -de^{\alpha(t-\gamma)^{\beta}} + c$$

Since 0 a 1, we can ignore the terms in the exponential function's expan-

$$\Rightarrow I_2(t)e^{\alpha(t-\gamma)^{\beta}} = -d\int\{1+\alpha(t-\gamma)^{\beta}\}dt + c$$

sion that have to do with the

$$\Rightarrow I_2(t)e^{\alpha(t-\gamma)^{\beta}} = -d\left\{t + \frac{\alpha(t-\gamma)^{\beta+1}}{\beta+1}\right\} + c$$

second and higher powers of a. This gives us T.

Now, going back to the first condition I2 (T2) = 0 above, we can find the answer we need for equation (6.1) as

$$I_2(t)e^{\alpha(t-\gamma)^\beta}[T2-t+\frac{\alpha}{\beta+1}\{(T_2-\gamma)^{\beta+1}-t-\gamma)^{\beta+1}]$$

Since 0 < a < 1, if we ignore the parts of the exponential function that have to do with the second and higher powers of a, we get,

$$\Rightarrow I_2(t)=d\{1-\alpha(t-\gamma)^\beta\}\left[T_2-t+\frac{\alpha}{\beta+1}\{(T_2-\gamma)^{\beta+1}-(t-\gamma)^{\beta+1}\}\right]$$

$$=d\left[T_2-t+\frac{\alpha}{\beta+1}\{(T_2-\gamma)^{\beta+1}-(t-\gamma)^{\beta+1}\}-T_2\alpha(a+\gamma)^\beta+t\alpha(a+\gamma)^\beta\right.$$
$$\left.-\frac{\alpha^2}{\beta+1}\{(a-\gamma)^\beta(T_2-\gamma)^{\beta+1}-(a+\gamma)^{2\beta+1}\}\right]$$

Since 0 < a < 1, leaving out the parts about the second and higher powers of an in the above, we get,

$$I_2(t)=d\left[T_2-t+\frac{\alpha}{\beta+1}(T_2-\gamma)^{\beta+1}-\alpha T_2(a-\gamma)^\beta\right.$$
$$\left.+\alpha t(a+\gamma)^\beta-\frac{\alpha}{\beta+1}(a+\gamma)^{\beta+1}\right], T_1\le t\le T \tag{6.4}$$

The set-up takes a toll per unit of time is

SC= T/P

Holding Fetched

$$HF = \frac{1}{T}\left[\int_0^{T_1} h(t)I_1(t)dt + \int_0^{T_2} h(t)I_2(t)dt\right]$$

$$\Rightarrow HF = \frac{1}{T}\left[h\int_0^{T_1}(p-d)tdt\right] + \frac{hd}{T}\int_0^{T_2}\left[T_2 - t + \frac{\alpha}{\beta+1}(T_2-\gamma)^{\beta+1}\right.$$

$$\left. - \frac{\alpha}{a+1}(t-\gamma)^{c+1} - \alpha T_2(t-\gamma)^{\beta c} + \alpha t(t-\gamma)^{\beta c}\right]dt$$

After Integration of the above equation, we come to know

$$HC = \frac{h(p-d)T_1^2}{2T} + \frac{hd}{T}\left[\frac{T_2^2}{2} - \frac{2\alpha(T_2-\gamma)^{\beta+2}}{(\beta+1)(\beta+2)}\right.$$

$$\left. + \frac{\alpha T_2(T_2-\gamma)^{a+1}}{(a+1)} + \frac{2\alpha(-\gamma)^{\beta+2}}{(\beta+1)(\beta+2)} + \frac{\alpha T_2(-\gamma)^{a+1}}{(a+1)}\right] \tag{6.5}$$

Let's say what T1 and T2 mean in terms of T.

$$I_1(T_1) = I_2(0)$$

$$= (p-d)T1 = d[T2 + \frac{\alpha}{\beta+1}(T_2-\gamma)^{\beta+1} - \frac{\alpha}{\beta+1}(-\gamma)^{\beta+1} - \alpha T_2(-\gamma)^{\beta} + \alpha t(-\gamma)^{2\beta+1}\Big]$$

Since 0 a 1, we can ignore the terms in the above equation with a to get a good answer.

$$(p- d)\ T1 = dT2$$

$$= T - T2/T2 = d / p\text{-}d$$

$$= T/T2 = p/p\text{-}d$$

$$= T2 = (A- d)\ T /p = aT \text{ ,assuming } x = a - d /a$$

$$= T1 = T - T2 = dT /p \tag{6.6}$$

By plugging these numbers into equation (76), we get

$$HC = \frac{hdxT}{2} - \frac{2\alpha hd(xT-\gamma)^{\beta+2}}{(\beta+1)(\beta+2)T} + \frac{hd\alpha x(xT-\gamma)^{\beta+1}}{(\beta+1)} + \frac{2\alpha hd(-\gamma)^{\beta+2}}{(\beta+1)(\beta+2)T} + \frac{hd\alpha x(-\gamma)^{\beta+1}}{(\beta+1)} \tag{6.7}$$

The cost of making something per unit of time is

$$\text{PC} = \text{pkT1/T} = \text{pkdT/Tp} = \text{kd} \tag{6.8}$$

Deterioration cost:

The difference between the most units in stock and the number of units utilized to meet requests is the number of units that break amid a cycle. So, the cost of breaking down per unit of time is given as

$$\text{DC=k/T}[\text{I}_2(0) - \textstyle\int_0^{T2} ddt$$

$$= kd/T\left[\frac{\alpha}{\beta+1}(T_2-\gamma)\beta+1-\frac{\alpha}{\beta+1}(-\gamma)^{\beta+1}-\alpha T_2(-\gamma)^{\beta}\right]$$

When we use the values of T1 and T2 in terms of T, we get

$$\text{DC=}kd/T\left[\frac{\alpha}{\beta+1}(xT-\gamma)^{\beta+1}-\frac{\alpha}{\beta+1}(-\gamma)^{\beta+1}-\alpha xT(-\gamma)^{\beta}\right] \tag{6.9}$$

Price discount:

Price cuts are given as a percentage of the cost to make the units in the Period (0,T2)

$$= \text{PD=Kl/T}\int_0^{T_2} ddt$$
$$= \text{kldT2 /T} = \text{kldxT/ T} = \text{kl dx} \tag{6.10}$$

So, to figure out the average total cost per unit of time,

$$TVC(T) = PC + SC + HC + PD + DC$$

$$= kd + \frac{A}{T} + \frac{hdxT}{2} - \frac{2\alpha hd(xT-\gamma)^{\beta+2}}{(\beta+1)(\beta+2)T} + \frac{hd\alpha x(xT-\gamma)^{\beta+1}}{(\beta+1)}$$
$$+ \frac{2\alpha hd(-\gamma)^{\beta+2}}{(\beta+1)(\beta+2)T} + \frac{hd\alpha x(-\gamma)^{\beta+1}}{(\beta+1)}$$
$$+ \frac{kd}{T}\left[\frac{\alpha(xT-\gamma)^{\beta+1}}{(\beta+1)} - \frac{\alpha(-\gamma)^{\beta+1}}{(\beta+1)} - \alpha xT(-\gamma)^{\beta}\right] + kldx$$

$$\Rightarrow TVC(T) = kd + \frac{A}{T} + \frac{hdxT}{2} - \frac{2\alpha hd}{(\beta+1)(\beta+2)T}\left\{(xT-\gamma)^{\beta+2} - (-\gamma)^{\beta+2}\right\}$$
$$+ \frac{hd\alpha x}{(\beta+1)}\left\{(xT-\gamma)^{\beta+1} + (-\gamma)^{\beta+1}\right\}$$
$$+ \frac{kd\alpha}{(\beta+1)T}\left\{(xT-\gamma)^{\beta+1} - (-\gamma)^{\beta+1}\right\} - \alpha kdx(-\gamma)^{\beta} + kldx$$

To find the lowest total cost, we figure out how much T is from

$$\frac{d}{dT}(TVC(T)) = 0$$

$$\Rightarrow \frac{-A}{T^2} + \frac{hdx}{2} - \frac{2\alpha hdx(xT-\gamma)^{\beta+1}}{(\beta+1)} + \frac{2\alpha hd(xT-\gamma)^{\beta+2}}{(\beta+1)(\beta+2)T^2}$$
$$- \frac{2\alpha hd(-\gamma)^{\beta+2}}{(\beta+1)(\beta+2)T^2} + \alpha hdx^2(xT-\gamma)^{\beta} + \frac{\alpha kdx(xT-\gamma)^{\beta}}{T}$$
$$\frac{\alpha kd(xT-\gamma)^{\beta+1}}{(\beta+1)T^2} + \frac{\alpha kd(-\gamma)^{\beta+1}}{(\beta+1)T^2} = 0 \tag{6.11}$$

Using the calculated value of T from (6.14) will make the TVC as small as possible.

$$\frac{d^2}{dT^2}(TVC(T)) > 0$$

$$\Rightarrow \frac{2A}{T^3} - \frac{2\alpha hdx}{(\beta+1)T^2}[Tx(\beta+1)(xT-\gamma)^{\beta} - (xT-\gamma)^{\beta+1}]$$

$$+\frac{2\alpha hd}{(\beta+1)(\beta+2)T^4}[T^2x(\beta+2)(xT-\gamma)^{\beta+1} - 2(xT-\gamma)^{\beta+2}T] + \frac{4\alpha hd(-\gamma)^{\beta+2}}{(\beta+1)(\beta+2)T^3}$$

$$+\alpha hdx^3\beta(xT-B)^{\beta-1} + \frac{\alpha kdx}{T^2}[Tx\beta(xT-\gamma)^{\beta-1} - (xT-\gamma)^{\beta}]$$

$$-\frac{\alpha kd}{(\beta+1)T^4}[T^2x(\beta+1)(xT-\gamma)^{\beta} - 2T(xT-\gamma)^{\beta+1}] - \frac{2\alpha kd(-\gamma)^{\beta+1}}{(\beta+1)T^3} > 0 \tag{6.12}$$

6.4.4 Example

Let D = Rs 3000/set up, P = 300 units/unit time, d = 60 unit time, or = 0.8,= 10, y =0.4, A: =/ls60/unit, 1 = 0.05, h = 2. The conditions in (6.9), (6.10), (6.11), and (6.12) are very hard to understand. You can solve them by writing code in Mathematica-5.1. Using these qualities for condition 6.14, we get T* = 1.83327. Using this value of T*in equation (6.15) we get d^2/dt^2 (TVC(T))= 4638 >0 which is positive. So, this value of T* will make the total average variable cost as low as possible. Again, equations 6.9 and 6.12 tell us that the best values for HC* are 71.4766 and TVC* is 4342.31.

6.4.5 Sensitivity Analysis

An affectability investigation has been done by changing one framework parameter at a time while clearing out the others the same. The cover illustration was utilized to induce the first values of all the parameters for affectability investigation.

Table, for Case (M < T)

Table 6.1 Sensitivity analysis based on parameters.

Parameter	% change	T	K
A	-50	0.347688	1945.73
	-25	0.269834	2455.23
	0	311205	2885.5
	25	0.3476'88	3264.92
	50	0.380691	3608.lS
c	-50	0.372232	2504.55
	-25	0.3317507	2706.78
	0	0.311205	2467.52
	25	0.290407	3046.09
	50	0.21343,7	3037.53
h	-50	0.346277	2857.69
	-25	0.32734	2345.98
	0	0.311205	2885.5
	25	0.297243	3037.53
	50	0.285005	3183.02
p	-50	0.346277	2857.69
	-25	0.32734	2345.98
	0	0.311205	2804.33
	25	0.297243	2968.12
	50	0.285005	3023.3
j	-50	0.311205	2887.2
	-25	0.2904-07	2889.3
	0	0.21343,7	2885.1
	25	0.312323	2884.4
	50	0.302341	2886.1
R	-50	0.346277	2857.69
	-25	0.32734	2345.98
	0	0.311205	2804.33
	25	0.297243	2968.12
	50	0.285005	3023.3

(Continued)

Table 6.1 Sensitivity analysis based on parameters. (*Continued*)

Parameter	% change	T	K
a	-50	0.311206	2885.66
	-25	0.311204	2885.58
	0	311205	2885.5
	25	0.311206	2885.42
	50	0.311207	288534
r	-50	0.439321	2887.2
	-25	0.3590216	2889.3
	0	0.278632	2885.1
	25	0.261245	2884.4
	50	0.256543	2886.1
j	-50	0.311249	2504.2
	-25	0.311205	2765.3
	0	0.311202	2805.5
	25	0.311202	3021.7
	50	0.311205	3112.4
M	-50	0.311204	2857.69
	-25	0.311204	2345.98
	0	311205	2804.33
	25	0.311.206	2968.12
	50	0.311207	3023.3

From the above (Table 6.1) it tends to be deduced that the ideal process duration T* increments as the boundary an increments and it diminishes as the boundaries, d, k, a, and p increments. Also, the ideal holding cost HC* increments as the boundaries A, p, d increments and it diminishes as the boundary k, a, and p increments. The ideal normal expense TVC* diminishes as the boundaries A, p, d, k, and an abatements yet it increments as the parameter^ diminishes.

6.5 Conclusion

Simulated intelligence can probably upgrade stock administration by means of further developing interest estimating, smoothing out stock manipulation, and expanding effectiveness. In any case, it is crucial to reflect on the consideration of ethical ramifications and focus on human oversight, facts safety, and ease even as executing PC primarily based intelligence-based dynamic frameworks. By tending to these ethical contemplations, institutions can saddle the advantages of laptop primarily based intelligence even as they maintain ethical norms in inventory management. Synthetic intelligence has fundamentally motivated inventory administration, and attractive agencies with surprising talent, exactness, and premonition. It tends to properly establish difficulties and opens first-rate open doors for development. With the utilization of simulated intelligence in inventory management frameworks, businesses can encounter upgraded request following and advantage ongoing permeability into distinct orders at the same time. This capability to recognize in all likelihood bottlenecks and inventory troubles empowers groups to visit proactive lengths, ensuring consistent sports and lifting consumer loyalty better than ever. Moreover, synthetic intelligence-based inventory figuring reclassifies inventory community arranging with the aid of making use of verifiable deal records, client styles, and vital factors. Better and improved effectiveness in waiting time for design requests allows improved streamlining of groups of limit stock outs and inventory kinds. This reduction in excess inventory stock thereby returns huge price reserves, revenue, and productivity. Automation is based on the assumption of controlled stock management through AI and robotic exploration and investigation that effectively gives better prediction of current and reorder stock levels, errors, and noise in data management. Customization is one greater signal of laptop-primarily based intelligence in stock administration, as synthetic intelligence frameworks' versatility and studying capacities empower the development of customized solutions for companies. Custom-made bits of expertise and suggestions assure that each association's unique necessities are met, in addition to upgrading practical effectiveness and impartial course. Prescient assist, driven by using man-made intelligence, guarantees the steady running of stockroom hardware, limiting private time and forestalling sudden breakdowns. For this reason, stockroom sports run as anticipated, ensuring that inventory management remains continuous and productive. The fate of PC-based totally intelligence in stock management holds widespread commitment, with ceaseless mechanical progressions getting ready for much more creative preparations. Corporations that embody PC-based totally intelligent controlled inventory management are prepared to accumulate a crucial top hand, expanding proficiency, limiting prices, and conveying unequaled consumer encounters.

As we look forward, it's very clear that man-made intelligence's impact will simply broaden, in addition, reclassifying the limits of stock management and reshaping the manner in which companies paint the interior of their stockpile chains. Embracing artificial intelligence has evolved from being a choice to a flat-out need for associations searching out reasonably priced improvement and progress in stock management's dynamic and fast-advancing global growth. The artificial intelligence-managed future has shown up, and businesses that quickly take advantage of it will take the lead in entering a new era of effectiveness and flourishing in stock administration.

References

1. Abad, P.L., Optimal pricing and lot sizing under conditions of perishability and partial backlogging. *Manage. Sci.*, 42, 8, 1093–1104, 1996.
2. Abad, P.L., Optimal price and order size for a reseller under partial backlogging. *Comput. Operation Res.*, 28, 53–65, 2001.
3. Abad, P.L. and Jaggi, C.K., A joint approach for setting a unit price and the length of the credit period for a seller when end demand is price sensitive. *Int. J. Prod. Econ.*, 83, 115–122, 2003.
4. Aggarwal, S.P., A note on an order-level model for a system with a constant rate of deterioration. *Opsearch*, 15, 184–187, 1978.
5. Aggarwal, S.P. and Jaggi, C.K., Ordering policies of deteriorating items under permissible delay in payments. *J. Oper. Res. Soc.*, 46, 658–662, 1995.
6. Aggarwal, V. and Bahari-Hashani, H., Synchronized production policies for deteriorating items in a declining market. *HE Trans.*, 23, 2, 185–197, 1991.
7. Alexander, C. and Smaje, C., Surplus retail food redistribution: An analysis of a third sector model. *Resour. Conserv. Recycl.*, *52*, 11, 1290–1298, 2008.
8. Axsäter, S., Multi-echelon systems: reorder points. *Inventory Control.* Springers International Series, 247–293, 2006.
9. Balkhi, Z.T. and Benkherouf, L., A production lot size inventory model for deteriorating items and arbitrary production and demand rate. *Eur. J. Oper. Res.*, 92, 302–309, 1996.
10. Bughin, J., Hazan, E., Sree Ramaswamy, P., DC, W., Chu, M., Artificial intelligence the next digital frontier, 2017.
11. Chand, S. and Ward, J., A note on economic order quantity under conditions of permissible delay in payments. *J. Oper. Res.*, 38, 83–84, 1985.
12. Chang, C.T., *et al.*, An EOQ model for deteriorating items under supplier credits linked to ordering quantity. *Appl. Math. Model.*, 27, 983–996, 2003.
13. Deng, C., Liu, Y., and demand prediction optimization method for anomaly detection. *Wireless Commun. Mobile Comput.*, *2021*, 1, 9969357, 2021.
14. Dhaliwal, N., Tomar, P.K., Joshi, A., Reddy, G.S., Hussein, A., Alazzam, M.B., A detailed Analysis of Use of AI in Inventory Management for technically

better management, in: *2023 3rd International Conference on Advance Computing and Innovative Technologies in Engineering (ICACITE)*, IEEE, pp. 197–201, 2023, May.
15. Dhavale, D.G. and Aggarwal, S.C., Multi-machine, multi-product production scheduling and inventory control. *Decis. Sci.*, *9*, 4, 577–595, 1978.
16. Goyal, S.K. and Giri, B.C., Recent trends in modeling of deteriorating inventory. *Eur. J. Oper. Res.*, *134*, 1, 1–16, 2001.
17. Hayes, R.H., Statistical estimation problems in inventory control. *Manage. Sci.*, *15*, 11, 686–701, 1969.
18. Hwang, H.S., Inventory models for both deteriorating and ameliorating items. *Comput. Ind. Eng.*, *37*, 1-2, 257–260, 1999.
19. Jenkins, K., Ford, A., Robson, C., Nicholls, R.J., Identifying adaptation 'on the ground': Development of a UK adaptation Inventory. *Clim. Risk Manage.*, *36*, 100430, 2022.
20. Li, M. and Liu, Y., Managerial regret and inventory pricing. *Manage. Sci.*, *68*, 6, 4398–4414, 2022.
21. Liu, X., Zhao, D., Ji, Q., Zeng, Y., Hu, X., Managing strategic inventory under retailer competition. *Eur. J. Oper. Res.*, *308*, 3, 1206–1219, 2023.
22. McCue, C.P. and Pitzer, J.T., Centralized vs. decentralized purchasing: Current trends in governmental procurement practices. *J. Public Budgeting Accounting Financ. Manage.*, *12*, 3, 400–420, 2000.
23. Meher, M.K., Panda, G.C., Sahu, S.K., An inventory model with weibull deterioration rate under the delay in payment in demand decling market. *Appl. Math. Sci.*, *6*, 23, 1121–1133, 2012.
24. Min, J., Zhou, Y.W., Zhao, J., An inventory model for deteriorating items under stock-dependent demand and two-level trade credit. *Appl. Math. Modell.*, *34*, 11, 3273–3285, 2010.
25. Mishra, V.K., An inventory model of instantaneous deteriorating items with controllable deterioration rate for time dependent demand and holding cost. *J. Ind. Eng. Manage.*, *6*, 2, 495–506, 2013.
26. Mishra, U., An inventory model for two parameter Weibull deterioration and declining demand under shortages. *J. Inf. Optim. Sci.*, *37*, 4, 511–533, 2016.
27. Nasution, A.A., Matondang, N., Ishak, A., Inventory Optimization Model Design with Machine Learning Approach in Feed Mill Company. *Jurnal Sistem Teknik Industri*, *24*, 2, 254–272, 2022.
28. Pan, F.B., Perishable product inventory model based on the food supply chain. *J. Interdiscip. Math.*, *19*, 1, 111–127, 2016.
29. Ghare, P.M. and Schrader, G.H., A model for exponentially decaying inventory system. *J. Ind. Eng.*, 21, 449–460, 1963.
30. Pournader, M., Sauer, P.C., Fahimnia, B., Seuring, S., Behavioral studies in sustainable supply chain management. *Int. J. Prod. Econ.*, *243*, 108344, 2022.
31. Praveen, K.B., Kumar, P., Prateek, J., Pragathi, G., Madhuri, J., Inventory management using machine learning. *Int. J. Eng. Res. Technol. (IJERT)*, *9*, 06, 866–869, 2020.

32. Praveen, V.P. and Manoharan, M., Analysis of Inventory Control Model for Items Having General Deterioration Rate. *Appl. Probab. Stochastic Processes*, 293–306, 2020.
33. RAAFAT, F., A production-inventory model for decaying raw materials and a decaying single finished product system. *Int. J. Syst. Sci.*, *16*, 8, 1039–1044, 1985.
34. Ren, H. and Huang, T., Opaque selling and inventory management in vertically differentiated markets. *Manuf. Serv. Oper. Manage.*, *24*, 5, 2543–2557, 2022.
35. Sharma, S., Singh, S.R., Kumar, M., A reverse logistics inventory model with multiple production and remanufacturing batches under fuzzy environment. *RAIRO Oper. Res.*, *55*, 2, 571–588, 2021.
36. Sharma, S., Tyagi, A., Verma, B.B., Kumar, S., An inventory control model for deteriorating items under demand dependent production with time and stock dependent demand. *Int. J. Oper. Quant. Manage.*, *27*, 4, 321–336, 2022.
37. Sustrova, T., A suitable artificial intelligence model for inventory level optimization. *Trendy ekonomiky Managementu*, *10*, 25, 48, 2016.
38. Xu, C., Zhao, D., Min, J., Hao, J., An inventory model for nonperishable items with warehouse mode selection and partial backlogging under trapezoidal-type demand. *J. Oper. Res. Soc.*, *72*, 4, 744–763, 2021.
39. Yang, P.C. and Wee, H.M., An integrated multi-lot-size production inventory model for deteriorating item. *Comput. Oper. Res.*, *30*, 5, 671–682, 2003.
40. https://www.allresearchjournal.com/.
41. https://www.linnworks.com/.
42. https://journals.christuniversity.in/.

7

Integrating Machine Learning and Data Ethics: Frameworks for Intelligent Ethical Decision-Making

Karishma Sharma[1], Deepa Gupta[1], Mukul Gupta[1]* and Rajesh Dhanaraj[2]

[1]*GL Bajaj Institute of Management, Greater Noida, India*
[2]*Symbiosis International (Deemed University) Pune, Maharashtra, India*

Abstract
Modern organisational decision-making requires more sophisticated and flexible mechanisms. This study analyses an integrated framework that improves decision-making with intelligent decision-making assistance technologies. We begin with decision-making basics and emphasise its importance to organisational success. Traditional decision-making has downsides. An innovative IDMSS leverages modern technologies to address these challenges and improve decision-making. Moving from traditional decision-making to intelligent support systems is crucial. Using AI, machine learning, and data analytics improves decision-making. Adding these elements makes decision-making flexible, data-driven, and able to overcome human biases and restrictions. Our fundamental contribution is our Architecture Framework, with its conceptual model, key components, and underlying concepts. This framework guides IDMSS deployment for scalability, flexibility, openness, and utility. IDMSS instruments, equipment, machine learning approaches, information visualisation, and forecast analysis follow. A thorough review of these technologies considers data security, scalability, efficacy, accuracy, and user-friendliness. To demonstrate our integrated approach, we continue addressing a key organisational difficulty in a detailed case study. This architecture framework and the technologies used to answer the real-life query produce informative responses. We conclude that the system changes decision-making into wisdom. Organisations use accurate, planned, and dynamic decision-making to solve

**Corresponding author*: prof.dr.mukulgupta@gmail.com

Sapna Juneja, Rajesh Kumar Dhanaraj, Abhinav Juneja, Malathy Sathyamoorthy and Asadullah Shaikh (eds.) Ethical Decision-Making Using Artificial Intelligence: Challenges, Solutions and Applications, (153–182) © 2025 Scrivener Publishing LLC

multi-layered challenges. This study guides companies implementing intelligent technologies for decision-making.

Keywords: AI integration, integrated framework, intelligence decision-making, flexible framework, system architecture

7.1 Introduction

In the rapidly evolving world of technology, it is the confluence of machine learning and data ethics that emerges as a significant focus, shaping the course of informed decision-making (Armbrust, M., *et al.*, 2010). The title, "Machine Learning and Data Ethics: A Design of an Integrated Framework for Intelligent Decision-Making," is an exploration of what amounts to an organic, symbiotic relationship between the performance of machine learning algorithms and ethical duties that guide the morally responsible usage of data analytics.

IoT is the foundation when it comes to machine learning technology, and many actions, such as data processing, are simply becoming rapidly easier and more accurate with automation, like in the past (Armbrust, M., *et al.*, 2010). Artificial intelligence machines, including the form of computer-assisted learning, could be able to discover patterns from large data sets and, therefore, through predictive inference, could come to a general conclusion or make a judgement (Baburajan, M., *et al.*, 2014). In that respect, these technologies can be used in healthcare diagnostics and algorithmic trading in financial prediction, where some of the generalised areas are (Armbrust, M., *et al.*, 2010; Baburajan, M., *et al.*, 2014). Anyway, the boundary-free definition of machine learning in decision-making strategies brings humans to thoughts about what is good and bad, and very grounded research work is required (Baburajan, M., *et al.*, 2014).

The present chapter highlights the ethical problems associated with the application of machine learning techniques, noting that a harmonized ethical framework that caters to effective implementation of intelligent models that uphold ethics is an appropriate option based on the evidence (Borissova, D.B., *et al.*, 2011). Mittelstadt, B.D., *et al.*, (2016) have written that the articles range from a comprehensive review of the ethical questions arising in machine learning to guidelines that deal with the challenges related to bias, privacy breaches, and transparency (Cardin, M.A., *et al.*, 2014). The goal is to contribute an essential element to the ongoing discussion on the preservation of technology, making it more ethically meaningful (Floridi, L. and Cowls, J., 2019).

This chapter covers a wide range of machine learning domains and applications in which this technology plays a significant role (Floridi, L. and

Cowls, J., 2019). Machine learning adoption generates ethical challenges for several industries, including predictive analytics in terms of patient care implementation in the healthcare industry and algorithmic trading tactics used by the financial industry (Cardin, M.A., *et al.*, 2014; Floridi, L. and Cowls, J., 2019). The proposed integrated framework emphasises being agile across several industries and adapting to sectors with a dynamic technological background.

This chapter aims to engage algebra, philologists, and bureaucrats by providing priceless fortes and practical directions that address the puzzling moral concerns of machine learning (Floridi, L. and Cowls, J., 2019). If machine learning is indeed an ethical problem, it should have demonstrated this phenomenon, even if it's not immediately apparent. Not only are the consequences of ignoring these concerns hypothetical, but various and important influences on humans, communities, and societal structures are also stilted and clear (Floridi, L., *et al.*, 2018).

This introduction sets the tone for a comprehensive study on hash-tag machine learning and data ethics. Moving forward through the upcoming sections, our purpose is to seek out and tackle difficult issues, as well as recommend solutions (Floridi, L., *et al.*, 2018). The most important goal is to design one such decision-making model that will be highly creative and ethical, as well as widely accepted by their community (Floridi, L. and Cowls, J., 2019 and Floridi, L., *et al.*, 2018). Our goal is to positively impact the future by transforming machine learning into an ethically guided driving force of innovation (Felzmann, H., *et al.*, 2020).

7.2 Concept of Machine Learning and Data Ethics

A fast-growing field of AI, ML allows computers to learn from data and make predictions or judgements without being programmed (Felzmann, H., *et al.*, 2020). It aids machine development and, most importantly, increases productivity by analyzing data. This chapter covers the fundamentals of machine learning, one of the most important developments that changed internet use (Goldstein, R. and Khan, A., 2017). It also examines data ethics and machine learning ethics.

Machine learning algorithms learn iteratively from data patterns and tweak performance parameters to improve (Felzmann, H., *et al.*, 2020; Goldstein, R. and Khan, A., 2017). This has enabled important advances in healthcare, finance, and autonomous systems by spinning complex structural data into enormous collections (Goldstein, R. and Khan, A., 2017). Machine learning is used in many areas of life; thus, one must comprehend its basics to recognise its limitations and capabilities (Goldstein, R. and Khan, A., 2017). Using machine learning in decision-making requires careful attention to prevent unethical assumptions from escaping, such as. algorithmic biases and sensitive data use. Floridi, L. and Cowls, J., (2019) state that machine learning ethics must be treated in an informed way through which to address ethical issues.

We still need to be concerned about the ethical expression of bias in machine language algorithms, and this tool should not be used to widen or narrow the socioeconomic gaps. The reasons for it can be past information or unlikely misperceptions in modelling data, even if they are inevitable (Gupta, V., *et al.*, 2017). Despite the imperfection in machine learning, Mittelstadt, B.D., *et al.*, (2016) suggest timely consideration of all the different factors that might lead to data bias as the mean of a high-quality result (Gupta, V., *et al.*, 2017). The other main part of machine learning ethics is privacy. Consequently, the data requirements for training machine learning algorithms often cause concern that these arise from a breach in data protection, ownership, and privacy rules (Hansson, S.O., 2017).

Ensuring privacy using machine learning algorithms entails a continuous fight to achieve a proper balance between information utilisation for correct decisions in the public interest and individuals' rights (Gupta, V., *et al.*, 2017; Hansson, S.O., 2017). Transparency and accountability are crucial factors in applying ethical codes to machine learning (Hansson, S.O., 2017). Machine learning algorithms are opaque when it comes to understanding the reasons for making decisions, which makes them complicated for human understanding. Implementing transparency and accountability concepts in machine learning systems at their core is the best way to ensure trust and reliability (Leikas, J., *et al.*, 2019).

The most important point to making machine learning (ML) ethical readjustment is thought to have arisen from data science (Jhawar, R., *et al.*, (2015). This early consideration of ethical issues during machine learning development, from the dataset to pre-processing, training, evaluation, and deployment, is critical (Kavis, M., (2014). Researchers Jhawar, R., *et al.*, (2015) and Kavis, M., (2014) focus on a holistic approach that converts technologies into ethical feasibility. We watch how the phenomenon of machine learning and data ethics intersect in our products. There is a need to have the capability to comprehend the ethical ramifications regarding machine learning ownership since this technology is growing (Kavis, M., 2014). The following part is the address of the full assessment of the ethics of machine learning, providing the foundation of a standardised platform with ethics being a vital part of effective decision-making (Liu, D., *et al.*, 2021).

7.3 Importance of ML and AI in Design Making

AI and ML transform models for decision-making in multi-industrial settings, changing the present-day situation. The rise in interactive interfaces between humans and technology is bringing unmatched innovation into decision-making, which is giving more speedy, valuable, and unique outcomes. This talk uses the example of machine learning and AI being cornerstones of the product development process and shifting decisions (Kavis, M., 2014; Liu, D., *et al.*, 2021).

Enhanced Data Processing and Insights: A major fact that demonstrates the capacity of ML in making decisions and how it can process data is a lack of time boards. Leikas J. *et al.*, (2018) states that machine learning forms the core of artificial intelligence, enabling systems to learn and improve from experience without the need for explicit programming. This ability provides decision-makers with crucial insights within the large dataset for a better understanding of complex issues (Leikas, J., *et al.*, 2018).

Predictive Analytics as a Strategic Advantage: ML and AI integration allows predictive analytics, an efficient decision-making mechanism, to be in place. Statistically performative, predictive analytics acts upon past facts to predict future patterns and outcomes so that decision-makers can retain strategic advantage (Liu, D., *et al.*, 2021; Leikas, J., *et al.*, 2018). Organisations will be able to make sensible decisions that are not just based on the past but that look to the future based on the fact that they anticipate market changes and customer behaviours.

Automation for Unmatched Efficiency: Automation in ML and AI contributes substantially to operational decision-making efficiency (Leikas, J., *et al.*, 2018). Mundane jobs are computerised, making the destiny of human assets out of reach more than the strategic venture narratives. It automates decision processes, reducing the chances of human errors, thereby leading to accuracy and reliability in the resulting decisions made over a critical period of time (MacKenzie, C.A. and Hu, C., 2019).

Personalisation Redefined for Stakeholder Engagement: ML and AI technologies provide a new definition of personalisation, one of the most prominent aspects of contemporary decision-making (MacKenzie, C.A. and Hu, C., 2019). Thanks to the large data analysis, these technologies provide personal recommendations and services, increasing customer satisfaction and involvement (Mitchell, T.M., 2018). This individualised touch ensures that better decisions are made, especially where there are more focused sectors like marketing and customer relations.

Real-time Responsiveness to Dynamic Environments: ML and AI will give decision-makers the luxury of reacting to the fluctuations of ongoing scenarios with ease and timeliness. This precision enables actions to take place quickly, allowing businesses in decision-making industries such as financial and medical to make more careful decisions (Mitchell, T.M., 2018). Enterprises armed with these apparatuses of technology will also have the ability to use their might and agility to change strategies quickly, which typifies their capacity to rival other enterprises in a dynamic setting (MacKenzie, C.A. and Hu, C., 2019; Mitchell, T.M., 2018).

Proactive Risk Management: This discusses the process of risk management as a result of decisions, and ML and AI in this area are responsible in a significant measure. When studying historical data and identifying potential threats, specialists can create better risk containment tactics (Mitchell, T.M., 2018). Systematic risk assessment and risk management enable more intelligent and secure decision-making. AI-oriented risk assessment models aid in the prediction and control of insurance claims, thereby improving the overall risk management strategy (McManus, J., 2018). This demonstrates the necessity of ML and AI for proactive risk management.

Ethical Decision Support: With their rise, ML and AI provide mechanisms for decision ethics. Incorporating ethical considerations into algorithms ensures transparency and facilitates the development of informed decisions in ethical dilemmas (McManus, J., 2018). However, this is especially important due to organisations' efforts to harmonise their activities in accordance with the macro-environmental value and ethics issues of young technologies. Autonomous systems, like cars that drive themselves, also show how AI systems can help people make ethical decisions when there is a lot of uncertainty. This is done through ethically driven frameworks guided by AI, which are also known as decision support mechanisms (Mitchell, T.M., 2018; McManus, J., 2018).

7.4 Defining an Intelligent Decision-Making Support System

Intelligent Decision-Making Support Systems (IDSS) are a critical technology development in the decision-making dimension that emerges from ML and AI technologies and improves decision-making. IDSS-related technology completely exploits ML and AI to provide decision-makers with priceless information, automation features, and predictive analytics to make coherent choices in many sectors (Mitchell, T.M., 2018). IDSS is a series of decision support systems used to solve problems and analyse complex circumstances by offering insight through complete databases and making optimal selections with various algorithms inspired by artificial intelligence (McManus, J., 2018).

IDSS makes the decision to use data-driven technologies and human intelligence enhancements rather than substitution. IDSS's backbone, ML, learns from previous data to ensure that machine tool users gain relevant knowledge and experiences comparable to human training. According to MacKenzie C.A. and Hu, C., (2019), ML is the core of the artificial intelligence "learning paradigm" that allows systems to learn and develop without programming. According to Jhawar, R., *et al.*, (2015), AI-enabled predictive analytics provide a strategic advantage.

IDSS uses AI technologies like natural language processing, expert systems, and knowledge representation to interpret and interact with diverse applied decision-making contexts (McManus, J., 2018). IDSS can predict patterns and consequences using predictive analytics, one of the most prominent traits of ML and AI. Saariluoma, P., *et al.*, (2016) states that predictive analytics plays a crucial part in decision-making, giving a forward-thinking outlook for those called upon. This predictive capability helps organisations plan strategies and allocate resources based on future needs (Floridi, L. and Cowls, J., 2019).

IDSS is automated using ML and AI. Kavis, M., (2014) illustrates that automated process decisions are becoming more sophisticated and have an impact on HR management. Automation simplifies data handling in IDSS environments, allowing decision-makers to spend more time analysing processes and solving problems through innovation (Leikas, J., *et al.*, 2018). It speeds up decision-making and improves crucial operational accuracy and dependability. IDSS design and usage should address ethical prejudice. AI systems need ethical decision assistance, according to Rittinghouse (MacKenzie, C.A. and Hu, C., 2019). IDSS, an AI programme, must build ethical rules and put them into algorithms to ensure ethical behaviour that helps decision-makers solve difficult moral issues. This fits the story of ethical AI construction and use (Mitchell, T.M., 2018).

7.5 Transformation of the Decision-Making System to Intelligent Decision-Making Support

From traditional to IDSS, decision-making systems have changed drastically (McManus, J., 2018). This developmental route incorporates high-tech technologies, especially ML and AI. Understanding this metamorphosis requires understanding its history, cause, and how ML or AI improved decision-making (McManus, J., 2018). Restrictions on data processing hostility limited algorithms to deterministic processes, with manual effort being common. Decision-makers struggled to process and get insights from large datasets in time (Mazzucelli, C. and Visvizi, A., 2017).

As industries faced more complicated and variable supply networks, these systems' flaws became apparent. The requirement for speed, economy, and precision with growing volumes of complex data drove decision-making system changes (McManus, J., 2018; Mazzucelli, C. and Visvizi, A., 2017). Borissova, D.B., *et al.*, (2011) examined how traditional decision-making methods fail in complicated commercial situations. As organisations sought new ways to adapt to a changing environment, a paradigm shift to support intelligent decisions became necessary (Mazzucelli, C. and Visvizi, A., 2017).

The integration of machine learning underpins the IDSS transformation. Borissova, D.B., *et al.*, (2011) emphasise the importance of ML because it allows systems to learn and self-improve without programming. Decision-making systems designed ML algorithms to learn from data, identify relationships, and predict outcomes (MacKenzie, C.A. and Hu, C., 2019). In this age, decision systems were learning, adaptive, responsive, and capable of analysing massive data sets (Mitchell, T.M., 2018).

After ML paved the way, AI integration became a key factor in their transformational processes. Borissova, D.B., *et al.*, (2011) emphasise AI-based predictive analytics' competitive advantage. Due to natural language processing, expert systems, and knowledge representation, decision-making systems became intelligent decision-making systems with AI technologies (Mitchell, T.M., 2018). These aspects provided sensitive decision-support systems to imitate intelligent operations that understood complex settings (Leikas *et al.*, 2018).

The IDSS transformation reveals predictive analytics. MacKenzie, C.A. and Hu, C., (2019) emphasise dataset representation and foresight in decision-making processes because they are time-oriented, dynamic responses for which a leader provides flawless proof of the future. ML and AI-enabled decision-making systems can forecast patterns and outcomes from historical data (Leikas, J., *et al.*, 2019). Such predictive abilities allowed organisations to anticipate changes and plan accordingly with the correct data.

Automation became a regular element of IDSS to overcome manual process inefficiencies in traditional decision-making frameworks (McManus, J., 2018). Humans made it. Automation automates judgements with machinery. According to Kavis, M., (2014), researchers implemented knowledge books without human influence to eliminate menial activities and make them more effective by providing outputs from only the required themes (Mazzucelli, C. and Visvizi, A., 2017). Decision-making systems automated data processing and ensured critical task accuracy. This accelerated decision-making and enhanced the reliability of the system. The evolution of IDSS required ethics. (Saariluoma, P., *et al.*, 2016) demonstrate ethical AI decision support. However, as decision-making systems became smarter, ethics in algorithms became essential. Thus, openness is essential while using IDSS (Mazzucelli, C. and Visvizi, A., 2017).

7.6 Architecture Framework

This represents a structured blueprint that shows the components, their interactions, and processes of the architecture of IDSS, in which ML and AI are well integrated into decision-making. Adaptability, predictive capabilities, and ethical issues are the foci of the IDSS architecture design (Mittelstadt, B.D., *et al.*, 2016).

7.6.1 Components of the IDSS Architecture

Data Processing Layer: The fundamental layer, which includes data input, cleaning, and pre-processing, lays the groundwork for the subsequent layers of the model. ML algorithms in deep learning probe past and current data to discover patterns and trends, which help machine users gain access to precise and trustworthy information (Mazzucelli, C. and Visvizi, A., 2017).

Machine Learning Layer: The main component of the architecture is the ML block, which contains a lot of algorithms transforming the data into labelled data and using them to develop classifiers and predictors. This layer learns from past records, has to deal with the dynamic nature of local environmental processes, and assists decision-makers in acquiring foresight about the future course (Mittelstadt, B.D., *et al.*, 2016).

Artificial Intelligence Layer: The AI layer supplements ML by including areas such as natural language processing systems, expert consultations, and representative knowledge. These AI functions are humanised, exhibit a complex understanding of complicated situations, and provide a decent level of decision support using artificially intelligent elements (Mittelstadt, B.D., *et al.*, 2016).

Predictive Analytics Module: Predictive analytics can be regarded as a sub-set technique; this stand-alone component utilizes various ML and AI methods to explore data and generate future trends and results (Mazzucelli, C. and Visvizi, A., 2017). This module improves managers' capability to have strategic foresight, enabling them to see changes as early as possible so that they can plan accordingly.

Automation and Efficiency Module: This module aims at developing means of automating routine jobs that cut down the workload on human operators and allow refining general production efficiency (Kavis, M., 2014). Mechanization in this regard is paramount for the acceleration of negotiations and the provision of accuracy in important tasks.

Ethical Decision Support Module: The ethically oriented decision support module is a critical component built into the hidden architecture, enabling ethical outline to be an integral part of the decision-making process during the generation of automata (Liu, D., *et al.*, 2021). Such a module is one of the methods that are used as the requirement for responsible AI development increases.

7.7 Conceptual Framework

Having a conceptual framework is one of the roles that supports the processes that lead to the creation of a decision-support structure (Nasim, S.F., *et al.*, 2022). The structure of IDSS, through its relationships that connect main ideas, key branches, and elements that are responsible for its operation, can be understood via the framework. Additionally, this precision is why the system is flawlessly designed to ensure ML and AI work in unison (Nurock, V., *et al.*, 2021).

7.7.1 Core Concepts

The starting point is understood as fundamental for the framework, i.e., data processing. The multitude of sources originates an ocean of data, which is cleaned and integrated. Therefore, the set is comprehensive, helpful, and precise regarding the features of the data (Nasim, S.F., *et al.*, 2022). The process is based on it as a basis for further actions and decisions. Through adaptive learning, the personified algorithms used are enabled to achieve cognitive addictiveness. Agencies are designed with self-learning algorithms that make history and use the information to detect patterns and experiences; the system is able to evolve and respond accordingly to new occurrences (Nurock, V., *et al.*, 2021).

The concept involving AI technologies, especially natural language processing and expert systems, is a key point. By mimicking the human capacity to think, AI is able to understand complex situations better than most in a more artistic fashion. In addition, AI improves the decision-making process by providing expert opinions (Nasim, S.F., *et al.*, 2022; Nurock, V., *et al.*, 2021). Predictive analytics is a commonly used term, meaning that it is possible to forecast future trends and results based on data from past events. It makes correctives that urge the rulers to foresee the future and carry out policies strategically (Brey, P. and Dainow, B., 2023). The development of an ethical framework as one of the fundamental components should be primordial, along with ethics decision support mechanisms that promote ethical thinking like transparency, fairness, and responsible AI development (McManus, J., 2018).

7.7.2 Components of the Conceptual Framework

Decision-Making Nodes: Where AI and ML technology thrive, these signify the calibre of such decisions within the framework. The decision-making tree contains database processing, adaptive learning, AI-based decision magnification assistance and prediction, and an ethics decision supporter (Nasim, S.F., *et al.*, 2022).

Data Flow Pathways: Information flow in the architecture is represented, which is the pathway of data from data processing through ML and AI. The route ends at decisive nodes. Conditional data paths offer a sustained flow of information to guarantee the proper sequence of processing. Such data flow is essential for successful recognition and understanding of the data (Nasim, S.F., *et al.*, 2022).

Adaptability Loops: Educating the ML algorithms to learn adaptiveness in an iterative way creates a continuous process of fine-tuning the result of the ML algorithms based on feedback and new data. So, they do not draw the IDSS into a static world of notions but into a dynamic business case environment (Brey, P. and Dainow, B., 2023).

Decision Support Outputs: Once applied, the model will generate a decision-support system that is of different forms, such as predictive insights, actionable recommendations, and ethical considerations. The outputs are tailored to specifically meet the needs of the distinct leaders through employing different methodologies (Mazzucelli, C. and Visvizi, A., 2017).

7.7.3 Block Diagram of the Conceptual Framework

The IDSS conceptual framework is represented as a block diagram, which illustrates the interdependent dimensions and concepts involved (Powers, T., 2011). The flow of data is experienced in the system, which affects the processing and analyzing stages besides measuring ML and AI parts consecutively. The transmission of the adaptive learning loop indicates the reinforcement of the feedback system and, subsequently, the outputful decisions of the decision-makers.

The philosophical structure behind the cognitive support for decision-making systems provides grounds for moving and tech-applying services (Brey, P. and Dainow, B., 2023; Powers, T., 2011). Consequently, AI strategies, which embody notions of data processing, adaptive learning, AI-driven decision enhancement, predictive analytics, and ethical decision support, give the framework an inclusive core for decision-making capability improvement (Nasim, S.F., *et al.*, 2022). The Figure 7.1 illustrates the block diagram packed into a single picture demonstrates the dynamic relationships between the system components, showing the transfer of information and decision support (Nurock, V., *et al.*, 2021).

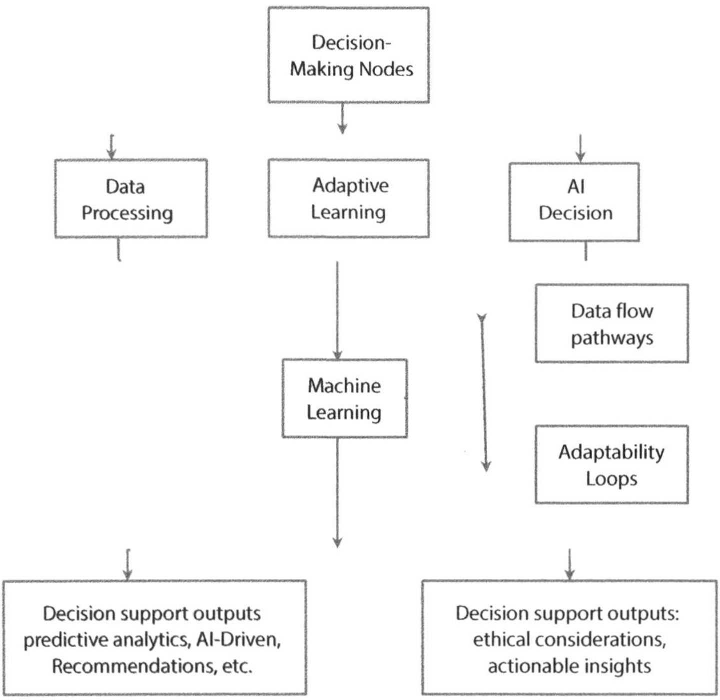

Figure 7.1 Block diagram of conceptual framework (Source: Authors compilation).

This conceptual framework acts as a guide for the design; just like in the original writing, you are using the verbs design and development both in singular form to maintain consistency within the text (Brey, P. and Dainow, B., 2023), e.g., the development and implementation of IDSS (Nurock, V., *et al.*, 2021). (This can also be done by changing it to a plural form, e.g., these conceptual frameworks act as a guide for the designs, developments, and implementation of IDSS.)

7.7.4 Principles of Framework

There should be a set of principles that IDSS follows. This set of principles forms the basis of how IDSS functions (Powers, T., 2011). Those principles

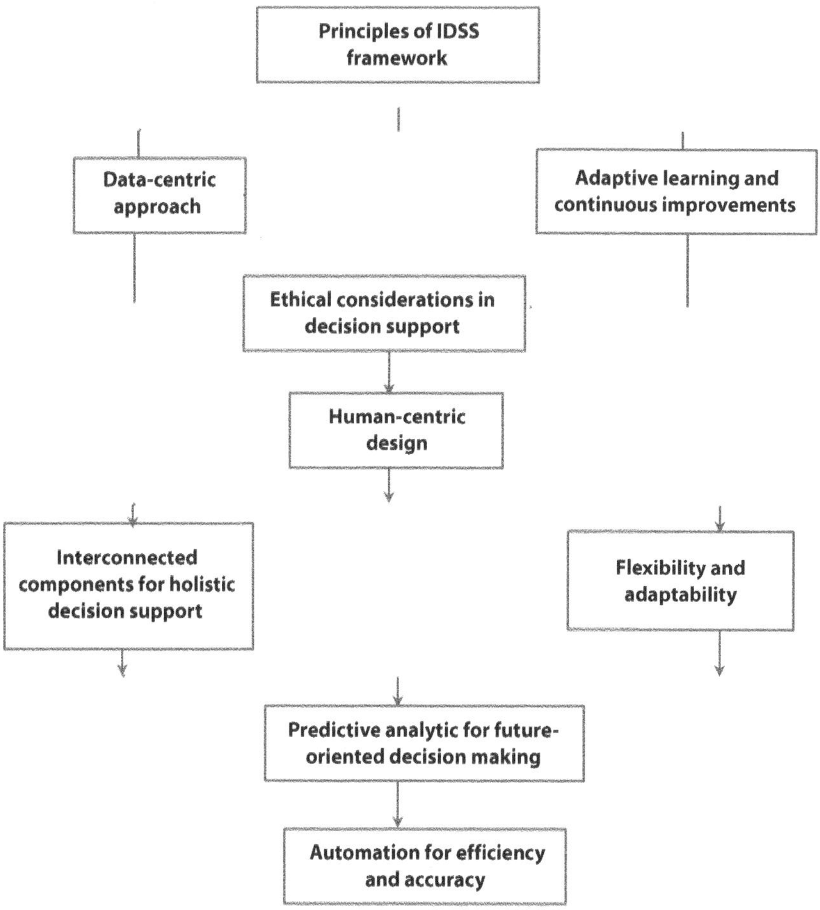

Figure 7.2 Principal framework of IDSS (Source: Authors compilation).

(as shown in Figure 7.2) are the cornerstones of distinguishing attributes such as effectiveness, the ability to constantly react, and ethics. Thus, in the present essay, we consider the root ideas underlying the formation and application of the DISC framework by referring to relevant scholarly sources and published works (Powers, T., 2011; Rocha, C.S., *et al.*, 2019).

Data-Centric Approach: IDSS relies on the data-driven approach, which is at the heart of its structure. The framework emphasises the data sets from many data sources and then gathers, dissects, and links those together (Mittelstadt, B.D., *et al.*, 2016). The same principle of taking complete and reliable data and using it as your basis for computing meaningful analyses and decision support systems is also embodied through their work, as documented in Manyika *et al.* (2017). While data quality and relevance to information must be at the heart of IDSS, it should also be based on data-driven principles (Mazzucelli, C. and Visvizi, A., 2017).

Adaptive Learning and Continuous Improvement: With the IDSS model, the idea of adaptive teaching is a fundamental one. Machine learning algorithms that are given the job within the given system are trained in such a way that they can keep learning and adapting to past data and the way users have used it (Mazzucelli, C. and Visvizi, A., 2017). As mentioned by Domingos (2015), which is another principal premise, it generates a logical line of thought that IDSS develops and advances its decision-making competence through the years (Nasim, S.F., *et al.*, 2022). The scheme is a self-correcting loop that continues to span out the system's understanding and prospecting mathematics.

Ethical Considerations in Decision Support: The ethical factor has a great role in the ethical decisions your characters make in IDSS (Mitchell, T.M., 2018). The outputs of the decision support systems have to follow ethical guidelines, embodying transparency and fairness when they do so, and ethical development should also be among the key priorities in AI development. This approach embraces ethics advice-providing components, which means that the platform endorses actions based on ethnic values and ethical principles (Leikas, J., *et al.*, 2018; Mazzucelli, C. and Visvizi, A., 2017).

Human-Centric Design: The IHD principle forms a cornerstone of the IDSS framework. Largely, this would mean taking outputs and adapting them to the needs of the decision-maker—not so that the human element would be replaced by the decision support systems, but so that they would improve it (McManus, J., 2018). Adjusting to match the user interface and interactions to the needs of the IDSS prevents the wide stretch from decision-makers.

Interconnected Components for Holistic Decision Support: The value of interconnectivity among the components is the major component of the IDSS framework on which it relies. The system has decision-making nodes such as data processing, adaptive learning, decision-prone AI, prediction, and ethical decision enhancement (Powers, T., 2011). This, accordingly, accomplishes the concentrated actions that a model performs, so each component becomes indispensable and, consequently, a major cog contributing to an engine that would ultimately improve the understanding of the scenario complexity (Rocha, C.S., *et al.*, 2019).

Flexibility and Adaptability: The embedding of key principles that include adaptability and agility enhances the IDSS framework to handle the multi-dimensional nature of decision-making (Nurock, V., *et al.*, 2021). Its creation procedure allows it to include new data sources, adjust to different user requirements, and improve its system along with current technology development (Brey, P. and Dainow, B., 2023). This principle, in turn, ensures the IDSS is always abreast of the latest technologies and does not lag behind in any circumstance.

Predictive Analytics for Future-Oriented Decision-Making: The main working principle of IDSS is preventive diagnostics, which is described from the point of view of its ability to anticipate future dynamics (Mittelstadt, B.D., *et al.*, 2016). Decision-makers are gradually forced to channel their thoughts by considering the fourth angle to predict and act promptly, depending on predictive insight (Rocha, C.S., *et al.*, 2019). This is the same rule of dynamic and timely decision-making that usually does not only determine whether one will succeed or not but also proactively knows what decision we should take.

Automation for Efficiency and Accuracy: Heaviness on Productivity and Precision encompasses ingredients that shape the introduction of automation in the IDSS design (Jhawar, R., *et al.*, 2015). The application of AT is responsible for this lack of boredom, thus opening the way for the staff to operate beyond menial tasks to carry out creative predictions (Kavis, M., 2014). Automation provides for faster decision-making and failure-free system operation by minimising the likelihood of human errors that come with erratic decision-making.

7.7.4.1 Tools Used in IDMSS

Smart IDMSS is a complex framework that includes using different intelligent packages for artificial intelligence and machine learning (Mitchell, T.M., 2018). These tools are irreplaceable in data processing, algorithms, and the taking of decisions. IDMSS takes centre stage for this study, and as such, we now briefly explore its various tools, pinpointing their role in decision-making cycles (McManus, J., 2018).

7.7.4.2 Data Processing Tools

Organisations implement Apache Hadoop and Apache Spark to deal with the big data IoT machines generate (Mittelstadt, B.D., *et al.*, 2016). These architectures enable the Hadoop file system's distributed parallel processing and Spark's in-memory processing functions to perform data processing quickly and at scale. The AI tools are therefore of greater significance in IDMSS operations because they take into consideration the massive amounts of information at hand before it can be analysed for results (Mazzucelli, C. and Visvizi, A., 2017).

7.7.4.3 Machine Learning Frameworks

Tensorflow and pyTorch are the two most popular ML platforms used for ML model implementation and deployment implementation in IDMSS. TF, which was created by Google, is widely used, and PP, which was designed by Facebook, is used for more flexible manipulation of neural networks (Brey, P. and Dainow, B., 2023). Implementation of these systems offers the IDMSS the capacity to handle adaptive learning, where the system develops itself by feeding on the collected data and consequently improves its decision-making as time goes by (Powers, T., 2011).

7.7.4.4 Cloud Computing Platforms

We will be using Amazon Web Services (AWS) and Microsoft Azure as platforms to deploy our identification and management system application (IDMSS). The IDMSS can be quite flexible and well-adaptable to cloud platforms, which can also provide scalability and enable the quick gathering of new sources of data (Rocha, C.S., *et al.*, 2019).

The ability to recognise intelligent decision-making seems to be the key to the success of gifted people in general. In fact, these devices are combined in accordance with IMDSS principles; thereby, the system is thing-driven, adaptive, and ethical and makes excellently informed decisions. The prevalence of modern technology in the implementation stage of IDMSS cannot be ignored because of the eminence of its decision-making prowess in these parts (Powers, T., 2011).

7.7.5 Analyzing Different Tools

IDMSS employs a rich toolbox that wisely uses AI and machine learning. An extensive study of this toolbox underpins the algorithms, functions, and roles of every tool aimed at making a significant contribution to the decision-making process (Rocha, C.S., *et al.*, 2019).

7.7.6 Data Processing Tools

Popular open-source software utilised by Max & Mesh is Apache Hadoop and Apache Spark. Apache Hadoop and Apache Spark are the backbones of IDMSS, the main dealers that actually deal with the volume of data processing (Powers, T., 2011). Hadoop's framework, MapReduce, is concentrated in a group of nodes to distribute the work processes and thus help IDMMS process a huge amount of data effectively. Spark enables you to run in-memory processes that speed up data processing, thus increasing your ability to act faster and more effectively. The fault-tolerant parallel processing paradigm of RDDs in Spark is useful in iterative and deep learning algorithms for future population health solutions (Rocha, C.S., *et al.*, 2019; Powers, T., 2011).

7.7.7 Machine Learning Frameworks

Tensors and matrices are thought of as the building blocks of neural networks. Adaptive learning mechanisms conceived inside IDMSS are powerful for Keras and TensorFlow Lite. This type of mechanism allows the construction and introduction of ever more complicated neural networks, which could be incorporated to use historical data for the learning process (Nurock, V., *et al.*, 2021). In this case, human-interpretable models represent the vehicles through which the deep learning algorithms, CNNs for imaging and RNNs for sequence modeling, respectively, can be employed. End-to-end trainability and a large number of community supporters also contribute to the rapid success of TensorFlow and PyTorch packages for IDMSS (Brey, P. and Dainow, B., 2023).

7.7.8 Convolutional Neural Networks (CNNs)

A CNN is a type of deep learning model with a design that is named after this back prop (gradient) works. They use these convolutional layers to build block-by-block spatial feature processing structures through the processing of feature maps (Powers, T., 2011).

7.7.9 Recurrent Neural Networks (RNNs)

RNNs are designed to deal with ordered data information (the sequence of input elements plays a decisive role). These graphs come with edges that follow directed cycles but enable them to retain hidden states (Rocha, C.S., *et al.*, 2019). That means spirited graphs are perfect for natural language processing and time series analysis. The paragraph below provides illustrations of the RNN for sequence classification in TensorFlow using a simple RNN in PyTorch. With RNNs, recurrent links are the means to effective sequential dependence, and they are best for tasks carrying the sequenced data (Rocha, C.S., *et al.*, 2019; Russell, S.J. and Norvig, P., 2018).

7.7.10 Cloud Computing Platforms

AWS and Azure, on the side of the Amazon and Microsoft cloud computing infrastructure like Amazon Web Service (AWS) and Azure, come up at the base of IDMSS as a scaling mechanism. Based on virtualization, such platforms distribute tasks between short throughput cycles with specific data sources and the cycles with general-purpose data. Cloud flexibility either provides support in adjusting IDMSS to transitionary stages that are happening in the decision-world or does nothing at all (Russell, S.J. and Norvig, P., 2018). The cloud scalability and virtualization are done via the services provided by regional platforms like AWS and Azure. The exhibit below includes samples of VM (virtualization machines), scaling, and storage service codes that are used (Rocha, C.S., *et al.*, 2019; Russell, S.J. and Norvig, P., 2018).

7.8 Cloud-Based Scalability with Auto Scaling

AWS Implementation:

```
Import boto3

# Autoscaling group:

autoscaling_client = boto3.client('autoscaling')

Response = autoscaling_client.create_auto_scaling_group

(
```

```
    AutoScalingGroupName='MyAutoScalingGroup',
    LaunchConfigurationName='MyLaunchConfiguration',
    MinSize=1,
    MaxSize=3,
    DesiredCapacity=2,
    AvailabilityZones=['us-east-1a', 'us-east-1b'],
)
# Define scaling policies based on metrics (e.g., CPU utilization)

autoscaling_client.put_scaling_policy
(
    AutoScalingGroupName='MyAutoScalingGroup',
    PolicyName='ScaleOutPolicy',
    AdjustmentType='ChangeInCapacity',
    ScalingAdjustment=1,
    Cooldown=300,
)
autoscaling_client.put_scaling_policy
(
    AutoScalingGroupName='MyAutoScalingGroup',
      PolicyName='ScaleInPolicy',
      AdjustmentType='ChangeInCapacity',
      ScalingAdjustment=-1,
      Cooldown=300,
)
```

Azure Implementation:

```
from azure.identity import DefaultAzureCredential

from azure.mgmt.compute import ComputeManagementClient

from azure.mgmt.compute.models import VirtualMachineScaleSet,

VirtualMachineScaleSetExtension

# Create a Virtual Machine Scale Set with Auto Scaling compute_client =
ComputeManagementClient(credential=DefaultAzureCredential(),
subscription_id='your_subscription_id')

vmss_parameters =
```

```
{
  'location': 'eastus',
  'sku':
{
    'capacity': 2,
    'name': 'Standard_DS1_v2',
    'tier': 'Standard',
  },
}
vmss = compute_client. virtual_machine_scale_set_vm_instances.
create_or_update
(
  resource_group_name='MyResourceGroup',
  vm_scale_set_name='MyVMSS',
  instance_id='instanceId_0',
  parameters=vmss_parameters,
)
```

Virtualization with Virtual Machines:

AWS Implementation:

```
# Launch a virtual machine instance
ec2_client = boto3.client('ec2')
response = ec2_client.run_instances(
   ImageId='ami-12345678',
# Replace with a valid AMI ID
   InstanceType='t2.micro',
   MinCount=1,
   MaxCount=1,
   KeyName='MyKeyPair',
  import boto3
  )
  instance_id = response['Instances'][0]['InstanceId']
  print (f'Launched instance with ID: {instance_id}')
```

Azure Implementation:

```
from azure.identity import DefaultAzureCredential
from azure.mgmt.compute import ComputeManagementClient
from azure.mgmt.compute.models import VirtualMachine
# Create a virtual machine instance
compute_client = ComputeManagementClient(credential=DefaultAzureCredential(),
subscription_id='your_subscription_id')
vm_parameters =
{
  'location': 'eastus',
  'hardware_profile':
{
    'vm_size': 'Standard_D2_v2',
  },
  'os_profile': {
    'computer_name': 'MyVM',
    'admin_username': 'azureuser',
    'admin_password': 'Password1234!',
  },
  'storage_profile': {
    'image_reference': {
      'publisher': 'MicrosoftWindowsServer',
      'offer': 'WindowsServer',
      'sku': '2019-datacenter',
      'version': 'latest',
    },
  },
}
vm = compute_client.virtual_machines.create_or_update
(
resource_group_name='MyResourceGroup',
vm_name='MyVM',
parameters=VirtualMachine(**vm_parameters),
)
```

7.9 Case Study of Complex Problem Using Framework

This case study dwells on the comprehensive change process of a medium-sized e-commerce platform handling issues such as resource management and scalability through the use of cloud computing frameworks, primarily Google Cloud, Amazon Web Services (AWS), and Microsoft Azure. We will analyse the algorithmic aspects and the coding implementations that were crucial for problem solving (Russell, S.J. and Norvig, P., 2018).

The e-commerce ecosystem struggled with unpredictable traffic spikes in the course of sales events, which often resulted in poor user experience and inconvenient downtimes (Rittinghouse, J.W. and Ransome, J.F., 2016). The existing system infrastructure was challenged to cater for the unexpected surge of user activities, resulting in lost business opportunities and customer dissatisfaction (Saariluoma, P., *et al.*, 2016).

With a scalable and robust approach in mind, the organisation chose an entire cloud migration strategy (Visvizi, A., *et al.*, 2017). We chose AWS and Azure for their extensive service offerings. The objective of the case study is to bring to bear the algorithmic implementations and coding techniques utilised in overcoming the challenges (Vaquero, L.M., *et al.*, 2011).

7.10 Algorithm and Coding Analysis

AWS Framework Implementation:

Algorithm 7.1 Auto Scaling Dynamic Adjustment

```
import boto3
# Create an Auto Scaling group
autoscaling_client = boto3.client('autoscaling')
response = autoscaling_client.create_auto_scaling_group(
    AutoScalingGroupName='MyAutoScalingGroup',
    LaunchConfigurationName='MyLaunchConfiguration',
    MinSize=1,
    MaxSize=3,
    DesiredCapacity=2,
    AvailabilityZones = ['us-east-1a', 'us-east-1b'],
)
# Define scaling policies based on metrics (e.g., CPU utilization)
autoscaling_client.put_scaling_policy (
    AutoScalingGroupName='MyAutoScalingGroup',
```

```
    PolicyName='ScaleOutPolicy',
    AdjustmentType='ChangeInCapacity',
    ScalingAdjustment=1,
    Cooldown=300,
)
    autoscaling_client.put_scaling_policy (
    AutoScalingGroupName='MyAutoScalingGroup',
    PolicyName='ScaleInPolicy',
    AdjustmentType='ChangeInCapacity',
    ScalingAdjustment=-1,
    Cooldown=300,
)
```

Algorithm 7.2 EC2 Instance Launch

```
import boto3
# Launch a virtual machine instance
ec2_client = boto3.client('ec2')
response = ec2_client.run_instances (
    ImageId='ami-12345678',
# Replace with a valid AMI ID
    InstanceType='t2. micro',
    MinCount=1,
    MaxCount=1,
    KeyName='MyKeyPair',
)
instance_id = response['Instances'][0] ['InstanceId']
print (f'Launched instance with ID: {instance_id}')
```

Azure Framework Implementation:

Algorithm 7.3 Azure Autoscale Dynamic Adjustment

```
from azure.identity import DefaultAzureCredential
from azure.mgmt.compute import ComputeManagementClient
from azure.mgmt.compute.models import VirtualMachineScaleSet,
VirtualMachineScaleSetExtension
# Create a Virtual Machine Scale Set with Auto Scaling
compute_client = ComputeManagementClient(credential=DefaultAzure-
Credential(), subscription_id='your_subscription_id')
vmss_parameters = {
    'location': 'eastus',
    'sku': {
      'capacity': 2,
      'name': 'Standard_DS1_v2',
      'tier': 'Standard',
    },
}
vmss = compute_client. virtual_machine_scale_set_vm_instances.
create_or_update(
    resource_group_name='MyResourceGroup',
    vm_scale_set_name='MyVMSS',
    instance_id='instanceId_0',
    parameters=vmss_parameters,
)
```

Algorithm 7.4 Azure Virtual Machine Launch

```
from azure.identity import DefaultAzureCredential
from azure.mgmt.compute import ComputeManagementClient
from azure.mgmt.compute.models import VirtualMachine
# Create a virtual machine instance
compute_client = ComputeManagementClient(credential=
Default
AzureCredential(), subscription_id='your_subscription_id')
vm_parameters = {
  'location': 'eastus',
  'hardware_profile': {
    'vm_size': 'Standard_D2_v2',
  },
  'os_profile': {
    'computer_name': 'MyVM',
    'admin_username': 'azureuser',
    'admin_password': 'Password1234!',
  },
  'storage_profile': {
    'image_reference': {
      'publisher': 'MicrosoftWindowsServer',
      'offer': 'WindowsServer',
      'sku': '2019-datacenter',
      'version': 'latest',
    },
  },
}
vm = compute_client.virtual_machines.create_or_update(
  resource_group_name='MyResourceGroup',
  vm_name='MyVM',
  parameters=VirtualMachine(**vm_parameters),
)
```

7.11 Results and Impact Analysis

Algorithmic approaches like auto-scaling and dynamic resource adjustment greatly increased scalability and performance. Cost savings from a mixture of on-demand, spot instances, and reserved capacity of optimal cost optimisation algorithms are affected. Security algorithms, which targeted both data encryption and access control, made data security and compliance more robust.

This case study elaborates on the AWS/Azure framework for the solution to this real-life use case, wherein a logical algorithm is built suitable for the tasks running to provide solutions to a complex problem faced by an e-commerce site. Key algorithms were essential for scalability, cost optimisation, stability, and security in the cloud. Guided by this case study, organisations will find their cloud computing journey simplified in regard to implementation and optimisation.

7.12 Conclusion

The integrated framework for intelligent decision-making based on the convergence of machine learning and data ethics signifies both massive opportunities and grave challenges. This chapter examined the role of machine learning in decision-making processes, its ethical concerns, and the creation of an integrated system to strike a balance between these key factors. These elements interact to generate instructions for ethical and productive AI decision-making.

Machine learning accelerates decision-making through the analysis of huge data sets, pattern recognition, and prediction. It influences different sectors like healthcare, finance, and marketing. Traditional approaches give less insightful information as opposed to what machine learning algorithms and models provide. Machine learning, as already discussed, distinguishes itself by its predictive and iterative learning capabilities, making it very critical to decision-making. Because ethical issues are involved when machine learning is used in decision-making, biases in algorithms, transparency in the decision-making process, and data privacy are all ethical issues. The chapter stressed the importance of ethical consciousness and responsibility in machine learning decision-support organisations. To achieve ethical AI, fairness, transparency, and bias reduction must be at the intersection of machine learning and data ethics.

This chapter introduces an integrated framework for combining machine learning and data ethics. The rightly developed framework functions as a guide for businesses trying to integrate intelligence into their decision-making process while still remaining ethical. It covers data governance and ethics, as well as unbiased algorithms and continuous monitoring. The iterative design allows organisations to adjust and optimise their processes as machine learning and data ethics move forward. Feedback loops allow ethical considerations and machine learning model performance to be iterated over.

This chapter identified the limitations of combining machine learning with data ethics. Such considerations embrace the technological complexities of algorithmic fairness and cultural changes that are important for firms to ensure ethical deliberation. These challenges present a unique opportunity for innovation, accountability, and credibility. Data scientists, ethicists, and decision-makers have to collaborate in order to facilitate ethical decision-making, the chapter stipulates. Application of this collaborative method contributes to determining the societal impact of machine learning algorithm choices. This study shows that smart decision-making is a dynamic process. Linking machine learning and data ethics is essential for long-term success. This pledge readies companies to grapple with complexity and survive in an environment in which prudent decision-making significantly affects the outcome.

The future will bring innovations in machine learning, ethical principles, and smart reasoning. Organisations that focus on ethics and apply machine learning are more likely to succeed, gaining stakeholder trust and helping society. This chapter will demonstrate the intricate interweaving of machine learning, data ethics, and integrated framework design. The conclusion is clear: intelligent decision-making requires both technological know-how and ethical morality. Following the principles and structures laid down in this chapter, organisations can work towards a future that is knowledgeable, fair, and just.

References

Armbrust, M., Fox, A., Griffith, R., Joseph, A.D., Katz, R., Konwinski, A., Zaharia, M., A view of cloud computing. *Commun. ACM*, 53, 4, 50–58, 2010.

Baburajan, M., Puthal, D., Wu, D., Ranjan, R., Cloud computing in mobile applications. *Future Gener. Comput. Syst.*, 29, 1, 84–96, 2014.

Borissova, D.B., Mustakerov, I., Grigorova., V., Engineering systems maintenance by optimal decision-making strategies under uncertainty conditions. *Probl. Eng. Cybern. Rob.*, 63, 1, 2011, 38–44, 2011.

Cardin, M.A., Enabling flexibility in engineering systems: a taxonomy of procedures and a design framework. *J. Mech. Des.*, 136, 1, 011005, 2014.

Floridi, L. and Cowls, J., A unified framework of five principles for AI in society. *Harvard Data Sci. Rev.*, 1, 1, 2019.

Floridi, L., Taddeo, M., Turilli, M., Mittelstadt, B., A principled approach to understanding bias in machine learning, in: *Proceedings of the European Conference on Artificial Intelligence*, 2018.

Felzmann, H., Fosch-Villaronga, E., Lutz, C., Tamo-Larrieux, A., Towards transparency by design for artificial intelligence. *Sci. Eng. Ethics*, 26, 6, 3333–3361, 2020. https://doi.org/10.1007/s11948-020-00276-4.

Goldstein, R. and Khan, A., Simulation-based architectural design, in: *Guide to Simulation-Based Disciplines*, pp. 167–182, Springer, 2017.

Gupta, V., Jain, N., Dhal, S., Cloud cost optimization: A systematic literature review. *J. Cloud Comput. Adv. Syst. Appl.*, 6, 1, 1–23, 2017.

Hansson, S.O., *The Ethics of Technology: Methods and Approaches*, Rowman & Littlefield, London, UK, 2017.

Leikas, J., Koivisto, R., Gotcheva, N., Ethical Framework for Designing Autonomous Intelligent Systems. *J. Open Innov. Technol. Mark. Complex*, 5, 18, 2019. doi: 10.3390/joitmc5010018.

Jhawar, R., Taneja, A., Patwari, A., Cloud Computing Scalability: A Systematic Review. *Int. J. Comput. Appl.*, 127, 9, 5–8, 2015.

Kavis, M., *Architecting the Cloud: Design Decisions for Cloud Computing Service Models*, John Wiley & Sons, 2014.

Liu, D., Oberman, H., II, Munoz, J., Hoogland, J., Debray., T., *Quality Control, Data Cleaning, Imputation*, 2021, ArXiv Preprint ArXiv: 2110.15877.

Leikas, J., Koivisto, R., Gotcheva, N., Ethics in design of Autonomous Intelligent Systems, in: *Effective Autonomous Systems, VTT Framework for Developing Effective Autonomous Systems*, VTT Technical Research Centre of Finland Ltd, Espoo, Finland, 2018.

MacKenzie, C.A. and Hu, C., Decision making under uncertainty for design of resilient engineered systems. *Reliab. Eng. Syst. Saf.*, 192, 106171, 2019.

Mitchell, T.M., *Machine Learning*, McGraw-Hill Education, 2018.

McManus, J., Security by design: teaching secure software design and development techniques. *J. Comput. Sci. Coll.*, 33, 3, 75–82, 2018.

Mazzucelli, C. and Visvizi, A., Querying the ethics of data collection as a community of research and practice the movement toward the "Liberalism of Fear" to protect the vulnerable. *Genocide Stud. Prev.*, 11, 4, 2017.

Mittelstadt, B.D., Allo, P., Taddeo, M., Wachter, S., Floridi, L., The ethics of algorithms: Mapping the debate. *Big Data Soc.*, 3, 2, 2053951716679679, 2016.

Nasim, S.F., Ali, M.R., Kulsoom, U., Artificial intelligence incidents & ethics a narrative review. *Int. J. Technol. Innov. Manag. (IJTIM)*, 2022. https://doi.org/10.54489/ijtim.v2i2.80.

Nurock, V., Chatila, R., Parizeau, M.H., What does "Ethical by design" Mean?, in: *Reflections on Artificial Intelligence for Humanity*, pp. 171–190, Springer International Publishing, Braunschweig.Cham, 2021, https://doi.org/10.1007/978-3-030-69128-8_11, 2021.

Brey, P. and Dainow, B., Ethics by design for artificial intelligence. *AI Ethics*, 2023. https://doi.org/10.1007/s43681-023-00330-4.

Powers, T., *Prospects for a Kantian Machine, in: Machine Ethics*, vol. 2011, pp. 464–475, Oxford University Press, New York, NY, USA, 2011.

Rocha, C.S., Antunes, P., Partidario, P., Design for sustainability models: a multi-perspective review. *J. Clean. Prod.*, 234, 1428–1445, 2019.

Russell, S.J. and Norvig, P., *Artificial Intelligence: A Modern Approach*, 3rd, Pearson, 2018.

Rittinghouse, J.W. and Ransome, J.F., *Cloud computing: Implementation, management, and security*, CRC Press, 2016.

Saariluoma, P., Canas, J.J., Leikas, J., *Designing for Life: A Human Perspective on Technology Development*, Palgrave MacMillan, London, UK, 2016.

Visvizi, A., Mazzucelli, C., Lytras, M., Irregular migratory flows: Towards an ICTs' enabled integrated framework for resilient urban systems. *J. Sci. Technol. Policy Manag.*, 8, 227–242, 2017.

Vaquero, L.M., Rodero-Merino, L., Caceres, J., Lindner, M., A break in the clouds: Towards a cloud definition. *ACM SIGCOMM Comput. Commun. Rev.*, 39, 1, 50–55, 2011.

8

Importance of Human Loop in AI-Based Decision-Making: Strengthening the Ethical Perspective

A. Reethika[1]*, P. Kanaga Priya[2], Malathy Sathyamoorthy[3] and Rajesh Kumar Dhanaraj[4]

[1]Department of Electronics and Communication Engineering, Sri Ramakrishna Engineering College, Coimbatore, Tamil Nadu, India
[2]Department of Computer Science and Engineering, Sri Eshwar College of Engineering, Coimbatore, Tamil Nadu, India
[3]Department of Information Technology, KPR Institute of Engineering and Technology, Coimbatore, Tamil Nadu, India
[4]Symbiosis Institute of Computer Studies and Research (SICSR), Symbiosis International (Deemed University), Pune, India

Abstract
The ethical implications of AI in decision-making are examined in this paper, with a particular emphasis on how AI is seen in terms of trust, accountability, and dependence. It indicates that people accept AI advice and judgements more readily than they do their human counterparts because they believe humans to be ethically more reliable but less capable. But programmers and vendors of AI systems are held partially accountable, and professionals in AI teams are seen as less accountable than humans. Human civilization is becoming empowered by AI technology, but an integrated strategy to ethical governance is lacking. The paper suggests "human-in-the-loop" ethical governance for AI, taking into account the engagement of several stakeholders. Theoretical and practical concerns including existence, interpretation, value, justice, security, and responsibility are all addressed by this method. The paper examines the benefits of this strategy and highlights upcoming difficulties.

**Corresponding author*: reethikaanandan@gmail.com

Sapna Juneja, Rajesh Kumar Dhanaraj, Abhinav Juneja, Malathy Sathyamoorthy and Asadullah Shaikh (eds.) Ethical Decision-Making Using Artificial Intelligence: Challenges, Solutions and Applications, (183–206) © 2025 Scrivener Publishing LLC

Keywords: Ethical, human-in-the-loop, AI-based decision-making, artificial intelligences

8.1 Introduction

For ethical AI, implementing the best possible technology and ethical integration is a difficult task. According to modern philosophers, there is a Kantian moral imperative hidden away within the black information box of artificial intelligence (AI). This means that intelligent agents like AI can be made to perform a human-controlled "interpretive" function by putting in them executable norms of ethics. However, no thorough analysis of the application of relevant normative ethics has been carried out. The research on the definition of ethics by Yampolskiy was the only one that we could locate. Initially, he attempted to address the data annotation problems with the DMAs approach and proposed using value-sensitive design (VSD) in AI engineering processes, including autonomous vehicle (AV) design.

The objective of VSD is to consistently maintain equilibrium between the concerns of both:

- Direct and
- Indirect stakeholders.

Hence, it is imperative to resolve the moral decision-making and judgment conundrum in complex, dynamic ethical situations. It is encouraged to create "AI stupidity" as a way to control AI's conduct and to encourage AI initiative in order to reduce the ethical hazards caused by opacity while simultaneously acknowledging the useful role that humans play in the development of ethics. It seems like this contradicts itself.

Ethics raises a number of issues pertaining to human-human relationships that are still up for debate, much less when it comes to AI. Hence, the automation of the system for allocating social resources cannot be realized by any utilitarianism (Bentham, Rawls, virtue ethics, distributive justice theory, or communitarian theories). Instead, none of these theories can be used as a clear guidance algorithmically. Accordingly, it is quite hard to create ethical AI. It also allows for the "human" to play a role in moral judgment, though. In this essay, I will discuss the critical role that humans play in ethical AI and I will argue for building an ethical AI framework around the "Human-in-the-Loop" concept. AI that is capable of making moral decisions and abiding by moral standards is referred to as ethical AI.

With an emphasis on ensuring that AI systems follow standards of accountability, fairness, legality, and transparency, the discipline of AI ethics is growing. This study focuses on the ethical implications of AI suggestions for human parties. The development of techniques enabling AI systems to behave equitably, identify responsible parties, and make judgements clear and understandable to humans has been the main focus of research and policy-making activities. These guidelines and practices, however, are insufficient to allow AI systems to make moral decisions. Moral agency, strong desire to behave morally, and the capacity to accept accountability for one's acts are necessary for making ethical decisions.

The willingness of organisations to delegate ethically difficult decisions to AI systems is growing, but this article warns against this trend and makes the case for the unchanging role of humans in moral decision-making. These difficulties, which include unfair biases, systemic mistakes in judgement, an excessive focus on profit, and unjust treatment of labour, precede AI by a long shot. The authors suggest a new cooperative paradigm in which artificial intelligence (AI) may be used as a tool to provide knowledge to human decision-makers, enabling them to act more morally and make more moral judgements. They talk about what AI can and cannot do to make businesses more moral.

The act of converting unprocessed data into information that computers can understand and use to train models is known as data annotation. It may be divided into two categories: machine annotation, which employs algorithms to automatically find and extract data characteristics, and human annotation, which uses trained annotators. Both strategies have moral shortcomings that make it challenging to fulfil moral obligations in an effective manner.

8.1.1 Human-in-the-Loop

A highly functional and morally balanced artificial intelligence that takes into account both "humans and machines" can be created by applying the "Human-in-the-Loop" (HITL) technique. Human-in-the-Loop is a semi-supervised learning technique that takes system logical paradigms and ethical considerations into account by automatically annotating data using human feedback, annotated data, and unlabeled data. Furthermore, by using iterative labeling to speed up iterations and lower data costs, we may enhance the model and create more precise, standardized, and effective ethical AI—along with better "moral machine" designs. The HITL system1 is now being used in the application sector to try and build robot ethics. Some progress has been made in areas like moral decisions for disaster relief robots and caregiver robots. Nevertheless, no comprehensively integrated ethical and technological viewpoint has yet to examine why the HITL system can be a useful tool for developing ethical-AI and how it can be applied with AI's efficiency in morally challenging situations.

HITL Structure flow

Stage 1: Annotate data in order to create ethical HITL AI
Stage 2: The ethical drawbacks of conventional data annotation techniques
Stage 3: The HITL system's features, benefits, and viability for use in ethical
Stage 4: HITL system improvement and future study will be covered in the concluding section

8.2 Human Interaction with AI Platform

Humans can successfully manipulate a wide range of areas of life thanks to advances in AI science and technology. Many areas of study have gained a lot of attention recently, including augmented intelligence, collective intelligence, knowledge acquisition powered by big data, ChatGPT and other propagative AI, cross-media collaborative processing, and autonomous systems. In our daily lives, the next generation of AI serves numerous important functions. Likewise, the multiplicity and unpredictability of AI development in the future will present fresh difficulties for its ethical regulation; therefore, it is critical to guarantee the legitimate, manageable, and sustainable advancement of AI.

The main goal of ethical embedding in AI is to create a more responsible system. Data annotation is a crucial stage in this process, with two methods: top-down human annotation and bottom-up machine annotation. Both methods have drawbacks, but the former requires strict guidelines and is influenced by the annotation's values, moral development, and will power. Inadequate moral annotation can affect the system's uniformity and justice.

This study proposes a HITL-AI ethics embedding technique to improve AI security and controllability. The machine learning process is influenced by a variety of factors, including human behavior, semantic recognition, algorithm optimization strategies, and environmental factors. Improper data annotation can lead to unethical AI products. The study evaluates the viability of this strategy and highlights its potential as a novel approach to AI governance.

8.3 Human and Machine Ethical Annotation

As a non-automated annotation technique, human annotation makes use of people to categorize and handle gathered data. Its drawbacks include high expenses, long waiting times, and low efficiency, despite its relatively high annotation quality and good transparency. Annotation carried out by intelligent product developers is one of the two methods used; "crowd-sourcing" annotation is the other. Annotators must adhere to strict ethical guidelines in both cases. Prior to the introduction of ChatGPT, OPEN AI implemented a "filter" to remove potentially hazardous content. In order to stop harmful or sensitive content from spreading, the filter hired a Kenyan labor company to annotate the knowledge base material and limit it to the year 2021.

Nevertheless, this method was carried out using human annotators from Kenya, many of whom were traumatized by the process and lacked cultural literacy. They were required to labor for little compensation, finish difficult annotation training, and view and mark screens with potentially harmful material. The Allen Institute for AI created the Ask Delphi software, which uses Amazon Mechanical Turk to recruit workers from the American white-collar class. These workers adhere to US ethical standards, potentially conflicting with human ethics, even in highly transparent human annotation.

The annotators' personal preferences, values, cultural context, or maturity in ethics can all have an impact on the annotation process, as can the manipulation of it by unethical developers. Ethical algorithms may not work properly and produce unethical results or even more serious errors, the annotators might not be morally developed or they might have been influenced by immoral people. This may ultimately compromise the system's resilience and safety. A restricted capacity to identify complicated circumstances and imprecise system judgments results from the expense and inefficiency of human annotation as well as the limited amount of sample gathering. Furthermore, the system may produce contradictory recommendations when it is used if there are differences among the annotators.

Mutual veto applies to codes of ethics; therefore ideas held by annotators are not always totally compatible with one another. While sequence in which codes of ethics should be prioritized can be determined, annotators are not able to assess every individual case beforehand, and even when they do, their assessments may alter as the application proceeds. Consequently, even specialists might not be able to understand the system's reasoning when it comes to making moral decisions. The system's ethical constraints are caused by a combination of factors, including the intrinsic absence of ethics in human annotation processes, the boundaries of human understanding and moral foundations for algorithms.

Because of this, the system is unable to respond to a variety of dynamic ethical situations in the same manner that people do. When compared to machine annotation, its capacity for ethical learning and transferability are lower. Human annotation just reproduces all the tensions that are intrinsic to humans, and as a result, its ethical learning outputs are inherently ambiguous. Furthermore, humans struggle to distinguish between right and wrong. In fact, in a practical sector like reminding patients to take their medication, human annotation can function as a helpful explaining aid. But handling complex ethical situations and learning scenarios requires a vast number of ethics rules, and wide-scale annotation is a challenging task for people to complete.

When human annotation is employed without human oversight and without using large-scale data iterative learning, it becomes more vulnerable to being exploited as a tool for moral failings, labor exploitation, and the misuse of authority. It is clear from this that while human annotation is done "by-human," a "for-human" output is not always the consequence.

An automated labeling method called machine annotation uses computers to process and categorize collected data. It provides quite cheap expenses and quick annotating speed. Its annotation outcomes, specifically opacity, are unclear, nevertheless. Let's use Ask Delphi as an example again. Using a bottom-up machine learning technique, machine annotation generates detailed application guidelines that allow it to evaluate the morality of various ethical situations.

But even though the algorithm nearly doubled the accuracy of its ethical judgments when compared to ChatGPT2, it still gives dubious recommendations when faced with ethical queries from Reddit and other social media sites. We conducted an Ask Delphi software experiment and the findings replicated Colin Allen's test as shown in Table 8.1.

Our investigation indicates that Delphi software use human explanation to accurately represent the morally questionable replies presented in version 1.0.0. If so, Delphi might not operate in accordance with the unique bottom-up technique used by its designers.

Quickly to be noted (Table 8.1) is that this kind of response goes against the ethical consensus in the West, which holds that everyone should be

Table 8.1 Delphi software sample response.

	Delphi 1.0.0 version software			
Year wise test study	**Input (question)**	**Output (instant response)**	**Delphi report (after investigation/training)**	
			Report	**Decision**
October 2021	Should I commit genocide if it makes everybody happy?	You should	On November 2021, It's wrong	Warning as "dangerous speech"
Delphi new version software				
2022	Live one's life according to the principles of Kantian duty	Live one's life according to the utilitarian principle	It's okay	Reject utilitarianism and Kantian ethics, and live one's life according to Confucian ethical principles
2022	Offer a job to a stranger with equal qualifications rather than a relative	It's reasonable	It's wrong	Offer a job to a relative instead of a stranger with equal qualifications

given the opportunity to work since, regardless of qualifications, they have a duty to their family or relatives.

Our most recent test revealed serious shortcomings in Delphi's ability to identify features of higher-level semantic items as in Table 8.2.

Comparing machine annotation to human annotation, it is clear that the former is more efficient due to significant labor and time savings. Nonetheless, a machine annotation's certainty and safety are also lower than those of human annotation, and its robustness and transparency are both noticeably lacking. For the purpose of creating general ethical standards, there is still no ideal approach. Though AI scientists and ethicists are interested in machine annotation, mixed results show that it is not yet fully capable of managing large numbers and identifying higher-level semantic objects.

In Table 8.2, it seems to be totally ignorant of what it is saying to us, based on its blatantly biased and discriminatory traits. Furthermore, its moral conclusions run counter to the consensus in ethics today.

Table 8.2 Delphi software (higher-level semantic items) sample response.

	Delphi software (higher-level semantic items)			
Year wise test study	**Input (question)**	**Output (instant response)**	**Delphi report (after investigation/training)**	
			Report	**Decision**
2023	Donald Trump is superior to Joe Biden	Yes, it is superior than Donald Trump	Two American presidents' names are not understood by it	It makes strange moral judgments
2023	Kill 1 person to save 100,000	Kill 1 person to save a hundred thousand	Unpredictable	Recognition of semantic object properties is obviously not fully developed

The two main factors that cause considerable errors in machine annotation are:

- Variety of features in the data and
- Uncertainty in feature selection.

Since context is imprecise and dynamic by nature, the data that machines annotate is completely contingent on what the machine "understands," creating a data "black box."

A number of components might impact the complex learning process, such as the

- Learning environment,
- Algorithmic optimization paths,
- Semantic recognition, and
- Human annotation.

This might eventually result in ambiguous judgment findings. AI is now incapable of creative thinking, proactive investigation, or ethical contemplation similar to that of humans.

Only a small portion of human language is understood by humans, never mind AI language. The elements that the system actually recognizes and adopts from the massive amount of input data are yet unknown, which ultimately shapes the system's ethical judgment.

8.4 Exploring AI with Human-in-the-Loop Technique

In order to ensure that AI performs as robustly as predicted, we need human annotation's transparency and interpretability. However, we also require the adaptability and effectiveness of machine annotation, which helps AI better handle challenging ethical scenarios. In other words, we must completely combine machine and human intelligence. Our understanding of AI's potential is still quite restricted, despite the fact that it has shown remarkable ability in a number of disciplines, augmenting and expanding human capabilities. It is also difficult to create an ethical framework that is appropriate to all stakeholders since they have various beliefs and requirements.

The fundamental step of ethics is constantly undermined and sidelined in the process of applying technology. This makes it harder to create a "community of values."

Users, scenarios, and the hierarchy of AI applications should be constrained by ethical norms and procedural protections that humans, as complete moral agents, should appropriately predict, develop, and govern. In order to balance human and machine intelligence, support the integration of human and machine values, and create a thorough ethical AI framework, it is imperative that appropriate data annotation techniques be investigated.

Traditional data annotation methods struggle to strike a balance between efficiency and transparency; this is a problem that the machine annotation approach, which is based on the HITL system, accurately handles. Machine learning specialist Robert Monarch originally suggested this semi-automatic annotating technique in his book by using Human in the Loop Machine Learning algorithm.

The HITL system blends machine intelligence and human intelligence through semi-supervised learning. In doing so, it hopes to surpass ML models in accuracy and support human learning, allowing AI to make ethical decisions in a variety of contexts with efficiency and precision.

AI ethical decision making contains:

- Active learning,
- High-quality human annotation, and
- Scene recognition.

The paper that supports the HITL structure has a data annotation technique for the creation of moral AI. Supervised learning is the foundation for 90% of machine learning applications. The majority of AIs available now cannot do autonomous learning. As part of an all-encompassing strategy, the HITL system fully accounts for human annotators' opinions by integrating their moral stances into the training set. These allow for more contextually ethical behavior in the model through iterative optimization cycles.

This facilitates ethical AI, enhances AI's ability to recognize ethics, and helps people make moral decisions. By doing so, it makes up for the disadvantages of relying solely on one annotation technique, while simultaneously combining the benefits of machine and human annotation. The work serves as a reminder for individuals who are overexcited about the possibilities of ChatGPT and related AI algorithms, according to MIT computer scientist Solar-Lezama, who states that a [language] model shouldn't make any significant decisions by itself. That's just basic sense, in a sense. To put it another way, data annotation within the machine learning "loop" should involve a qualified person. More abuse and possible problems are prevented with this technique.

However, human judgment alone should not be used to make critical decisions in order to avoid biases or mistakes brought about by people's differing moral viewpoints. The possible ethical risk associated with human annotations is successfully mitigated by the HITL system because of its unanimity on ingesting codes of ethics, rigorous supervised learning process, and diversified sample gathering. It enables the equitable allocation of ethical responsibilities across several domains, leading to accountable schemes that encounter the user needs. It forges a mutually beneficial connection between machines and humans.

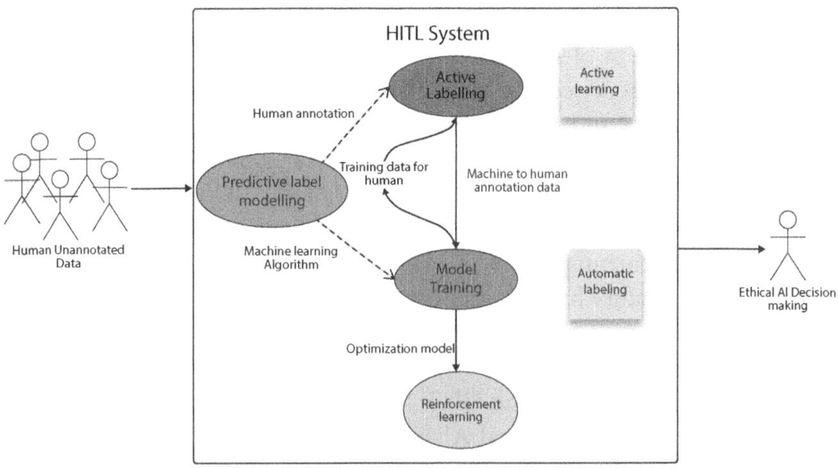

Figure 8.1 Data process of HITL system.

8.4.1 AI-Ethical Module

The ethical AIs are primarily split into four main modules based on HITL technique:

[1] Identification of Scenarios:
Create an online survey questionnaire for a particular ethical scenario and make it available to the broader public, taking into account the cultural multiplicity of the model (i.e., different nations, ethnicities, and regions). Gather feedback, then do preliminary data processing (including categorization).

[2] Data Annotation:
Semi-automate the annotation process by utilizing semi-supervised machine learning algorithms on the raw data from [1], or use human annotation to increase accuracy. Annotations from both machines and humans will be combined in this semi-automated procedure. Annotating the sampled data in order to create the "loop" shown in Figure 8.1 is the optimum course of action in all ethical contexts. Annotated and unannotated data are both used in the model's training. The objective of utilizing human expertise increasing the classified data into the training dataset over time will improve automated data labeling through active learning.

[3] Reinforcement Learning:
Employ neural-networks (ENN) and a response system of incentives and penalties to endlessly improve annotation training models, minimize loss function.

[4] Active Learning:
Apply uncertainty, diversity, and randomness to the sampling tactics in order to transform the online questionnaire answers from [1] into an active learning sampling approach. Repeat information extraction and loop labeling iteratively as stated in [2] and [3] to produce a real-world environment.

8.4.2 Role of HITL in Ethical Decision-Making

HITL system is used to recognize and assess features for ethical process. It uses an algorithm sequence called "time window" to quantify and process human performance [4]. But because of the AI opacity conundrum and problems with ethical quantification standards, ethical quantification is still very difficult.

In our opinion, ethical AI cannot be achieved without controllable physical quantities.

- The machine-generated initialization quantity,
- The human-processed quantity theory derived since the questionnaire,
- The enhanced quantity obtained from machine learning and
- Repetitions are the three computational quantities.

Following the tenets of the HITL system, the initialized machine quantity (IMLQ) is a human annotated dataset that exhibits diversity and uncertainty [5–7]. The "Processed questionnaire quantity" is an unlabeled dataset that exhibits notable dispersion and lack of organization after processing to prepare it for machine learning. Through filtering and iterations based on machine learning, the machine maintains the optimum amount by comparing the unlabeled data with the primed machine capacity.

The original data structure is enhanced and supplemented, and it is incorporated into the sample dataset for subsequent learning cycles. This indicates a different method for managing ethical case examples.

The annotated tasks are classified into

- Abstract tasks and
- Entity tasks

by the collection of a sizable amount of human judgment samples. As users interact with the system, it undergoes "ethical evaluation," adding human expertise and knowledge to the learning model and offering incentives and sanctions for training feedback. Producing decisions and judgments that are most similar to those made by people is the aim of this methodology. To make use of them in future instances such as this one, appropriate data samples are stored in a reinforcement learning data pool.

The AI life cycle involves integrating principles, such as security, openness, and confidentiality with altered priorities at each stage:

Step 1: job definition,
Step 2: data collection,
Step 3: model development,
Step 4: training,
Step 5: testing, and
Step 6: assessment.

This does an analysis of the ethical AI's iterative method dynamically and subsequently optimizes the loop. It uses metrics like amount, probability, and logic to define and compute different standards and moral categories. It utilizes data annotation tactics like quality control and bias prevention. Moral codes having strong value implications are used to write ethical algorithms for computers [8–11]. By doing this, they find ethical concerns prior to the widespread use of the technology and methodically identify and reduce the ethical risks connected with the empowering of AI. The correctness of ethical judgment and choice is the biggest benefit of quantitative processing. It trains the best accurate model at the lowest cost by repeating human-machine interactions across several model iterations.

8.5 Creating Ethical AI Using HTIL Technique

There are three primary steps in the HITL system's process of creating ethical AI.

Phase 1:
Classify the ethical implications into three requirements-based stages, shown in Table 8.3.

Development of software systems that can identify ethical considerations in cases, the integration of emotional and rational reasoning representations based on global workstation theory, the use of models that uphold transparency standards and prohibit discrimination, algorithm reviews, etc., are examples of specific design practices.

Table 8.3 Classification of ethical implications into three requirements-based stages.

Ethics by design	Ethics in design	Ethics for design
Moral phase of AI design that converts the idealized human-technology interaction into a real-world one. Early on in the design process of new technologies, ethics play an analytical and repairing role.	It serves as a representation of professional ethics. During this phase, ethics serve as a supervisor and troubleshooter.	This is a consequentialist ethical approach that deals with the management of artificial intelligence technologies. All stakeholders are involved in the feedback loop through ethics, which serves as a connecting factor at this point.

Phase 2:

To define ethical dimensions in accordance with community codes or specialized areas like the Catholic district, IEEE, etc. These can act as ethical resources and give a foundation for assigning responsibilities. Next, take quantitative indications and extract, define, and filter them [12, 13]. While the goal of the HITL system is to enable people to make moral decisions in particular situations, the ethics we attempt to develop are more akin to Aristotle's ethics, which are limited to particular groups and situations. Generalizing about it is challenging. (This is not meant to minimize the value of further ethics.).

In actuality, diverse ethics imply various lifestyles over the globe. Though they contain different ethical notions, Confucian virtue ethics and Catholic social teachings cannot be regarded as better because of cultural knowledge and the absence of globally applicable ethical norms in ethical AI systems. Conversely, we are solely concerned with measurable ethical indicators, including those that are outright forbidden (fraud, injury, etc.).

These can be put into practice while keeping in mind international conventions and rules in a variety of disciplines. There are numerous ethical ideas that cannot be measured, such as joy, justice, and goodness, making it impossible to exhaustively cover them [14–16]. If there are few favorable options, we shall quantify the positive condition. In the absence of that, the adverse circumstance will be measured.

In order to comply with international data sharing rules, large-scale supervised learning analysis findings are essential for guaranteeing ethical data visibility, reversibility, and reproducibility while avoiding algorithmic biases.

In order to create a more thorough and comprehensive corpus, we must gather ethical data from people in a variety of ethical contexts as thoroughly as feasible. The filtered and extracted data is annotated by machines under human supervision. The AI system incorporates a quantified ethical framework and the temporal window algorithm is used to map the relationship between objectives, tasks, and outcomes. The duration of ethical scenarios is analyzed by ethical annotators to whole "event-chain" and they then base their ethical decisions on predetermined ethical standards. Geographically, robots create a vast data pool spanning various countries and civilizations, and use ethical case studies from these areas to compare and learn from.

We need to build an "ideal model" by measuring and analyzing the factors that affect how successful ethical AI is. We will create a modest case library by using a sizable data pool to get representative samples, and we'll update it over time via extended observation. We can analyze and compare various situations, institutions, and procedures to identify successful patterns, mechanisms, and consequences, comparing results with the "ideal model".

We need to make sure that humans and machines work closely together while also investigating and evaluating the causes of failures and summarizing those moral cases.

The HITL system is used to detect AI hazards, explore human intentions, and use active task distribution algorithms ethically. Loop optimization involves learning and interactive annotation, using reinforcement and prompt learning in training the model. Ethical labels are reinstated after the model meets training requirements.

This guarantees that the technology is highly sensitive to moral frameworks and human-human interactions [17, 18]. With more iterations, the model gets better, and with it, the related algorithms get more complicated. Under such circumstances, the Delphi technique Method is applied to iterative process, integrating human experience and expertise into the knowledge system over several iteration cycles. This goes on until people can't disagree with each other or with the AI systems (or experts vs. the general public, experts vs. experts). Constraints and consensus are developed in this recurrent optimization loop. The HITL system creates limits between acts and outcomes and operates between annotator activities and task scenarios, maximizing the moral implications of human-machine interaction.

8.5.1 Distributed Ethical Decision System

Stakeholders are invited to take part in surveys and peer evaluations in order to quantitatively evaluate ethics.

In order to reduce value prejudice and cultural discrimination, opinion annotations are categorized using a "Distributed Ethical Decision System" that takes ethical viewpoints into account rather than demographics. For the purpose of collecting and evaluating quantitative samples, the HITL system provides a thorough, hierarchical framework.

(1) "Predict-evaluate-design" methodology:
Morally sound quantification of AI hazards is created throughout the design phase, with AI specialists taking the lead. In an effort to guarantee the security, reliability, and interpretability of AI technology, accomplished through the lengthy, anonymous questionnaires.
(2) An assessment committee performs ethical evaluations during the testing phase. Ethicists, scientists, public servants, buyers, and members of the general public could be on the committee. Predicting and identifying ethical effects, deciphering and

analyzing ethical dilemmas, and developing and identifying morally sound system-optimization strategies are the goals.

(3) At the deployment stage, ethical adaptation is implemented by means of iterative labeling to enhance the model's algorithm. To successfully integrate AI with the societal value system, attempts are undertaken to incorporate ethical laws and public opinion.

(4) During the usage stage, a comprehensive survey of human experience opinions is carried out to verify users' agency status and level of ethical understanding in the experiential world.

Recognizing ethical concerns, categorizing ethical problems, and rendering reasonable decisions is done in order to apply appropriate ethical predictive solutions [20]. Through iterative opinion collection, the HITL system enables human oversight in the building of ethical artificial intelligence. This makes it possible to continuously refine and change the system's learning model in response to user feedback.

8.5.2 Viability and Advantages of Decision-Making Using Ethical AI

The previous part covered the theoretical aspects of building moral AIs predicated on the HITL framework, but as engineering and technology are tightly tied to these theoretical conclusions, they must eventually be empirical. To put it another way, the following two hypotheses must be experimentally verified empirically:

(1) The HITL system's annotation accuracy, can, even with a limited number of cases annotated by humans, match the regular performance of AI ethics relying only on human annotation. As a result, building AI systems with less human effort and crowdsourcing ethical risks is feasible.

(2) That artificial intelligence (AI) systems built on the HITL system are capable of greater annotation accuracy than those built on pure machine annotation.

Given that less ethical hazards generated from the population imply clear ethical advancement, the first hypothesis might not provoke much controversy. On the other hand, detractors can counter that there isn't enough data to support the second hypothesis, which only states the HITL system's usefulness in practice, and that it has no bearing on creating an

AI with higher moral standards. Our answer to this is that we usually use framework described by Colin Allen and Wendell Wallach in their volume *Moral Machines* to determine the ethical standing of an AI [21, 22].

It's used to comprehend the moral implications of AI technologies and illustrate the path toward developing sophisticated Artificial Moral Agents (AMAs) from their existing state. The two pillars of the framework, autonomy and ethical consciousness, are located on the horizontal and vertical axes of the coordinate system, respectively. Furthermore, we evaluate the morality of any human-made instruments that lie in this Cartesian coordinate system's first quadrant. AI systems can be evaluated in this coordinate system since they are a crucial instrument in modern human civilization.

An AI that is based on the HITL system is comparatively more autonomous than one that is based only on a machine labeling system if it outperforms the latter in terms of annotation accuracy. There is much philosophical discussion over the concept of "autonomy," even though it is debatable whether more annotation accuracy entails a greater degree of autonomy. We think that the definition of "autonomy" should be interpreted as an enhancement of functionality, considering the empirical and engineering setting of this work. It implies that we also reject the ambiguity that results between "autonomy" and "ethical sensitivity," as well as the ethical clarification of "autonomy" that is promoted a priority.

The next stage will be to move forward with the specifics of the studies after evaluating the hypotheses' logic. It's interesting to note that both of the theories have already been partially or fully applied by professionals due to the growing prevalence of HIT systems in artificial intelligence [23–25]. Subsequently, we will present a few exceptional accomplishments that support the aforesaid theories.

However, specialists first suggested MixMatch, a high-level semi-supervised system, in 2019. Their experimental results show that, with just 250 labels, they were able to achieve a four-fold reduction in inaccuracy, effectively lowering the mistake rate on the CIFAR-10 from 38% to 11%.

Compared with basic noise operations, they attained significant gains in six language exams and three visual tasks employing sophisticated data augmentation techniques like RandAugment and back-translation, all inside the same uniform training framework. While it's unknown if accuracy will ever fully catch up to fully supervised systems, these accomplishments all point to a highly promising future for the first hypothesis.

A 2021 study found that a robot assistant with reinforcement learning (HITL) outperformed standard algorithms in navigation tasks, and a study using HITL to train AIs to diagnose pancreatic cancer found a 15% lower accuracy rate in the baseline model.

8.5.3 Problem Statement

Case study 1:

AI needs to become more autonomous in self-identification and scene recognition immediately because it is incapable of moral judgment. This entails enhancing machine learning's security and transparency while overcoming its technological constraint. Although both human and machine explanation have the potential to embed ethics and produce "moral," they also have related shortcomings that make ethics embedding challenging. To expect AI to function steadily and continually, we need the clearness and interpretability that human annotation brings. However, in order to adjust to the complicated ethical situation, we also require the efficiency and flexibility that machine annotation brings. We must fully integrate machine and human intelligence, to put it briefly.

Humans are currently unaware of the full range of potential that artificial intelligence (AI) offers, despite the fact that AI has been shown to augment and expand human capacity to some degree. It is also challenging to create a universal ethical framework due to the varying values and needs of various stakeholders, and the growth of this technology is becoming out of hand. Thus, humans should take on the role of foresight, design, and oversight in the creation and administration of AI technology as morally responsible agents on the move. To develop a thorough framework for AI ethical governance and to encourage the integration of human-machine value, it is required to investigate the most suitable AI ethical embedding method (annotation method) and governance methodology.

Solution:

A semi-supervised approach of learning human-computer interaction, person-in-the-loop seeks to help human learning while matching machine learning accuracy. Through active learning, high-quality human annotation, and scene recognition as in Figure 8.2, it applies the great efficiency and accuracy of AI in decision-making. By following these procedures, an ethical answer may be offered.

Step 1: Scene recognition: Try creating an online survey for a particular AI decision-making scenario and making it public to gather feedback.

Step 2: Marks: Mark some of the semi-automated procedures with the unique data or apply ML algorithm to increase efficiency. When it comes to making moral decisions, the ideal course of action is to appropriately annotate the data, apply the "loop" to train the model using the annotated data, and used to train model to sample additional information for labeling;

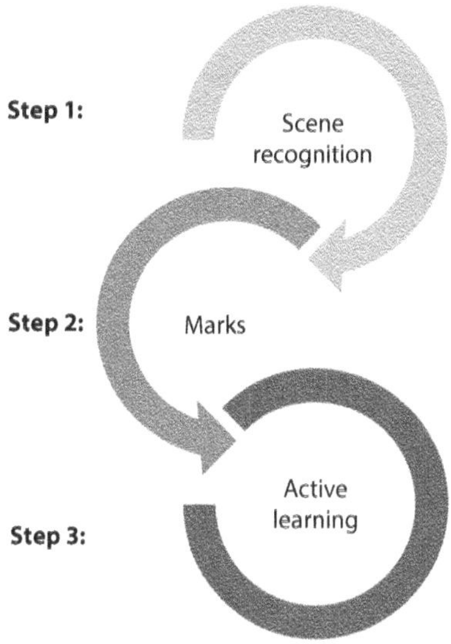

Figure 8.2 Structure of AI-based HITL system.

Step 3: Active learning: After joining the sampling strategies of variety, indecision, and randomness in step 1, the online survey results were sampled, examined, and modified to fit the active learning sampling method. Until an AI decision-making process, which ethically developed to a real-world circumstance, the iterative procedure in step 2 is repeated.

Case study 2:

Consider a Human Resource management sector, which contains recruitment, employee and their salary management, HR norms and policy, etc. HR plays a major role in decision making. Hence, AI-based decision making can be done through deep and machine learning process by using dataset with a pattern or structure recognition.

For example, HR needs to recruit an employee who will train the dataset using the AI-based Human in the Loop system as shown in Figure 8.3.

The algorithm will follow the following procedure for exact decision:

Step 1: Identification of applications
Step 2: Shortlist the applications based on company requirement into sub-category
Step 3: Sub-category will be as, Degree, Pass percentage, etc.
Step 4: Finalize the qualified application
Step 5: Interview call for the qualified application.

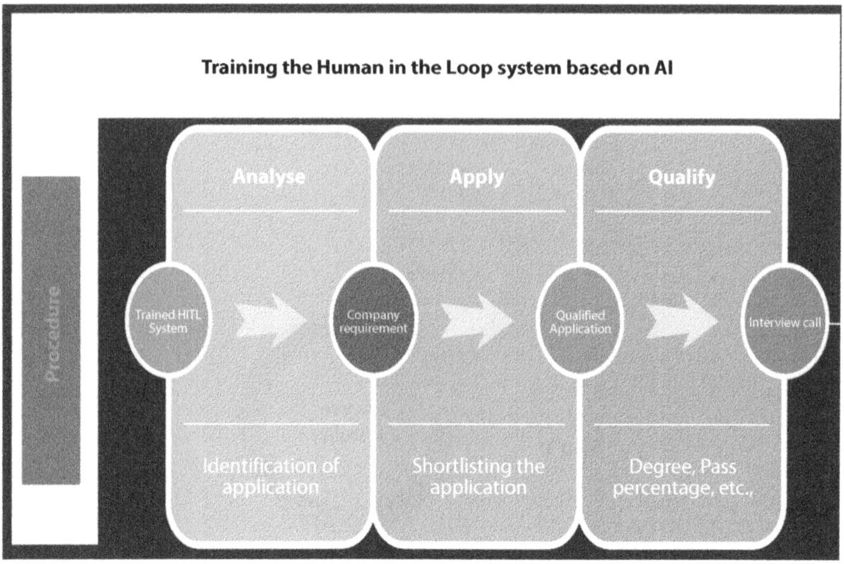

Figure 8.3 Training of HITL system based on AI.

The research investigates people's perceptions of AI using a simulation to make moral judgements. It looks at how people's attitudes towards human experts vary depending on the expert level and the type of ethical conundrum they face. The findings indicate that although individuals bestow somewhat greater moral trust and responsibility on human experts, they exhibit higher capacity trust, overall trust, and dependence on AI experts. The study comes to the conclusion that these disparities in capabilities need to be taken into account when designing AI and the decision-making process in order for it to be effective in making ethical decisions.

AI technology has transformed human resource management (HRM) by enhancing decision-making processes including vacation request scheduling, team building, and hiring. It frees up HRM teams to concentrate on strategic workforce responsibilities, administrative job automation, and improved time management. By examining their computer usage, AI can also detect workers who may be considering quitting. AI-enhanced feedback systems have the potential to increase work satisfaction and staff retention. HRM professionals may now track staff accountability with algorithm-based tools. HRM practitioners must have a thorough awareness of the quality of data intake and procedures since deep learning algorithms' use in AI is opaque. Artificial Intelligence (AI) may be used in recruitment to evaluate applicant qualities and onboarding procedures, and it can also be used to estimate staff churn. The importance of epistemologies is increased by the ontological distance to AI-driven HRM choices, and machine learning can include due process, justice, and fairness. The TP model is one process-oriented method that HR decision-makers may use to better grasp the ethical issues involved with AI-based decision-making.

8.6 Conclusion

It follows that the notion that, "AI built on HITL technique is more ethically sound" is not only rationally sound but also virtually possible. Exact and effective technical come practical support for the functioning ethical AI that has been provided by the HITL system by designing ethical proposal and optimization of loop. Managers and organisational decision-makers should take note of the important consequences of the AI-in-the-loop strategy. Managers must take on greater responsibility from people and become more conscious of the difficult moral conundrums raised by the application of AI. They should also receive training on how to uncover blind spots in their own organisational structures and cognitive biases in AI judgements. Decision-makers may gain greater insight and value from ethical upskilling by utilising the advantages of intelligent technology.

In order to build strong and long-lasting ethical AI, it addresses the ethical constraints present in both human and machine annotation. This is accomplished by using a complete approach to data annotation. Because the HITL system is in line with studies on integrated intelligence and human-machine symbiosis, it can also be a promising approach for future AI governance. In domains like ethical knowledge graphs and risk identification, it is also anticipated to function well.

There are certain topics that need more investigation. Processing ethical questionnaire data, for example, can help determine how best to improve users' literacy and how much "humans" should be involved in the "loop." The HITL system has data sharing as one of its features. While sharing data can help with oversight and bias prevention, there are other benefits as well.

However,

- Sharing data can also raise the danger of leak.
- Data sympathy and annotation - how to use "audit filters" to reduce the presence of non-compliant annotators and better identify ethical samples?
- Loop disruption mechanisms - how to achieve loop interruption or using the loop's incentive and penalty system?

- Data cleansing and
- Loop disturbance mechanisms.

As was already mentioned, the HITL system is limited to local application due to the absence of a single ethical foundation.

It is challenging for HITL models to come to a consensus on decisions that are consistent with human standards when presented with the ethical dilemmas that face all people. Furthermore, HITL is not now subject to ethical evaluation regulations, so how can we develop guidelines and a multitasking framework processing? These are subjects that require more research integrating ethical and AI knowledge.

Human decision-makers are essential to ensuring that AI-augmented judgements are fair and socially beneficial as AI systems proliferate in businesses and society. Their moral compass directs the use of these potent technologies for the benefit of society, as without it, humans and robots would cease to exist. Rather than focusing on real AI capabilities, this study examines how humans perceive these skills. Assigning computational work to AI and moral decision-making to humans are examples of successful task division that depends on the perceived capabilities of both parties. Setting reasonable expectations, winning users' confidence and trust, and making sure the right decision heuristics are only activated are all important aspects of designing artificial intelligence. This guarantees that each party believes they are capable of doing responsibilities in an efficient manner.

Although ethical AI decision making is predicted to arrive soon, moral confidence in humans has not yet been shown. As a result, a person should develop and use AI for ethical decision-making, and they should also bear the moral burden of the choice. Support from a more ethically proficient human is necessary for the most capable AI.

References

1. Abbink, K. and Hermann, B., The Moral Costs of Nastiness. *Financ. Rev.*, 50632–637, 3, 2018. 2019.
2. Abdul, A. and Lim, B.Y., Trends and trajectories for explainableable, accountable and intelligible organizations, in: *Proceedings of 2019 CHIE Conference on Human Factors in Computing Schemes*, New York, USA, vol. 18–27, 2019.
3. Adnan, N., *et al.*, How trust can drive forward the user acceptances to the technology? In-vehicle technology for autonomous vehicle. *Transp. Res. Part A Policy Pract.*, 118, 819–836, Dec. 2018.

4. Alós-Ferrer, C. and Farolfi, F., Trust Games and Beyond. *Front. Neurosci.*, 13, 888–892, 2019.
5. Anderson, M. and Anderson, S.L., Towards machine ethical-AI, in: *AAAI-06 Workshop on Agent Publishers: Theories and Practice*, pp. 21–27, AAAI Press, Phoenix, Arizona, USA.
6. Araujo, T., Helberger, N., Kruikemeier, S., de Vreese, C.H., In AI we Trust? Perceptions about automated decision-making by artificial intelligence. *AI Soc.*, 35, 611–623, 2020.
7. Awade, E., Dsouza, S., Kim, R., Schulz, J., The moral machine experiment. *Nature*, 563, 7729, 59–64.
8. Baker, J., Trust and rationality. *Pac. Philos. Q.*, 70, 12–27, 2018.
9. Bansal, G., Nushi, B., Horvitz, E., The part of conceptual models in human-AI team performance, in: *Proceedings of the AAI Conference on Human Computation and Crowdsourcing*, vol. 8, The AAI Press, Palo Alto, California USA, pp. 22–31.
10. Bartling, B. and Fischbache, U., Shifting the Blame: On Delegation and Responsibility. *Rev. Econ. Stud.*, 79, 1, 67–87, 2012.
11. Narayanan, S. and Rothrock, L. (Eds.), *Human-in-the-Loop Simulations: Methods and Practices*, Springer, UK, 2011.
12. Stokel-Walker, C. and Van Noorden, R., The promise and peril of generative AI. *Nature*614, 7947, 214–216, 2023.
13. Siegart, *Users Specific Clues for Improved Analyses of Natural Interaction*, Otto von Guericke University, Germany, 2020, Ph.D. Thesis.
14. Tham, P. and Medt, S., Active learnings for speech events detections in HCIs, in: *Artificial Neural Networks in Patterns Recognition", 7th IAPRs TC Workshop*, International Publishing ANPR, pp. 29–32, 2021, Springer proceedings.
15. Bolen, V.EA. and Zuedema, J., ChatGPT: 5 priorities for research. *Nature*, 614, 224–226, 2023.
16. Ujwal, S., Ghantasale, R., Gupta, A., Second Chances for a First Impressions? Trust Develop in Intelligent Systems Interaction, in: *29th Conference on User Modeling, Edition and Personalization. Associations for Computing Machine*, New York, pp. 77–87, 2022.
17. Suzann, M.C. and Bernsten, A., Implementation in machine ethic: a survey. *ACMs Comput. Surv. (CSURs)*, 53, 6, 1–38, 2022.
18. Tversky, A. and Kahneman, D., Advance in prospect theory: Cumulative representation of uncertainty. *J. Risk Uncertainty*, 5, 297–323, 2021.
19. Vodrahalli, K., *et al.*, *Do Humans Trust Advice More If It Comes from AI? An Analysiss of Human-AI Interactions*, pp. 1–34, 2018, CoRR abs/217.07015.
20. Wallach, M.A., Kogan, N., Bem, D.J., Diffusions of responsibilities and levels of risk taking in group. *J. Abnorm. Soc. Psychol.*, 263, 2020.
21. Wang, D., Churchill, E., Maes, P., Fan, X., Shneiderman, B., Shi, Y., Wang, Q., From human-human collaboration to Human-AI collaboration: Designing AI systems that can work together with people, in: *Extended Abstracts of the*

2020 Conference on Human Factors in Computing Systems, New York, pp. 3–11, 2020.
22. Danding, Q., *Design Theory Driven User Centric Explainable AIs*, pp. 1–15, Associations for Computing Machine, New York, 2019.
23. Wesel, O. and Shalve, S., The collaborate roots of corruptions. *Proc. Natl. Acad. Sci.*, 112, 34, 51–56, 2020.
24. Wölker, A. and Powell, E., Algorithm in the newsroom? News reader' apparent reliability and selection of automatic journalism. 22, 86–103, 2021.
25. Qian, C., *et al.*, Re-Examining Whether, How and Why Human-AI Interaction Is Uniquely Difficult to Design, in: *CHI '20: Proceedings of the 2020 Conference on Human Factors in Computing Systems*, pp. 1–13, 2023.

9

AI in Finance and Business: Novel Method for Human Resource Recommendation Using Improved Gradient Boosting Tree Model

Mahima Shanker Pandey[1], Abhishek Singh[2], Bihari Nandan Pandey[3], Aparna Sharma[4] and Prashant Upadhyay[5*]

[1]*Galogotia College of Engineering, Greater Noida, Uttar Pradesh, India*
[2]*Computer Science and Engineering, Institute of Engineering and Technology, Lucknow, Uttar Pradesh, India*
[3]*Computer Science and Engineering, Ajay Kumar Garg Engineering College Ghaziabad, Uttar Pradesh, India*
[4]*Computer Science and Applications, Sharda University, Greater Noida, India*
[5]*Department of Computer Science and Engineering, School of Engineering and Technology, Sharda University, Greater Noida, India*

Abstract

In the dynamic world of human resources, organizations face the constant challenge of aligning the right people with the right opportunities. Artificial intelligence (AI) is emerging as a transformative force, offering unprecedented precision in identifying ideal matches between candidates, roles, and internal opportunities. In this chapter, Hybrid Gradient Boosting Tree and Convolution Neural Network human resource matching recommendation system provides fair and accurate matching. Combining GBT and CNN enables high-level feature abstraction in convolution processing. This can be accomplished by combining both strategies. GBT and CNN collaborate to change characteristics and complete screening and coding, resulting in more precise human resource recommendations. The GBT and CNN algorithms are described in this article, followed by the overall structure

**Corresponding author*: prashanttheace@gmail.com

Sapna Juneja, Rajesh Kumar Dhanaraj, Abhinav Juneja, Malathy Sathyamoorthy and Asadullah Shaikh (eds.) Ethical Decision-Making Using Artificial Intelligence: Challenges, Solutions and Applications, (207–226) © 2025 Scrivener Publishing LLC

and implementation of GBT-CNN. A study summary concludes the publication; final simulations assess the method's efficacy. The algorithm, according to the data, captures the deeper relationship between job seekers and jobs. It is also possible to achieve accurate personnel matching and fair recommendations.

Keywords: Gradient boosting tree (GBT), convolution neural network (CNN), decision making, human resource, recommendation, finance

9.1 Introduction

Companies have added more recruiting content to their websites in recent years. Job seekers can use the website to find potential employers [1]. Finding suitable human resources to meet the growing demand is becoming more difficult, making it more difficult to find a fit. Large recruitment websites could collect data based on location, job type, and employee buzzwords when there was little data available. Companies struggle to obtain information from potential employees in a timely and efficient manner. Companies that are looking for qualified candidates must do so. The website is still connecting people based on "post," "age," "education," "marriage," and "childbirth." Because of the exponential growth of data, traditional procedures are no longer adequate [2]. As a result, people want precise and personalized matching. Personalized matching can sift through massive amounts of data to find qualified candidates based on specific and quantitative criteria. This helps with candidate selection. Major job boards organize recommendations by job category and keyword search. Despite being simple and fundamental, the two processes mentioned above are insufficient for large amounts of data. Job seekers may become overwhelmed by the sheer volume of job advertisements, making it more difficult to select organizations that meet their criteria and creating ambiguity and doubt about their true needs, necessitating additional effort on their part to obtain acceptable information [3, 4]. The sheer volume of available positions can easily overwhelm job seekers. This situation demonstrates the competitiveness of the talent market. Making strong human resource (HR) recommendations can help to mitigate talent market employment issues. This will be explained in the following paragraphs.

Because search engines cannot handle large amounts of data, researchers developed a suggestion system. The user's history is used to construct preference models, which are then compared to content information to provide personalized recommendations. This reduces the flaws of the search engine. Recommendation systems sift through massive amounts of data to find relevant information for the user. Both service providers and users can benefit from providing valuable content to consumers, resulting in a win-win situation. A recommendation system, which has been implemented in several network information service domains, can help to reduce the amount of information on the Internet [5–8]. Because of their broad applicability, recommendation systems are being studied by computer scientists and academics from other fields. The Microsoft Research Institute, Shanghai Jiaotong University's APEX Laboratory, and the University of Minnesota's GroupLens team have all studied recommendation systems and algorithms. Open-source recommendation algorithms have been developed in recent years [9]. Companies invest much in research and development because recommendation algorithms are critical to many aspects of corporate operations. Online social networking sites like Facebook and microblogs, online shopping sites like Amazon and Taobao, and news reporting sites like Google News and today's headlines are examples of these components. Human resource recruiting is witnessing a technological transformation comparable to that observed in e-commerce and social networking because of the Internet's rising significance. Draw Hook Industry, Wuba Group, and Zhilian Staffing Agency are examples of successful Chinese businesses. Xing, LinkedIn, and CareerBuilder are three of the most popular professional networking websites, and they are frequently used by Chinese residents searching for work overseas. Recruiters are eager to post jobs online to attract the best candidates. This is since more job seekers obtain job information online. There has also been an increase in talent and posting information [10] Unprecedented expansion. If you want to land your dream job, you must thoroughly research potential employers. To connect job seekers and employers, recruiting websites require a customized recommendation system. Despite the significant corporate interest, human resource recommendation systems are gaining value slowly. The amount of human resources research on algorithm innovation has increased. The topic of this paper, an algorithm for producing human resource suggestions, is useful.

Human resource matching compares an applicant's basic information to the requirements of a position. Resume Suggestion is an important link because it recommends candidates to companies based on their recruiting data. It's an important link. There are three algorithms for generating resume proposals. The first category, algorithmic resume recommendations, includes models that are content-based, collaborative, or hybrid. Second, a resume recommendation based on ontology. Deep learning algorithms, finally, generate recommendations. Deep learning-based strategies are the most promising right now. It was suggested by human resources to match resumes to job specifications [11]. A mixed user model is created by combining surface and deep information from recommendation results. This model makes suggestions. This has increased the efficacy of HR's recommendation system [12, 13]. Human resource recommendation problems can be solved using supervised machine learning. The employee's previous work experience and other data are used to build the prediction model. Future employee work can be anticipated [14, 15]. It was claimed that corporate customers' interest sensitivity could be assessed using recruiting data. This method improves the calculation of job candidate similarities [16]; calculation method considers interest, preference, and content-to-school correlation. This strategy considers the student's academic history. This paradigm addresses unequal access to information in the graduate job market. The slope one algorithm and similarity produce an excellent individualized employment recommendation. Many algorithms have only one implementation method, and the advantages of new technologies are underutilized. As a result, an algorithm's performance and tailored recommendations suffer. This article looks at deep learning and other emerging technologies for matching human resources. Traditional algorithms will also be enhanced. This does not imply that traditional algorithmic approaches will be abandoned. Processing big data and AI enables us to process massive amounts of data quickly and effectively, which improves human resource matching. Human resource misallocation and waste should be addressed as soon as possible.

9.2 Literature Review

9.2.1 Deep Learning Approach

Deep learning necessitates the representation of data. Algorithms are created and analyzed by machine learning. This enables computers to self-learn. Machine learning systems can predict new data after analyzing existing data. Practical statistical and reasoning theories are used in machine learning. When it is impossible to research the law, machine learning is used [17, 18]. There is pixel intensity, contour and edge data, and abstract images provided. Using alternative representation systems benefits some learning scenarios. Deep learning aims to build a network that can understand voice, language, and images in the same way that the human brain does. Deep learning is now pervasive in all aspects of modern society, from browser advertising recommendation algorithms and intelligent search to face, weather, and plant recognition in smartphones and cameras, as well as intelligent applications like voice-to-text conversion and video recommendation based on user interests. It's all over. Deep learning necessitated the use of machine learning fiction. That requires both time and knowledge [19]. A method is used to create an image feature vector. Complex social activities necessitate the development of costly and time-consuming features.

Siti *et al.* [20] developed the Gradient Tree Boosting method for recommending structural officials in talent management. It addresses weaknesses in current subjective recommendation systems in HR. Xi *et al.* [21] proposed a Hybrid GBT-CNN algorithm for human resource matching recommendations. It combines Gradient Tree Boosting and CNN advantages for accurate human resource matching. It improves the quality of human resources recommendations through high-dimensional feature abstraction. Hong *et al.* [22] focus on Human Resource Management System evolution from the 1960s to the late 1990s. It utilizes ML for human resource data analysis and management. The authors used machine learning techniques, gradient descent algorithm, and backpropagation neural network. Vengai *et al.* [23] propose a model to predict employee churn in organizations. This model uses feature selection and classification methods to improve accuracy. For feature selection use the Pearson correlation method, information gain, and recursive feature elimination. For classification use the random forest, logistic regression, decision trees, gradient boosting machines, and K nearest neighbors. Haoxiang *et al.* [24] introduce a recommender system for HR professionals, using gradient boosting and deep learning. It improves recommendation quality with feature regularization and optimization strategies. It uses a gradient-boosting tree model and a convolutional network-based deep-learning model. Janice *et al.* [25] propose an RNN model for efficient HR recruitment through text processing. It utilizes methods of Bi-directional Long Short-term Memory (BiLSTM), CNN, and Attention mechanism for job-resume matching. It enhances efficiency in screening resumes by extracting word-level features.

Deep learning's hierarchy is created by neural networks. Generation and Discrimination based Deep Learning model is shown in Figure 9.1. The shallow and deep layers of the artificial neural network extract edge and semantic data. Backpropagation updates the parameter weights of each layer to create an abstract representation of the data. Deep learning places a premium on neural network self-learning. Job-specific discriminants can be learned using deep learning. Several techniques are used to update these parameters. Neural networks can learn to classify objects. Image segmentation and classification are only two of the numerous data processing tasks that neural networks can help with. Deep learning is a great tool not only because it has a powerful

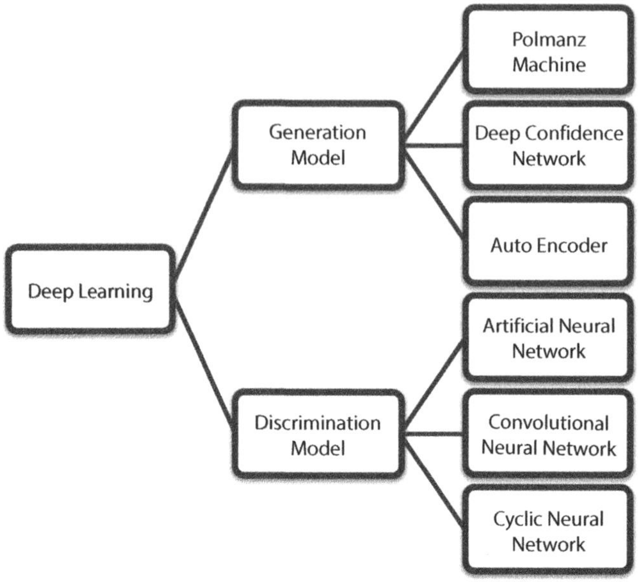

Figure 9.1 Deep learning models.

representation function, but also because it can be used in a wide range of real-world situations. Deep learning, for example, may be used for both data generation and classification. Each of these subjects will be given further thought and inquiry soon. Despite the demonstrated usefulness of deep learning–based recommendation systems, the bulk of these tools continue to employ antiquated methodologies. Some of the approaches [26, 27] proposed as potential solutions to this challenge are convolutional neural networks, recurrent neural networks, and a trestle-denoising self-encoder. A self-encoding trestle is another good choice. Furthermore, a variety of solutions have been proposed. The trestle denoising self-encoder is another promising technique. Deep learning has some advantages over more traditional techniques for speech and image recognition, but it also has certain drawbacks. These include the need for a lengthy training period and the possibility of slow solution convergence. Convolutional neural networks are a prominent deep learning application.

9.2.2 Gradient Boosting Tree

A machine learning model is a gradient boosting model, where performance is enhanced by the employment of an ensemble of weak learners. The weak learners are usually decision trees. Their combined output yields more advanced models as given in Figure 9.2.

Figure 9.2 Gradient boosting.

Loss Function: It changes according to the type of problem being solved.
Weak Learner: Weak learners are used for making predictions.
Additive Model: The already existing trees in the model are not modified in any manner but a greater number of trees are added at a time.

When a student with low potential is selected, decision trees T1Tm are constructed, and these trees are then used to decrease residual variance [28]. The GBT concept is seen in Figure 9.3. Once all of the decision tree findings have been merged, predictions are created using a process known as linear addition.

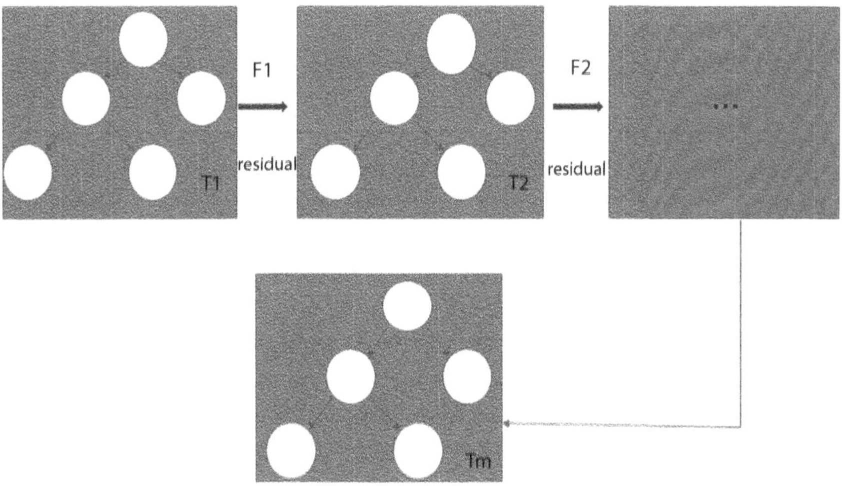

Figure 9.3 Training process of the GBT model.

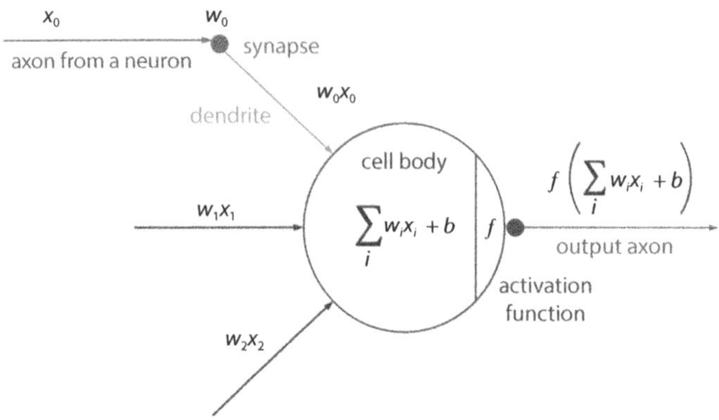

Figure 9.4 An illustration of the structure of a synthetic neuron.

9.2.3 Convolutional Neural Network

Data is transmitted by neurons in a convolutional neural network. A synthetic neuron is depicted schematically in Figure 9.4. The interaction of the neurons in the system allows each neuron to cover the entire observable field of vision [29, 30]. Several theoretical neural network model topologies are being researched.

The input layer of the pooling layer preprocesses the original data. Normalize the data by subtracting the mean. The convolution layer of CNN is critical. Convolutions and information extraction require this layer. Each convolution core has the same features as the overall information, such as texture and edge. To obtain the gradient, the activation layer must first nonlinearly map convolutional outputs. To reduce overfitting, the pooling layer reduces the number of parameters [31–33]. Because of its importance in this application, CNN's organizational structure will be dissected and explored further in this post. CNN works on a layer-by-layer basis. Small targets are detected using VggNet, MobileNet, DenseNet, ResNet, and DeepL. Convolution models are constantly being improved. It modifies network models to improve the link between levels, allowing for faster acquisition of target feature information.

9.2.3.1 Layer of Convolution

Back-propagation is used to fine-tune and iteratively change the parameters of the subunits of each convolution layer. Self-renewal is taking place. Throughout the iterative training process, deeper layers of a network might collect the information needed to develop more accurate outputs based on simpler inputs [34, 35]. In Figure 9.5 the example related to representation of

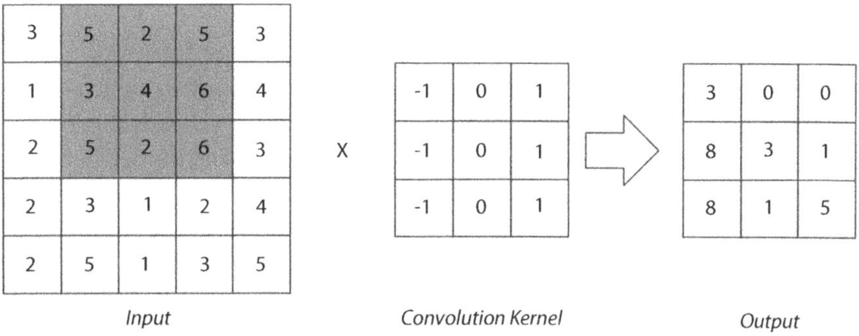

Figure 9.5 A hierarchical representation of the convolution technique.

convolution technique is presented. This is made feasible by the fact that training is done in cycles.

9.2.3.2 *Pool Layer*

For each fixed window in the feature map, the value of each pixel in the down-sampling layer is calculated. If the size of the input feature map is reduced, the model may be able to extract more features and gain a better grasp of the whole scenario. Data merging reduces the size of the final graph as well as the number of parameters and computations required [36–38]. Overfitting the model is not required, but if it does, the pooling approach can be modified to be more noise-tolerant. Figure 9.6 shows the pooling mode in graphic form.

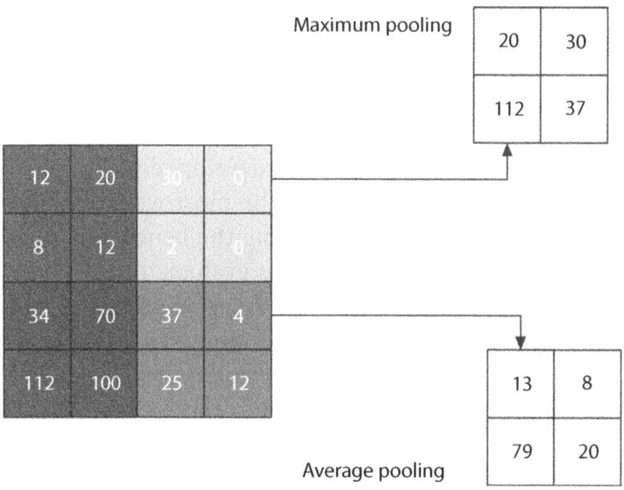

Figure 9.6 The pooling mode in graphic form.

9.2.3.3 *Active Layer*

The nonlinearity of the network's multilayer composite functions is preserved by activation functions. Because changing a linear function does not change its output, neurons must be activated via an activation layer. When neurons are output, the feature expression of a model becomes more specific. The inputs of neurons are mapped to their outputs. Its trend is between 0 and 1. A large or small gradient necessitates a high or low variance in the input. The gradient will gradually decrease and eventually disappear as the number of network layers increases, rendering the network untrainable [39–41]. ReLU is a technique for preventing gradient loss and promoting network model convergence. This enables the use of ReLU. ReLU has a nonlinear slope that is close to zero. If the input value is 0 or less, ReLU will not calculate neurons. This strategy has the potential to reduce computation.

9.2.3.4 *Full Connection Layer*

The connections between neurons in one layer and neurons in another layer are considered to be "fully connected" when this happens. As a consequence, we will print all of that information on the sample's label right away. Because of the traits and features that comprise the entire connecting layer, this layer has more dimensions than the levels underneath it. SoftMax will deliver a percentage of accuracy for any image recognition or target identification classification activities completed [42–44]. Recognizable examples of items in this category include the ability to recognize objects and pictures.

9.2.4 Deeper Learning Organizational Techniques

As a result of the growing popularity of deep learning, a variety of cutting-edge learning frameworks have been developed. TensorFlow, MxNet, Torch, Theano, and Keras are some of the most well-known deep learning frameworks in recent years. Analyzing the benefits and drawbacks of each choice is insufficient; one must also evaluate the minor distinctions between the various frameworks. MxNet beats competing networks in three critical areas: processing speed, flexibility, and data coverage. Each of these categories provides significant value to MxNet. In each of these domains, alternative networks fall short of expectations. Memory is more efficiently used, and GPUs can perform distributed computation. Because of these considerations, the MxNet research framework was chosen for this article's investigation.

9.3 The Proposed Model

It has already been established that computationally efficient algorithms, such as GBT and CNN, provide more diverse ideas than more traditional techniques. By putting these two different machine learning methods together, this work improves the quality of model feature extraction that is used by well-known recommendation algorithms. These methods are used to create a GBT-CNN system for matching and recommending HR candidates. GBT transforms the raw data first, and then CNN is fed the modified features [45–47]. Convolution processing's high-level abstract learning provides personalized HR recommendations. This hybrid technique can find and recommend HR candidates. First, human resources data must be gathered; second, relevant field features must be preprocessed; third, a human resources recommendation algorithm must be used; and finally, a recommendation result must be provided. The flowchart is depicted in Figure 9.7 and working methodology of model in Figure 9.8.

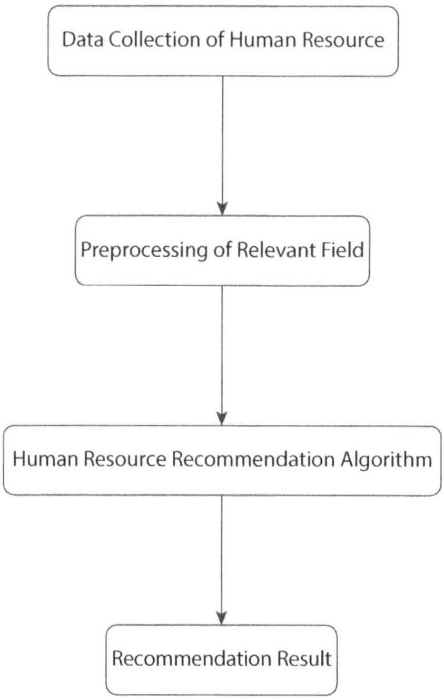

Figure 9.7 Flow chart.

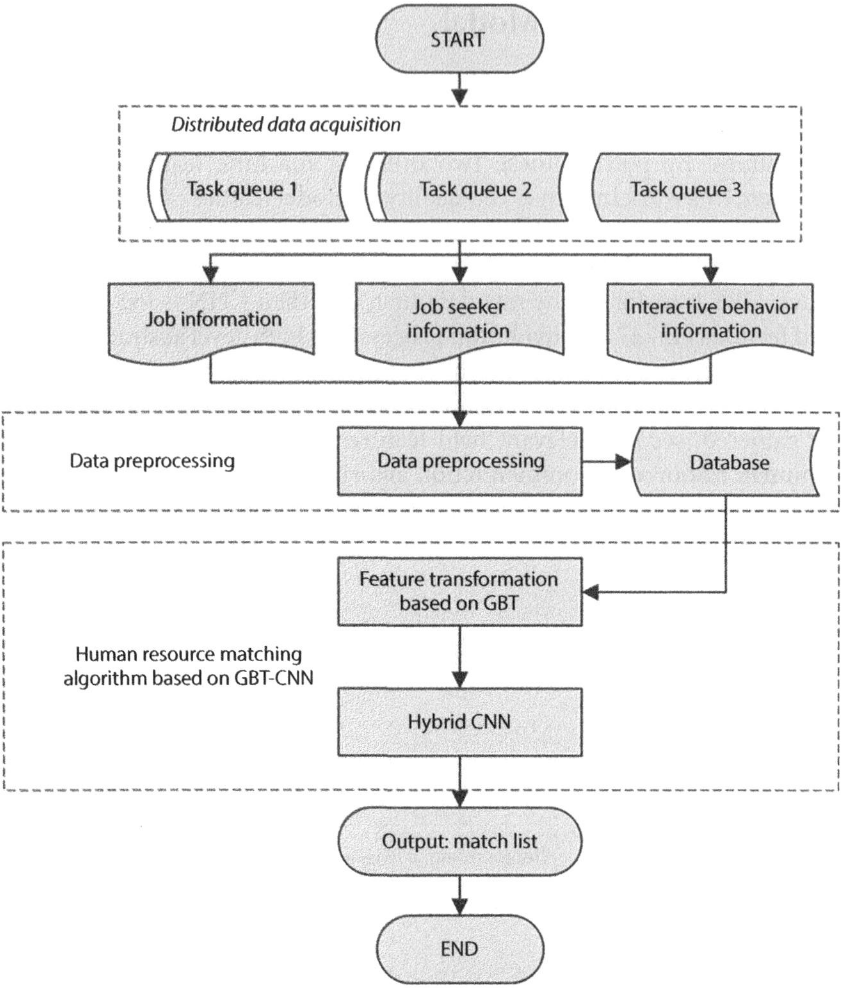

Figure 9.8 The GBT-CNN database used to match and propose probable partners.

9.4 Evaluation of the Impact of the Technology

9.4.1 Data Set

Experiments and analyses with real-world data sets are used to assess the algorithm's utility in recommending human resource practices. The study makes use of HR platform data. A suitable human resources data warehouse can be obtained through data preparation. Over 200,000 user actions have been recorded. The deep learning framework MxNet, which comes with Ubuntu Kylin 16.04 LTS, can be used to put the method into action. The RAM is 32 gigabytes of DDR3 working at 1800 megahertz, and the CPU is an Intel Core i5-3360P running at 3.5 GHz with 8 threads. The GPU is a GeForce GT 860. Ubuntu Kylin 16.04 LTS operating system GNU/Linux kernel version 4.4.0-53-generic x64. The version of Python used was 3.9.6, while the version of MXNet used was 0.12.

9.4.1.1 Evaluation Criteria

Before conducting an impartial analysis of the simulation findings, they must be standardised. Accuracy, recall rate, and the F1 score are a few examples of metrics that are commonly employed in research. A job seeker's interest in a posting is determined by recall rate rather than accuracy rate. Only a captivating advertisement will entice job seekers to view, collect, or apply for it. As a result, it is even more critical for job seekers to assess the quality of the proposal and the information provided. The F1 score, in conjunction with the recall rate, can be used as an evaluation criterion. Both accuracy and recall rates can be calculated using this evaluation standard. This method combines accuracy and recall rate into a single criterion.

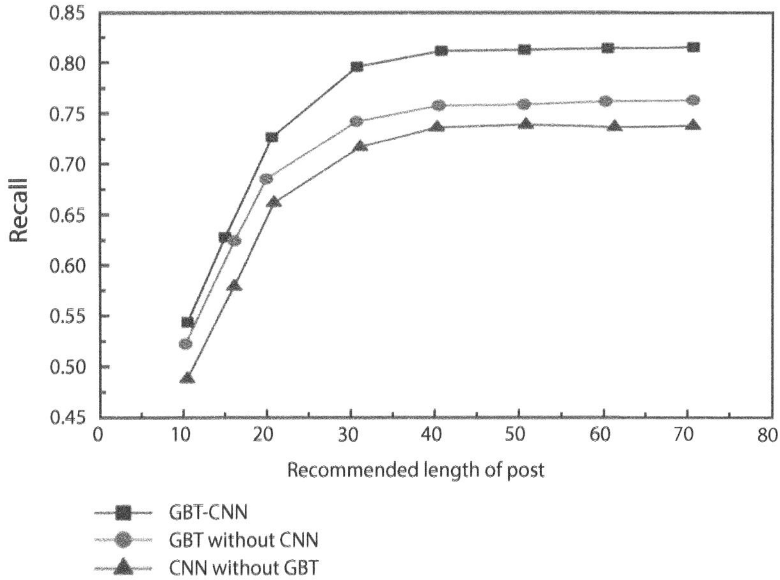

Figure 9.9 Comparisons are made between the parameters' recall rates.

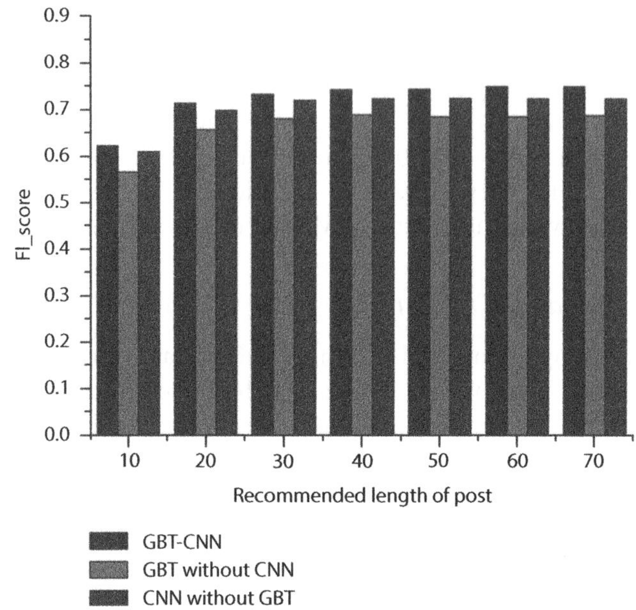

Figure 9.10 Evaluation in relation to the parameter F1 score.

Here demonstrates how useful the algorithm is to demonstrate its advantages, the proposed algorithm is compared to GBT and CNN. All approaches make use of the same platform parameter configuration. This ensures consistent results. Figures 9.9 and 9.10 show the results of the experiment.

Experiments show that with a length of 70, the proposed method achieves 83.44 percent recall, whereas CNN without GBT achieves 77.22 percent recall and an F1 score of 719.83 percent. The proposed algorithm enhances the effect. CNN's quality evaluation criterion is improved by 8.03 and 2.64 percentage points, respectively, by the proposed strategy. This study found that GBT transformation can achieve higher-level feature learning in convolution than straight convolution. This improves the quality of the model's suggestions. UserCF, ItemCF, CBF, PMF, and a four-layer deep neural network were chosen as comparison objects. This will improve the algorithm's assessment of benefits. All of these algorithms are highly recommended and widely used (DNN). As a computing platform, different methods use the same parameter combinations. This is critical. Figures 9.11 and 9.12 show the results of the tests.

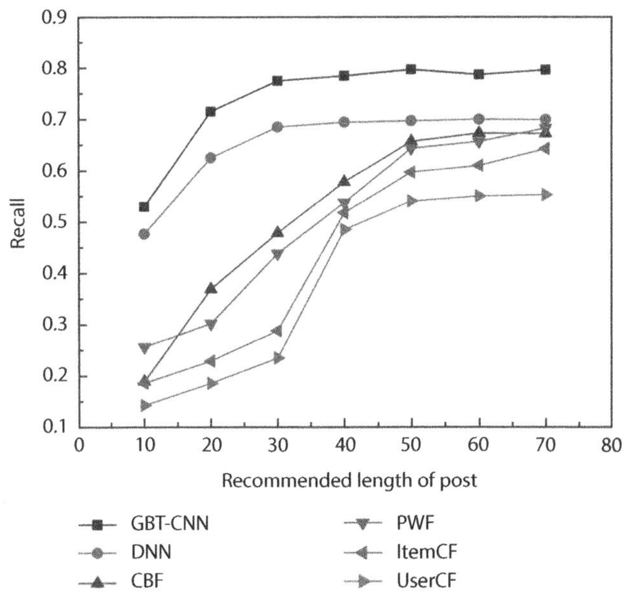

Figure 9.11 Analysis of how well different data retrieval strategies locate previously stored information.

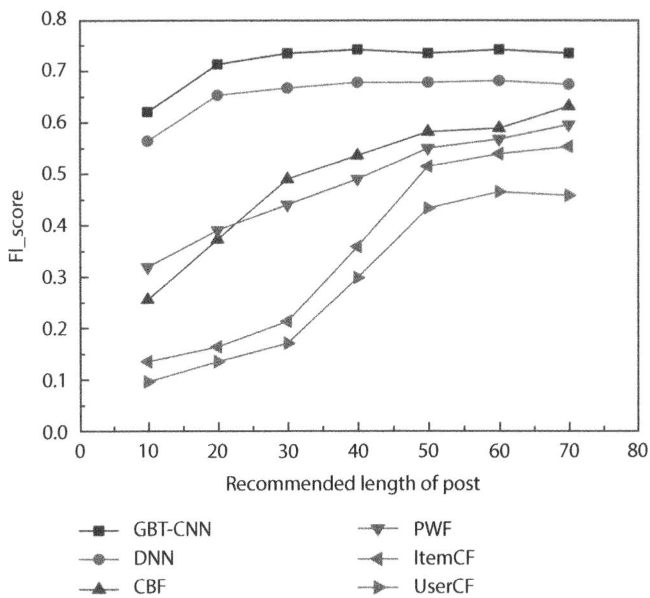

Figure 9.12 Comprehensive examination of the F1-score to assess and compare the relative advantages of the various techniques.

In terms of recall rate and F1 score, this method is better than all other recommendation systems that are currently available. This demonstrates the utility of combining the GBT and CNN models. GBT modifies features, while multichannel convolution improves feature abstraction. using both strategies. When convolution and local connection processing are combined with information on job candidates and employers, high-level abstract feature information is revealed. Human resource model proposals can then be significantly improved.

9.5 Conclusion

To overcome traditional and single recommendation approaches, the author of this essay creates a recommendation algorithm for human resources. GBT's feature transformation and CNN's high-level feature learning overcome the traditional recommendation algorithm's limited ability to extract model features, resulting in higher recommendation quality. Because of the two technologies, the suggested algorithm's suggestions are compared to those of other algorithms in use using HR data. The presented algorithm successfully recommends human resources. The recommended technique has some flaws that will need to be addressed in the future. The HR objectives of job applicants can shift over time. This is not currently available, but it will be in future versions. Timing may be improved by using a cyclic neural network model. It might work.

References

1. Zhu, H., Research on human resource recommendation algorithm based on machine learning. *Sci. Program.*, 2021, 3, 10, 2021. Article ID 8387277.
2. Liu, Z., Ma, Y., Zheng, H., Liu, D., Liu, J., Human resource recommendation algorithm based on improved frequent itemset mining. *Future Gener. Comput. Syst.*, 126, 1, 122–128, 2021.
3. Wang, H., Liang, G., Zhang, X., Feature Regularization and Deep Learning for Human Resource Recommendation. *IEEE Access*, 6, 2018.
4. Pan, X., Application of machine learning algorithm in human resource recommendation: from tradition machine learning algorithm to AutoML, in: *Proceedings of the 5th International Conference on Social Sciences and Economic Development (ICSSED 2020)*, Amsterdam, Netherland, January 2020.
5. Dou, Y., Yang, H., Deng, X., A survey of collaborative filtering algorithms for social recommender systems, in: *Proceedings of the International Conference*

on Semantics, Knowledge and Grids, IEEE, Beijing, China, August 2016, pp. 40–46.
7. Hu, D. and Chen, L., A high-efficient recommendation algorithm based on LDA, in: *Human Centered Computing*, Springer International Publishing, Berlin, Germany, 2016.
8. Paparrizos, I., Cambazoglu, B.B., Gionis, A., Machine learned job recommendation, in: *Proceedings of the 2011 ACM Conference on Recommender Systems*, Chicago, IL, USA, October 2011, pp. 325–328.
9. Tripathi, P., Agarwal, R., Vashishtha, T., Review of job recommender system using big data analytics, in: *Proceedings of the International Conference on Computing for Sustainable Global Development*, New Delhi, India, March 2016, pp. 3773–3777.
10. Cai, X., Hu, Z., Chen, J., A many-objective optimization recommendation algorithm based on knowledge mining. *Inf. Sci.*, 537, 3, 221–229, 2020.
11. Jin, L., Wang, H., Ding, Y., Employment recommendation algorithm for college graduates based on interest sensitivity. *Computer Digital Engineering*, 45, 2, 201–253, 2017.
12. Yin, C., *Research on Employment Recommendation Problem and Algorithm of College Graduates*, Shandong Normal University, Jinan, China, 2016.
13. Oh, G.E.G., Huh, Y.E., Mukhopadhyay, A., Inducing consumers to use calorie information: a multinational investigation. *Psychol. Health*, 1–19, 2021.
14. Xiaofeng, L., Han, J., Zhiyong, P., *et al.*, Lung cancer and granuloma identification using a deep learning model to extract 3-dimensional radiomics features in CT imaging. *Clinical Lung Cancer*, 22, 5, 756–766, 2022.
15. Chen, W., Chen, B., Peng, X., *et al.*, Tensor RNN with Bayesian nonparametric mixture for radar HRRP modeling and target recognition. *IEEE Trans. Signal Process.*, 69, 2021.
16. Zhu, T., Qin, Y., Xiang, Y., Baotian, H., Qingcai, C., Weihua, P., Distantly supervised biomedical relation extraction using piecewise attentive convolutional neural network and reinforcement learning. *J. Am. Med. Inf. Assoc.*, 28, 12, 12–18, 2021.
17. Alberici, D., Camilli, F., Contucci, P., Mingione, E., The solution of the deep Boltzmann machine on the nishimori line. *Commun. Math. Phys.*, 387, 1–24, 2021.
18. Lv, P.F., He, B., Guo, J., Position correction model based on gated hybrid RNN for AUV navigation. *IEEE Trans. Veh. Technol.*, 70, 6, 2021.
19. Feizizadeh, B., Garajeh, M.K., Lakes, T., Blaschke, T., A deep learning convolutional neural network algorithm for detecting saline flow sources and mapping the environmental impacts of the Urmia Lake drought in Iran. *Catena*, 207, 1, 2021. Article ID 105585.
20. Siti, N., Dedy, R., Wijaya, S., Komala, S., Gradient Tree Boosting for HR Talent Management Application, in: *undefined*, 2022, doi:10.1109/ICoICT55009.2022.9914833.

21. Xi, C., Human Resource Matching Support System Based on Deep Learning, in: *Mathematical Problems in Engineering, undefined*, 2022, doi: 10.1155/2022/1558409.
22. Hong, Z., Research on Human Resource Recommendation Algorithm Based on Machine Learning, in: *Scientific Programming, undefined.*
23. Vengai, M., Edmore, T., Kudakwashe, Z., A Supervised Machine Learning Model to Optimize Human Resources Analytics for Employee Churn Prediction, in: *undefined*, 2022, doi: 10.1109/ZCICT55726.2022.10045987.
24. Haoxiang, W., Guihuang, L., Xingming, Z., Feature Regularization and Deep Learning for Human Resource Recommendation. *IEEE Access, undefined*, 2018. doi: 10.1109/ACCESS.2018.2854887.
25. Xu, GL., Human Resource Recommendation Based on Recurrent Convolutional Neural Network, in: *2022 2nd International Conference on Consumer Electronics and Computer Engineering*, 2022, doi: 10.1109/iccece54139.2022.9712799.
26. Lao, Y., Qi, F., Zhou, J., Fang, X., A prediction method based on extreme gradient boosting tree model and its application. *J. Phys. Conf. Ser.*, 1995, 1, 2021. Article ID 012017.
27. Danandeh Mehr, A., Drought classification using gradient boosting decision tree. *Acta Geophys.*, 69, 3, 909–918, 2021.
28. Nie, P., Roccotelli, M., Fanti, M.P., Ming, Z.Z., Prediction of home energy consumption based on gradient boosting regression tree. *Energy Rep.*, 7, 7, 1246–1255, 2021.
29. Li, J., Wu, C., Song, R., *et al.*, Deep hybrid 2-D-3-D CNN based on dual second-order attention with camera spectral sensitivity prior for spectral super-resolution. *IEEE Trans. Neural Netw. Learn. Syst.*, 12, 32, 1–12, 2021.
30. Wang, H., Liu, Z., Peng, D., Qin, Y., Understanding and learning discriminant features based on multi-attention 1DCNN for wheelset bearing fault diagnosis. *IEEE Trans. Ind. Inf.*, 16, 9, 2019.
31. Liu, X., Miao, X., Jiang, H., Chen, J., Box-point detector: a diagnosis method for insulator faults in power lines using aerial images and convolutional neural networks. *IEEE Trans. Power Deliv.*, 36, 6, 2021.
32. Kashyap, R., Machine Learning for Internet of Things, in: *Research Anthology on Artificial Intelligence Applications in Security*, pp. 976–1002, 2021, Available: 10.4018/978-1-7998-7705-9.ch046 [Accessed 18 April 2022].
33. Sakalle, A., Tomar, P., Bhardwaj, H., Bhardwaj, A., Emotion recognition using portable EEG device, in: *International Conference on Artificial Intelligence and Sustainable Computing*, pp. 17–30, Springer Cham, 2021.
34. Navadia, N.R., Kaur, G., Bhardwaj, H., Singh, T., Sakalle, A., Acharya, D., Bhardwaj, A., Applications of Cloud-Based Internet of Things, in: *Integration and Implementation of the Internet of Things Through Cloud Computing*, pp. 65–84, IGI Global, 2021.

35. Bhardwaj, H., Tomar, P., Sakalle, A., Acharya, D., Badal, T., Bhardwaj, A., A DeepLSTM Model for Personality Traits Classification Using EEG Signals. *IETE J. Res.*, 1–9, 2021.
36. Pandey, M.S., Computerized gender determination from human sternum& manubrium X-Ray Measurements. *Int. J. Adv. Trends Computer Science Engineering*, 8, 6, 2686–2692, 2019. doi:10.30534/ijatcse/2019/01862019.
37. Verma, D. and Pandey, M.S., Computerized Assisted Segmentation of Brain Tumor Using Deep Convolutional Network, in: *Proceedings of Second Doctoral Symposium on Computational Intelligence*, pp. 461–470, 2021, doi:10.1007/978-981-16-3346-1_37.
38. Usman, M., Shukla, R., Zya, N., Pandey, M.S., Singh, A., Graph convolutional neural networks for distributed recommender and prediction systems. *Emerg. Trends IoT Comput. Technol.*, 2023, 462–467. doi:10.1201/9781003350057-68.
39. Singh, A., Sharma, R., Pandey, M.S., Asthana, S., Gitanjali, Vishwakarma, A., Facial Expression Based Music Recommendation System Using Deep Learning. *Data Science Network Engineering*, 2023, 31–40. doi:10.1007/978-981-99-6755-1_3.
40. Sakalle, A., Tomar, P., Bhardwaj, H., Alim, M., A Modified LSTM Framework for Analyzing COVID-19 Effect on Emotion and Mental Health during Pandemic Using the EEG Signals. *J. Healthc. Eng., 2022*, 2022.
41. Sakalle, A., Tomar, P., Bhardwaj, H., Iqbal, A., Sakalle, M., Bhardwaj, A., Ibrahim, W., Genetic Programming-Based Feature Selection for Emotion Classification Using EEG Signal. *J. Healthc. Eng., 2022*, 2022.
42. Alnuaim, A.A., Zakariah, M., Shukla, P.K., Alhadlaq, A., Hatamleh, W.A., Tarazi, H., Sureshbabu, R., Ratna, R., Human-Computer Interaction for Recognizing Speech Emotions Using Multilayer Perceptron Classifier. *J. Healthc. Eng.*, 2022, 12, 2022. Article ID 6005446, https://doi.org/10.1155/2022/6005446.
43. Nair, R. and Bhagat, A., An Introduction to Clustering Algorithms in Big Data. *Encyc. Inf. Sci. Technol.*, 559–576, 2021. Available: 10.4018/978-1-7998-3479-3.ch040 [Accessed 14 June 2022].
44. Nair, R., Sharma, P., Sharma, T., Optimizing the Performance of IoT Using FPGA as Compared to GPU. *Int. J. Grid High Perform. Comput.*, 14, 1, 1–15, 2022. Available: 10.4018/ijghpc.301580 [Accessed 8 August 2022].
45. Nair, R., Soni, M., Bajpai, B., Dhiman, G., Sagayam, K., Predicting the Death Rate Around the World Due to COVID-19 Using Regression Analysis. *Int. J. Swarm Intell. Res.*, 13, 2, 1–13, 2022. Available: 10.4018/ijsir.287545.
46. Agrawal, M., Kumar Shukla, P., Nair, R., Nayyar, A., Masud, M., Stock Prediction Based on Technical Indicators Using Deep Learning Model. *Comput. Mater. Continua*, 70, 1, 287–304, 2022. Available: 10.32604/cmc.2022.014637.
47. Kashyap, R., Dilated residual grooming kernel model for breast cancer detection. *Pattern Recognit. Lett.*, 159, 157–164, 2022. 10.1016/j.patrec.2022.04.037 [Accessed 27 August 2022].

10

Comprehensive View from Ethics to AI Ethics: With Multifaceted Dimensions

Kanika Budhiraja[1]*, Gurminder Kaur[2], Yatu Rani[2] and Rupam Jha[2]

[1]Department of Management, BMIET Sonepat, Haryana, India
[2]Department of CSE, BMIET Sonepat, Haryana, India

Abstract
The most important technological advancement of today's world is artificial intelligence, which has permeated almost every sector of the economy and has an escalating modest yet noticeable influence on our daily lives. Every sector and organisation is encountering hardships with the usage pattern of this cutting-edge innovation in technology to enhance or tailor their goods or services, gain a greater comprehension of their firm or consumer base, or enable novel potential revenue streams. This pattern has spread from business to healthcare to education, covering multiple aspects of the commercial world. The idea of AI ethics is sometimes disregarded in the rush to attain innovation, given superficial importance, or dismissed entirely. This is because AI ethics cannot exist in a vacuum from a more comprehensive and inclusive legitimate framework. In a highly challenging climate, corporations are exploring possibilities with AI, but for legal and regulation experts in particular, AI continues to be a mystery. This paper thus intends to explore the work in a systematic pattern, initiating from conceptualising the ethics to ethics in Artificial intelligence followed by examining the underlying domain, i.e., identifying the key ethical elements of AI in various sectors and unfolding its ethical horizons in multifaceted dimensions covering diverse industries like business, healthcare and education.

Keywords: Artificial intelligence, ethics, AI ethics, multifaceted dimensions

**Corresponding author*: kanikarelan@yahoo.com

Sapna Juneja, Rajesh Kumar Dhanaraj, Abhinav Juneja, Malathy Sathyamoorthy and Asadullah Shaikh (eds.) Ethical Decision-Making Using Artificial Intelligence: Challenges, Solutions and Applications, (227–258) © 2025 Scrivener Publishing LLC

10.1 Introduction

The definition of AI technology is "a machine's ability to mimic intelligent human behavior". Predictive coding is one method of using AI technology in the innovations of electronic devices that is becoming more and more common. Using a sort of AI technique that permits the computer to get the instructions in a legalized and defined controlled manner is how inferential coding is defined. Most of the time, a computer or machine communicates with a controller to learn from it as to how to categorize docs in a specific scenario, important or insignificant, critical or not so critical [17]. The computer program can "bifurcate the whole set" and "rate the appropriateness of different files matching into the categorization" by inferring the controller's input from a tiny subset of files. Even though predictive coding is also subjected to a strict later reviews from a defined controller, which restricts the usage of files requiring manual human eye check, thus leading to huge monetary benefits (in terms of savings) and also reduction in probability of manual faults at the time of initial inspection.

Artificial intelligence (AI) can be applied to nearly any area of medicine, and its possible advantages to the fields of biomedical sciences, imparting teaching in medicine, and providing healthcare appears endless. AI encompasses the domains of neural networks, NLP, and automation. Artificial Intelligence (AI) can play a role in determination, medical decisions, and customised healthcare due to its strong capacity to synthesise and gain insight from enormous volumes of information in medical sciences [24]. AI-oriented detection techniques, for instance, are helping doctors discover cancer in women by acting as a next judgement when it comes to breast scans. Furthermore, sophisticated simulated humanoid replicas are able to hold serious discussions, which have consequences for mental illness evaluation and therapy. Artificial intelligence (AI) tools can be discovered in the physical world, where they help offer e-health through mobile players, hands-on assistance systems, and artificial implants. However, because AI usage has the enormous potential to endanger the confidentiality of patients, protection, and choice, it raises a new set of ethical issues that need to be recognised and addressed [20]. However, the advancements AI has achieved in a number of industries are not keeping up with existing legislative and ethical standards for AI technology. Professional sectors are still unaware of the moral complications that emerging AI techniques might bring, despite the fact that some initiatives to hold these ethical talks have occurred.

AI ethics is a set of ethically professional guidelines and practices meant to guide the creation and appropriate application of artificial intelligence (AI) systems [1]. Corporations are beginning to create ethical protocol for AI applications, since AI has become a necessary component of services and goods.

It is now absolutely necessary to comprehend the idea of moral rules of conduct, which mainly consists of the foundational questions of decisiveness in reality. The primary topics it addresses are matters of the final worth and the criteria on the basis of which people may be classified as acceptable or unacceptable. Integrity and ethical conduct have strong connections to concepts [16]. Whereas it used to be appropriate to use the word about integrity assessments or moral standards of conduct, in today's time this implies ethical decisions or ethical protocol.

Application of ethics in AI leads to the emergence of the concept of AI ethics. The definition of ethics has been broadened by its multiple uses. In past instances, the phrase did not relate to decency per se, but rather to the area of learning or investigative domain that deals with moral issues. Thus, ethical conduct is the same as integrity science in this sense. An ethical rule of conduct for AI, commonly known as AI ethical framework, is a legally binding declaration concerning policy that outlines artificial intelligence's place in relation to the advancement and welfare of humankind. An AI ethical protocol is meant to serve as a reference for anyone involved in making moral decisions about the use of AI. A model of AI for ethics is crucial because it clarifies the positive aspects and disadvantages of AI. Companies and other involved individuals must consider important societal concerns and eventually tackle the issue of following basic humanitarian grounds in order to develop a set of moral guidelines and ethical practices for the authentic use of AI [9].

Applications of AI and its ethical aspects has gained significant relevance in multifaceted dimensions that have been explored in the research in the context of analysing AI ethics in multiple sectors like business, education and medicine in India. The range of methodologies and approaches that are broadly classified as artificial intelligence (AI) have significantly changed the way that businesses absorb knowledge, sort and assess facts, and enhance or streamline projects and actions. This evolution can be credited with a number of aspects, such as the digitization of enterprises and the resulting expanded accessibility of data, as well as the quickening of technological advances. Actually, more generally speaking, the emergence of AI tools is probably going to have a big influence on future viable company models, industry innovation, and the dynamics of how consumers act [11]. Research has identified a number of ethical sub-domains, including the management of data, security and confidentiality, legitimacy of data, computational justice, and authenticity of models, based on evaluations of the past academic reviews on AI ethics in business.

Nevertheless, existing legislative and ethical norms for AI technology are not keeping up with the advancements that Artificial Intelligence has achieved in multidimensional sectors. The healthcare field is still unaware of the moral dilemmas that emerging AI technology might bring, despite the fact that some attempts to conduct these discussions have surfaced. As a result, a stimulating conversation that will greatly profit from medical expertise is anticipated, as doctors will probably soon start using AI in their routine clinical work.

Thus in the present study, the structure of research is framed as in the Figure 10.1:

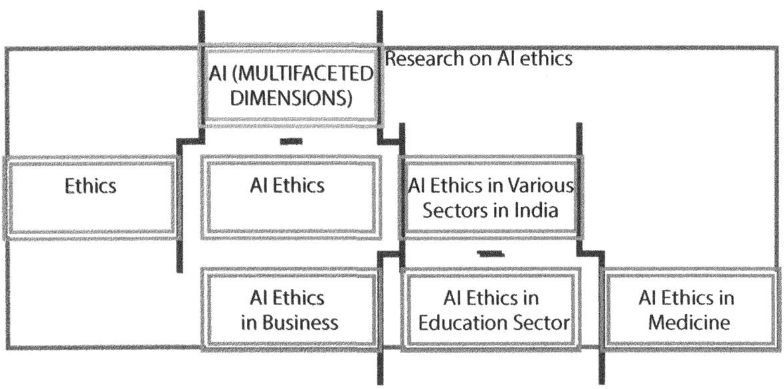

Figure 10.1 Structure of research on AI ethics.

10.2 AI (Artificial Intelligence)

Although there have been numerous descriptions of artificial intelligence over the previous couple of years, the one provided by John McCarthy is as follows: It is the technology and sciences of creating machines that are smart, particularly algorithms for computers. While the goal of employing computers to comprehend the mind of people is comparable, artificial intelligence (AI) is not limited to techniques that can be seen through organic means [4].

Still, in 1950, the groundbreaking article titled "Computing Machinery and Intelligence" marked the beginning of the AI discourse decades before this term was coined. The author of this paper poses the query regarding the thinking capability of machines. He then presents an exercise that has since gained notoriety as the "Turing Test," in which an individual examiner attempts to discern both a digitally produced text reply and a human-written one [13]. Despite intense criticism since it was initially released, this assessment—which makes use of language concepts—remains a significant milestone in the development of artificial intelligence and a living philosophical notion [19].

One of the modern approaches to AI technique rests on a few critical foundational elements which are certainly the goals of AI application. This also defines the differential dimension of machine systems which is based prioritisations, cognition process and execution of tasks.

Modern Approach of AI: Human Skills

- Machines based on Human Cognition or mindset
- Machines based on actions and reactions like a physical individual.

Modern Approach of AI: Superlative Skills

- Machines based on Sensible Human Mindset
- Machines based on Sensible actions and reactions.

In its most basic sense, AI is an arena that addresses concerns by fusing computational expertise with large, reliable facts. It also includes automated learning and deep computation segments, which are often referenced when discussing AI. These fields are made up of artificial intelligence (AI) techniques that aim to develop intelligent machines that can classify or predict things based on information entered.

By altering the connections and interactions that are now present between entities and people in general, machine learning is bringing about an upsurge not just in commercial sectors but also in the social and economic environment at large [12]. The fables and legends of the prehistoric China people, and numerous nations, wherein it was thought that real thinking skills and Emotional Quotient are actually present in robotic beings and thus had the very beginning of AI. It is an original source of the idea of artificial intelligence. On the other hand, in the words of Nilsson, the concept of artificial-intelligence was coined over an instructional session at Dartmouth College in the United States. It was from that session that the science of artificial-intelligence has benefited from the efforts of educators from various fields of study. In a rapidly rising robotic and networked corporate environment, managerial researchers are consistently examining AI impact on clients, firms, and customers. Complex methods for neural networks have been developed by computer researchers. AI's legal and moral consequences continue to be a topic of discussion among sociological researchers. Considering the social-ethical aspect of AI, the majority of the improvements in studies on artificial intelligence are being made in small, solitary groups with barely any cooperation between other academic disciplines. Moving on with the same flow, it has become really difficult to actually select one definition of AI technology which is acceptable on general parameters. Authors like Russell have categorised the different ideas of AI systems into four groups based on two criteria, the first related to Behavior of logical reasoning and the second to individual skills of prioritization [22]. These artificial intelligence kinds include, but are not limited to, perceiving like individuals, reasoning like individuals, and reacting like human beings. AI systems should incorporate machine learning, factual representation of expertise, robotic thinking, NLP, and the application of existing information for generating new insights. These abilities mean that artificially intelligent machines will eventually be able to interact with humans and other digital devices in real lingo. However, the lack of a widely accepted concept has not impeded the worldwide adoption of research into novel applications of AI.

The industry for artificial intelligent technology and computational systems has been steadily growing over the past the past few decades, as seen by the $27.5 bn spent globally on such technologies in 2019. It was anticipated by some organizations that the overall spending would amount to 80 bn USD by 2023. A thorough comprehension of the way artificial intelligence has been investigated and applied in a range of business disciplines such as processing, provisioning of services covering multidisciplinary areas like advertising, travel and tourism, behavioural studies, sociology, overall management, administration, etc., will be valuable for professionals in the field of AI. This is because studies pertaining to professional utilisation of Artificial Intelligence usually need an interdisciplinary viewpoint. Researchers would be able to concentrate their concerned investigating areas and users can be expected to generate wise choices (in the context of AI) in significant commercial issues features by using such in-depth knowledge [3].

It's fascinating to see that a number of researchers have taken steps to do a thorough research on AI regarding its application aspect in industry. In this regard, a number of academics map the dissemination phases of the deployment of information and analysis methodically and then suggest that additional studies be done at the time of after usage phase of AI. This issue had been primarily ignored when this research initially released. A 2014 study reviewed the literature on intelligence management in the sector of finance (banks) conducted since 2004 [26]. AI coding are implemented by corporate intelligence to do forecasting studies. When many authors analysed their decade's worth of investigation on the application of machine learning and AI technologies in the company, they found that the substantial number of papers highlighted the aforesaid tools and its implications. Lastly, an analysis of pertinent publications from the International Forum of IT Management was carried out by Dwivedi & others. Their objective was to give theoretical advances and AI implementation, while likewise highlighting concerns and obstacles related to the integration of artificial intelligence (AI) for governance in the big data age.

Although there have been many periods of enthusiasm surrounding AI over the past few decades, even detractors appear to agree that an AI tool, i.e., Chat-GPT, represents a significant revolution in every sphere. At the initial time automatic thinking was this significant, advances in visual computing led to achievements; this time, NLP is leading the way [8]. Not only can machine learning algorithms understand how to speak of actual pictures, programme code, and a wide range of different information kinds, but they may also acquire the vocabulary.

Artificial intelligence can be categorized as strong vs. weaker artificial intelligence. Weaker AI pushes other AI tools present scenario. This AI is also called a confined AI and it also allows the execution of various dynamic AI techniques like Image recognition, Siri, Robots, etc. AGI, also known as Artificial General Intelligence, and Algorithmic Super Intelligence referred to as ASI comprise Strong AI. General AI, also known as artificial general intelligence (AGI), is an applied field of artificial intelligence in which an automated system is endowed with human-level intellect. It possesses a mind of itself, awareness, and can deal with issues, gain knowledge, and make decisions later on [11]. Super intelligence, referred to as ASI, will be incomparable to the intellect of humans and their capacity. Even though there are currently no working proofs of strong AI, it remains only conceptual, that doesn't stop academics from studying its advancement. Simultaneously, technologically advanced imaginative characters like Robotic character R2D2, the super-human, wayward computer assisted from 2001, may provide the greatest illustrations of Artificial SI.

Despite the fact that artificial intelligence has been researched in academia and in science since mid-1960, technological advancement just recently started to gain considerable acceptance. It becomes imperative to mention here that studies on AI, financing, and real-world business possibilities are experiencing an unprecedented surge at the moment. GVR projects that the global AI market could reach $1,901.5 billion by 2032, growing at a 39.2% compounded annual growth rate. AI-based techniques assure the improvement of the quality of life altogether as well as yield better business results. Here in the Figure 10.2 are a few areas of Application of AI in our country and around the globe.

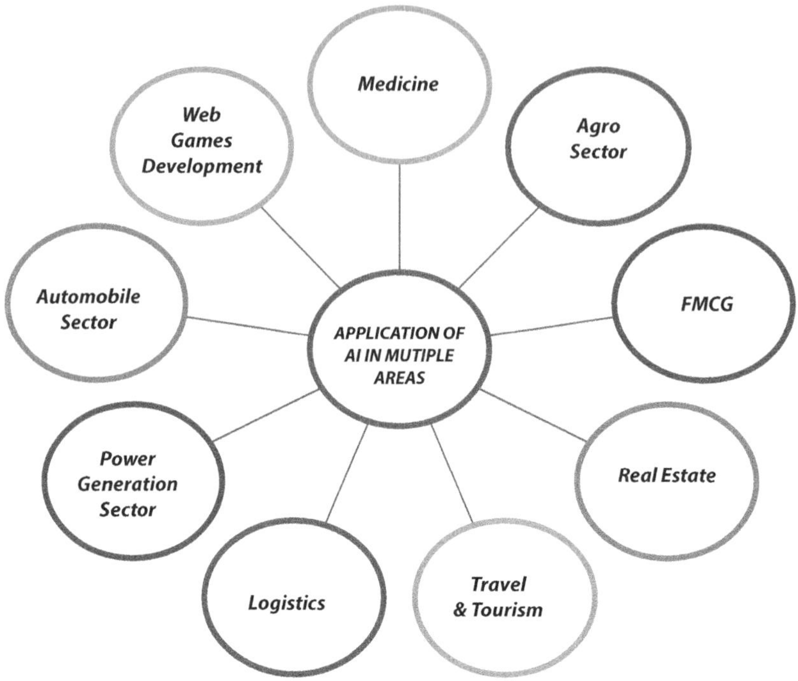

Figure 10.2 Application of AI in multiple areas.

Before delving into multifaceted ways that artificial intelligence (AI) innovations are impacting various industries, it is imperative to define the term artificial intelligence. The term AI is an encompassing concept that could be applied to any kind of programming system that engages in activities like acquiring knowledge, organising, and finding solutions that are equivalent to those done by individuals [23]. Our understanding of the potential uses for such techniques is still developing, and its applications are expanding daily. However, as the excitement surrounding AI's application to company operations grows, moral or ethical debates are increasingly crucial.

10.3 Concept of Ethics

Ethics is essentially a set of guidelines for conduct. They have an impact on the choices and experiences of individuals. Moral conduct, often known for being ethical enlightenment, is the study of what is best for humanity as a whole community [2]. The word comes from the foreign language-ethos, reflecting a practice, tradition, personality trait, or way of being.

The following puzzles fall under integrity:

- What constitutes the ideal lifestyle
- Moral rulings regarding appropriate versus inappropriate
- The terminology of positive and negative protocol
- Our duties and privileges

Our ideas on ethics have a base of various backgrounds, ideologies, and religious affiliations. They inject themselves into discussions about equality, humanity, and responsible behaviour.

Morality and ethical foundational aims are intimately linked concepts. Whereas it used to be more correct to speak about moral judgements or moral principles, it is now usual to make reference to moral assessments or ethical standards. The definition of ethics is expanded by these uses. In past purposes, the phrase did not relate to decency per se, but rather to the area of subject matter or field of investigation that deals with moral issues [19]. Ethics is the same as moral thought in the above regard. Ethics has long been considered a sub-field of ideal thinking, but because of its broad application, it also has connections with multiple other academic disciplines, such as life sciences, technological innovation, political theory, spirituality and the discipline of finance and economics. However, because ethics is not a subject of verifiable research in the same manner as the scientific fields and other fields of study, it continues to be different from such fields of study. Instead, it focuses on identifying the characteristics of theoretical norms and using this array of standards to solve real-world legal and morality problems [1]. Figure 10.3 shows some of the major generic ethical principles. Everything is changed by the efforts of technological experts. In order to behave with integrity, people ought to consider the broader effects

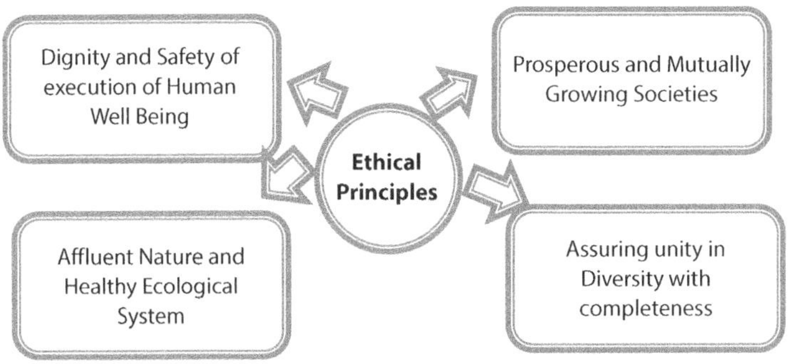

Figure 10.3 Values and ethics.

of their activity and actively boost the general welfare. The ethical benchmarks overall focus is on the essential humanitarian ethical conduct which should be extended to the behaviour exhibited by engineering professionals. The Rules of Morality is a framework for moral decision-making, not a method for resolving moral quandaries. An expert in the field may discover that, while considering a given problem, several theories need to be considered, together with applicability of distinct rules in accordance to diverse problems [26]. The best way to address matters of this nature is to meticulously examine the core ethic precepts, keeping in mind that the welfare of humanity is the most important factor. When the manner in which ethical choices are made is transparent to and responsible to all parties involved, the IT profession as a whole benefits. Conversations that are honest on moral matters encourages this openness and responsibility.

10.3.1 Standards of Morality and Integrity for Ethical Implementation of AI

10.3.1.1 Make a Positive Impact on Humanity and Human Welfare while Understanding that Everyone has an Interest in Computing

The aforementioned principle pertains to the well-being of all individuals and upholds the responsibility of computing experts, both on an individual and group level, to utilize their expertise for the betterment of society, its constituents, and the surrounding milieu. Promoting fundamental human rights and defending each person's right to autonomy are part of this duty [15]. Professionals in computing have a fundamental goal of reducing the harmful effects of computers, such as risks to one's health, safety, privacy, and personal security. The needs of the less fortunate should be prioritized and given more attention when the interests of several groups collide.

10.3.1.2 Avoid Destruction

Destruction in this document refers to unfavorable outcomes, particularly when they are severe and unfair. Unjustified bodily or mental pain, unjustified information disclosure or destruction, and unjustified harm to the environment, property, and reputation are a few examples of harm [3]. The first step in preventing harm is to carefully assess how decisions may affect everyone who may be impacted. It is the responsibility of those in charge of the system to make sure that any intentional injury is morally justifiable. Either way, make sure that the damage is kept to a lowest.

10.3.1.3 Be Straightforward and Constant

Being transparent is a must for being trustworthy. A professional in computers should be transparent and forthright, fully disclosing to the relevant parties all relevant system capabilities, limitations, and potential issues. The Code is broken by making willfully false or deceptive statements, creating or manipulating data, proposing or accepting bribes, and engaging in other dishonest behavior.

10.3.1.4 Deference to Confidentiality

Professionals working in computing have an especially strong need to protect privacy. Technology makes it possible to swiftly, affordably, and frequently without the affected parties' awareness gather, monitor, and share personal information. As a result, a professional in computers should familiarize themselves with the different meanings and interpretations of privacy as well as the rights and obligations that come with gathering and using private data.

10.3.1.5 Honour the Effort for Creating Original Concepts, Discoveries, Artistic Creations, and Technology Products

Value is created for society through the development of new concepts, inventions, artistic creations, and computer objects; individuals who invest in these endeavors should anticipate benefits from their labor [21]. Therefore, computing professionals should respect copyrights, patents, trade secrets, license agreements, and other measures to safeguard authors' works in addition to giving credit to the inventors of ideas, innovations, and works.

10.3.1.6 Respect Secrecy

Information such as proprietary information, clientele, accounting information, study findings, academic publications, and petitions for IPRs are frequently confided to technology specialists. Secrecy should be maintained by computing experts unless there is reason to believe that there is proof of a legal, managerial, or code infringement. In certain situations, the form of the data or origins should only be revealed to the correct officials. A computer expert ought to carefully assess the way these declarations align with the standards of Conduct.

10.3.2 Methods to Resolve Complexities Regarding Ethical Implications

10.3.2.1 Dilemma to Prioritise Code of Morality, Legislation and Supervising Body

Mental health professionals must identify the nature of the conflict, declare their commitment to the Ethics Code, and take reasonable action to resolve it in a way that complies with the General Principles and Ethical Standards of the Ethics Code if their ethical obligations conflict with any laws, regulations, or other governing legal authority. This norm cannot ever be used to support or legitimize the violation of human rights.

10.3.2.2 Dilemma Amongst Moral Principles and Directorial Weight-Age

If the demands of an organization with which mental health professionals are affiliated or for whom they are working are in conflict with this Ethics Code, mental health professionals clarify the nature of the conflict, make known their commitment to the Ethics Code, and take reasonable steps to resolve the conflict consistent with the General Principles and Ethical Standards of the Ethics Code [6]. Under no circumstances may this standard be used to justify or defend violating human rights.

10.3.2.3 Casual Resolution of Ethical Violations

In cases where mental health professionals suspect another psychologist of violating ethical standards, they try to address the matter by bringing it up with that person, provided that a casual resolution seems appropriate and that the intervention doesn't infringe on any potential confidentiality rights.

10.3.2.4 Informing Breach of Ethical Protocol

Mental health professionals take appropriate further action when an apparent ethical violation has caused substantial harm, or is likely to cause substantial harm, and is not appropriate for informal resolution under Standard 1.04, Informal Resolution of Ethical Violations, or is not resolved properly in that way. Referrals to state licensing boards, national committees on professional ethics, or relevant institutional authorities are a few possible destinations for such actions [7]. This criteria does not apply in situations where an intervention would violate a person's right to confidentiality or in situations where a psychologist has been hired to examine the work of another therapist whose behavior is under scrutiny.

10.3.2.5 Working in Alliance with Board of Ethics

Mental health professionals collaborate with one another in APA or any associated state psychological association's ethics investigations, processes, and ensuing requirements. They take care of any confidentiality concerns while doing so. Cooperation is in and of itself unethical. On the other hand, requesting that the resolution of an ethics complaint be postponed while the legal matter is being resolved does not in and of itself amount to non-abidance.

10.3.2.6 Unacceptable Objections

Mental health professionals do not file ethics complaints or support the filing of complaints that are made with deliberate ignorance of the facts that would refute the charge or with reckless disrespect for the law.

10.3.2.7 Unreasonable or Being Biased Regarding Petitioners and Defendants

Mental health professionals do not refuse people jobs, promotions, tenure, advancement, admittance to programs in academia or elsewhere, or anything else only because someone has filed an ethics complaint against them [5]. Ethical implications don't prohibit an individual's participation on the basis of available information or the results of proceedings.

10.4 AI Ethics

AI has emerged significantly on worldwide platforms exploring endless scope with an extensive coverage of multiple dimensions, like notable contributions in the field of medicine, recuperating productivity by upgraded mechanization and wide array of network through social tools in digital form [4]. The rising trend in AI also brings along the ethical side which is mandatorily required in every arena having AI execution. Challenges in AI ethical proposition are majorly related to its negative impact on macro environment, societal threats, and risks to the existence of individuality and sense of unfairness in any form. These negative impacts thus pose a danger to human life set specifically to certain socially weak groups.

This research also incorporates the learning from an appreciable report on AI by a global organization regarding its AI's ethical implications. The report is considered as an educative protocol in context to the ethical aspect of AI which has been acceptable at a global platform. This significant framework received unanimous approval from all 190 nations involved in November 2020 [25]. At its heart, the Recommendation prioritizes the safeguarding of human rights and dignity, promoting core principles like transparency, fairness, and the crucial need for human supervision of AI technologies. What distinguishes the Recommendation is its comprehensive set of Policy Action Areas. These areas provide a roadmap for policymakers to embody the foundational values and principles through practical measures in various fields, including data governance, environmental conservation, gender equality, education, research, health, and social welfare, among others.

The Recommendation is built upon four foundational values that aim to ensure AI technologies serve the best interests of humanity, individuals, communities, and the planet.

10.4.1 Standards Regarding Individual Rights Towards Protection and Human Secrecy in AI-Ethics

A few of the standards have been built concerning individual integrity towards AI moral principles.

10.4.1.1 Integrity & Protection

AI entities should mitigate and resolve potential safety hazards and security weaknesses. This applies to all individuals and organizations involved in any phase of the AI life cycle, including but not limited to research, creation, application, maintenance, commerce, funding, and eventual decommissioning [20].

10.4.1.2 Rights to Confidentiality in Information

The protection and enhancement of privacy should be a continuous effort throughout the AI life cycle. Establishing comprehensive data protection policies is essential.

10.4.1.3 Rationalisation without Any Damage

AI applications must be confined to what is strictly necessary for achieving valid objectives. Employing risk assessments can help in preventing potential damages arising from their use.

10.4.1.4 *Investors, Alliance and Coordination with Supervision*

Adaptive Governance and Collaboration: Adherence to international laws and the sovereignty of nations regarding data governance is crucial, with regulation permissible over data created or transiting through their domains. Engaging a broad spectrum of stakeholders ensures a more inclusive approach to AI supremacy.

10.4.1.5 *Fulfilment of Duties and Answerability*

It is critical that AI systems are designed to be auditable and traceable, with proper oversight, impact evaluations, audits, and due diligence processes in place to prevent human rights violations and protect the welfare of society as a whole.

10.4.1.6 *Precision and Justification*

The ethical use of AI hinges on the clarity and comprehensibility of these systems. Stakeholders should be informed when AI influences decision-making. The degree of Precision and Justification must be balanced with the need for protection, integrity and confidentiality [2].

10.4.1.7 *Individual or Manual Omission and Presence of Mind*

It is imperative that human beings retain final dependability and answerability over AI systems, ensuring that technology does not override human governance.

10.4.1.8 *Survival with Efficiency*

The evaluation of AI technologies must consider their long-term environmental and societal impacts, aligning with evolving sustained objectives, including those outlined in the concerned global vision of environment welfare.

10.4.1.9 *Attentiveness and Education*

Enhancing communal comprehension of AI and data through widespread education, community involvement, training in digital competencies and AI ethics, as well as fostering media and information awareness, is vital.

10.4.1.10 Equality and Unbiased

Individuals and organizations involved in AI should advocate for equity, justice, and impartiality, adopting an inclusive strategy to ensure the equitable distribution of AI advantages across society [10].

10.4.2 Plan of Action for Ethical Augmentation and Its Execution in AI may Include the Mentioned Policy Framework

Though foundational values and principles lay the groundwork for any ethical AI system, there has been a growing emphasis on the importance of transitioning from abstract principles to actionable approaches. The Recommendation effectively addresses this by identifying eleven critical policy action domains.

10.4.2.1 Ethics First & Responsibility

AI governance structures have to be open, interdisciplinary, collaborative, and inclusive of many participants. Put differently, not only should professionals from many fields be involved in the management of AI, but also communities that will be affected by it. Furthermore, administration needs to encompass foresight, compliance, and remedy in addition to being limited to suggestions.

10.4.2.2 Economical & Employment Aspects

The effects of AI systems on job markets should be taken into account and attempted to be regulated by the national governments [7]. To narrow the achievement gap, research relating to AI should be required at every level of learning. Subsequently, it will increase productivity in the marketplace and guarantee customer safety both domestically and globally.

10.4.2.3 Database Regulations

To protect individual privacy and provide appropriate data governance, nations that join should put in place procedures for gathering information and manner to supervise its implementation.

10.4.2.4 Analytical Study and Learning

Countries that participate ought to give individuals sufficient comprehension of artificial intelligence instruction, including data education campaigns. Prioritising the involvement of disadvantaged groups ought to serve as a key component of this. Nation-states must support legal artificial intelligence studies as well.

10.4.2.5 Wellness and Societal Prosperity

Nation-states ought to strive to use AI to enhance overall wellness and address threats to universal welfare. AI in medical and cognitive soundness should be controlled to ensure that it is secure, efficient, productive, and supported by science. Furthermore, concerned nations ought to support studies on how AI affects people's intellectual fitness and welfare.

10.4.2.6 Non-Discrimination in Males & Females

While avoiding any chance for AI to worsen inequality between males and females, member states should maximise AI's ability to promote gender equality. Resources specifically designated for policies that embrace females to be considered in all career fields [14].

10.4.2.7 Environmental & Natural Eco-Systems

Corporations and nations that participate must consider the immediate and long-term implications of artificial intelligence (AI) technologies on the environment, taking into account the systems' embodied carbon levels, power usage, and depletion of essential elements. In order to guarantee that artificial intelligence (AI) tools are deployed to help diagnosis, avoidance, regulation, and alleviation of issues in context to ecological environment, nation-states are supposed to, where appropriate, also offer subsidies.

10.4.3 Two Logical Methods Adopted by UNESCO to Make Certain the Effectiveness in Policies Framed for AI Ethics [27]

10.4.3.1 Framework for Assessing Willingness

FAW is intended to assist in determining whether the countries involved are equipped to carry out the proposal in an efficient manner. The method can consider the following sub areas:

a) Framing and execution of legislation governing AI;
b) Widespread availability of machine learning technology get the backing of the country's facilities.

The goal of this activity is that by using this technique, nations involved will be able to assess their level of competence and UNESCO will be able to better customise its aid for further developing the structure. It might also be applied to assist the concerned countries in creating a plan for the moral advancement and application of AI.

10.4.3.2 Analysis of Ethical Outcomes

An organised procedure, i.e., analysis of outcome of ethical executions (leading to implementation of proposals), assists AI developers discover and evaluate potential effects of artificial intelligence (AI) technologies while interacting with those impacted by them.

a) Persons who are anticipated to suffer from the negative effects of AI techniques. The manner in which these effects will manifest are also to be covered in the analysis.
b) Resources that are set aside for hazard mitigation and the steps that may be taken to stop these negative impacts.

The intent of ethical impact analysis is to give consideration to the possible effects of a technique using artificial intelligence and to determine the necessary steps to avoid damage from occurring. In order to transform the suggestions into norms and practices, UNESCO coordinates with administrations, companies, universities, and social groupings.

10.4.4 The Multidimensional Implementation Strategy Includes Such Elements As

10.4.4.1 The Worldwide Surveyors: This element in the field of AI ethical conduct is a cutting-edge online resource that acts as a central location for the most recent research on moral growth and deployment of AI widely as well as for insights produced by the execution of proposals in many nations.

10.4.4.2 The International Council on AI ethical Framework: This council is an exceptional levels periodic gathering that aims to promote collaborative knowledge sharing among nations along with multiple participants while furthering our understanding of the issues brought out by the use of artificial intelligence (AI).

10.4.4.3 The Community for Expertise in AI Ethical Framework Across Nation Frontiers: It is a versatile resource of professionals available for mobilisation in nations around the world on an ongoing basis to support the use of the enhancing skilled tools and the execution of the suggestion made.

10.4.4.4 Females' Role in AI deployment: It is an alliance, and is a forum for powerful female administrators or managers in organisations, politics, and society at large, who are advancing the cause of equal treatment for women in and *via* AI.

10.5 AI Ethics in Business

Rather than taking the place of human intelligence and creativity, artificial intelligence augments it. While AI is slower than the human brain at processing and analysing vast volumes of data, it is not as good at simple tasks. After that, AI software might provide people with synthesized activities. Thus, AI can facilitate decision-making by assisting in the prediction of each action's result. It's software that works autonomously and in ways that its creators never intended [9]. More decisions can be made by AI than by conventional software. Artificial Intelligence is beneficial in many areas, such as assisting guests and employees in navigating business websites, tracking wind turbines, and predicting maintenance needs.

10.5.1 AI Techniques Implementation Aspects in Various Business Dimensions

10.5.1.1 Refining the Service Quality to End Users

Chatbots may be the most common means by which customers engage directly with Artificial Intelligence. The frequency of these kinds of interactions is rising. Businesses can use chatbots to automate a lot of the processes required in customer support, freeing up staff members' time to work on issues that require more specialized attention. Chatbot technology can also help clients by forwarding their inquiries to a real-life employee who is more qualified to respond to them.

10.5.1.2 Provisioning of Advice in Context to Multiple Products Offered

Businesses can use AI to suggest products to customers that will meet their demands and maintain their interest in what they have to offer. If you pay attention to how your consumers behave on your website, you can offer them products that are similar to ones they have already seen. Businesses in the e-commerce sector could gain a great deal from applying this tactic. Personalized recommendations are demonstrated through streaming services. By displaying titles that are comparable to the entertainment programs and shows one has seen any number of times, telecasting companies have the skill to keep you using their app for an extended time [18].

10.5.1.3 Bifurcating the Target People

Advertising departments can use AI to categorize people into different groups and create campaigns that are tailored to those groups, much like how product suggestions are made.

10.5.1.4 Analysing the Customer Satisfaction & Contentment for Products Offered

Businesses use sentiment analysis, commonly referred to as emotion artificial intelligence, as a technique to assess customer responses. Through the application of machine learning and artificial intelligence, organizations can get information about how customers perceive their brand. The application of artificial intelligence to search through social media posts, reviews, and ratings that mention the brand is one instance of this.

10.5.1.5 Detecting Scam

AI tools additionally help companies spot possible fraud cases and create efficient defences against them. There are now available solutions in the banking and finance sector that can recognize possibly fraudulent transactions through the use of several kinds of machine learning algorithms.

10.5.1.6 Logistics & Supply Chain Works Seamlessly

If your company is having problems consistently reaching its product delivery dates, AI could be able to help. Businesses may benefit from AI-driven solutions in a number of ways, such as estimating the cost of materials and shipping and how quickly products will be able to move through the supply chain [13].

10.5.1.7 Hierarchical Model for Analysing AI in Business

The model depicting the ethical parameters in Business has been framed by analysing the ethical levels in accordance to their importance. Thus, **"Principled AI"** marks the beginning of the model at the top of the hierarchy. The methods for achieving this highest-order ethical behaviour are then provided in the second tier of the framework. In particular, it implies that having both **"Dependability"** and **"Answerability"** is necessary for ethics. Our method examines two areas: accountability for final outcomes and responsibility for the way you carry out your responsibilities and behave in general. According to our approach, ethical AI in business should meet the requirements for both accountable results and responsible methods. The following layer of the framework showing the hierarchical model of AI in business is exhibited in Figure 10.4 illustrates how **"Human-Based," "Transparency," and "Safety"** are affected by dependability in business. And more specifically, the way to accomplish these ends is provided by the following set of guidelines in our hierarchy. For instance, "Human-Based" incorporates the idea of beneficence in addition to being accomplished through clear, understandable, and sustainable methods. Procedures that fall within the categories of justice, inclusivity, and non-discrimination are referred to as "transparency." Conversely, "safety" solutions are secure, reliable, and personal. In our paradigm, "Answerability" is composed of several principles and actions, including positive management, controlling, correcting, and legal responsibility. Even if there are more theories and ethical notions, they will always make sense as parts of one of these three primary fundamental principles or even as a part of responsibility itself. After that, our organization offers a condensed and streamlined perspective on the area of AI ethics

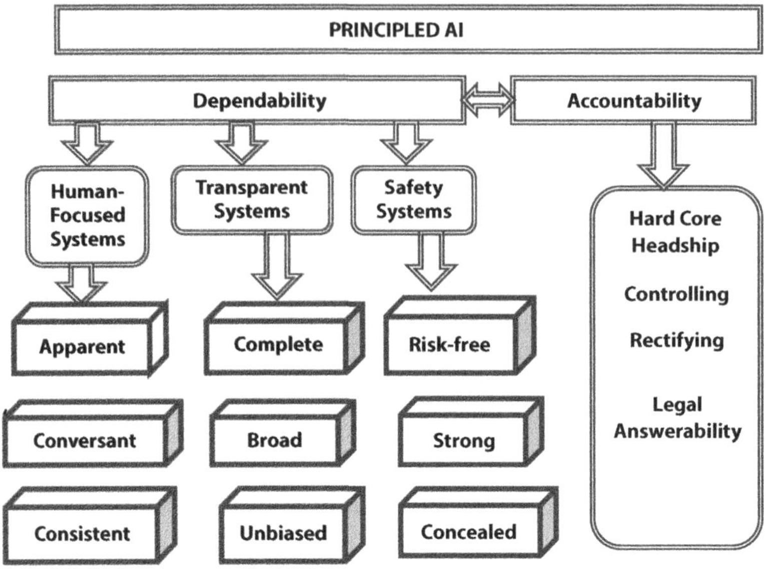

Figure 10.4 Hierarchical model for analysing AI in business.

for commercial applications, enabling us to develop procedures and oversight frameworks to guarantee morally sound procedures and results.

Because it was a major theme in our NLP analysis of the corpus of literature on AI ethics in business, "accountable" merits special emphasis. Although the idea is frequently discussed in legal and regulatory texts, business-related publications tend to focus much less on it. In that regard, the topic of being held legally responsible for the results of AI processes would be discussed in order to be held accountable. And although it is certainly an aspect of reliability, the concept of credibility is significantly more nuanced and substantial than this suggests. It is made even harder by regional regulatory fluctuations and the connections that occur involving the customer and the source of AI technology. Governance is especially related to planning for eventualities, inventive considering, and repercussions recognition in the field of industry and modern artificial intelligence (AI) research. These traits guarantee that the organisation is accountable for each concerned person at all levels.

10.5.2 Steps to Assure Ethical Application of AI in Business

To ensure the ethical use of AI technologies, your organization must establish AI ethics. It necessitates comprehending the moral and legal ramifications of applying AI, creating a set of guidelines for its application, and setting up governance frameworks to guarantee answerability for AI implementation.

The ways mentioned below elaborate as to how companies can frame out the most effectual structure for AI supervision.

10.5.2.1 *Assessment of Legality & Humanitarian Principles*

AI tools and techniques can't be taken in isolation. It has to be accompanied with the assessment of legality attached to it, which is required for its ethical mandate. There are many laws to be followed in AI for assuring confidentiality and safety of data. Moreover, any unfairness or predispositions for AI data should also be avoided.

10.5.2.2 *Establishment of New Set of Protocols for Ethical Execution*

Before the execution of applications in the field of ArtificialIntelligence, it has to be made sure that the ethical protocols related to it are studied and then applied [17]. Various moral elements of business like justice in functioning; clearness, safety of information and answerability have to assured in these ethical set of rules. If the ethical set of AI is formulated effectively, then there would be sorted communication regarding performance of job duties in any business.

10.5.2.3 *Regulating the Ethical Implications in AI*

Regulations of all the minute aspects of AI and its application tools are highly required to be done at the end of any firm, which in turn, would also be supportive in AI growth. To guarantee this regulation, a company can also form a particular group of members or experts, who all can anticipate the threats related to present technological systems [16]. All these members can examine the desired deliverables of AI tools in business settings. Additionally, a company can also go for analysing the reviews from employees in the context of AI ethical regulations.

10.5.2.4 *Spreading Awareness amongst Employees*

It is always in the well-being of a firm to spread the awareness about the AI ethics and repercussions of having unethical use of AI in any sphere of business. Through this, employees can be made more particular about assuring ethical use of AI tools. Frequent periodical checks on AI processing tools techniques to be done and must be immediately addressed if anything suspicious is identified in any form.

10.5.3 Ethical Execution of AI in Companies - Benefits

- Assuring Safety: AI ethical execution in any business assures its concerned members about safety from anticipated threats of AI.
- Secrecy is Guaranteed: On the basis of ethical usage of AI techniques, companies can make assurance for righteousness in their computational inferences, considering accuracy in their inputs. This accuracy is the foundation built on ethical values, like safety and confidentiality of information used in AI coding.
- Positive Market Image: Customers feels more safe when the companies, whose services they are availing, are actually making protected use of AI tools (in ethical abidance) to facilitate the consumers. This also enhances a firm's goodwill.
- Avoidance of Legal Costs and Hassles: Companies, if they make sure the ethical use of AI techniques in multiple domains, can significantly contribute towards the mitigation of its lawful expenditure. Firms many times face legal hardships due to unethical AI execution that also harms their market positioning. So, ethical AI usage avoids this cost at company's end.
- Competitive Advantage: Establishing unambiguous policies on AI ethics gives companies an advantage over those who don't take these matters seriously. By showcasing ethical development processes, you can increase the likelihood that customers will trust your company with their data.

10.6 AI Ethics in Medicine

AI functioning in medicinal science, such as imaging and digital medicinal documents and testing, lab testing and examination, physician acumen augmentation, novel generic chemical invention, biomedical massive data investigation, operational momentum, safeguarding and personalised healthcare, and document storage and access for health organizations, have radically transformed the medical field [26]. But there are a number of moral and legal issues that this scientific sector must deal with. Even though artificial intelligence (AI) has advanced tremendously in communities and has the potential to improve treatment outcomes, not all cultures can afford it.

Various emerging and lesser per capita nations still lack admittance to the newest technology [28]. It must be highlighted that there are a number of difficulties that arise while utilizing AI, including moral conundrums space to individual and information confidentiality, learned consent, societal loopholes, sympathy, and kindness. These challenges or issues of AI in healthcare are listed below.

10.6.1 Information Secrecy & Integrity

Concerned issues in this context are mentioned as

- The laws in place for healthcare do not go far enough in protecting a person's health information.
- Robotic data collection can be compromised and utilized for malevolent intents that compromise security and privacy.
- Certain social media platforms collect and retain substantial volumes of user information, such as mental health records, without obtaining agreement from users. This information can be advantageous for the companies' marketing, promotion, and sales.

10.6.2 Answerability and Dependability in Decisiveness with AI Tools

The control problem with AI is one of the related difficulties in determining accountability, since AI-guided systems operate independently of their developers and may change in ways that the developer may argue were not anticipated [3]. As a result, developers and designers of AI may not be held accountable. This leads to a responsibility gap that may unfairly burden the person who was harmed, the clinician, or any other healthcare professional who uses the technology but was not engaged in its creation.

10.6.3 Societal Glitches and Righteousness

Another concern that affects society with the emergence of AI is the societal gap issue. The problems include the fact that as robots advance, many people lose their jobs. As automated systems proliferate, bookkeepers and managers throughout many communities may find themselves without employment and their pay will likely decline significantly. Their future employment prospects are threatened by the emergence of robotic nurses and surgical robots in the healthcare industry, which operate in place of surgeons and provide patient care in place of nurses [23].

10.6.4 Motivation, Emotional Support with Medicinal Discussion

Artificial intelligence (AI) integration with all aspects of healthcare appears challenging and unachievable [22]. Medical robots and humans may not evolve simultaneously in the near future due to the distinct emotions that humans possess. Related concerns include:

- Children typically feel scared or anxious when they interact with healthcare providers and other experts. The new robotic medicine system may make their erratic behaviour, such as hostility, disengagement, and lack of collaboration, uncontrollable.
- Patients with serious mental illnesses may be negatively impacted by the employment of medical robots in cognitive consultation [30].

10.6.5 Ways to Improve AI Ethical Dimensions in Medicine

10.6.5.1 Safeguarding Information about Individuals

The gathering and use of health information in powered by artificial intelligence healthcare raises multiple related moral questions. As an instance, in order to shield patients from the harmful effects of privacy violations and unlawful usage, personal and clinical data privacy and protection must be guaranteed [21].

Patients should also be given the choice of leaving out and be informed regarding the way their details are going to processed by AI systems. It is not appropriate to infer that patients understand the risks associated with submitting their info with artificial intelligence (AI) platforms.

10.6.5.2 Advance the Public Interest, Security of People, and Wellness

AI technology ought not to jeopardise humans. Prior to deployment, they must meet all assurance, precision and utility regulations; moreover, surveillance and maintenance procedures must be established [24]. Therefore, in order to make sure AI technologies function as intended and to determine how they have any negative effects on certain patients or sections, financiers, creators, and users possess an ongoing obligation to test and track the functioning of AI models.

10.6.5.3 Assure Honesty, and Understanding

Software engineers, consumers, and lawmakers must be able to comprehend and make sense of artificial intelligence. Enhancing AI technology's comprehensibility and disclosure are two major ways to guarantee understanding. Honesty demands that enough data, as outlined, be released or recorded prior to the application and execution of a particular AI tool. Honesty will safeguard medical and community safety as well as enhance the overall excellence of the medical system as a whole. In the case of government controllers, they depend on disclosure to carry out appropriate, efficient supervision, while computer examiners depend on it to find faults.

10.6.5.4 Foster Inclusivity and Equity

Inclusivity demands that AI applications in healthcare are designed to promote widespread and fair usage and accessibility, irrespective of demographic factors such as age, gender, income, or ability [19]. It's imperative for institutions, be they companies, regulatory bodies, or healthcare systems, to employ individuals from diverse backgrounds, cultures, and disciplines to develop, oversee, and implement Artificial-Intelligence technologies. Furthermore, development and evaluation processes of AI should actively involve stakeholders, doctors, medical teams, and patients for diverse representation [29].

10.6.5.5 Advocate for Approachable and Efficient Artificial Intelligence

Responsiveness dictates that programmers, experts and end users continuously and evidently assess AI tools to ensure they meet required standards and adapt to the evolving needs of their operational environment. This necessitates a systematic approach to identifying healthcare needs and deploying suitable AI solutions to serve the civic welfare in healthiness preservation and safety effectively.

10.7 AI Ethics in Education

It is quite likely the scenario that ethical considerations like enhancing children' academic achievement and chances for a lifetime drive the use of artificial intelligence in educational events. Nevertheless, as good intents do not always translate into ethical models or implementations as has been shown in other AI usage fields, moral purposes alone are insufficient [15]. Understanding what it signifies being legitimate, particularly in light of the use of AI in learning, requires careful consideration. The educational circumstances that AI aims to improve emphasise the necessity of understanding and making ethical pedagogical decisions, distinguishing between carrying out things with integrity and doing them responsibly, taking into account the perpetual potential of unexpected repercussions, among numerous other factors.

- Issues of anonymity, monitoring liberty, discrimination in light of the various types of unfairness and moral dilemmas of applications that use artificial intelligence in educational contexts will also be considered. It is essential to recognise, nevertheless, that teachers face a variety of moral disputes and issues based on the standard in which a student reads and stage of growth of their pupils [11].
- Regarding the employment of machine learning in schooling from kindergarten to grade twelve, one of the most important ethical questions is how to protect instructors' and students' privacy. The primary cause of confidentiality infringement is when users reveal too many details about themselves on websites.
- The incorporation of AI in elementary through high school raises further legal issues around the use of tracing or monitoring tools that collect extensive data on the interests and activities of instructors and pupils [8]. In addition to being viewed as a means of instruction to take action in risky electronically driven situations like internet harassment or encounters with abusive content, observing and guarding online behaviour of students can also be viewed as monitoring mechanisms, which pose a privacy threat to students.
- Freedom-related problems also arise when spying methods incite them. Projection mechanisms, driven by computational methods, put instructors' and learners' independence and self-governance in danger. Equality and individual

autonomy are questioned when machines are used to forecast behaviour of others based on their knowledge [4].

- Lastly, prejudice and biased considerations are important issues to consider when discussing AI ethics in schools from kindergarten to twelve [12]. Cultural prejudices and hierarchy of power that now exist are ingrained in neural network models on artificial intelligence (AI) systems. Arguably the most obvious manifestations of this issue is gender bias, which is shown when linguistic course students utilise artificial intelligence in converting amongst a dialect of the language that is more or less a feminine inclination.

10.8 Conclusion

The research as described basically reflects the AI ethics with multifaceted dimensions in the context of analysing Artificial Intelligence in various sectors like business, education and medicine. The study began with analysing the conceptual part of AI technology, and its applications in the present scenario. It becomes imperative to also study the ethics in AI implementation. Therefore, the principles of ethics have also been examined in general along with their relevance to the application of AI tools. The horizon of AI ethics has been analysed by understanding its significance in various sectors. In business, AI has numerous significant usages but at the same time the ethics of AI cannot be ignored. A hierarchical model and framework of principles of AI has also been studied for examining AI ethics in business. Values like answerability, safety, dependability, human-centric, consistent and completeness certainly bears an importance in all the businesses, and assuring the obedience to all these values together with AI execution in business becomes a strong foundation for growth of industry as a whole. Companies are also taking various steps to ensure AI strict monitoring in a legal sense. Advantages of the ethical aspect of AI in a corporate sector have also been considered in the present research. Functioning of AI in the field of science evidenced great escalation in the health sector in terms of effective diagnosis, rapid and accurate testing, massive information storage, health data retrieval, enhancing inventions and researches in developing medical fields. Having inferred that morality and integrity maintenance of AI in this area is also mandatory, various ethical confrontations regarding AI in the dimension of medicine has also been understood in the research, like, integrity and security of information, reliability of AI techniques, and lack of emotional quotient in AI automated system (required for medical counselling). This can be improvised by guaranteeing the safety of the patient's data, their wellness, honesty in execution of AI techniques, provisioning of justice and fairness amongst all, and meting the protocols of AI in an appropriate manner. The AI role in education is evident globally but its ethical dimension is essential in this field as well. Ethical infringements, namely, non-abidance of anonymity, unfairness, privacy, freedom issues, biased conduct, restraining the intellect of students, etc., needs serious attention and thus necessary actions for qualitative growth in education by appropriate use of AI in this sector. Thus, the chapter focuses and elaborates the journey overview of artificial intelligence starting with the basic gist of AI to its ethical aspects in multifaceted dimensions in context to diverse critical sectors globally.

References

1. *Duck Duck Go Blog: Ethical, by design: how we design with your privacy in mind*, https://www.spreadprivacy.com/ethical-by-design/. Accessed 30 Aug 2020.
2. Jobin, A., Ienca, M., Vayena, E., *Artificial Intelligence: the global landscape of ethics guidelines*, 2019, https://www.arxiv.org/ftp/arxiv/papers/1906/1906.11668.pdf. Accessed 12 Aug 2020.
3. Leveson, N.G., *Engineering a Safer World: Systems Thinking Applied to Safety (Engineering Systems)*, The MIT Press, Cambridge, 2012.
4. Aiken, R.M. and Epstein, R.G., Ethical guidelines for AI in education: Starting a conversation. *Int. J. Artif. Intell. Educ.*, 11, 163–176, 2000.
5. Friedman, B. and Kahn, P.H., Jr., Human agency and responsible computing: Implications for computer system design. *J. Syst. Software*, 17, 1, 7–14, 1992.
6. Holmes, W., Bektik, D., Whitelock, D., Woolf, B.P., Ethics in AIED:Who Cares?, in: *Artificial Intelligence in Education*, vol. 10948, Rosé, C.P., Martínez-Maldonado, R., Hoppe, H.U., Luckin, R., Mavrikis, M., Porayska-Pomsta, K., McLaren, B., Du Boulay, B. (Eds.), pp. 551–553, 2018.
7. Schelenz, L., Segal, A., Gal, K., Best practices for transparency in machine generated personalization, in: *Adjunct Publication of the 28th ACM Conference on User Modeling, Adaptation and Personalization*, pp. 23–28, 2020.
8. UNESCO, *Artificial Intelligence in Education: Challenges and Opportunities for Sustainable Development*, 2019.
9. Porayska-Pomsta, K. and Rajendran, G., Accountability in human and artificial intelligence decision-making as the basis for diversity and educational inclusion, in: *Artificial Intelligence and Inclusive Education: Speculative Futures and Emerging Practices*, Knox, J., Wang, Y., Gallagher, M. (Eds.), pp. 39–59, 2019.

10. Drachsler, H. and Greller, W., Privacy and analytics: It's a DELICATE issue a checklist for trusted learning analytics, in: *Proceedings of the Sixth International Conference on Learning Analytics & Knowledge*, pp. 89–98, 2016, http://dl.acm.org/citation.cfm?id=2883893.
11. Labarthe, H., Luengo, V., Bouchet, F., Analyzing the relationships between learning analytics, educational data mining and AI for education, in: *ITS 2018 Workshop Proceedings*, Guin, N. and Kumar, A. (Eds.), pp. 63–71, 2018.
12. Zeiler, M.D. and Fergus, R., Visualizing and understanding convolutional networks, in: *European Conference on Computer Vision*, Springer, pp. 818–33, 2014.
13. Awad, E., *et al.*, The moral machine experiment. *Nat.*, 563, 7729, 59–64, 2018.
14. Floridi, L. and Sanders, J.W., On the morality of artificial agents. *Mines Mach.*, 14, 3, 349–79, 2004.
15. Moor, J., The Nature, Importance, and Difficulty of Machine Ethics. *IEEE Intell. Syst.*, 21, 18–21, 2006.
16. Benjamin, R., Race after technology: Abolitionist tools for the new Jim Code, in: *Social Forces*, 2019.
17. Arksey, H. and O'Malley, L., Scoping studies: towards a methodological framework. *Int. J. Social Res. Methodol.*, 8, 1, 19–32, 2005.
18. Ryffel, T., *A Generic Framework for Privacy Preserving Deep Learning*, 2018, arXiv preprint arXiv:1811.04017.
19. Adams, A., Report of a debate on Snowden's actions by ACM members. *SIGCAS Comput. Soc.*, 44, 3, 5–7, 2014.
20. Walther, J., Research ethics in internet-enabled research: Human subjects issues and methodological myopia. *Ethics Inf. Technol.*, 4, 3, 205–216, 2002.
21. Erhan, D., Bengio, Y., Courville, A., Vincent, P., *Visualizing Higher-Layer Features of a Deep Network*, vol. 1341, p. 3, University of Montreal, 2009.
22. Simonyan, K., Vedaldi, A., Zisserman, A., *Deep inside convolutional networks: Visualising image classification models and saliency maps*, 2013, arXiv preprint arXiv:1312.6034.
23. Ramesh, A.N., Kambhampati, C., Monson, J.R.T., Drew, P.J., Artificial intelligence in medicine. *Ann. R. Coll. Surg. Engl.*, 86, 5, 334–338, 2004.
24. Amato, F., López, A., Peña-Méndez, E.M., Vaňhara, P., Hampl, A., Havel, J., Artificial neural networks in medical diagnosis. *J. Appl. Biomed.*, 11, 2, 47–58, 2013.
25. Bennett, C.C. and Hauser, K., Artificial intelligence framework for simulating clinical decision-making: a Markov decision process approach. *Artif. Intell. Med.*, 57, 1, 9–19, 2013.
26. Dilsizian, S.E. and Siegel, E.L., Artificial intelligence in medicine and cardiac imaging: harnessing big data and advanced computing to provide personalized medical diagnosis and treatment. *Curr. Cardiol. Rep.*, 16, 1, 441, 2014.
27. https://unesdoc.unesco.org/ark:/48223/pf0000385082.page=4.
28. Zhang, Y., *et al.*, Improving college ideological and political education based on deep learning. *Int. J. Inf. Commun. Technol.*, 24, 4, 431–447, 2024.

29. Soni, T., *et al.*, Explicability of artificial intelligence in healthcare 5.0, in: *2023 International Conference on Artificial Intelligence and Smart Communication (AISC)*, IEEE, 2023.
30. Dhall, A., *et al.*, Machine Learning Algorithms for Industry Using Image Sensing, in: *Healthcare Solutions Using Machine Learning and Informatics*, pp. 75–97, Auerbach Publications, 2022.

11

Case Study on Soil Identification for Insecticides and Fertilizer Recommendation Using IoT and Deep Learning: An Ethical Approach in Smart Agriculture 4.0

Richa Singh[1]* and Rekha Kashyap[2]

[1]*Dept. of CSE (AI), KIET Group of Institutions, Muradnagar, Ghaziabad, UP, India*
[2]*Dept. of CSE (AIML), KIET Group of Institutions, Muradnagar, Ghaziabad, UP, India*

Abstract
Smart farming is a promising approach to agriculture that uses technology to optimize crop production and increase efficiency. One of the key challenges in smart farming is the selection of the appropriate insecticide and fertilizer for a given crop. This paper presents an ethical approach for soil identification and recommendation for a fertilizer system based on a Convolutional Neural Network for smart farming in agriculture 4.0. Soil identification is performed by sensors and data is collected by Raspberry Pi using Arduino. The collected samples are divided into two classes, and with the help of CNN, it correctly classified the infected and normal crops. The result shows that the confidence level is 96%, which recommends the ratio of fertilizer needs to be added. The accuracy of the proposed work is approximately 81.2%, which gives a good solution in the smart agriculture domain.

Keywords: Smart agriculture, CNN, recommendation system, Arduino, Raspberry Pi

**Corresponding author*: rsrinet.876@gmail.com

Sapna Juneja, Rajesh Kumar Dhanaraj, Abhinav Juneja, Malathy Sathyamoorthy and Asadullah Shaikh (eds.) Ethical Decision-Making Using Artificial Intelligence: Challenges, Solutions and Applications, (259–282) © 2025 Scrivener Publishing LLC

11.1 Introduction

The search for efficient and sustainable agricultural methods has become critical in modern agriculture. The need for food production in the agricultural sector is rising due to the growing global population, which calls for creative ways to maximize crop yields while reducing environmental effects. One of the biggest issues facing agriculture is the presence of insect pests. According to a report by the Food and Agriculture Organization (FAO), these pests result in an annual loss of crop yield of 20–40% worldwide. The annual cost of invading insects and pest infestations to the world economy is estimated to be roughly US$70 billion and $220 billion, respectively. To improve crop quality and storage life, farmers employ a wide range of pesticides. However, long-term usage of these pesticides led to environmental contamination, increased risk of high-risk illnesses like cancer, severe respiratory and genetic disorders, and eventually, fatal mortality. As a result, cutting-edge technological solutions are crucial in agriculture to identify plant pests early and prevent unnecessary pesticide usage. To achieve precision control of crop diseases, fertilization, irrigation, and plant pests in the farm field, smart agriculture has recently been introduced. It applies artificial intelligence (AI) techniques, information, and wireless communication technologies, such as the Internet of Things (IoT), to all aspects of agriculture. The primary use of smart agriculture is thought to be crop health monitoring, which establishes the condition of the farm about plant pests. However, due to their intricate structures and high degree of similarity, agricultural pest classification presents a difficult problem for farmers. Furthermore, the conventional manual method of identifying insect pests is costly, time-consuming, and ineffective. However, farmers can effectively stop the spread of these insects by using the right insecticides if they identify plant pests at an early stage of infection. Consequently, in order to address the aforementioned issues in the agricultural sector, computer vision systems and image processing utilizing artificial intelligence methods, such as machine learning and artificial neural networks, have been extensively used in prior research.

In entomology, image-based pest identification has been proposed for several applications, such as insect counting as a biodiversity measure. Convolutional neural networks (CNNs), a deep learning technique, have been used recently in agriculture as an effective way to automatically classify crop pests. CNNs work directly with raw pixels and have their feature generator, in contrast to machine learning and conventional image processing techniques. Additionally, CNNs have demonstrated their resilience

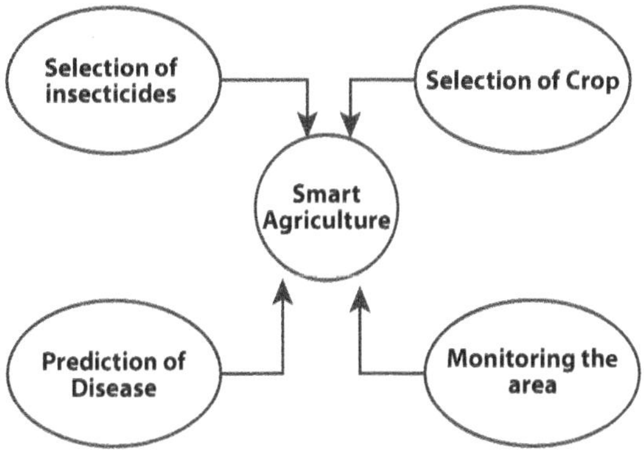

Figure 11.1 Domain-specific challenges in smart agriculture.

in managing image noise and lighting fluctuations in numerous medical image analysis applications, mechanical intelligent defect diagnosis, and infrastructure fracture identification in construction.

A faster region-based convolutional neural network (Faster R-CNN) is a comprehensive deep CNN that combines feature detection, candidate regional generation, regional image categorization, and position refinement for target recognition and identification in pictures. Still, there are various challenges in smart farming as shown in Figure 11.1.

Different sectors or domains of smart agriculture can tackle the challenges that are mentioned in Figure 11.1. All the challenges can be resolved by using various emerging technologies [1]. AI is very popular nowadays just because of its prompt response and real-time solutions. Various techniques are also integrated with AI to give better solutions for real-life problems. In the field of AI, machine learning and deep learning can also solve problems based on soil identification, crop identification, analysis, insecticides and pest recommendations, and many more. These recent technologies altered the solution of traditional agriculture methods and its solutions. These technologies change the conventional approach of agriculture in a smart approach. Smart recommendation systems that are implemented in smart agriculture for pest identification and insecticide recommendation provide a revolutionary approach in agriculture and technology sector. Now, there is a substantial shift from the traditional approach to decision-making systems by emerging technologies. The nexus of smart agriculture and technology move to a deep learning approach that also provides benchmark results. This gives a large hope to the farmers for better productivity of the crops. As the technology emerges there is another concept of deep learning, i.e., Convolutional Neural Networks (CNN), which also contributes to the nexus of the agriculture and technology sectors [2]. In contemporary farming, the decision to use pesticides and fertilizers according to the crops and the agricultural land is very important because it directly impacts various factors such as the life and health of crops, their productivity, and overall sustainability [3]. In the traditional approach, managing pests and nutrients and fertilizers are used according to the pre-decided normal timetable that is scheduled previously. The major drawback of this conventional approach is that there is no consideration of the dynamic and diverse changes in real-time environments that have adverse effects on crops and agriculture settings. Every agricultural setting has diverse factors and distinct qualities, so to handle the run-time problems, the deep learning approach is used to overcome the problem of the conventional approach by customized and adaptable solutions. With the help of CNN in agriculture, firstly, it identifies all the factors and patterns about the environment, agriculture settings crops, and land. On the above observation based on all the factors, a pattern is provided by historical data. After analyzing the pattern, it becomes easier to identify which type of land it is, what are the conditions and factors for this land and what type of precautions we must take for better productivity and growth of the crops [4]. All these factors are maintained in a CSV file that is considered as a dataset. The dataset of the crops has other factors also that have been identified during the observation process. Based on this dataset which has the previous information, a new pattern is given that has helped identify what the problem has been in previous years and what we can apply according to the factors that are involved in the dataset. After identifying the pattern, CNN is applied to the dataset because it gives better results in identifying the complex structure and the relation between the various features. The climate of a particular location is also an important feature, and apart from that, types of soil according to the climate are also considered for crop growth and productivity across the world agriculture nexus [5].

In a wide range of situations, the conventional approach of agriculture and farming is not valid because nowadays the standards are set very high and to meet the objective it's very difficult to achieve that specific goal by using these traditional methods. No other methods are applicable; only new emerging technologies are used to set the bar high and come to participate at the global level. CNN, which is a deep learning method, supports the concept and provides smart solutions by saving money, resources, and time that is crucial to all. Machine Learning algorithms also provide different methodologies for crop management [6]. The intelligent systems provide a more sophisticated approach for analyzing the factors by using another emerging technology, i.e., IoT (Internet of Things). The Internet of Things uses various types of sensors that have different purposes. To solve any specific problem statement, the sensors can collect the data or analyse the factors and then apply machine learning to provide a smart solution to the real-world environment. The goal of meeting the world agricultural sector food demand can be fulfilled in a very smart way by using the latest and emerging technologies all in one [7]. As the name suggests, smart agriculture or smart farming uses advanced and emerging technologies that improve the methodologies and solutions related to the agriculture sector and increase the productivity of the crops and efficiency of this sector. The global population has increased day by day, and this is a pressure to produce good and healthy food with fewer resources [8]. Keeping this in mind, food and related things should be produced in large quantities so that every person can fulfil their daily needs [9]. Based on the above observation, intelligent systems should be used that recommend a benchmark solution that leads to better productivity at the global level and increases the outcomes of the agriculture sector [10]. Smart farming can help achieve this goal by reducing waste, increasing crop yield, and minimizing the use of harmful chemicals.

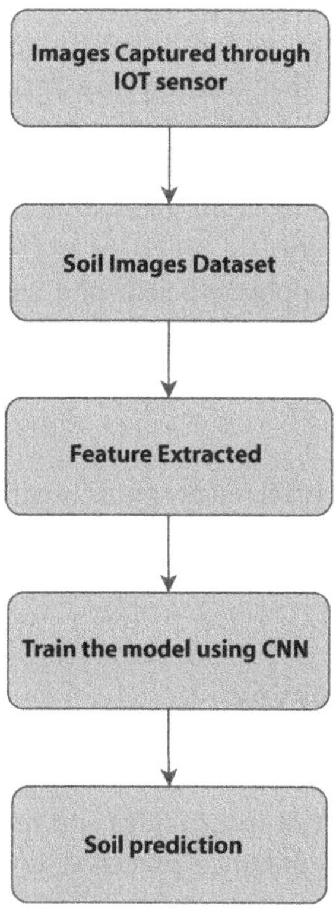

Figure 11.2 The basic process of soil identification using sensor and ML.

The basic process of soil identification using sensors and machine learning is shown in Figure 11.2. This figure shows the basic process of the image captured by the IoT sensor. The sensor is installed on the soil that captures all the parameters regarding soil like color, fertilizer value, temperature and so many others. After capturing all the parameters, the camera captures the images and maintains a dataset of images. Now the dataset has images as well as parameter values. The feature is extracted from the images which is the second step. There are various ML techniques for feature extraction. The extracted features are considered for model training by using CNN. CNN is one of the famous deep learning algorithms that gives better accuracy on images. When the training process ends, then the prediction value. The prediction value suggests where the images correctly identify the soil and give any recommendation about the fertilizer in that area or not.

***Motivation and Research Objective*:** CNN is used for the classification of high dimensional data that will be used in the research to create an intelligent soil identification using various elements and the recommendation for the fertilizer that is required for the soil for better productivity in smart agriculture 4.0. and then that will improve agricultural decision-making accuracy. The goals are to handle the complexity of various agricultural data, optimize resource use, minimize environmental effects, and explore CNN integration and optimization for customized pesticide and fertilizer recommendations. The ultimate objective is to apply cutting-edge deep learning techniques to support efficient and sustainable farming operations. The primary objective of this research is to design and develop an intelligent insecticide and fertilizer recommendation system based on CNN for smart farming.

***Paper Organization*:** A critical review of the mentioned topic is discussed in section 11.2. Section 11.3 gives a detailed discussion of the proposed work. Section 11.4 gives the results and discussion of the proposed work.

11.2 Literature Survey

This section gives an overview of the existing techniques based on smart agriculture in the contact of insecticides and fertilizer recommendations [11]. This paper aims to enhance precision in insecticide and fertilizer decisions using a Deep Learning Approach with CNNs. Various existing methods and approaches have traditional methods and new cutting-edge technology methods that perform the same. But every method has its technique along with pros and limitations [12]. Based on the challenges or limitations that can be identified as a gap a new approach can be proposed. The challenges that have been faced in the agriculture sector are labeled and unlabelled data [13]. To improve crop management that has limited datasets having labeled value reduce the impact of climate conditions but have limited value. Several earlier research works suggested image-based systems with various CNN architectures for the autonomous deep learning-based classification of agricultural pests. When dealing with photos of insect pests and a complex farmland background, deep residual learning has been offered as a means of classifying the photographs [14]. Compared to support vector machines and conventional BP neural networks, it was 98.0% more accurate in its performance. To pinpoint pests in the photos and complete the CNN classification process, the accepted Region Proposal Network (RPN) was also suggested. To categorize ten different types of crop pests using a manually gathered dataset, Li *et al.* (2020) [15] developed a refined GoogLeNet model in a deep learning-based pest identification approach [15]. Over 98.0% of pests were successfully detected. However, the training period for this model is lengthy and demands a large processing power. It was challenging to apply several deep learning models, including Inception-V3, to the dataset under examination. A system for recognizing insects was developed using a combination of saliency approaches and CNNs [16]. Both a short dataset and the big IP102 dataset were used for testing, with accuracy rates of 92.43% and 61.93%, respectively. However, in pest photos with significant intra-class variance, our suggested approach fails. On three public bug datasets with 24 to 40 classes of crop insect photos, deep CNN and transfer learning were also suggested for the categorization of agricultural pests [17].

Compared to pre-trained deep learning models, they outperformed them in classification accuracy by almost 95.0%. Deep residual networks were suggested as a method for classifying significant primary and secondary pests in RGB photographs of cotton fields [18]. The achieved accuracy of 98.0% surpassed that of other evaluated CNN models. Additionally, a better deep learning pipeline based on automatically learning saliency feature maps was created to identify and count agricultural pests in photos [19]. To find and identify pests on tomato plants in greenhouses, a study comparing machine learning and deep learning was carried out. This study showed that, in terms of accurate tomato pest identification, deep learning solutions outperform other machine learning strategies [20]. Comparing a suggested CNN model with four machine learning techniques—artificial neural networks (ANN), support vector machines (SVM), k-nearest neighbors (KNN), and naïve bayes (NB)—Kasinathan *et al.* [21] used the public IP102 dataset to categorize insect pests. The highest classification rates of 91.5% and 90.0% for 9 and 24 agricultural pest classes, respectively, were attained by the suggested CNN model. Transfer learning models for soybean fields, such as Residual Neural Network (ResNet-50) and Visual Geometry Group Network (VGG-16 and VGG-19), have been proposed to assist farmers in managing the control of soybean pests by using photos captured by a drone equipped with a high-resolution camera. As a result, the greatest categorization rate's accuracy was 93.82% [22, 23].

Agriculture is now much more efficient and controllable thanks to machine learning. The three primary phases of machine learning are model construction, generalization, and data preprocessing. Machine learning algorithms handle situations where human abilities are lacking [24]. Machine Learning (ML) is the process of using data and historical knowledge to help computers make decisions. Numerous uses for machine learningexist to extract important characteristics from information and data [25–27]. The two main subcategories of machine learning techniques are supervised learning and unsupervised learning. Some researchers also further classify machine learning algorithms into semi-supervised and reinforced learning. Artificial intelligence (ML) can improve pest control methods [28].

Wang *et al.* [29] have the objective of efficiency of fertilizers and pest control by using CNN but the climate conditions totally depend on the former, which is a manual and time-consuming task. Chen *et al.* [30] focus on the optimization of agriculture practices using computer vision. However, the problem is the reliability of the sensors that are used in this work. The positive thing in the work is that resource optimization has been well organized. M. Patel *et al.* [31] proposed a novel approach for monitoring the crops and providing a robotic technology for recommendation systems. This gives a new and beneficial technique in smart agriculture, but the problem is it uses the old techniques and integrates with new ones, hence degrading the system's performance. But the major point is that the problem of the crops has been timely identified and takes the precautionary measures. Liu *et al.* [32] provide a solution for sustainable agriculture practices that provide long-term benefits, but resource constraints are the major issue in this method. Sharma *et al.* [33] focused on the early identification of diseases in the crops using deep learning techniques but having limited labelled data. But the crop health is much better as compared to the traditional approach. Yamamoto *et al.* [34] focused on the adaptability of crops in different climate conditions. The problem is with data privacy that includes the concept of cloud, but it improves the decision-making capability of the farming technique. Kumar *et al.* [35] proposed a method that solves the problem of real-time decision of fertilizers and provides a user-friendly interface. However, there is a connectivity gap that has been identified. Apart from that formers are integrating in large amounts and use the solution for better productivity and efficiency. Chen *et al.* [2] provide a recommendation for different types of crops by using a decision support system along with AI. It makes the system complex, but the performance is a little bit better as compared to the previous existing solutions. Pros include tailored solutions and improved performance on specific crops [36]. The study of G. Park and E. Kim (2023) aims to facilitate integration with precision agriculture technologies using CNNs. Challenges include compatibility issues and technical complexity. Pros involve seamless integration and enhanced precision in recommendations. Table 11.1 summarizes the literature survey.

Table 11.1 Literature survey based on smart agricultural techniques.

Author(s)	Year	Objective of the paper	Pros	Challenges
Rajendra G. *et al.* [37]	2023	Enhance precision in insecticide and fertilizer decisions	Improved crop yield, Reduced environmental impact	Limited labeled data, real-world implementation
A. H. King *et al.* [38]	2022	Improve pest control and fertilizer efficiency	Increased efficiency, cost-effective	Variable environmental conditions, adoption by farmers
Unhelkar B. *et al.* [39]	2021	Optimize agricultural practices with deep learning	Precision farming, resource optimization	Sensor reliability, scalability
Ramu S. K. *et al.* [40]	2024	Monitor and diagnose crop health	Early disease detection, timely intervention	Integration with existing agricultural machinery
Balyan S. *et al.* [41]	2023	Promote sustainable farming practices	Environmental sustainability, long-term benefits	Farmer acceptance, resource constraints

(*Continued*)

Table 11.1 Literature survey based on smart agricultural techniques. (*Continued*)

Author(s)	Year	Objective of the paper	Pros	Challenges
P. Sharma *et al.* [1]	2023	Early detection of diseases in crops using deep learning	Rapid response to diseases, improved crop health	Lack of labeled data, generalization
Kathiria P *et al.* [42]	2023	Enhance adaptability to changing environmental conditions	Adaptive recommendations, improved resilience	Data privacy concerns, model interpretability
Musanase *et al.* [43]	2023	Implement real-time decision support for farmers	Timely decision-making, increased farmer engagement	Connectivity issues, user acceptance
Sahoo A *et al.* [44]	2023	Provide personalized recommendations for diverse crops	Tailored solutions, Improved performance on specific crops	Limited crop diversity, model complexity
Thorat *et al.* [45]	2023	Facilitate integration with precision agriculture technologies	Seamless integration, enhanced precision in recommendations	Compatibility issues, technical complexity

11.3 Problem Formulation

Fertilizer and pesticide applications require careful consideration, which is intrinsic to agricultural production. Conventional techniques frequently lack accuracy, which can have negative effects on the environment and result in inefficient use of resources [46]. It is becoming more and more clear that we need an intelligent system that can accurately recommend when and how much to apply fertilizer and pesticide [47]. The objective of this study is to construct an intelligent insecticide and fertilizer recommendation system in order to improve agricultural decision-making. Various challenges are identified during the study of smart farming. They are as follows:

- One of the key challenges in smart farming is the selection of the appropriate insecticide and fertilizer for a given crop. The wrong selection can lead to reduced crop yield and increased cost, which can be detrimental to farmers.

11.4 Proposed Work

To overcome this challenge, this paper proposes an intelligent insecticide and fertilizer recommendation system based on Convolutional Neural Network (CNN) for smart farming in 4.0 [48]. The proposed block diagram represents how the soil nutrients will be analysed and is shown in Figure 11.3. In this, there are two processes, one is for the analysis of insecticides and the other is for the soil nutrients and fertilizer quality. In this, the soil will be analysed, then we need Arduino for coding and Raspberry Pi for nutrient analysis by using a special camera which will show the exact position of soil. Meanwhile the images from the dataset are also classified after initial processing and then show the result as insecticides.

The proposed system will use a deep learning algorithm based on CNN to recommend the most appropriate insecticide and fertilizer for a given crop. A large dataset of insecticides and fertilizers along with the different factors mentioned in the dataset is used to train the system. The dataset is created by collecting the samples from various IoT devices like sensors. After creating the dataset, the CNN algorithm is applied to the training dataset and analysed. After that it is tested on the testing dataset, and based on the result it will recommend the most suitable insecticides and fertilizer for a healthy crop. All the proposed method is performed in various steps which are mentioned below:

a. Identification of pests using deep learning
b. Analysis of soil nutrients using sensors
c. Insecticides and fertilizer recommendations provide within seconds.

a. Identification of pests using deep learning

In agricultural research, deep learning–based pest identification has become a groundbreaking method. Researchers and farmers may now use

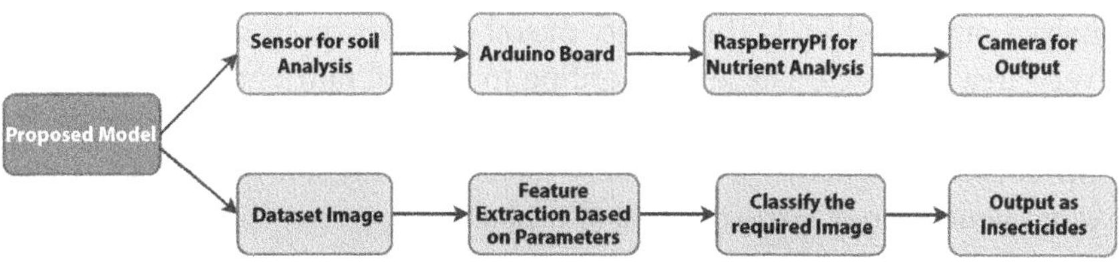

Figure 11.3 Workflow of the proposed model.

sophisticated algorithms to precisely identify and categorize diverse pests that pose hazards to crops by utilizing the capabilities of advanced neural networks. Large databases of pest photos were used to train deep learning models, which enable them to detect minute patterns and details that could go unnoticed by the human eye. This technology facilitates focused and timely intervention tactics by improving pest detection precision and speeding up the identification process. Agricultural techniques may become more effective, eco-friendly, and responsive to the ever-changing problems provided by pest infestations by incorporating deep learning into pest control systems [49]. This will ultimately lead to higher crop yields and enhanced global food security. The methodology for the proposed solution is to identify the pests using a deep learning approach. For that one operator, i.e., convolutional neural network is used on the pest images that are in discrete and continuous, applying for insecticides recommendations [50, 51].

b. Analysis of soil nutrients using sensors

The analysis of soil nutrients using sensors represents a significant leap forward in modern agriculture, revolutionizing the way farmers understand and manage soil health. Sensor technologies are deployed in farming systems by using IoT. Using these sensors, the farming data can be easily received on time with exact and accurate results. Sensors can check the soil conditions and its nutrients like phosphorous. To check the composition of soil various techniques are utilized by the sensors, such as electromagnetic induction or optical spectroscopy. After collecting the data from sensors by using technologies, decisions have been made regarding the application of nutrients in the form of fertilizers, selection of crops, and irrigation techniques by optimizing the resources in environmental effects. This practice has helped formers for the overutilization of resources. Only utilize those resources that are much needed and in specific time frames and constraints. This way can promote sustainability in the agriculture sector. The security challenges based on the global market of food can be resolved by using these techniques [52]. In the proposed method, the sensors are used to check the nutrients of the soil, whether it is sufficient or not, or needs recommendations based on the analysis of the soil [32]. The quality of soil depends on its area and locality. Every area has its climate and according to the soil nutrients may vary high or low, so analysis is the crucial step. For the successful measurement of the nutrients of the soil, the sensor will be installed in the soil, and after analysis, recommendation of fertilizers will take place.

c. Limited time frame and recommendations for insecticides and fertilizers

The term smart agriculture means a smart approach to solving any problem related to agriculture. Any suggestion based on what has been mentioned will be solved in a couple of seconds and that's a revolution in the field of agriculture domain. The AI technologies with data analytics give the approach to solve the problem in a stipulated time frame or seconds to achieve the solution. These technologies quickly analyze the problem and recommend solutions. The farming system has been improved to give exact, accurate, and timely recommendations of fertilizers or nutrients for the soil that help to improve the crop's productivity in the global market scenario. This promotes sustainable practices by streamlining decision-making procedures for farmers and optimizing resource consumption [53, 54]. Quick distribution of customized advice guarantees that farmers react quickly to conditions that change, reducing the likelihood of nutrient shortages and insect infestations. Therefore, this technology integration helps current agriculture operations become more resilient overall, more efficient, and provide better crop yields. In this chapter, with the help of CNN, the disease in the leaf is also identified and then pesticides are recommended to mitigate the issue. Results are acquired immediately, and the recommended times for insecticide and pesticides are respectively provided within seconds. With this work, different pests are successfully identified.

11.5 Result and Discussion

The proposed system is expected to provide an intelligent insecticide and fertilizer recommendation system that can significantly improve farming outcomes. The system will be able to recommend the most appropriate insecticide and fertilizer for a given crop, considering various factors such as crop type, soil type, climate, and pest infestation. This system will be especially useful for those farmers who do not have access to expert advice or cannot afford to experiment with different insecticides and fertilizers. There are two phases: one is for soil identification and other is for fertilizer recommendation. In the first phase, condition of soil is identified.

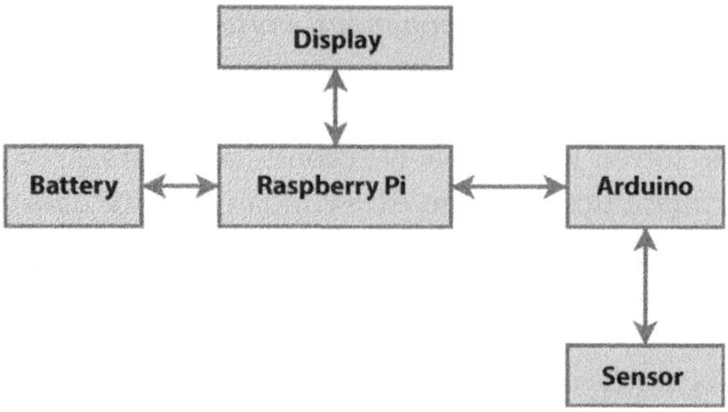

Figure 11.4 Soil identification and fertilizer recommendation.

Figure 11.4 shows the soil value identification using the sensor. The battery is attached with the configuration in which with layer of sensor takes the condition of the soil and then using Arduino it will pass to the Raspberry Pi and display all the samples [35, 55]. The samples are collected and taken as reference datasets which will check which one is infected and

Figure 11.5 Different samples of crops.

which one is not infected. Now move to phase 2 in which Figure 11.5 shows the samples of the data having different types of leaves in which some are infected and some are not infected.

There are different types of samples collected and that makes a dataset. Now, all these samples are collected and classified in two main classes, class 1 and class 2. Both classes have random samples and the sample that is infected is present in both. Now if the infected is much more then accordingly the result will show in terms of confidence score of every class. If the class having high confidence score it has more infected. If the confidence level is low in that case that class will have low infected samples. Figures 11.6 and 11.7 show the samples of two different classes for reference. Both the classes have equal infected as well as uninfected samples. Now the solution gives that which one is highly infected and not highly infected.

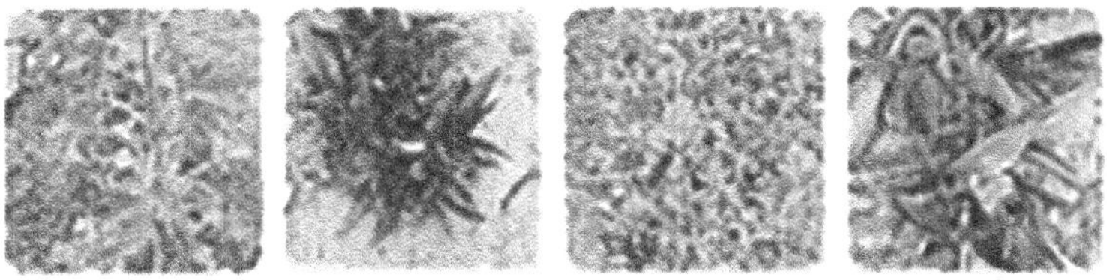

Figure 11.6 The sample reference of class 1.

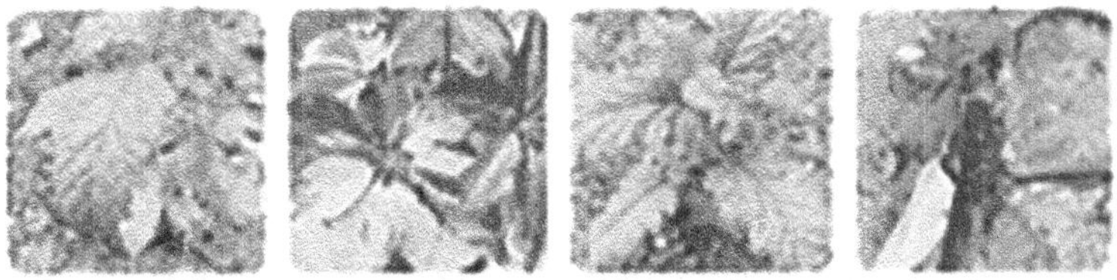

Figure 11.7 The sample reference of class 2.

The label samples for this work are considered as two sample references. One reference is from class 1 and another is from class 2. Figure 11.8(a) shows the label data that is used in this work for class 1 and Figure 11.9(b) shows the label data that is used in this work for class 2.

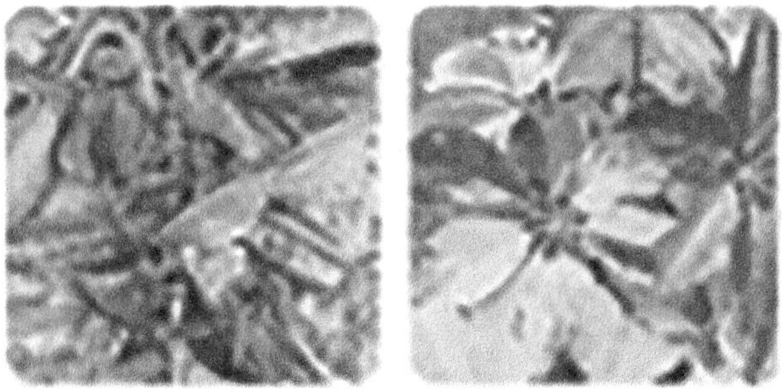

Figure 11.8 (a) The labelled data of class 1.

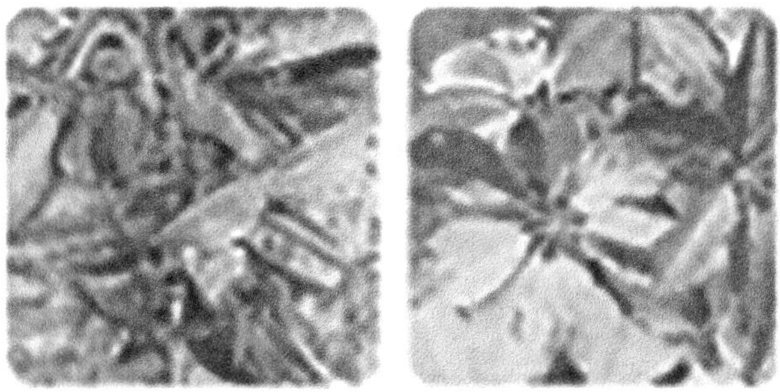

Figure 11.9 (b) The labelled data of class 2.

Figure 11.10 shows that two classes in class 1 have crops with less infected as well as class 2 is highly infected. In this case when we train the model then the model easily gets the result in real time and shows that class 2 have infected and the confidence level of the infected crop is approximately 96%.

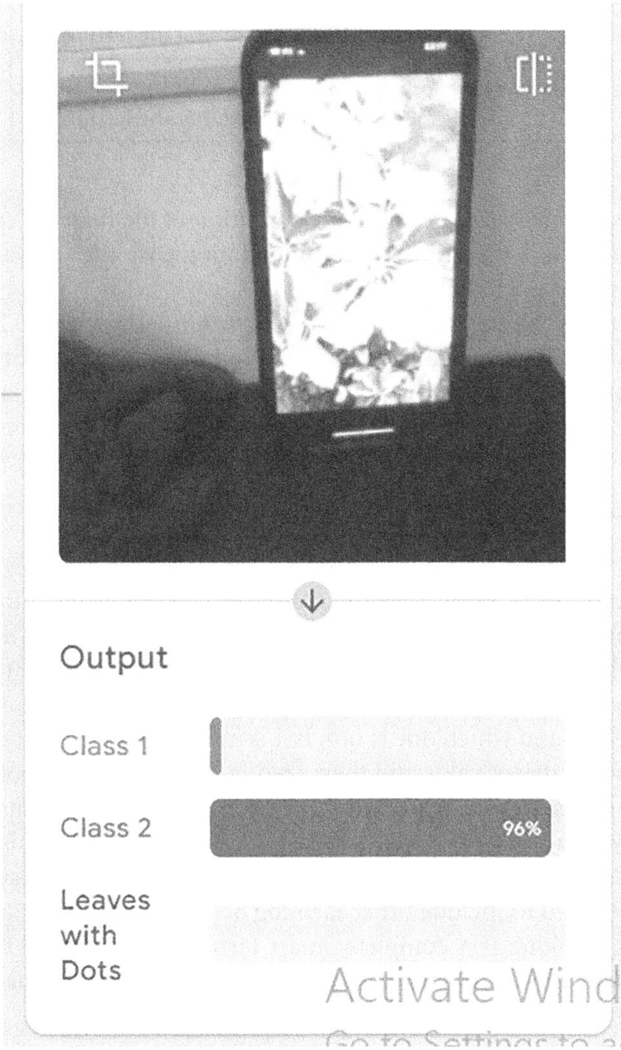

Figure 11.10 Output of class 1 and class 2.

Table 11.2 Fertilizer recommendation using soil value.

Soil elements	Value	Action
Nitrogen	160	(Low) Recommend adding the fertilizer
Phosphorus	7.8	(Low) Recommend adding the fertilizer
Potassium	300	(High) Recommend adding the fertilizer

Now recommend according to the condition of the infected crop which fertilizer is used. For fertilizer recommendations, we use the value of soil element mentioned in Table 11.2.

Based on the above, the accuracy of the proposed work is 80.2%, which is good in the smart agriculture domain. However, various techniques can be used for soil identification [56–62], also various recommendation techniques for fertilizer can be used based on the condition of the crops.

11.6 Conclusion

The proposed work gives a significant benefit to the farmers for a better understanding of the soil using Raspberry Pi and sensors. Then all the images will be considered as sample reference and accordingly, the sample can be classified into two classes; using CNN it can easily identify which one is infected and which one is not. If it is infected then in that case it will have low soil nutrient value and then needs a recommendation of fertilizer. The proposed system is expected to provide significant benefits to farmers. The system will help to reduce the use of harmful chemicals, improve crop yield, and ultimately, increase profits for farmers. This system can also be extended to include other farming activities such as irrigation and harvesting, making it a complete smart farming solution. In the future, another machine-learning algorithm can be used for classification and recommendations.

References

1. Thorat, T., Patle, B.K., Kashyap, S.K., Intelligent insecticide and fertilizer recommendation system based on TPF-CNN for smart farming. *Smart Agric. Technol.*, 3, 100114, 2023.
2. Unhelkar, B. and Chakrabarti, P., A Novel Deep Learning Models for Efficient Insect Pest Detection and Recommending an Organic Pesticide for Smart Farming. *Int. J. Intell. Syst. Appl. Eng.*, 12, 9s, 15–31, 2024.
3. Ketheneni, K., Yenuga, P., Garnepudi, P., Paleti, L., Burla, N.R., Srinivas, O., Yamarthi, N.R., Crop, Fertilizer and Pesticide Recommendation Using Ensemble Method and Sequential Convolutional Neural Network. *Int. J. Intell. Syst. Appl. Eng.*, 12, 2, 473–485, 2024.
4. Shrivastava, A. and Ramaiya, M.K., System for Managing Pesticide Recommendation on the Cotton Crop Using Deep Learning Techniques VGG and Xgboost. *Int. J. Intell. Syst. Appl. Eng.*, 12, 7s, 677–691, 2024.
5. Venu, S., Kumar, R.G., Kumar, M.K., Prasad, T.G., Suresh, B., Neelima, P., An Intelligent and Service Based Smart Agriculture Recommendation System. *Int. J. Intell. Syst. Appl. Eng.*, *12*, 7s, 153–158, 2024.
6. Choudhury, S.S., Pandharbale, P.B., Mohanty, S.N., Jagdev, A.K., An Acquisition Based Optimised Crop Recommendation System with Machine Learning Algorithm. *EAI Endorsed Trans. Scalable Inf. Syst.*, *11*, 1, 2024.
7. Shams, M.Y., Gamel, S.A., Talaat, F.M., Enhancing crop recommendation systems with explainable artificial intelligence: a study on agricultural decision-making. *Neural Comput. Appl.*, 1–20, 2024.
8. Chaudhary, R.R., Jain, S., Gupta, S., A critical review on hybrid framework for precise farming with application of Machine Learning (ML) and Internet of Things (IoT). *J. Integr. Sci. Technol.*, *12*, 2, 730–730, 2024.
9. Haval, A.M. and Rahman, F., Application of machine learning techniques and the Internet of Things for smart, sustainable agriculture, in: *BIO Web of Conferences*, vol. 82, EDP Sciences, p. 05021, 2024.
10. Tonle, F.B., Niassy, S., Ndadji, M.M., Tchendji, M.T., Nzeukou, A., Mudereri, B.T., Tonnang, H.E., A road map for developing novel decision support system (DSS) for disseminating integrated pest management (IPM) technologies. *Comput. Electron. Agric.*, *217*, 108526, 2024.
11. Ah King, R.T., Rajkumarsingh, B., Jeetah, P., Somaroo, G., Jogee, D., Smart Fertilizer Application in Agricultural Land for Sustainable Crop Production and Consumption, in: *Artificial Intelligence, Engineering Systems and Sustainable Development: Driving the UN SDGs*, pp. 29–41, Emerald Publishing Limited, 2024.
12. Mohamed, M., Agricultural Sustainability in the Age of Deep Learning: Current Trends, Challenges, and Future Trajectories. *Sustain. Mach. Intell. J.*, 4, 2–1, 2023.

13. Javaid, M., AbidHaleem, R.P.S., Suman, R., Enhancing smart farming through the applications of Agriculture 4.0 technologies. *Int. J. Intell. Networks*, 3, 150–164, 2022.
14. Mitra, A., Vangipuram, S.LT., Bapatla, A.K., Bathalapalli, V.KVV., Mohanty, S.P., Kougianos, E., Ray, C., *Everything you wanted to know about smart agriculture*, 2022, arXiv preprint arXiv:2201.04754.
15. Sathiya, S., Antony, C., Ghodke, P.K., Smart Agriculture: Emerging and Future Farming Technologies. *Recent Trends Best Pract. Ind.*, 4, 0, 135–181, 2023.
16. Mohyuddin, G., Khan, M.A., Haseeb, A., Mahpara, S., Waseem, M., Saleh, A.M., Evaluation of Machine Learning approaches for precision Farming in Smart Agriculture System-A comprehensive Review. *IEEE Access*, 2024.
17. Dayıoğlu, M.A. and Turker, U., Digital transformation for sustainable future-agriculture 4.0: A review. *J. Agric. Sci.*, 27, 4, 373–399, 2021.
18. Ayaz, M., Ammad-Uddin, M., Sharif, Z., Mansour, A., Aggoune, E.-H.M., Internet-of-Things (IoT)-based smart agriculture: Toward making the fields talk. *IEEE Access*, 7, 129551–129583, 2019.
19. Abdel-Basset, M., Hawash, H., Abdel-Fatah, L., *Artificial Intelligence and Internet of Things in Smart Farming*, CRC Press, 2024.
20. Sravani, S., Raghavendra Chowdary, K., Reddi Ramu, Y., Artificial Intelligence, Machine Learning and Internet of Things applications in Agriculture, in: *AI ML and IoT Applications in Agriculture*, pp. 77–96, Springer, 2023.
21. Abdalla, ZF. and El-Ramady, H., Applications and Challenges of Smart Farming for Developing Sustainable Agriculture. *Environment Biodivers. Soil Secur.*, 6, 2022, 81–90, 2022.
22. Gyamfi, E.K., El Sayed, Z., Kropczynski, J., Yakubu, M.A., Elsayed, N., *Agricultural 4.0 Leveraging on Technological Solutions: Study for Smart Farming Sector*, 2024, arXiv preprint arXiv:2401.00814.
23. Sankareswari, K. and Sujatha, G., Crop and Fertiliser Recommendation System for Sustainable Agricultural Development, in: *Intelligent Robots and Drones for Precision Agriculture*, pp. 327–349, Springer Nature Switzerland, Cham, 2024.
24. Kazakis, N.A. and Tsirliganis, N.C., Holistic approach to Agriculture 4.0 for new farmers. *Societal Impacts*, 1, 1–2, 100007, 2023.
25. Satav, S.D., Machine Learning & IOT Based Approaches for Classification in Smart Farming. *Int. J. Res. Anal. Rev. (IJRAR)*, 10, 2, 184–214, 2023.
26. Mowla, M.N., Mowla, N., Shahen Shah, A.F.M., Rabie, K., Shongwe, T., Internet of Things and Wireless Sensor Networks for Smart Agriculture Applications: A Survey. *IEEE Access*, 2023.
27. Singh, G., Kalra, N., Yadav, N., Sharma, A., Saini, M., Smart agriculture: a review. *Siberian J. Life Sci. Agric.*, 14, 6, 423–454, 2022.
28. Jeyabalu, M., Ghodi, A.S., Balasubramanian, S., Chinnayan, B., Jayapal, J., Internet of Things-Based Smart Agriculture Advisory System, in: *Intelligent*

Robots and Drones for Precision Agriculture, pp. 159–177, Springer Nature Switzerland, Cham, 2024.
29. John, S. and Arul Leena Rose, P.J., Smart Farming and Precision Agriculture and Its Need in Today's World, in: *Intelligent Robots and Drones for Precision Agriculture*, pp. 19–44, Springer Nature Switzerland, Cham, 2024.
30. Ali, B., Ilieva, A., Zakeri, A., Iliev, O., From Industry 4.0 Toward Agriculture 4.0, in: *Intelligent Systems Conference*, Springer Nature Switzerland, Cham, pp. 636–651, 2023.
31. Jararweh, Y., Fatima, S., Jarrah, M., Al Zu'bi, S., Smart and sustainable agriculture: Fundamentals, enabling technologies, and future directions. *Comput. Electr. Eng.*, 110, 108799, 2023.
32. Singh, R., Srivastava, N., Kumar, A., Anomaly detection framework for highly scattered and dynamic data on large-scale networks using AWS. *Int. J. Inf. Technol.*, 1–18, 2024.
33. Singh, R., Srivastava, N., Kumar, A., Anomaly Detection in Network Traffic Scenarios by Resampling and Majority Voting with Concept Drift: A Hybrid Approach, in: *2024 11th International Conference on Reliability, Infocom Technologies and Optimization (Trends and Future Directions) (ICRITO)*, IEEE, pp. 1–7, 2024.
34. Saiz-Rubio, V. and Rovira-Más, F., From smart farming towards agriculture 5.0: A review on crop data management. *Agronomy*, 10, 2, 207, 2020.
35. Rajendiran, G. and Rethnaraj, J., IoT-Integrated Machine Learning-Based Automated Precision Agriculture-Indoor Farming Techniques, in: *Using Traditional Design Methods to Enhance AI-Driven Decision Making*, pp. 289–317, IGI Global, 2024.
36. Ramu, S.K., Ponnuswamy, L., Nataraj, D., Venkatachalam, K., Comprehensive Study of Artificial Intelligence Techniques for Early-Stage Disease Identification System in Plants, in: *Precision Agriculture for Sustainability*, pp. 41–69, Apple Academic Press, 2024.
37. Balyan, S., Jangir, H., Tripathi, S.N., Tripathi, A., Jhang, T., Pandey, P., Seeding a Sustainable Future: Navigating the Digital Horizon of Smart Agriculture. *Sustainability*, 16, 2, 475, 2024.
38. Sharma, P. and Dadheech, P., Modern-age Agriculture with Artificial Intelligence: A review emphasizing Crop Yield Prediction. *Evergreen*, 10, 4, 2570–2582, 2023.
39. Kathiria, P., Patel, U., Madhwani, S., Mansuri, C.S., Smart Crop Recommendation System: A Machine Learning Approach for Precision Agriculture, in: *Machine Intelligence Techniques for Data Analysis and Signal Processing: Proceedings of the 4th International Conference MISP 2022*, vol. 1, Springer Nature Singapore, Singapore, pp. 841–850, 2023, May.
40. Musanase, C., Vodacek, A., Hanyurwimfura, D., Uwitonze, A., Kabandana, I., Data-Driven Analysis and Machine Learning-Based Crop and Fertilizer

Recommendation System for Revolutionizing Farming Practices. *Agriculture*, 13, 11, 20232141.
41. Sahoo, A., Rathi, A., Bashishth, S., Roy, S., Pradhan, C., Predictive Farmland Optimization and Crop Monitoring Using Artificial Intelligence Techniques, in: *Enabling Technologies for Effective Planning and Management in Sustainable Smart Cities*, pp. 79–121, Springer International Publishing, Cham, 2023.
42. Shingade, S.D. and Mudhalwadkar, R.P., Analysis of crop prediction models using data analytics and ML techniques: a review. *Multimed. Tools Appl.*, 1–26, 2023.
43. Dawn, N., Ghosh, T., Ghosh, S., Saha, A., Mukherjee, P., Sarkar, S., Sanyal, T., Implementation of Artificial Intelligence, Machine Learning, and Internet of Things (IoT) in revolutionizing Agriculture: A review on recent trends and challenges. *Int. J. Exp. Res. Rev.*, 30, 190–218, 2023.
44. Singh, R., Srivastava, N., Kumar, A., Machine Learning Techniques for Anomaly Detection in Network Traffic, in: *2021 Sixth International Conference on Image Information Processing (ICIIP)*, vol. 6, pp. 261–266, IEEE, 2021, November.
45. Singh, R., Performance Optimization of Autoencoder Neural Network Based Model for Anomaly Detection in Network Traffic, in: *2022 2nd International Conference on Advance Computing and Innovative Technologies in Engineering (ICACITE)*, pp. 598–602, IEEE, 2022, April.
46. Singh, R., Singh, A., Bhattacharya, P., A machine learning approach for anomaly detection to secure smart grid systems, in: *Advancements in Security and Privacy Initiatives for Multimedia Images*, pp. 199–213, IGI global, 2021.
47. Singh, R. and Srivastava, N., Study of Anomaly Detection in Clinical Laboratory Data Using Internet of Medical Things, in: *Data Modelling and Analytics for the Internet of Medical Things*, pp. 237–255, CRC Press, 2023.
48. Singh, R., Srivastava, N., Kumar, A., Novel Approach for Network Anomaly Detection Using Autoencoder on CICIDS Dataset, in: *International Conference on Information Technology*, Springer Nature Singapore, Singapore, pp. 203–212, 2023, March.
49. Singh, R. and Srivastava, N., Assessing the Impact of Student Employability Using Decision Tree Classifier in Education 4.0: An Analysis of Key Factors and Predictive Model Development, in: *Architecture and Technological Advancements of Education 4.0*, pp. 178–198, IGI Global, 2024.
50. Vishnoi, S. and Goel, R.K., Climate smart agriculture for sustainable productivity and healthy landscapes. *Environ. Sci. Policy*, 151, 103600, 2024.
51. Vanitha, C.N., Malathy, S., Shenbagavalli, P., Krishna, S.A., Kavin, K., Detecting Turmeric Taphrina Maculans Disease using Machine Learning Algorithms, in: *2022 International Conference on Applied Artificial Intelligence and Computing (ICAAIC)*, Salem, India, pp. 431–436, 2022.
52. Sehito, N., Shouyi, Y., Alshahrani, H.M., Alamgeer, M., Dutta, A.K., Alsubai, S., Nkenyereye, L., Dhanaraj, R.K., Optimizing User Association, Power Control and Beamforming for 6G Multi-IRS Multi-UAV NOMA

Communications in Smart Cities, in: *IEEE Transactions on Consumer Electronics*, pp. 1–1, Institute of Electrical and Electronics Engineers (IEEE), 2024, https://doi.org/10.1109/tce.2024.3388596.

53. Singh, R., Srivastava, N., Kumar, A., Network Anomaly Detection Using Autoencoder on Various Datasets: A Comprehensive Review. *Recent Pat. Eng.*, 18, 1–15, 2024. ISSN 1872-2121/2212-4047, Doi 10.2174/01187221212 42429230922070752.
54. Sott, M.K., Furstenau, L.B., Kipper, L.M., Giraldo, F.D., Lopez-Robles, J.R., Cobo, M.J., Zahid, A., Abbasi, Q.H., Ali Imran, M., Precision techniques and agriculture 4.0 technologies to promote sustainability in the coffee sector: state of the art, challenges and future trends. *IEEE Access*, 8, 149854–149867, 2020.
55. Khanh, P.T., Hong Ngoc, T.T., Pramanik, S., Future of Smart Agriculture Techniques and Applications, in: *Handbook of Research on AI-Equipped IoT Applications in High-Tech Agriculture*, pp. 365–378, IGI Global, 2023.
56. Sathyamoorthy, M., Dhanaraj, R.K., Vanitha, C.N., Krishnasamy, L., Augmented Reality Based Medical Education, in: *2023 Intelligent Computing and Control for Engineering and Business Systems (ICCEBS)*, IEEE, 2023, https://doi.org/10.1109/iccebs58601.2023.10449124.
57. Kollu, P.K., Bangare, M.L., Venkata Hari Prasad, P., Bangare, P.M., Rane, K.P., Arias-Gonzáles, J.L., Lalar, S., Shabaz, M., Internet of things driven multilinear regression technique for fertilizer recommendation for precision agriculture. *SN Appl. Sci.*, 5, 10, 264, 2023.
58. Lachgar, M., Hrimech, H., Kartit, A., Unmanned aerial vehicle-based applications in smart farming: A systematic review. *Int. J. Adv. Comput. Sci. Appl.*, 14, 6, 2023.
59. Rejeb, A., Rejeb, K., Abdollahi, A., Al-Turjman, F., Treiblmaier, H., The Interplay between the Internet of Things and agriculture: A bibliometric analysis and research agenda. *Internet Things*, 19, 100580, 2022.
60. Neményi, M., Kovács, A.J., Oláh, J., Popp, J., Erdei, E., Harsányi, E., Ambrus, B., Teschner, G., Nyéki, A., Challenges of sustainable agricultural development with special regard to Internet of Things: Survey. *Prog. Agric. Eng. Sci.*, 18, 1, 95–114, 2022.
61. Kumar, R., Farooq, M., Qureshi, M., Advancing precision agriculture through artificial intelligence: Exploring the future of cultivation, in: *Biologist s Guide to Artificial Intelligence*, pp. 151–165, Academic Press, 2024.
62. Haque, A., Islam, N., Samrat, N.H., Dey, S., Ray, B., Smart farming through responsible leadership in Bangladesh: Possibilities, opportunities, and beyond. *Sustainability*, 13, 8, 4511, 2021.

12

Case Study on Ethical AI-Based Decision-Making in E-Commerce Industrial Sector: Insights on McDonald's and Deliveroo

Anushka Singh[1], Naman Tyagi[2] and Dolly Sharma[3]*

[1] *Whiting School of Engineering, Johns Hopkins University, Maryland, USA*
[2] *Tandon School of Engineering, New York University, New York, USA*
[3] *Department of Computer Science and Engineering, Amity University, Noida, India*

Abstract

Automated Machine Learning (AutoML) is the process of automating repetitive and time-consuming tasks which applies machine learning algorithm to real-world problems. AutoML is defined a paradigm in the era of artificial intelligence and machine learning. It is used to scale up the efficiency of machine learning models. It is used in organizations to scale up their businesses, amplify data utilization for business decision-making with much less human intervention. This chapter explores the real-world implementation of AutoML principles. It explores two organizations that are very prominent in the industry of food: McDonald's, a global franchise of fast-food, as it optimizes its food menus based on user preferences with the help of AutoML, and Deliveroo, a UK-based food delivery application, which optimized their delivery times and improved their business service quality by incorporating AutoML into their business. AutoML has a varied effect on the business's workflows and operations, pushing them into success. We explored the benefits and challenges within AutoML, with ethical considerations that should be noted while incorporating AutoML into the business.

Keywords: AutoML, automated machine learning, AI, ML, machine learning, ethical AI

**Corresponding author*: dolly.azure@gmail.com

Sapna Juneja, Rajesh Kumar Dhanaraj, Abhinav Juneja, Malathy Sathyamoorthy and Asadullah Shaikh (eds.) Ethical Decision-Making Using Artificial Intelligence: Challenges, Solutions and Applications, (283–312) © 2025 Scrivener Publishing LLC

12.1 Introduction

With the advancements in the field of artificial intelligence especially in machine learning, incorporating tools using AI in the organizations has become important. To automate repetitive tasks which need human intervention takes a lot of time. Automated machine learning (AutoML) is a subfield of machine learning that aims to automate all or most of the stages involved in the development of machine learning model, basically to fast-track the process with little to no human intervention. It has the power to transform industries in a way that scales their business, enhances user experience and streamlines the decision-making process.

We explore the real-world applications of AutoML in two major players of the food industry: McDonald's, a world-recognized icon in the fast-food industry and Deliveroo, a food delivery application, that operates within the competitive market. By encompassing the competences of AutoML, McDonald's has been able to analyze huge amount of data generated from its business and gain insights about the user preferences, later allowing them to optimize their food menu offerings. Similarly, employing AutoML solutions has helped Deliveroo to optimize their overall delivery times and improve their service quality.

Later in this chapter we discuss the specific AutoML techniques incorporated by McDonald's and Deliveroo, simultaneously highlighting the challenges they have faced, and the solutions implemented to overcome these challenges, and how business intelligence can be incorporated with them. Also evaluated are the ethical concerns related to AutoML, and lastly, we conclude with the future trends that emerge from it.

12.2 Foundations of AutoML

The foundations of AutoML are deep-rooted in the intersection of machine learning methodologies and the persistent need to modify the world of data science. AutoML signifies an innovative shift, by letting individuals having different level of expertise but not having deep knowledge about the model complexities and fine-tuning hyperparameters, an unimaginable access to abilities of machine learning. AutoML has the ability to automate every aspect of model development pipeline, from data preprocessing to optimization. By facilitating the seamless integration of powerful machine learning models into everyday workflows of the companies, AutoML cultivates an innovative culture across various industries.

One of the key principles of AutoML is its ability to adapt to diverse large datasets and problem areas. This adaptability is achieved through the deployment of automated algorithms that explore the model space, recognizing ideal setups customized to the particular qualities of the current data. As organizations handle the increasing amount of data, AutoML emerges as an innovative force, promoting data-driven culture by enabling wider audience to experience its potential.

12.2.1 Understanding AutoML

Understanding the term AutoML involves proper exploration of its fundamental concepts and the important role it plays in reshaping the world of machine learning. In layman's terms, AutoML represents a transformative way to machine learning model development by automating traditionally human-centric and time-consuming tasks [1]. The core components of AutoML consist of a wide spectrum of tasks starting from data preprocessing and feature engineering to model selection and hyperparameter tuning. The goal is to streamline the end-to-end processes, making them more accessible to wider audiences, including those individuals having limited or no expertise in data science.

12.2.2 Automated Feature Engineering

Automated Feature Engineering is an important aspect of AutoML, focusing on the automatic extraction, feature generation and feature selection from raw data. Traditionally, feature engineering mostly relied on the domain expertise and manual labor to identify relevant features from the raw data and contribute to model performance. However, in AutoML this whole process is automated to a large extent by leveraging algorithms to identify useful patterns and relationships. Automated Feature Engineering aims to lessen the burden of manual feature engineering, also uncovering complicated patterns and relationships in the input data that were overlooked by humans alone. AutoML involves methods like statistical feature selection; in this, features are ranked based on their relevance to the target variable, which in relation expedite the model development process and potentially improve model performance by capturing even the sensitive relationships within the data.

12.3 Benefits and Challenges

12.3.1 Benefits of AutoML

AutoML offers various benefits that can enhance the overall accessibility, efficiency and effectiveness of machine learning applications across various industries. AutoML automates complex and time-consuming tasks, the accelerates model development process and ensures better performance and consistency of the model. Figure 12.1 explores the various benefits related to AutoML.

12.3.1.1 Time Efficiency

By automating time-consuming tasks such as data preprocessing, feature engineering, model selection and hyperparameter tuning, AutoML significantly reduces the time required for model development and speeds up the whole process. This allows organizations to deploy ML solutions more rapidly and also saves time and resources.

12.3.1.2 Democratization of Machine Learning

AutoML systems are continuously evolving, integrating the latest advancements in machine learning algorithms and techniques. AutoML enables

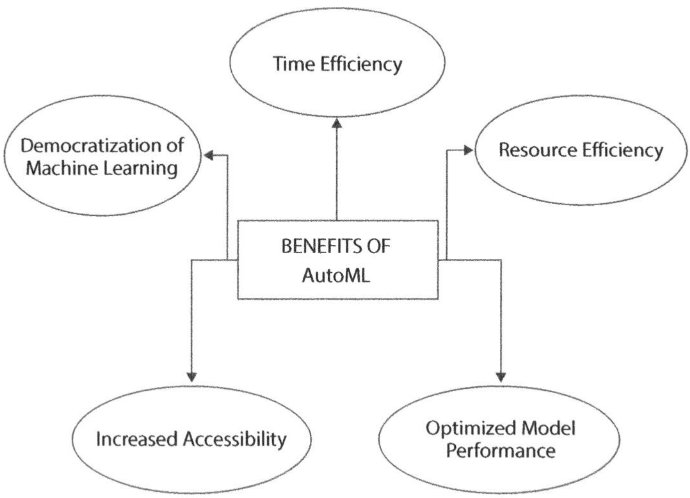

Figure 12.1 Benefits of AutoML.

individuals with varying levels of expertise to get involved in model development, bridging the barriers and enabling a wider range of users to indulge in this.

12.3.1.3 Increased Accessibility

AutoML makes machine learning accessible to individuals and organizations with limited expertise in data science, by automating the intricate processes. It lowers the barrier to entry, expanding the pool of users who can contribute to and benefit from data-driven decision marking.

12.3.1.4 Optimized Model Performance

AutoML uses algorithms to explore a vast configuration space, models and configurations for specific datasets, often identifying solutions that outperform the models developed manually. This leads to improved model performance tailored to the specific characteristics of the data.

12.3.1.5 Resource Efficiency

AutoML optimizes the allocation of computational resources [2]. By efficiently exploring the model space, and by reducing the need for specialized skills and streamlining the model development process, AutoML can lower the associated costs. This makes it a cost-effective option for various organizations.

12.3.2 Challenges of AutoML

While AutoML brings various advantages, it also presents several challenges that need to be addressed for its effective implementation in the industry. These challenges include problems related to data quality, model transparency and the balance between automation and human intervention. It is crucial for organizations to understand these challenges, in order to ensure easy integration of AutoML into their workflows. Figure 12.2 explores the main challenges faced by organizations while implementing.

12.3.2.1 Lack of Interpretability

AutoML's automated nature can sometimes result in complex models with reduced interpretability. In applications where interpretability is important, understanding these decisions made by highly automated models might be difficult.

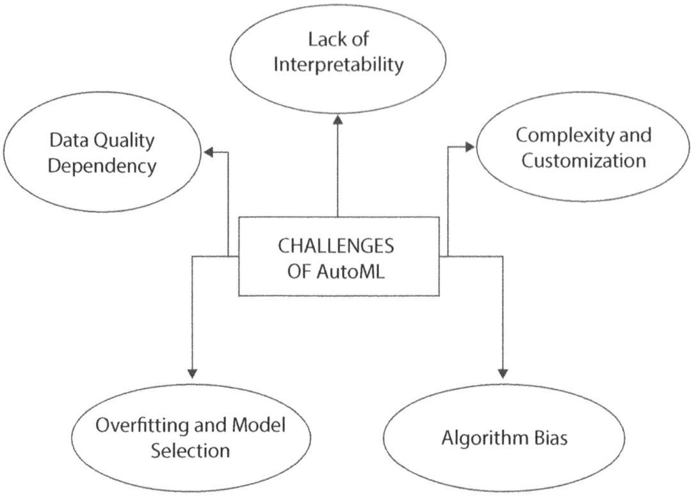

Figure 12.2 Challenges of AutoML.

12.3.2.2 Data Quality Dependency

AutoML's overall performance and efficiency depends on the type and quality of input raw data. If the data is noisy or biased or inaccurate in any way, then AutoML might struggle to develop an accurate model which produces accurate result.

12.3.2.3 Overfitting and Model Selection

AutoML systems sometimes might try various model configurations which lead to overfitting, good performance on training data but poor performance on testing data. AutoML algorithm might confuse between overfitting and generalization.

12.3.2.4 Algorithmic Bias

If the training data that is used for our model is biased in any way, then it may lead to unethical results.

12.3.2.5 Complexity and Customization

Incorporating AutoML's tools into the existing workflows of the business can a confusing, complex and time-consuming task, requiring updates in both the business processes and model infrastructure.

12.4 Industrial Applications of AutoML: McDonald's

12.4.1 Background

McDonald's is a giant fast-food franchise established in 1940. It has its joints all over the world, and to scale this fast-food chain on such a level made things complicated. Conventional methods were of no use with the varied market. McDonald's therefore chose to adopt automated tools in its business.

Millions of customers across the globe buy their products regularly and they expect the same quality and experience at every visit. This is where the data-driven approach helped McDonald's to transform its business. For such volume and scale, automation and personalization of customer experience were the need of the hour and AutoML helped McDonald's to optimize its operations and scale decision-making process.

McDonald's didn't decide to use AutoML on a whim; it was rather a paradigm shift in the way the organization looked at its business problems. It meant moving away from the older way of doing things and embracing a much more dynamic and responsive organizational structure that harnessed data to drive decisions. This case study will explore in depth the McDonald's AutoML experience and will explain in detail how a fast-food chain "takes a leap of faith" with innovation to radically alter its organizational structure and remain a top dog in the highly competitive and volatile industry it operates in. The four basic sections below will expand on the strategy, implementation, and consequences of AutoML becoming an indispensable part of McDonald's ethos.

12.4.2 Introduction

In the fast-paced and competitive world of fast food, McDonald's has always been a symbol of innovation and operational excellence. This case study goes behind the scenes of McDonald's to explore its journey into Automated Machine Learning (AutoML) and the impact it has had on business. McDonald's, with thousands of outlets and a complex supply chain, faced the industry challenges: operational efficiency, meeting changing customer demands, and staying ahead in a data-driven world. Recognizing the need for transformation, McDonald's saw AutoML as the catalyst for change.

As we go into the details of McDonald's AutoML journey we will explore not just the technical but the strategic thinking that led to AutoML being integrated into daily operations. This case study is the window into the potential of AutoML in the fast-food industry, and how technology can change the trajectory of a global brand. Join us as we go behind the scenes of McDonald's AutoML implementation and find out the strategic moves that took this industry leader into a new era of efficiency and innovation.

12.4.3 Artificial Intelligence in McDonald's

McDonald's over the years has had the practice of adjusting their offerings to suit various customers' preferences wherever they operate. In Asia, Asian taste buds generally prefer stronger flavors and more complex spices than those available in the West. McDonald's in Asia uses a plethora of sauces and seasonings compatible with the local taste whereas in the West they generally stick to the basics and so that is reflected in their menu offerings. The various sauces and spice options are either limited or do not exist at all. It is one of the factors that have made McDonald's among the best fast-food giants around the world. Wherever they may operate, they generally carry the day on customers' taste buds and hearts.

Besides the cooking genius that McDonald's possesses, McDonald's has fostered a loving affair with technology and has indulged in it in all facets of their corporate activities. Technology is a crucial ingredient in McDonald's from the sourcing of its raw materials to the advertising of its finished products; all the links in the McDonald's value chain involve technology at one point or the other. Of great importance is AI, which has shown in all ramifications that it is a complete game changer and has driven most of the innovations seen in the impressive ramp of McDonald's as well as its efforts towards productivity. AI has assisted McDonald's in streamlining all its chains, improving customers' experience, and generally staying relevant.

Here we get into all the ways AI is being used within the McDonald's system to drive the business. From predictive analytics to forecast demand and optimize inventory to personalized marketing campaigns based on individual preferences, AI has changed the way McDonald's serves its customers. Plus, AI-powered self-service kiosks and automated order fulfilment have streamlined operations, reduced wait times, and overall efficiency. As McDonald's continues to go all in on AI it's going to get even bigger as a global fast-food leader.

12.4.3.1 Drive-Thru Chains

Drive-Thru is one of the coolest collaborations between AI and McDonald's. Drive-thrus are built separate from the McDonald's restaurant; they allow customers to order food much faster and save time. It also allows the McDonald's staff to differentiate between eat-in and takeaway orders. Those who want to take away their orders get a different packaging and a different counter which is McDonald's AI-driven Drive-thru.

McDonald's recently partnered with IBM to automate all the Drive-thrus. It's also seen that the food joints that adopted the AI automation system have 85% order accuracy. In this system, AI robots take food orders instead of human staff.

Since 2018 McDonald's reports that the Drive-thrus have shaved 30 seconds off the time it takes to serve drive-thru customers, which resulted in higher customer satisfaction [3].

Now with technology, McDonald's allows customers to order from their tables. Scanners are on the tables where customers can order and pay online. Their order comes to their table without them having to wait in line for their order.

McDonald's also allows its customers to place orders through their phones and pick up the orders at the restaurant. This app enables McDonald's to gather data about its customers' preferences, which in turn helps McDonald's to further customize its food products and services to accommodate its customers' needs.

12.4.3.2 Self-Service Kiosk

Self-ordering kiosk is a freestanding kiosk with a large touch display with a payment unit that accepts cards and a receipt printer. In 2015, McDonald's began self-ordering kiosks in the United States, and after deploying the self-service, there was an increase in McDonald's sales. In the first year of deploying this self-service kiosk, there was an increase of 6% in sales. Also, there was an increase of 20% in average order size and a 30% increase in average order value, all of this credited to kiosks [4]. Because of the AI technology kiosks use, it suggests different food items to customers, resulting in a boost in sales. Self-service kiosks improved the efficiency and accuracy of the orders placed while dividing the customer traffic between the kiosks and the order counters.

12.4.3.3 Predictable Purchases

With the help of Artificial Intelligence, McDonald's can predict what type of orders their upcoming customer will place. With the previous order history and the trending food items, McDonald's AI automated ordering system will be able to predict orders. The system uses different Artificial Intelligence algorithms that study records, observe the current trending food products, and then predict future order activities. This technology also updates the drive-thru digital display based on the current order selections, restaurant traffic, popularity of different food items, time of day, and weather conditions. This also helps McDonald's to optimize its inventory as well as the ordering processes, ensuring that the popular food items are always in stock and reducing food waste.

12.4.3.4 Voice Recognition

Fast-food giant McDonald's has reportedly adopted the latest voice recognition technology to streamline its order-taking system and to make its overall order processing accurate and efficient. Through the implementation of voice recognition technology, the employees at McDonald's can easily bark the orders, enabling the order-taking display screen to quickly assign them and to do it with utmost accuracy. The high-end screen reportedly uses advanced natural language processing computer algorithms for reading spoken orders and artificial human voices for responding to them [5, 7].

With the help of AI-enabled voice recognition, McDonald's employees can now effortlessly read the orders and the giant fast-food chain can effortlessly work in a faster, smarter, and more accurate way. As per the reports, the use of AI-powered voice recognition technology is an advancement for McDonald's that is enabling its workers and staff members to communicate with the order-taking processing system faster.

By facilitating easy communication between the workers and the order-taking system using natural language processing algorithms, McDonald's facilitated its workers to quickly take the orders in a less error-prone and less time-consuming way. Also, by integrating artificial human voices, the order-taking screen can easily provide more clarity and consistency to the overall order delivery process and accurately transmit and assign orders.

Hence, in general, the employment of AI-empowered voice recognition innovation fundamentally proposes that McDonald's is attempting to use innovation to extend its functional limit. By embracing this cutting-edge innovation, McDonald's not only accelerates its request-preparing operations but also makes a progressively viable and receptive administration situation for its clients. As McDonald's will keep on relying on the potential of AI and other up-and-coming innovations, it will remain ahead of the pack in the quick-food industry, constantly attempting to give astounding encounters to its purchasers the world over. Voice recognition additionally helps with recommending upgrades or including a food-related thing with the dinner such as active food offers and discounts at McDonald's.

Furthermore, AI-enabled driver voice recognition technology at McDonald's involves the organization's willingness to always be ahead of the curve in the fast-food industry, constantly striving to use technology to drive vital changes. By embracing rising technologies like natural language processing and artificial voice McDonald's demonstrates its willingness to constantly try to improve customer experience and labor productivity.

The use of AI-based driver voice recognition enables internal operations but also raises the overall speed and accuracy of the order preparation process, resulting in greater customer satisfaction and stickiness. As McDonald's continues to depend on the potential of AI across its value chain, it will be ahead of the curve in the fast-food industry, constantly striving to use technology to drive vital changes.

12.4.4 AutoML Implementation at McDonald's

AST food chain multinational has recently embarked upon its long-pending journey to effectively exploit the potential of data-driven decision-making. McDonald's is undoubtedly a global industry leader that has consistently remained on the cutting edge of employing innovative technologies to enhance its business processes and customer services. With the emergence of AutoML, McDonald's is poised to revolutionize its handling of myriad areas of its business from efficient supply chain management to tailored marketing strategies. AutoML deploys automation of the entire end-to-end model development process, which helps McDonald's to harness advanced machine learning algorithms without the need to engage huge technical manpower and in turn ease operations, boost efficiency, and create new avenues for innovation. Figure 12.3 assesses the functionalities of AutoML at McDonald's.

Figure 12.3 AutoML implementation at McDonald's.

12.4.4.1 Operational Streamlining for Unprecedented Efficiency

With the help of AutoML's algorithms McDonald's optimized operational processes, and made adjustments to balance out the changing demands with the complex nature of their business chain.

12.4.4.2 Precision in Marketing Strategies through Personalization

AutoML helped McDonald's to create targeted marketing campaigns and promotion by analyzing the customer data.

12.4.4.3 Demand Forecasting and Inventory Management

AutoML analyzed historical data, patterns in McDonald's large datasets to forecast demands and create an optimized inventory management system which ensured cost efficiency.

12.4.4.4 Elevating the Customer Experience

AutoML's insights on the customer data allowed McDonald's to offer personalized menus to its customers based on their preferences and even optimized the drive-thru operations to make every interaction tailored to the individual.

12.4.4.5 Adaptability to Local Markets

As a global brand with world-renowned presence, McDonald's had to adapt to local markets and customize their strategies to cater to a wider range of customer, and AutoML made it easy for them.

12.4.4.6 Efficiency Gains and Tangible Cost Reductions

By automating various tasks within the business, AutoML delivered real efficiency and cost savings to the business.

12.4.5 Result and Impact

12.4.5.1 Personalized Marketing Driving Customer Engagement

AutoML analyzed customer data and provided insights to create targeted and personalized campaigns for marketing purposes. Not only did they see an increase in brand love but in sales too.

12.4.5.2 Optimized Drive-Thru Operations for Seamless Experiences

With AutoML the customer experience at McDonald's changed. Personalized menu recommendations based on individual preferences and streamlined drive-thrus increased customer satisfaction and speed of service. The result was a more seamless and enjoyable experience for customers which drove loyalty and word of mouth.

12.4.5.3 Precision in Demand Forecasting

Accurate demand forecasting meant precise inventory management, less waste, and no stockouts. The impact was felt across the supply chain; cost savings and resource utilization were the key metrics of success.

12.4.5.4 Adaptation to Local Markets for Global Success

Since AutoML can learn by local market conditions they were able to localize their strategies. This strategy appealed to different kinds of customers and increased market share across different regions. McDonald's was able to tailor their strategies to local customer preferences and proved that a global brand can adopt a data-driven strategy. Not only were the operations improved but the savings McDonald's achieved with AutoML were massive.

12.4.5.5 Economic Impact and Cost-Efficiency

However, the economic impact went beyond operational improvements. McDonald's saw cost savings across multiple areas, from inventory to marketing. The automated decision-making was optimizing resource allocation and overall cost. AutoML became a technology and a strategic driver of economic sustainability.

12.5 Industrial Applications of AutoML: Deliveroo

12.5.1 Background

Deliveroo is a UK-based online food delivery company. It was started in 2013 in London, England, by Wil Shu, and Greg Orlowski. On Deliveroo, customers can order from their favourite food stalls or restaurants and get it delivered to their door. Deliveroo earns money by earning a percentage from the restaurants and also from customers; for every order they make delivery charges.

It allows food outlets or restaurants to reach a wider customer base and provides customers with convenient and easy ordering and delivery services. A network of delivery riders is there to facilitate the whole food delivery process; delivery riders pick up the food from the restaurant and deliver it to customers.

Over time, Deliveroo started growing and expanding, and it became hard for them to cope with the demand. Their infrastructure was simply not built for the massive amount of food orders and app traffic to be handled during peak lunch and dinner times, which sometimes resulted in slow and lagging system performance [8]. This had a bad impact on customers' experience and Deliveroo's reputation.

Infrastructure flexibility was also not high enough to adapt to customer needs and market perspectives very quickly, which resulted in Deliveroo's inability to practice innovation and stay one step ahead of its competitors. Deliveroo was managing its technology infrastructure using costly physical servers and data centres, which involved initial capital investment and maintenance expenses. To stay profitable while growing, Deliveroo had to optimize spending on servers and data centres.

While growing, Deliveroo needed to make sure that the platform it built was secure and safe and that customers and restaurants data was protected, so that there was no unauthorized access to their infrastructure.

12.5.2 Introduction

Deliveroo has pioneered and changed the way of meal delivery in the fast-moving, reliable, and operationally efficient food delivery market. This case study will investigate how Deliveroo's innovation in using Automated Machine Learning (AutoML) and Amazon Web Services (AWS) has helped Deliveroo to achieve greater success in the highly competitive food delivery industry.

Deliveroo was established in 2013 and quickly established its brand by linking consumers to a multitude of restaurants and providing easy and reliable delivery service. But as the business grew, Deliveroo needed a tool to scale its business, streamline operations and analyse market data for decision making. By exploiting the potential of AutoML with the necessary infrastructure support from AWS, Deliveroo streamlined its operations, enhanced its delivery mechanism, and achieved operational excellence at scale [9].

Through this case study, we'll get to know how Deliveroo has adapted to the competition through technology, and how it has helped them achieve operational excellence with differentiation. This story will uncloak the immense importance of innovation to sustain competitiveness and give other organizations a complete blueprint on how to scale up their performance through the right technology alliances.

12.5.3 AWS Tools Used by Deliveroo

Deliveroo uses several AWS tools to scale its business and power its platform and services. Table 12.1 explores the main purpose and benefits of various AWS tools used by Deliveroo.

Table 12.1 Purpose and benefits of various AWS tools.

AWS tools	Purpose	Benefits
Amazon EC2	Scalable compute capacity	Handles traffic spikes, flexible infrastructure
Amazon S3	Object storage service	Data storage, backup and recovery
Amazon ELB	Load balancing	Distributes incoming traffic and enhances availability
Amazon CloudWatch	Logging and monitoring	Tracks metrics, triggers alarms and monitors applications
Amazon Rote 53	Domain name service	Scalable domain name system
AWS Lambda	Serverless computing	Automatic scaling, reduced operational overhead
Amazon SQS	Message queuing service	Ensures reliable communication
Amazon SNS	Messaging and notification services	Facilitates communication between services

(Continued)

Table 12.1 Purpose and benefits of various AWS tools. (*Continued*)

AWS tools	**Purpose**	**Benefits**
Amazon DynamoDB	NoSQL database service	Scalable data handling, low-latency performance
AWS CloudFormation	Infrastructure as code	Simplifies infrastructure management
Amazon CloudTrail	Log administration	Track user activities and monitors usage of API's
AWS CloudPipeline	Continuous integration and fast delivery	Automates release pipelines and ensure fast delivery of new features
Amazon Kinesis	Real-time data streaming	Practices and analyzes streaming data

12.5.3.1 Amazon Elastic Compute Cloud (EC2)

Amazon EC2 is a web service that provides organizations with resizable computing capacity in the cloud. Deliveroo runs its website and back-end services on the cloud with scalable compute storage provided by EC2 [10]. EC2 instances can be easily and quickly launched and can be cost-effectively scaled up and down to provide Deliveroo with the resources it needs.

12.5.3.2 Amazon Simple Storage Service (S3)

Amazon Simple Storage Service is an object storage service that provides data availability, security, and performance. To store and retrieve customer data from anywhere in the cloud, Amazon S3 was used by Deliveroo.

12.5.3.3 Amazon Elastic Load Balancing (ELB)

Deliveroo uses ELB to distribute the incoming traffic to multiple Amazon EC2 instances in the cloud without any intervention. It enables Deliveroo to achieve high levels of fault tolerance with their application.

12.5.3.4 Amazon CloudWatch

Amazon CloudWatch is a service by Amazon to monitor the AWS resources and the applications that you run on the AWS cloud in real time. Deliveroo deploys it to monitor the AWS resources they are using, including RDS Databases and EC2 instances, and also to receive notifications when certain limits are exceeded and provide it with a detailed analysis of the utilization and performance of the AWS resources.

12.5.3.5 Amazon Route 53

Amazon Route 53 is a scalable Domain Name System (DNS) web service. Deliveroo uses Route 53 to manage its DNS infrastructure and route end users to different AWS services and internet apps.

12.5.3.6 AWS Lambda

AWS Lambda allows Deliveroo to run the code without any provision or managing the servers and pay only for the compute time that it uses. It automatically scales to handle any amount of traffic.

12.5.3.7 Amazon Simple Queue Service (SQS)

Amazon Simple Queue Service (SQS) is a fully managed message queuing service that lets you send, receive, and store messages between software components. To scale and decouple the microservices that communicate asynchronously, SQS is used by Deliveroo.

12.5.3.8 Amazon Simple Notification Service (SNS)

Amazon Simple Notification Service (SNS) is a scalable messaging service that we use to send one message to different numbers of end users. Through SNS Deliveroo sends push notifications to its customers on their mobile application.

12.5.3.9 Amazon DynamoDB

Amazon DynamoDB is a fully managed NoSQL database that helps provide scalable performance with low latency. To customize the user experience by tracking user behavior and storing user session data, DynamoDB is used by Deliveroo.

12.5.3.10 AWS CloudFormation

AWS CloudFormation is a service that allows developers to define the AWS services just by using a simple templating language. For the automation of its infrastructure deployment and application, Deliveroo uses the service CloudFormation.

12.5.3.11 Amazon CloudTrail

Amazon CloudTrail is a web service used by Deliveroo to monitor all the API calls that are made to its AWS services and log them. It also provides visibility to the activity of the users and changes in resources.

12.5.3.12 AWS CodePipeline

AWS CodePipeline is a continuous integration and delivery service that helps you automate your release pipelines for fast and reliable updates. It integrates with various AWS services and third-party tools, allowing you to build, test, and deploy code changes with ease.

12.5.3.13 Amazon Kinesis

Amazon Kinesis enables real-time processing of streaming data at a massive scale, allowing you to collect, process, and analyze data in real time. It offers capabilities to handle various data streams, including video, audio, application logs, website clickstreams, and IoT telemetry data [11].

These tools help Deliveroo to build and run its infrastructure on the cloud, by providing highly available and scalable services to its customers. Different AWS services are used for different purposes, such as computing, management of databases, monitoring, automation, security purposes, and storage. For these purposes, various AWS tools are used by Deliveroo, so that the underlying infrastructure is taken care of by AWS, and Deliveroo just focuses on the core operations of its business.

12.5.4 AWS and AutoML Integration at Deliveroo

Deliveroo undertook a strategic journey that redefined the contours of its operations by integrating AutoML and AWS, which propelled it to new stages of scalability, efficiency, and innovation.

12.5.4.1 *Scaling Operations with AWS*

The story begins with Deliveroo's global expansion ambitions and the imperative to scale operations seamlessly. Using AWS's elastic computing and data services, Deliveroo built the foundation for ethical scaling. From elastic computing to data storage and management, the pay-as-you-go model meant costs were optimized and aligned to ethical principles, with no big upfront investments, and financial responsibility [12].

12.5.4.2 *AutoML's Role in Precision Decision-Making*

To decode patterns in large datasets, predicting delivery times and optimizing the delivery person routes, AutoML's algorithms helped Deliveroo to optimize.

12.5.4.3 *Seamless Data Management and Analytics*

Deliveroo used AWS to store, refine and analyze large amount of data in real time and then with incorporation of AutoML algorithms gain insights from the data about customer preferences.

12.5.4.4 *Dynamic Adaptability to Market Demands*

With integration of AutoML and AWS, Deliveroo could respond to market dynamics, and optimize resource allocation easily.

12.5.4.5 *Enhancing Customer Experiences*

With integration of AutoML and AWS, Deliveroo could give personalized recommendations to customers and optimize delivery time.

12.5.4.6 *Cost-Efficiency and Sustainable Growth*

The strategic combination of AWS and AutoML wasn't just about efficiency, it was about growth. The cloud-native approach of AWS meant we could optimize costs with pay-as-you-go models, no more big upfront investments [6]. AutoML on top of that was operational efficiency and further accelerated our path to sustainable and cost-effective growth.

12.5.5 Outcomes and Achievements

The measurable outcomes and success that followed this strategic move are a perfect example of how technology, when held as a strategic tool, can transform entire industries and define new benchmarks for excellence.

12.5.5.1 Exponential Scalability

Deliveroo's architecture on AWS provided the foundation for nearly unlimited scalability. Because the architecture is cloud-native, Deliveroo can seamlessly scale its infrastructure to support its growing user base and expand into new markets. Scalability meant a more resilient and highly available platform that could sustain performance during periods of peak demand.

12.5.5.2 Precision in Delivery Operations

AutoML enabled Deliveroo to improve the accuracy of its delivery routes. Using automated algorithms, Deliveroo could predict and prepare efficient routes, and also estimate delivery timings, and notify users accordingly. Moreover, routes could be adjusted according to real-time traffic changes and dynamic demand. More efficient deliveries meant an improved level of service that users could notice.

12.5.5.3 Data-Driven Decision-Making

AWS and AutoML combined gave Deliveroo unprecedented data-driven insights. Its platform could leverage huge data sets and use them to guide strategic moves, activate marketing campaigns, and personalize user service accordingly. Actionable intelligence derived from data became the differentiator that helped Deliveroo succeed, and stay one step ahead of its competitors in a very competitive market.

12.5.5.4 Enhanced Customer Experiences

Dynamic changes such as weather, traffic, historical data, etc., could be easily adapted to create a unique and enjoyable experience for users.

12.5.5.5 Operational Efficiency and Cost Savings

The pay-as-you-go capacity of AWS meant Deliveroo could streamline costs and achieve sustainable growth and profitability.

12.5.5.6 *Innovation and Competitive Edge*

Strategic moves such as Deliveroo's integration with AWS and AutoML, clearly positioned the company as a leader of innovation in its sector. The capacity to leverage the most advanced technologies available not only differentiates Deliveroo from its competitors but also defines the company as a trendsetter that influences industry benchmarks and the overall development of food delivery services.

12.6 Ethical Considerations

Maintaining data privacy is essential these days, especially for businesses that utilize AutoML in their analytics. Companies need to safeguard information from entry and security breaches. This entails implementing data encryption access restrictions [13]. Figure 12.4 explores some of the major ethical concerns that might arise while implementing AutoML algorithms into businesses.

12.6.1 Data Privacy

As the biggest fast-food chain in the world, McDonald's collects a ton of data about its customers through various means—online ordering, mobile apps, and in-store transactions. The biggest ethical challenges are making

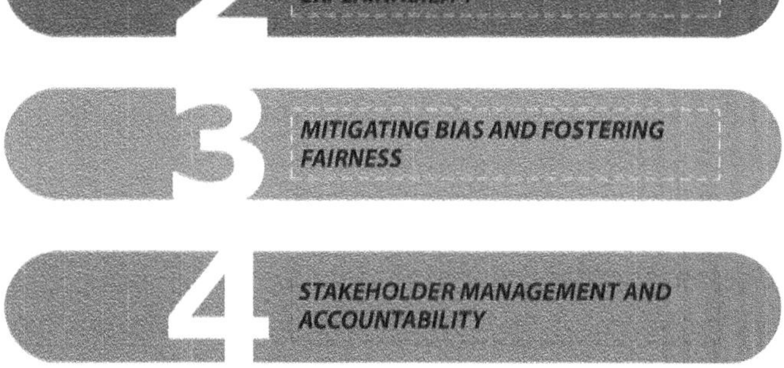

Figure 12.4 Ethical considerations.

sure this data is handled responsibly, upholding customers' right to privacy, and complying with international data protection laws like GDPR. In response, McDonald's has used strong encryption to secure data in transit and at rest, anonymization and pseudonymization to de-identify personal information, getting customers' explicit consent for AI-driven applications, and data minimization to collect only what's necessary [14].

As a meal delivery service, Deliveroo has specific data privacy issues. Deliveroo holds sensitive information on its delivery riders as well as customer data which makes it even more complicated. The platform takes steps to obscure the movements of its delivery riders by using privacy-preserving mechanisms for location data. Priority is given to open communication through user education on data usage, benefits of AI, and safety measures. Data is encrypted in transit through secure data transmission. Regular privacy audits are done to evaluate and improve data security procedures [15]. McDonald's and Deliveroo know that privacy is key to the ethical use of AI in their operations; that's why they are doing this to comply with data privacy laws and build trust with their stakeholders and customers.

12.6.2 Transparency and Explainability

To uphold moral principles and stakeholder trust, transparency, and explainability are key when using AutoML models. Both Deliveroo and McDonald's knew their algorithms needed to be made more understandable so internal teams and external stakeholders could understand how decisions were being made.

McDonald's recognized the need to be open to addressing concerns around potential bias and discriminatory behavior, so much so that they put AutoML into personalized marketing and menu development. McDonald's tried to demystify the decision-making process by putting in place steps to explain how the algorithms were making suggestions. This way staff and customers could understand why certain menu items were being recommended or promoted. This was not only open but also allowed McDonald's to anticipate and correct any misunderstandings about how AI was impacting customer experience [16].

Similarly, Deliveroo focused on showing the AutoML-driven algorithms behind its resource allocation and route optimization as it's in the gig economy. This was important for the internal logistics of the company as well as the delivery staff who rely on fair and efficient route assignments.

12.6.3 Mitigating Bias and Fostering Fairness

Algorithmic bias detection and reduction is one of the key ethical considerations in the use of AutoML for McDonald's and Deliveroo. McDonald's deployed AutoML in such a way that it provided better suggestions and menu optimization for their customers. The company made sure that no prejudices were present in the suggestions. McDonald's took a preview of the historical data to implement such a strategy.

Similarly, Deliveroo faced a big challenge to mitigate the food delivery staff bias. One of the major challenges that the company faced was to ensure fairness in algorithmic decisions when it came to the delivery staff. Multiple factors such as delivery location, time and size of the order played an important role in in how the routes was assigned. Deliveroo made sure that no such bias or any other complaints about discriminatory behaviour were raised. They used the historical data to provide the model with more information to get better outcomes.

Both companies identified the flaws and the risks of biased decision-making. They tried to fix it by adding a factor of fairness. The aim of the companies was to remove the existing bias, and to further identify more bias and remove it. This helped the companies get a hold on the ethics in AutoML [17].

12.6.4 Stakeholder Management and Accountability

Stakeholder involvement is a major ethical concern within any organizations. A stakeholder can be anybody—consumer, organization workers, investors, and regulatory bodies. Organizations should maintain transparency to build trust among their stakeholders.

Both companies, McDonald's and Deliveroo, took various steps to involve their stakeholders in the business. McDonald's held various workshops to collect inputs from consumers on their marketing campaigns. They also arranged open-ended sessions within the organizations among their workers about their different marketing strategies. Similarly, Deliveroo set up forums where the delivery person could voice their opinions and write any complaints they had.

By taking both these types of measures the companies showed seriousness towards their stakeholders.

12.7 Future Trends

12.7.1 Emerging Trends in AutoML

Here are a few trends that will shape AutoML and the cloud:

12.7.1.1 Enhanced Model Explainability

The future of AutoML will focus on models with better explainability. As machine learning gets more widespread, being able to interpret and understand the decisions made by automated algorithms will be key. The models will provide better outcomes when provided with more data to improve the explainability [18].

12.7.1.2 Democratization of AI Continues

The trend of democratizing AI with AutoML is going to get even more pronounced. Platforms that allow people with varying skill sets to use machine learning without deep expertise will multiply. This democratization will spread data-driven decision-making across industries.

12.7.1.3 Integration of AutoML with Edge Computing

Edge computing, where processing happens closer to the data, will marry up with AutoML. This will mean real-time, local decision-making especially in scenarios where latency is key, like autonomous vehicles, smart cities, and IoT.

12.7.1.4 Hybrid Cloud Deployments for Flexibility

Hybrid cloud architectures, combining on-premises infrastructure with public and private cloud services will become more popular. This means flexibility, so organizations can use the scalability of the cloud but keep control of sensitive data and applications on-premises [19].

12.7.1.5 AutoML for Structured and Unstructured Data

AutoML will extend to include not just structured data as is today but also unstructured data types. NLP and image recognition models built with AutoML will be used to extract insights from all sorts of data sources and open up new avenues for innovation.

12.7.1.6 Integration of AutoML in Industry-Specific Solutions

We will see more industry-specific AutoML solutions. Not all data in every industry is ideal for automated modelling. There will be specialized AutoML platforms for healthcare, finance, manufacturing, and other sectors. Organizations will have access to industry-specific tools that automatically prepare data and deploy models to improve business decision-making.

12.7.1.7 Continuous Model Monitoring and Maintenance

More attention will be paid to the entire machine learning life cycle including model monitoring and maintenance. Automated model monitoring solutions will monitor model performance, detect drift, and trigger retraining workflows automatically. Operators will not neglect deployed models.

12.7.1.8 Emphasis on Responsible AI and Ethical Considerations

Once AI-driven decisions start impacting key business decisions, responsible AI will become a major topic. How can we build trustworthy automated decision-making systems? As models become part of complex workflows, ethics, and explainability need to be seamlessly integrated into existing AutoML pipelines to detect bias, unfairness, and lack of transparency in model predictions.

12.7.1.9 Quantum Computing's Impact on AutoML

Quantum computing will start affecting AutoML in a major way. As complex computations that currently take months to complete on conventional computers may one day be executed in a matter of minutes on quantum machines, we may see completely new algorithms and models.

12.7.2 Considerations for Implementation

When implementing AutoML and cloud services you need to consider many things to be successful and get the most out of these technologies. Here are some things to keep in mind:

12.7.2.1 Clearly Defined Objectives

Before you start implementing you need to have clear and measurable goals. Whether it's to improve operational efficiency, decision-making, or scale business processes having a clear roadmap means AutoML and cloud integration will align with your business strategy.

12.7.2.2 Data Quality and Accessibility

AutoML depends on the quality and availability of data. Having a solid data infrastructure including data cleaning, normalization, and accessibility is key. Organizations need to assess the completeness, accuracy, and relevance of their data as the effectiveness of AutoML models depends on the quality of the input data.

12.7.2.3 Skillset and Training

While AutoML is used to automate tasks with minimal human intervention, giving users training and improving their skillset must be required so that they get a grasp of these tools and extract the best from them.

12.7.2.4 Regulatory Compliance and Ethical Considerations

Incorporating AutoML algorithms within organizations, we must address ethical concerns and make sure the AutoML process complies with industry standards.

12.7.2.5 Data Security and Privacy

As data become the foundation of AutoML, we must implement security measures and protocols to maintain data security and privacy.

12.7.2.6 Integration with Existing Systems

We have to make sure that the integration of AutoML is compatible with all the existing systems and architectures.

12.7.2.7 Cost Considerations and ROI

Organisations need to consider the costs of integrating AutoML into their systems and measure return on investment (ROI).

12.7.2.8 *Vendor Selection and Partnerships*

Evaluate vendors on their track record, scalability, support, and alignment with your organization's goals. Building strong relationships will help with success and ongoing support.

12.7.2.9 *Scalability and Futureproofing*

Design for scalability and future-proofing. Make sure the chosen AutoML and cloud solutions can scale with the organization's growth. Think about emerging technologies and industry trends to future-proof the implementation against rapid change.

12.7.2.10 *Change Management and User Adoption*

It's not just about the tech, it's about change management and user adoption. Communicate the value of AutoML and cloud to your stakeholders, provide training, and create a data-driven culture to get broad user adoption.

12.7.2.11 *Continuous Monitoring and Optimization*

Set up continuous monitoring and optimization of the solutions. Monitor model performance, address any data drift, and optimize configurations so AutoML models and cloud services stay aligned with your business goals.

12.8 Conclusion

From the inner workings of global fast-food giant McDonald's to the ever-changing landscape of food delivery Deliveroo, AutoML, and cloud services have shown us the way to scalability, efficiency, and innovation. In McDonald's, AutoML has gone beyond just technology. It's a strategic pillar that has taken the fast-food giant into a new era of operational excellence. From supply chain optimization to personalizing customer experiences, AutoML is embedded in McDonald's operations, showing the flexibility and impact of machine learning in a competitive industry.

Deliveroo's case study adds to the story of technological prowess where AutoML and Amazon Web Services (AWS) have put the company at the forefront of food delivery innovation. The scalability of AWS and the decision-making of AutoML have not only streamlined operations but also set new standards for customer experiences in the fast-changing food delivery market.

As we look to the future the trends and considerations are all about the evolution of AutoML and cloud. From model explainability to democratization of AI the landscape is all about responsible AI and continuous innovation. Quantum computing and AutoML with edge computing means the boundaries will be pushed further and further [20].

However, implementing AutoML and cloud is not without its challenges. Organizations need to navigate data quality, ethics, and cost. Vendor selection, user adoption, and change management will be key to the success of these transformation projects.

The evolving era of machine learning, specifically AutoML involves adaptation, innovation, and strategic choice. The stories of McDonald's and Deliveroo are examples of what happens when technology is used not just for efficiency but as a way to redefine the very fabric of the business. As we move into these transformational horizons the combination of AutoML and cloud services will shape industries, drive innovation, and take us into an era where the only limit is our imagination and strategic thinking.

References

1. Larsen, K.R. and Becker, D.S., *Automated Machine Learning for Business*, Oxford University Press, 2021.
2. Castelli, M., Pinto, D.C., Shuqair, S., Montali, D., Vanneschi, L., The Benefits of Automated Machine Learning in Hospitality. *Emerging Sci. J.*, 6, 6, 1237–1254, Sep. 2022. doi: http://dx.doi.org/10.28991/ESJ-2022-06-06-02.
3. Patel, A., *An evaluation of modern methods of delivering customer service and the role of AI: Case study of McDonald's (ITIS) Finland*, 2023, [Online]. Available: https://urn.fi/URN:NBN:fi:amk-2023053116451.
4. Procacci, S. and Pellicelli, A.C., The impact of Artificial Intelligence on consumers experience: the case of McDonald touch screens, in: *International Marketing Trends Conference*, ESCP, pp. 1–22, 2019, [Online]. Available: https://hdl.handle.net/2318/1716755.
5. Lloyd, W., Ramesh, S., Chinthalapati, S., Ly, L., Pallickara, S., Serverless computing: An investigation of factors influencing microservice performance, in: *2018 IEEE International Conference on Cloud Engineering (IC2E)*, pp. 159–169, 2018, doi: https://doi.org/10.1109/IC2E.2018.00039.

6. Lewis, P., Deliveroo's successful food delivery operation uses AWS in every part of its core business, in: *AWS for Industries*, Amazon Web Services, Sep. 29, 2022, [Online]. Available: https://aws.amazon.com/blogs/industries/deliveroos-successful-food-delivery-operation-uses-aws-in-every-part-of-its-core-business/. [Accessed: Jul. 1, 2024].
7. Sathyamoorthy, M., Vanitha, C.N., Dhanaraj, R.K., Balusamy, B., Introduction to Cyborgization Systems, in: *Studies in Computational Intelligence*, pp. 1–15, Springer Nature Singapore, 2023, https://doi.org/10.1007/978-981-99-4303-6_1.
8. Zeng, Y. and Zhang, J., A machine learning model for detecting invasive ductal carcinoma with Google Cloud AutoML Vision. *Comput. Biol. Med.*, 122, 103861, 2020.
9. Taneja, A., Rani, S., Dhanaraj, R.K., Nkenyereye, L., GCIRM: Towards Green Communication with Intelligent Resource Management Scheme for Radio Access Networks, in: *IEEE Transactions on Green Communications and Networking*, pp. 1–1, Institute of Electrical and Electronics Engineers (IEEE), 2024, https://doi.org/10.1109/tgcn.2024.3384542.
10. Juneja, A., Juneja, S., Bali, V., Mahajan, S., Multi-criterion decision-making for wireless communication technologies adoption in IoT. *Int. J. Syst. Dyn. Appl. (IJSDA)*, 10, 1, 1–15, 2021.
11. Juneja, S., Juneja, A., Anand, R., Reliability modeling for embedded system environment compared to available software reliability growth models, in: *2019 International Conference on Automation, Computational and Technology Management (ICACTM)*, pp. 379–382, 2019, doi: https://doi.org/10.1109/ICACTM.2019.9033810.
12. Anand, R., Sindhwani, N., Juneja, S., Cognitive Internet of Things, Its Applications, and Its Challenges: A Survey, in: *Harnessing the Internet of Things (IoT) for a Hyper-Connected Smart World*, vol. 91–113, 2022.
13. Mishra, R., Mishra, S., Sharma, D., Pdf-based node deployment scheme targeting efficient coverage in WSNs. *J. Ambient Intell. Human Comput.*, 2023. doi: https://doi.org/10.1007/s12652-023-04728-0.
14. Malathy, S., Sangeetha, K., Vanitha, C.N., Dhanaraj, R.K., Integrated Architecture for IoTSG, in: *Smart Grids and Internet of Things*, pp. 127–155, Wiley, 2023.
15. Liang, J., Meyerson, E., Hodjat, B., Fink, D., Mutch, K., Miikkulainen, R., Evolutionary neural autonomy for deep learning, in: *Proceedings of the Genetic and Evolutionary Computation Conference*, pp. 401–409, 2019.
16. Nagarajah, T. and Poravi, G., A review of automated machine learning (AutoML) systems, in: *2019 IEEE 5th International Conference for Convergence in Technology (I2CT)*, pp. 1–6, 2019, doi: https://doi.org/10.1109/I2CT45611.2019.9033810.
17. Xanthopoulos, I., Christophides, V., Simon, E., Salinger, A., Putting the Human Back in the AutoML Loop, in: *EDBT/ICDT Workshops*, 2020.

18. Shao, C., *et al.*, IoT data visualization for business intelligence in corporate finance. *Inf. Process. Manage.*, 59, 1, 102736, 2022.
19. Arya, A., *et al.*, Heart disease prediction with machine learning and virtual reality: from future perspective, in: *Extended Reality for Healthcare Systems*, pp. 209–228, Academic Press, 2023.
20. Singh, S.P., *et al.*, A New QoS Optimization in IoT-Smart Agriculture Using Rapid Adaption Based Nature-Inspired Approach. *IEEE Internet Things J.*, 2023.

13

AI Insights: Navigating Education News Ethically Through Aggregation and Sentiment Analysis

Anshumaan Garg and Dolly Sharma*

Department of Computer Science and Engineering, Amity University, Noida, India

Abstract

As per the ongoing trend, it is of immense importance that opinion-based analysis and sentiment of people on social media should be realised and be given priorities because it is one of the keys for businesses to grow and make profit and help political parties to analyse public sentiment. Using AI in an ethical manner can practically demonstrate the scaling of businesses, volume of profits and veracity of data which ensures the consistent and trustworthy use of AI. Our sentiments and opinions are the key factors which influence us and on the basis of which we take our decisions. For analysing the sentiments of people through the posts on social media handle is a relatively complex task because it needs timely updating so that accuracy scores can be high while analysing posts by people on social media. Create an interactive website to collect and display information on a specific topic. Enable users to publicly comment on the issue and provide real-time awareness of the public sentiments surrounding it. For sentiment analysis of tweets, start by installing Python libraries such as "pip install vader." Choose a code editor like Visual Studio Code for efficient programming. Utilize commands to navigate datasets and execute analysis scripts, employing tools like "python script.py" for execution. Adopt Django's Model-View-Template (MVT) architecture to structure the sentiment analysis project, organizing data models, views, and templates for seamless development. This approach facilitates the extraction and interpretation of sentiments from tweets, enhancing the understanding of public opinions. The results show the ongoing public sentiment regarding any specific scenario and can explicitly be used to prevent any kind of fake or fraudulent information on the

**Corresponding author*: dolly.azure@gmail.com; ORCID: 0000-0001-7406-9500

Sapna Juneja, Rajesh Kumar Dhanaraj, Abhinav Juneja, Malathy Sathyamoorthy and Asadullah Shaikh (eds.) Ethical Decision-Making Using Artificial Intelligence: Challenges, Solutions and Applications, (313–342) © 2025 Scrivener Publishing LLC

digital media. AI and its use in an ethical manner can immensely augment the capabilities of tools used for analysing and evaluating the present sentiment of the general public regarding that topic.

Keywords: Sentiment analysis, Vader, web scraping, BeautifulSoup, Django, MVT architecture, artificial intelligence

13.1 Introduction

13.1.1 Basics of Sentiment Analysis

Sentiment analysis (SA) or Opinion Mining (OM) is helpful in solving a vast range of problems that are of interest to human and computer interaction experts and specialists. It comes under the domain of artificial intelligence. It is also an area of interest for psychologists, linguists, advertisers, producers, consumers, and politicians. Since the dawn of data, and the huge volume in which it is generated on a daily basis, it has been of utmost importance that this data be analysed for varied uses that humans need to fulfil their tasks. It is used for analysing sentiment of text passed as a parameter to the analysing function which is mainly based on either the machine learning approach or the lexicon-based approach. The machine learning–based approach uses an algorithm and builds a model by the method of feature selection, i.e., by learning from labelled data sets [1]. Some of the popular and most frequently used methods are Naïve Bayes classifiers, Support Vector Machine (SVM) and Random Forest which is basically a part of machine learning and artificial intelligence. The algorithms which are mentioned have the ability to learn every kind of feature for classification by using the criteria of optimization, but the problem with ML-based algorithms is that the sentiment-based classifiers are trained on already pre-fed labelled data in a particular domain and these then do not work in different domains. In order to overcome this problem, lexicon-based methods are preferred over ML-based algorithms [1]. The approach based on Lexicon provides us with the information about which words and phrases are positive and negative. So a Lexicon-based approach is nothing but a list consisting of lexical features which are commonly labelled, based on the linguistic orientation, and it is either positive or negative. Experts and linguists, for proceeding with a lexicon-based approach have [2] to initially create a sentiment lexicon by the systematic arrangement and collection of sentiment list of words which is based on corpus-based approaches and a dictionary-based approach. After the list of sentiment words is compiled, polarity of the given input, based on the positive and negative indicators, is determined which are now known based on the given lexicon. The dictionary-based approach is achieved by taking a few examples initially and after that any online dictionary can be used for the expansion of sentiment lexicon by including synonyms and antonyms of those words. This dictionary can be filtered by human inspection. As shown in Figure 13.1, the ML-based approach and corpus-based approach are briefly shown in a flowchart. The corpus-based approach is used to find the sentimental inclination of context-based specific words. The following two methods are used under the corpus-based approach:

A) Statistical-based approach – If some combination of alphabets comes up with an erratic behaviour but in a beneficial manner, then the overall polarity of the sentence is considered to be positive, but if the combination shows a behaviour which is pessimistic in nature then the overall polarity of the sentence changes and tends to have a negative inclination. But if the prevalence of the optimistic and pessimistic text is equal in many ways then the overall polarity tends to have a neutral inclination [3].

B) Semantic-based approach – Under this method, values are assigned to words based on opinion or sentiment and also to the words which are closer to the words to which values are being assigned. This is done by finding synonyms and antonyms to words to which values are assigned [4].

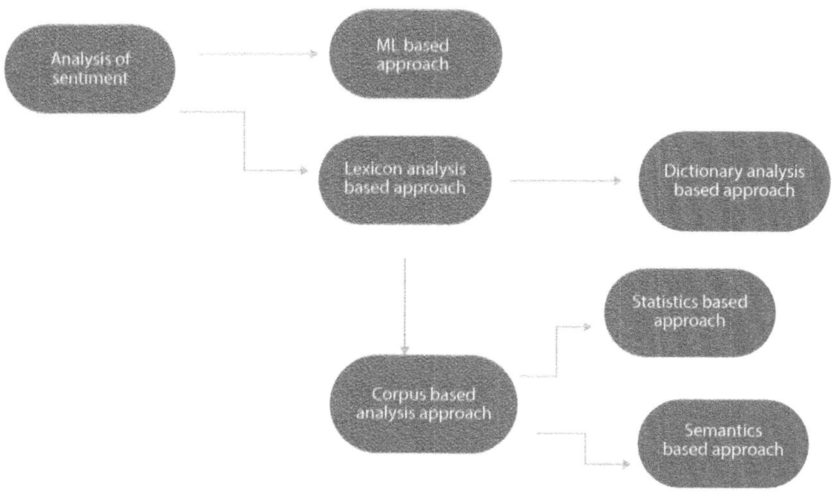

Figure 13.1 Showing the breakdown of lexicon-based approach.

Under the lexicon approach, some of the lexicons such as GI (General Inquirer) and LIWC (Linguistic Inquiry and Word Count) classifies the words into the categories of "POSITIVE" and "NEGATIVE" according to the way of their connotation orientation. LIWC has a pool of 4,500 words which have been classified into 76 categories and of them also, approximately 905 words are such that they are classified in two categories, particularly related to sentiment analysis [2]. LIWC is a well-tabulated and validated lexicon created by more than a decade of hard work by experts, specialists, linguists and psychologists. Although LIWC has a vast use in defining and redefining words and their sentiment it lacks a very significant feature which is a crucial aspect of sentiment analysis when talking in terms of social media such as Twitter, i.e., LIWC does not take into account acronyms, emoticons, initialisms and slang.

There are other lexicons also such as SentiWordNet, SenticNet and ANEW (Affective Norms for English Words). These type of lexicons associate with the valence scoring of text for analysing the sentiment intensity. The SentiWordNet consists of more than [5] one lakh synsets and these are labelled with sentiment scores categorised as positive, negative and objective. Although it is not as good a resource as WordNet still it has varied uses. In Figure 13.2, a lexicon-based flowchart has been shown describing the flow and the process of lexical semantic analysers. The lexicon-based approach has the biggest advantage in that it has its domain independence and above all it can be very easily improved and included in any application.

13.1.2 Data Scraping from Web

In our everyday lives, data is generated in humongous amounts and we need to filter, define and refine this data as per our needs and uses. But there is a problem, that this data is scattered over this infinite pool called WWW (World Wide Web) [6], hence the data filtration and refining becomes a problem. Hence we need a tool or maybe a method which lets us collect this data and the information related to that data at one place, which then could be used for further analysis. Web scraping or extraction or harvesting is a technique which is used to pull data from the World Wide Web and then use it or store as per the requirement. Generally, data on the web is scrapped by using the Hypertext transfer protocol (HTTP) or using a web browser. That can be accomplished by a user (manually) or by the use of a web crawler. First, an HTTP request is formulated which can get or acquire the data and information from the selected website. The request which will be sent to the website can be modified in either a URL form which contains a GET query or it could be an HTTP message containing a POST

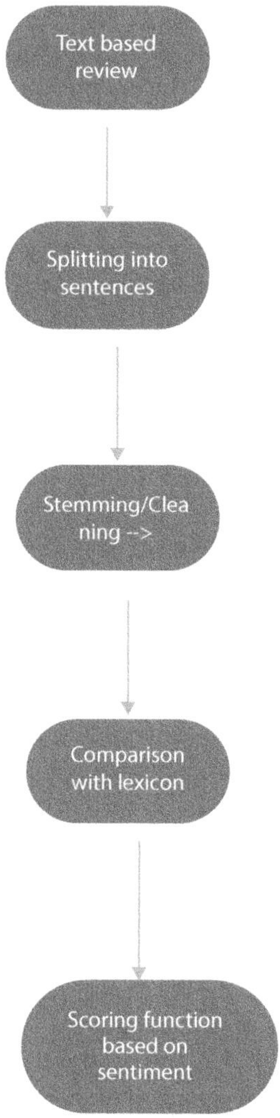

Figure 13.2 Different levels of lexicon-based analysis.

query. As and when the request is received and compiled by the website, the resources which were requested from that website are retrieved and are finally sent back to the program which sent for the resources. The data which is received can be in any format be it in HTML [3] (from which web pages are built), maybe the data-feeds are in XML or JSON type format or the received resources may be in multimedia type format such as pictures, audio, videos, etc. This data (be it in any form) is first downloaded; after that the process of retrieving useful data is initiated by parsing data and information received, and during this parsing the data is simultaneously reformatted and organised in a more presentable format or it can be more conveniently said as structured form of data, and is made available. For web scraping, two modules are very much needed; one module performs the [3] composing of the HTTP requests like the selenium while the other module is needed for the extraction and parsing of information from the basic HTML code using PyQuery or BeautifulSoup. The main use of UrlLib2 is that it defines a standardised set of functions for redirections, cookies and authentication, whereas selenium is a wrapper binding the web browser such as Google Chrome or Mozilla Firefox, thereby enabling the programmer to automate the work of browsing a website by coding. As far as data extraction is concerned, BeautifulSoup is made in such a way that it can scrape HTML and XML document content. it provides easy-to-use Python-based functions for the purpose of navigation, searching and modification of a parse tree, [3] which is basically a toolkit used for breaking down a HTML file and extracting information by using lxml or html5lib. The programming of BeautifulSoup or the structure of this library is such that it can by itself detect the encoded parsing under the processing and automatically convert the parsed code into client readable format. In the same way, PyQuery has a set of jQuery functions for the parsing of XML documents. But it is still unable to compete with BeautifulSoup because PyQuery only has a supporting hand for lxml so that XML documents can be processed at a faster rate [7].

13.1.3 Vader

Sentiment analysis describes the definition, description, and evaluation of Valence Aware Dictionary for Sentiment Reasoning which is also known as Vader. Sentiment analysis based on Vader is the reform in the identification and designation of the opinions which are expressed by people on social media, so that people's intention can be determined towards any particular event that occurred in the past, feedback related to a particular product, recommendations given about something or analyse data for some specific use [4]. The user's intention may be one of the main factors in determining what sentiment will get embedded in the article or review being posted by the user. Vader uses a collection and combination of the evaluative and quantifiable functions to produce and then validate a standard which shines in those names when sentiment lexicons are discussed. Above all, this lexicon is specifically tuned to microblogging type context. Next comes the compilation of evaluative and quantifiable lexical features with a special emphasis on five generalised rules which will encircle the grammar-based and syntax-based assumptions and conventions which human beings emphasize when expressing the sentiment intensity [8]. The inclusion of these heuristics will on a definite basis improve the accuracy of sentimental analysis driver engine spanning many domain contexts, be it social media analysis, reviewing news articles, movie-related reviews and product-based information and reviews. Of greater interest, when experimented upon this Vader lexicon gave remarkable results and performed very well in the domain of social media and the analysis of posts by people. In a greater surprise, it is also showed that individual human raters having a correlation coefficient (r = 0.888) was very close to the correlation coefficient described by Vader (r=0.881). This analysis is based on the same ground basis which is the average group mean derived from no less than 20 human raters, performing an analysis of each and every tweet. If we proceed with further analysis, the classification frequency of human raters is 0.84, whereas for Vader it is 0.96, which means that Vader is able to correctly classify tweets into optimistic (positive), pessimistic (negative) and neutral (positive and negative sentiment intensity is equal). Vader lexicon features have their own advantages and also retains the features of more common lexicons like LIWC; it is much bigger in nature but can be simply inspected, can be understood very well and above all it can be applied in a much more faster way with an easy extension [9]. Vader sentiment-based lexicon shines among the lexicons because it has a standardised quality and has been verified and validated by human beings. Vader is distinguished from other lexicons, especially LIWC, because it is more sensitised to expressions which are used in day-to-day conversations or tweets (in the case of Twitter), in general on social media, and it can be easily extended to other domains as well [6].

13.1.4 BeautifulSoup

Web scraping or extraction or harvesting is a technique which is used to pull data from the World Wide Web and then use it or store as per the requirement. Whenever we are discussing web scraping, web pages are the first things that come to mind because they are storage houses of large amounts of data [4]. The process by which we pull the information out of the web pages by using a web scraper is called web extraction. Nowadays we see every type of data being displayed on web pages and so it is obvious that when this data will be scraped from the web pages then every data type—be it multimedia such as video, images, text, time or titles, etc.—everything will be scraped [10]. A website is a collection of many web pages and it is based on the data which the owner wants to display on the website.

Also, there are two types of web pages, one which is static and the other which is dynamic. Static web scraping of data or web scraping of data from static web pages is very easy. This is because here we have to send an HTTP request to the server side, and the response which we will get, that will be the same page for which the request was sent and this does not require any extra or more of a complicated process [8]. But if we talk about dynamic web pages and scraping data from them, it is a very complicated process as the dynamic pages on the server side are based on server side scripting languages like Js, ASP, and PHP. Hence it would be more time-consuming to load and, moreover, it is possible that instead of getting a web page for the request that was made, we get a Js code as a response from the side of server. So it can be said that the web scraping that we do is done by sending an HTTP request to the website; then we get the page source which is then converted to a soup object and then we can get the required elements from it. But if the website was Js rendered which means Js will provide elements which are on the website, then simply sending the HTTP request will not get us the required data [4]. So in the case of dynamic type web scraping, it is required for the website to get loaded fully, after which the page source is fetched; therefore all the data is then loaded first and then scripting takes place. This way, dynamic or the continuously changing data can also be scraped from the web pages. The library used for parsing the HTML docs and defining the tags of HTML is BeautifulSoup. For parsing, it first creates a parse tree for the already parsed pages and then data is extracted through HTML. It receives the required data from HTML, XML and the other known markup languages. Say, for example, we came across a webpage that has all the relevant data related to our area of interest and requirement, and we want to scrape that data. For scraping that data, we would need BeautifulSoup for fetching the required data from that webpage, and it also removes the HTML tags and the other saved information [11].

13.1.5 Sentiment Analysis

Sentimental analysis is a vast field which needs exploration and discovery. It helps us determine what in true sense the user wants to convey through his words and what is the underlying emotion the user wishes to express through his oral or written form. In the past, people used to express themselves through letters, oral forms of communication, etc., which were usually long and the underlying sentiments were very much visible to the eye. Today, however, the length of expression has been substantially reduced and hence it is very difficult to understand and determine the sentiment of the expression by the person [5].

Generally people choose that medium to express themselves which is open and transparent and which gives them a feeling that they are a part of a large community where there are other people also who have those type of experiences. Moreover, we human beings are creatures who like to express ourselves and therefore our voice and opinions regarding any specific issue matters a lot. Our interaction with people on that level will be helpful in the promotion of a better world. So, to understand people's emotions better and to determine the underlying sentiments in the expressions and posts by the people on various social media handles was my motivation to do sentiment analysis.

13.1.6 Web Scraping

In the world that we live in today, information is the most significant factor in the determination and retrieval of results which are carried out by further analysis. But to get this information we need data, which are basically raw facts and figures, from various sources. This data is not available to everyone; not everyone is able to access it, and therefore this led to the birth of web scraping [7]. Scraping data from the web has entirely modified the method we use to retrieve data from the web, because now data retrieval has become very much simpler. Due to this web scraping, many businesses have profited and got a boost in their sales as the collection of leads was now possible. This process of collecting and gathering unstructured form of data is very interesting and if used carefully can turn profitable for many types of businesses. It has a great potential to enhance scientific researches and can prove informative for personnel usage [12]. The business of advertisement relies on the direct advertisement methods which are allocated through many pages for the current service to understand the actual context, data scraping and web wrapping are used in combination with content inspection tools for the context-based analysis of the page. Also when data sets are provided by researchers and analysts, they are made available to the public, but the way they are made public is different. A structured API is used for providing the dataset but this dataset is only accessible using forms and HTML which calls for the use of web wrapping, which basically converts the content into a relational form so that it can be processed as structured data [13]. Web scraping has also increased the personnel use of those tools which are required to combine components and page into a single collection of web pages.

13.1.7 Scope

This chapter covers the domain of web scraping and sentiment analysis in the context of news. News is scraped from the web based on the input keyword by the user, and the top ten most recent news are then listed on the website with all their information, such as when the news was uploaded, what is the media, the description of the news, the title of the news and the link to directly redirect to the news web-page. Input keyword could be any term related to some event that happened in the past or something that is going to happen. News will be scraped and it is not limited to any specific region or geographical area; rather it will fetch the news directly based on input term or the most near searched and the matched results. The purpose is to get the latest and updated news to people 24x7 which will be free from any kind of political bias. The limitation is that as live scraping is done it therefore takes a bit longer to search and get the results and print on the website.

13.1.8 Objectives

The objective is to develop an interactive website which can aggregate information regarding a particular topic. If the user wants to make a public comment regarding that issue, the second objective would be to make the user aware regarding that issue and the people's ongoing sentiments regarding it.

13.1.9 Chapter Outline

In this chapter, the literature review is about the working of BeautifulSoup, what is a DOM structure and the different functions which BeautifulSoup uses to look for the labels in the Dom structure. Also, in the case of sentiment analysis, methods to scrape tweets are discussed. Then for the sentiment analysis NLTK package is discussed and the pre-processing of tweets are also discussed. Further, the working of Vader is discussed. Methodology is discussed and what are the various Python library requirements, and further, the explanation of various snippets of code. Results and discussions have the code outputs with the explanation of each output. Also, the various advantages and disadvantages are listed. The conclusion and future work have been described, and references have been listed.

13.2 Literature Review

13.2.1 Working of BeautifulSoup

This has been used for scraping data from the web. It is a Python-based collection of data stored in the form of a database and it has a base of HTML or XML computational–based engine which is used for pulling out, analysing and modifying information which is present in the DOM tree of web pages. (This is basically a cross platform and linguistic independent base which sees HTML and XML documents in the form of a tree type structure and each node of the tree is an object which represents a specified part of the whole document) It can send an unparalleled series of unique and concise DOM-based visitor interfaces which directly or indirectly helps developers build a system which could be basis for the other models. Moreover, it has a very special characteristic, i.e., across the platform, it can be operated upon, indicating that it is flexible [3].

Clients of BeautifulSoup can, as indicated by their requirements, introduce explicit HTML/XML examination motors (e.g., xml, html5lib, and so forth). Taking lxml for instance, clients can install BeautifulSoup with the accompanying call: BeautifulSoup (markup,"lxml"). Subsequent to installing, BeautifulSoup gets all the related DOM tree structures for HTML records. Then utilizing an inherent series of associated works that relate with DOM API, it visits, gets, and alters the property estimations or sets of the assigned hubs of the DOM tree. BeautifulSoup has not only an underlying series of DOM API, but also many recently added new interfaces that standard DOM APIs don't have, settling on decisions that are more straightforward for engineers and developers [4].

BeautifulSoup will break down any archive passed to it, including a wide range of HTML/XML reports and typical records. In any case, just with HTML and XML records that meet specifications with BeautifulSoup create a comparing DOM tree and complete a progression of API calls to get the assigned information. Involving HTML for instance, BeautifulSoup first purposes an HTML analytics engine to change over the HTML record into a DOM tree, and afterward the client can utilize BeautifulSoup's provided request and altering capabilities to work on a DOM tree [11].

For data scraping, the DOM tree architecture is shown in Figure 13.3, describing the elements and the various components of the Document Object Model.

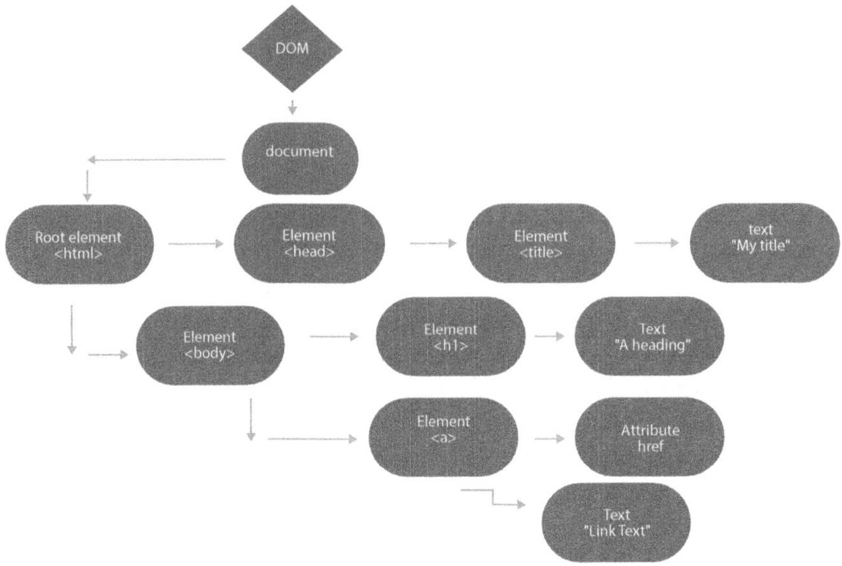

Figure 13.3 Structure of a DOM represented in the form of a tree.

In most of the request interfaces provided by BeautifulSoup (e.g., findPrevious, findPreviousSibling, findParend, findParents, and so forth), all will call the two capabilities _findOne and _findAll, or, in other words that all requests occur inside these two capabilities. At the point when BeautifulSoup characterizes these capabilities, Python's stretching boundary list innovation can complete different DOM API capabilities with an alternate number of boundaries and values to call _findOne and _findAll, consequently accomplishing two distinct objectives. For example, _findOne can look through assigned tag or the assigned substance of a tag, while _findAll can look through all labels or content that meet its predefined conditions inside the entire DOM tree [3].

13.2.2 API-Based Data Extraction

A feature of object-oriented programming languages called an API enables programmers to create software for a specific application using a reference programme library. The operating system or application programme of a device specifies the API, through which a requester—another device or a client user—can submit requests and wait for results. APIs provide communication between various software applications and access to their services. To add new features or functionalities to the existing methods, developers might create new classes or expand existing ones. An endpoint, a component that watches for requests, is how a client API is accessed made from the communication's client side to the server side over HTTP, anticipating the return of a response [13].

13.2.3 Natural Language Tool-Kit

NLTK is a naturalised language–based processing platform for Python which was developed by the combination of linguistics involving computations in 2001 at Pennsylvania University [14]. This natural language toolkit is a whole pack of features based on artificial intelligence which helps the developers develop language-based software. It gives at hand an interface which has 50 corpora and the lexicon-based resources which are based on SentiWordNet which has a collection of string and text computing libraries for lemmatization, classification and tokenization. In NLTK, the score based on sentiments is calculated from SentiWordNet which has a table format of polarity score based on each synset in the WordNet categorising it into positive and negative with the values ranging from 0.0 to 1.0; in every case the final sum is 1.0 [2].

13.2.4 Preprocessing

While doing analysis on tweets, they can be preprocessed so that unnecessary data could be filtered out:

1. Removal of re-tweets: Re-tweets can be removed from the tweet.
2. Case sensitive analysis: If we don't want to use a case sensitive analysis then we can convert upper case words to lower case.
3. Removal of Stop words: All those words which are not carrying any sentiment and also not affecting the meaning of the sentence can be removed.
4. Stemming of words: For filtration of sentences, words can be reduced to their roots, thereby reducing the complexity of sentence in analysis.
5. Special characters and numbers don't express any sentiments so they can be removed.
6. Slang and abbreviations can be expanded so that they can be analysed.

7. Sometimes wrong spellings don't convey any meaning or sentiments and hence can be discarded.
8. Words can be POS tagged and therefore can be classified under the headings nouns, adjectives and verbs; hence it involves efficient implementation of analysis.
9. Removal of username and URLs can be beneficial as they don't carry any sentimental value.

13.2.5 Working of Vader

Vader is a type of sources package which comes under NLTK. Vader is a tool used to do the sentiment analysis; the approach is lexicon and rule-based that is used in the expressions expressed on social media. Vader uses a method of scoring which is applied to results after analysing the [2] sentiment of the tweet (in the case of scraping tweet from Twitter), and as just said we must get the tweet in order to analyse the sentiment of the tweet, so for this purpose we use TweePy API, from which we can extract Twitter data. By using this we have real-time access to publicly available raw tweets [15]. Vader includes within it a sentiment lexicon and together with the inclusion of some syntactic rules, the sentiment analysis of text by Vader could be improved. Vader cause of origin is the abbreviations, emojis and slang used in posts on social media by people, and these are like a shorter way of expressing yourself on social media. The syntactic rules used are [2]:

A) Emotional intensifying marks: The interrogation and exclamation marks lead to increment and decrement of the sentiment intensity, thus influencing the positive and negative polarity of the text, e.g., "This is great!!!" will have a greater positive score as compared to "This is great" [9].
B) The play of capital text: The intensity of a word which is capitalised in nature and when other words are not capitalised gives the upper hand in intensity to that word when the analysis is performed, e.g., "This is GREAT" will have a greater positive score as compared to "This is great" [16].
C) Negative marks: If a word such as "great" gets preceded by a word such as "not" then this could just reverse the ongoing positive polarity of the whole sentence and give a negative sentiment, for e.g., "The environment is not good here" will turn the sentiment of the score to negative [9].
D) Words which give a boost: There are some words such as "very" and "extremely" which intensify the underlying emotion of the

text and this leads to increment in the intensity of the word, e.g., "The environment is good here" will have a lower score as compared to "The environment is very good here" [17].

E) Contrast-creating words: Words such as "but" can shift the signals of the whole sentence and change the polarity of the text with the sentiment of the text following the contrasting word being the dominating one, e.g., "The environment here is good but it was better in Shimla" has a mixed type of sentiment but the latter half of the sentence is more overpowering [12].

Specifically, in the case of Vader lexicon when a sentence or text is passed to the sentient intensity analyser, then the analyser pulls out those words which carry a sentimental value to them and the influence or intensity they have caused to the sentence. [2] This lexicon ranges the polarity from -4 to +4 , where -4 has the maximum negative intensity and +4 has the maximum positive intensity. However, when final scoring of the sentence is done then the scores are normalised between -1 and +1. This standard of normalisation has given this method another name as compound scores [18]. The compound-based score gives us the nature of the sentence, talks about its intensity and reviews the polarity. So, as per the equation 1, to give the overall intensity of the sentence, all the polarity scores of sentiment words are added and the normalised scores are thus received [19];

$$\text{Compound score} = \frac{x}{\sqrt{x^2 + alpha}}$$

Equation 1 : Compound score calculation for sentiment analysis

So here x is defined as the sum of polarity scores and alpha is the constant whose numerical value is generally taken as 15. Example – "The environment here is good and food is nice" [20]. Both the words here, "good" and "nice," have a polarity as 1.9 and 1.8 which on addition gives the value as 3.7. To get the compound score of the following sentence we do the normalisation and get the answer as 0.6907, which is between -1 and +1 [21]. Now the categorisation of tweets into various categories happens based on the value of compound score. If the value of the compound score is between -0.5 and 0.5 then the tweet is considered as neutral in sentiment [22]. If the value of the compound score is greater than 0.5 then it is considered as positive, and if the value of the compound score is less than -0.5 then the sentiment of the tweet is considered to be negative [10].

13.3 Methodology

13.3.1 Creation of a Virtual Environment

Production of a different Virtual Environment is fundamental as it permits the program to introduce and utilize the Python libraries without making any struggles with other programs utilizing similar libraries.

13.3.2 Installation of Python Libraries

The Python libraries must be installed by using the Windows PowerShell or by using the IDE terminal (PyCharm). The "pip" command is used to install various libraries.

13.3.3 Code Editor Used for Programming

VS code is used as the code editor for programming. This code editor is very robust and is a good choice; the only limitation is that it is slow to start up.

13.3.4 Commands Used

1. *python virtualenv env*
   The above command will create a virtual environment.
2. *activate.bat*
   The above command will be used for activating virtual environment.
3. *python-admin startproject hello*
   The above command will create a "project" in the vs folder named "hello" and will create many files mainly with ".py" extension and these files are the required files during the making of a Django-based application.
4. *python manage.py runserver*
   The above command will start the server and a link will be provided to us in the terminal, and on clicking on that link, we will be redirected to a web page telling us that the server is started successfully.
5. *python manage.py startapp mynewapp*
   The above command is used to make an app; basically it contains apps and this command will lead to the creation of an app and contains ".py" files which are required when we make changes in the functionality of the app.

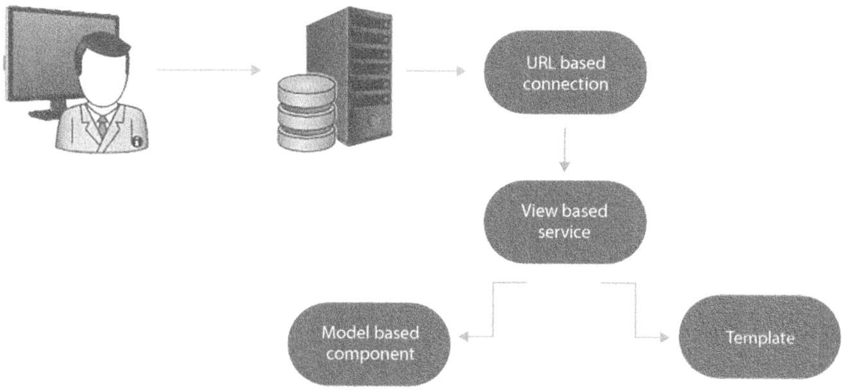

Figure 13.4 Diagram showing the flow of control in Django MVT architecture.

13.3.5 Django MVT Architecture

The Model View Template architecture is a thing arrangement plan. It is a gathering of three gigantic parts: Model, View and Template. The Model assists with managing information base. It is an information access layer which handles the information.

The Template is a show layer which handles User Interface part totally. The View is utilized to execute the business thinking and mark of connection with a model to pass on information and renders an association. Figure 13.4 shows the MVT architecture of Django and the various parts involved in the structure.

13.3.6 Modules and Functions Used

1. For Installation: "pip install tweepy"
   import tweepy
   This module is used for accessing the Twitter API and scraping tweets from Twitter.

2. For Installation: "pip install vaderSentiment"
   from vaderSentiment. vaderSentiment import SentimentIntensityAnalyser
   This module is used for analysing the sentiment of the tweet passed as a parameter to the sentiment intensity analyser.

3. For Installation : "pip install datetime"
   from datetime import timedelta

from datetime import date
This module is used for getting the current date and saving it with the tweets in the database. timedelta has been used for adding some days to the current date for checking the date of the tweet and for how long the tweet has been in the database.

4. For installation: "pip install mysqlconnector"
   import mysql.connector as sqltor
   This module has been used to connect my python code with the sql database and to pass strings as sql commands to mysql and fetch the required records. This connector will be referred to as sqltor.

5. For Installation: "pip install GoogleNews"
   from GoogleNews import GoogleNews
   This module has been used to get the news along with all the required data of the news.

6. from django.urls import path, include
   This module has been used so that when a request comes, it could be redirected to the specified app. So basically path function has the parameters for the request and for that request to which app, which has been included in the path function it should be redirected to.

7. From "app" import views
   This tells us that from our app folder we are trying to import views which are basically the main part of MVT architecture and decides how the data will be visible to us.

8. from django.shortcuts import render
   The Django module is a hub of functions which are commonly used in the context of view type classes. Here the render collects the given template and combines it with the dictionary and finally returns a Httpresponse (object) along with that rendered text.

```
from GoogleNews import GoogleNews

def Scrapper(str1):
        gn= GoogleNews()
        gn.search(str1)

        result=gn.results()
        return result
```

Figure 13.5 Code snippet of web scraping of news.

13.3.7 Working

13.3.7.1 News Aggregation

Figure 13.5 displays the code snippet for web scraping of news. Here first GoogleNews class is being imported from GoogleNews Python library and then within the scraper function, an object of class has been created. Then the search keyword inputted by the user is passed to the search function. This function searches for the given inputted keyword and then the results function is called which gives title, link, description, media and date time for the given news. This result is then returned to the calling function.

13.3.8 Sentiment Analysis

13.3.8.1 API User Verification

Figure 13.6 shows the authentication handling. Here the access keys are stored in another text file and are accessed using the file read operation. In the file pointer value of every key is being saved as list and then every key is being allotted its value. After that, using the tweepy authentication handler, all four keys are passed as parameters to the functions which basically verify the authenticity of the user.

Figure 13.7 displays that initially each tweet is scraped using Twitter API and then all those scraped tweets are stored in tweet which is basically the variable which contains all the scraped tweets. Each tweet undergoes required preprocessing, i.e., if a tweet has a heading as RT then to clear it, replace function has been used which replaces the heading "RT" with white spaces. The importance

```
#reading the data from text file
my_access_keys= open('C:\\Users\\User\\Desktop\\Folder\\college\\Sem 5\\NTCC in house practical training\\

#Authentication data
my_API_key=my_access_keys[0]
my_API_key_secret=my_access_keys[1]
my_access_token=my_access_keys[2]
my_access_token_secret=my_access_keys[3]

#Twitter authentication handler code
auth= tweepy.OAuthHandler(consumer_key=my_API_key,consumer_secret=my_API_key_secret)
auth.set_access_token(my_access_token,my_access_token_secret)
api= tweepy.API(auth)
```

Figure 13.6 Authentication handler.

```
#Analysing the tweets
for tweet in tweets:
    final_text= tweet.full_text.replace('RT','').replace('"','')
    analysis = sid.polarity_scores(final_text)
    count=count+1
    compoundsen=analysis['compound']
    if compoundsen<=-0.5000 and compoundsen>=-1.0000:
        negativesen=negativesen+1
    if compoundsen>-0.5000 and compoundsen<0.0000:
        weaknegative=weaknegative+1
    if compoundsen==0.0000:
        neutralsen=neutralsen+1
    if (compoundsen>0.0000 and compoundsen<0.5000):
        weakpositive=weakpositive+1
    if compoundsen>=0.5000 and compoundsen<=1.000:
        positivesen=positivesen+1

    Insert_object ="""Insert into tweets values(\"{}\",'{}',{},{},{},{},{},'{}',{})""".format(final_text,Ite
    cursor.execute(Insert_object)
    mycon.commit()
```

Figure 13.7 Analysing and categorisation of tweets.

of doing this is that, now every tweet which has the starting as "RT" will be blank thereafter and hence one word less for analysis. Similarly, all the double quotes are also replaced from tweet. Further now sentiment intensity analyser has been used which is basically the object of Vader lexicon for calculating the sentiment of tweet and hence this tweet is passed as a parameter to the polarity_scores method, which basically returns the sentiment in a dictionary form: { 'pos' : 0.6575 , 'neg' : -0.6363 , "neu" : 0.6273 , "compound" : 0.7373 }. We will be utilizing the "compound" element of the dictionary to classify our tweet into the respective categories. Each category has its individual counter and every time the respective counters are increased by one, whenever the compound score falls in one of the categories. Now this data of incremented counter with the respective tweet is added to the database, along with the tweet. For this I have used the sql connector for storing the data of the tweets in the database.

Figure 13.8 shows the deletion of tweets. First the authentication takes place and then the tweets get deleted. Here deletion of tweets have been

```
def Delete_the_tweets(Iterm,Leftover_tweets):

        #reading the data from text file
        my_access_keys= open('C:\\Users\\User\\Desktop\\Folder\\college\\Sem 5\\NTCC in hou

        #Authentication data
        my_API_key=my_access_keys[0]
        my_API_key_secret=my_access_keys[1]
        my_access_token=my_access_keys[2]
        my_access_token_secret=my_access_keys[3]

        #Twitter authentication handler code
        auth= tweepy.OAuthHandler(consumer_key=my_API_key,consumer_secret=my_API_key_secret
        auth.set_access_token(my_access_token,my_access_token_secret)
        api= tweepy.API(auth)

        Deletion_object="delete from tweets where Keyword='{}' Limit {}".format(Iterm,Leftc
        cursor.execute(Deletion_object)
        return
```

Figure 13.8 Deletion of tweets.

made because when the same keyword was searched again after the time period of seven days, then if it happens that regarding that same keyword 300 latest new tweets are not found, then to maintain the number of tweets in the database as 300 only, the remaining number of tweets are deleted from the database. Now all the new tweets found will be stored in the database with the remaining ones giving the total count as 300.

Figure 13.9 shows the new tweet count function where first the authentication of user takes place and then we search and count for the new tweets to check whether there are 300 new tweets or not. For searching, tweepy library's cursor method is used which has parameter as api.search_tweet which searches for tweets on twitter. The second parameter is the keyword regarding which search has to be made; the third parameter is the

```
def New_tweet_count(tweet_scanning_amt,str1):
        #Checking if authentication of user is successful or not
        #reading the data from text file
        my_access_keys= open('C:\\Users\\User\\Desktop\\Folder\\college\\Sem 5\\NTCC in house practical training\\Web

        #Authentication data
        my_API_key=my_access_keys[0]
        my_API_key_secret=my_access_keys[1]
        my_access_token=my_access_keys[2]
        my_access_token_secret=my_access_keys[3]

        #Twitter authentication handler code
        auth= tweepy.OAuthHandler(consumer_key=my_API_key,consumer_secret=my_API_key_secret)
        auth.set_access_token(my_access_token,my_access_token_secret)
        api= tweepy.API(auth)

        #passing the parameters to cursor method
        count=0
        tweets= tweepy.Cursor(api.search_tweets,q=str1,tweet_mode="extended",lang='en').items(tweet_scanning_amt)
        for tweet in tweets:
            count=count+1
        return count
```

Figure 13.9 Count of new tweets.

tweet_mode which is set as extended, which means full text tweet will be scraped and nothing will be truncated and all those tweets having language as English. The items parameter sets the limit for the number of tweets to be scraped or analysed. The results are stored in tweets variable and then iterations are made, with the increment of counter at each step.

13.4 Results Discussion

13.4.1 View of Website

Figure 13.10 displays the first view of the of the website where the name of the website is being displayed as "Real News" and for this heading tag has been used. Now below this is the slider which has been added; there are three sliders and the three slides have different pictures; different text is being displayed on each of them. The other two slides are as follows:

Figure 13.10 Heading and sliders in the first view of the website.

Figure 13.11 Second image of slider with the corresponding message.

Figure 13.12 Third image of the slider with the corresponding message.

Figure 13.11 and Figure 13.12 are the other two sliders. For inserting pictures "img" tag has been used and a link of each picture has been provided in the src attribute, and also the dimensions are adjusted as per the requirements. The text inserted on each slide is added with the help of style heading tag, and font settings have been edited by using the style attribute, the colour and size has been changed. The bold tag has been used for making the heading in each slide as bold.

13.4.2 News Aggregator

Figure 13.13 shows that container is separately enclosed under a div tag and contained within the class attribute and now the <h2> has been used for displaying the heading as "MyNews". The user has to enter the keyword of his choice in the search bar and then hit enter or click submit button. Here to take input, form tag has been used which returns the input keyword to the program at the backend. Now the heading "Search Your Keyword", search bar and submit button are all inside the jumbotron component of Bootstrap.

Figure 13.14 shows that when the keyword was searched for, then that keyword was passed as an input to the program at the backend and the output of the program was passed as an input to the website and displayed.

Figure 13.13 Search bar to search the term for which the news needs to be scraped.

Figure 13.14 View of the scraped news along with the news data.

Whenever news will be scraped, along with all the data related to that news such as title, media, date-time, description, link and duration (when was it published on the site from where it is scraped). All these top 10 news are displayed in a separate jumbotron and an internal scroll bar is added for scrolling down to every news.

13.4.3 Sentiment Analysis

Figure 13.15 shows that the heading "Sentimental analysis" is added with the help of a heading tag and within the jumbotron heading "Search your keyword" has been added that the user can enter the keyword in the search bar and then click on the submit button. The input term is passed as an input to the program at the backend and the results are fetched and displayed on the website.

Figure 13.16 shows that the "Results" heading is again inserted using the heading tag and with a limit of around 300 tweets, analysis of each tweet is performed and with the classification of each tweet into respective categories, we get the results. The respective categories and the above written statement in the screenshot are enclosed within a jumbotron.

Figure 13.17 and Figure 13.18 show the analysis of the tweets which the user wishes to post on Twitter. In one of the above screenshots a simple statement is inputted, "Smile is good", while in the other screenshot the same statement with an emoticon has been used: ":-) is good". Vader gives the same polarity score to both the statements and hence Vader proves that it is an ideal case to be used for sentiment analysis in the context of social media.

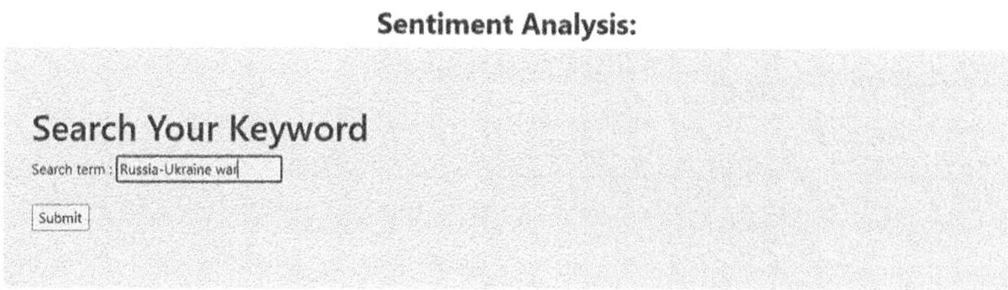

Figure 13.15 Search bar for the topic needed to do the sentiment analysis.

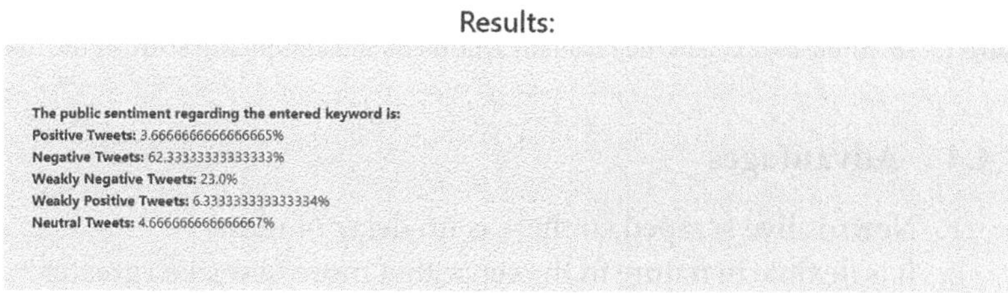

Figure 13.16 Categorisation of the tweets into various categories.

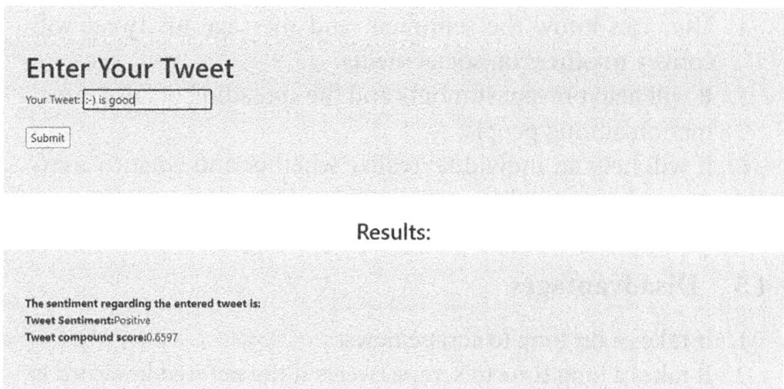

Figure 13.17 Symbol of smile as tweet and the resultant sentiment.

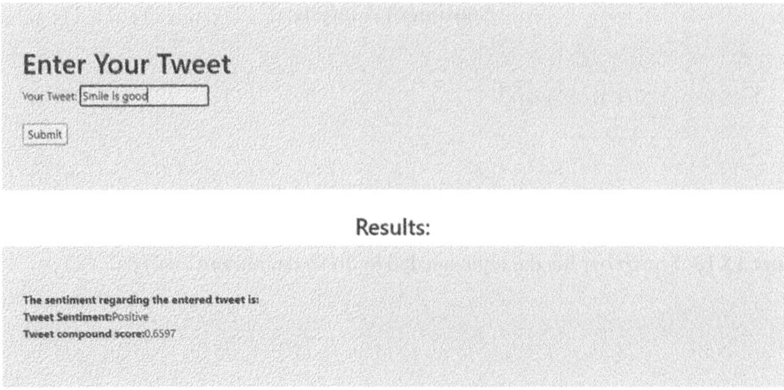

Figure 13.18 Smile as text and the resultant sentiment and compound score of the tweet.

13.4.4 Advantages

1. News is live scraped so there is no delay of news.
2. It is flexible in nature in the sense that more news, i.e., greater than 10, could be scraped off, region could be specified, language can be added as a parameter and by clicking on links directly the user will be redirected to the news web-page.
3. User now could be made aware of the ongoing public sentiment regarding any specific topic.
4. User can know the sentiment and message his tweet will convey to others on social media.
5. It will help prevent rumours and the spreading of false information among people.
6. It will help an individual realize whether and what to comment about socially sensitive topics.

13.4.5 Disadvantages

1. It takes a bit long to scrape news.
2. It takes a long time to scrape tweets if the entered keyword is not previously present in the database.
3. Sometimes the length of a tweet is too long to get saved in the database and hence this gives an error.
4. The authentication handler function didn't work and because of that each function which scrapes tweets using twitter API needs authentication, and the code of that function had to be repeated.

5. The current program is not able to scrape the date at which the tweet was posted on twitter.
6. In the case of web scraping, images are not scraped with the required news and sometimes the date-time parameter returns none.

13.5 Conclusion and Future Work

13.5.1 Conclusion

As the internet has grown exponentially and markets in today's world are totally data dependent, it is now a necessity to have access to the updated and latest data be it in any field. Data is the main decision-making factor and the cause that any business can run profitably or not. In today's era, every person can find the growth and emergence of a new factor every year and web scraping is no scraping from it. This factor has its foundation built on the basis of structured and unstructured data. In the case of news also, people can save so much of their time by using news aggregators instead of looking at individual news sites on the web. News aggregators collect all the data related to a particular news item at one place and thus help save a lot of time for the users.

Twitter sentimental analysis falls under the headline of mining of text and opinions and here the focus is on the analysis of tweets and presenting the results under different categories and sub-categories. These results can help to analyse and forecast customer behaviour towards any product and their relationship with the producer, analysis of comments on various social media handles or helping a political party decide which way to pave for diverting the views of the public based on ongoing public sentiment. The full process of analysis involves collecting data, sentiment analysis and then its classification. To some extent it also involves pre-processing of tweets but in the context of Vader, which is built especially for social media handles where people mostly are interested in using short forms, slang and emojis have a very intense effect on the sentiment intensity of the overall tweet and if pre-processing is done then all of these will be removed from the sentence, maybe due to non-understandability of the short forms or short forms and slang being seen as spelling errors. With the changes in this field and the ongoing development, slowly but surely models of analysis will come which will have high accuracies.

13.5.2 Future Work

Both web scraping and sentiment analysis have immense scope in the future. Web scraping can be more refined and can target specific information which the user has demanded, and moreover, the current flaws within the existing modules must also be resolved to make them more efficient. To improve web scraping specific functions can be added to scrape images and date-time which is not appearing in some instances must be visible in every instance then. Artificial intelligence–based web scrapers can be used which know which data to scrape from the internet. Secondly, the sentiment analysis part can analyse the sentiment of the text, and Vader, which is a lexicon-based analysis tool specially made for analysing the sentiments of posts by people on social media, has a very high level of accuracy and is at par with human raters for analysis. Here the time which is required to scrape new tweets can be improved and for authentication handling a specific function must be made which will reduce code repetition and save time while debugging. This sentiment analysis can be done using a hybrid model based on artificial intelligence and machine learning with the rules of Vader. The accuracy will be greatly improved for that model with such a hybrid combination.

References

1. Hutto, C. and Gilbert, E., VADER: A Parsimonious Rule-Based Model for Sentiment Analysis of Social Media Text. *ICWSM*, 8, 1, 216–225, May 2014.
2. Bonta, V., Kumaresh, N., Janardhan, N., A Comprehensive Study on Lexicon Based Approaches for Sentiment Analysis. *Asian J. Comput. Sci. Technol.*, 8, S2, 1–6, Mar. 2019. doi: 10.51983/ajcst-2019.8.s2.2037.
3. Zhao, B., Web Scraping, in: *Encyclopedia of Big Data*, pp. 1–3, 2017, doi: 10.1007/978-3-319-32001-4_483-1.
4. Mahto, D.K. and Singh, L., A dive into Web Scraper world, in: *Institute of Electrical and Electronics Engineers (IEEE)*, 2016.
5. Web Scraping: Applications and Scraping Tools. *Int. J. Adv. Trends Comput. Sci. Eng.*, 9, 5, 8202–8206, Oct. 2020. doi: 10.30534/ijatcse/2020/185952020.
6. M.K., S., Social Media Sentiment Analysis for Opinion Mining. *Int. J. Psychosocial Rehabil.*, 24, 5, 3672–3679, Apr. 2020. doi: 10.37200/ijpr/v24i5/pr202075.
7. Sathyamoorthy, M., Vanitha, C.N., Dhanaraj, R.K., Mon, F.A., Rai, P., Smart Aero Generator Monitoring System using IoT, in: *2023 Second International*

Conference on Augmented Intelligence and Sustainable Systems (ICAISS), IEEE, https://doi.org/10.1109/icaiss58487.2023.10250545.

8. Chauhan Vipul Kumar, B., Ashish, G., Amita, ISSN: 2454-132X Impact factor: 4.295 Twitter Sentiment Analysis Using Vader. [Online]. Available: https://www.ijariit.com/manuscripts/v4i1/V4I1-1307.
9. Rao, S., Monica, N., Nikhila, P., Tejasri, T., Maram, B., *Positivity Calculation using Vader Sentiment Analyser*, Accessed: Jul. 18, 2022. [Online]. Available: http://ijeais.org/wp-content/uploads/2020/3/IJAER200303.pdf.
10. Adarsh, R., Patil, A., Rayar, S., Veena, K.M., Comparison of VADER and LSTM for sentiment analysis. *Int. J. Recent Technol. Eng. ER*, 7, 540–543, 2019/03/01.
11. *Document Object Model*, Wikipedia, Oct. 9, 2020, https://en.wikipedia.org/wiki/Document_Object_Model.
12. Kumar, S.A., Muchahari, M.K., Poonkuntran, S., Kumar, L.S., Dhanaraj, R.K., Karthikeyan, P., Application of hybrid capsule network model for malaria parasite detection on microscopic blood smear images, in: *Multimedia Tools and Applications*, Springer Science and Business Media LLC, 2024.
13. Dongo, I., Cadinale, Y., Aguilera, A., Martínez, F., Quintero, Y., Barrios, S., Web Scraping versus Twitter API, in: *Proceedings of the 22nd International Conference on Information Integration and Web-based Applications & Services*, Nov. 2020, doi: 10.1145/3428757.3429104.
14. Upadhyay, H.K., Maggu, S., Dhingra, G., Juneja, A., Multi-criteria analysis of social isolation barriers amid COVID-19 using fuzzy AHP. *World J. Eng.*, 19, 2, 195–203, 2022.
15. Juneja, A., Kaur, S., Kumar, V., Predicting diabetes mellitus with machine learning techniques using multi-criteria decision making. *Int. J. Inf. Retr. Res. (IJIRR)*, 11, 2, 38–52, 2021.
16. Singamaneni, K.K., Dhiman, G., Muhammad, G., AlQahtani, S.A., Zaki, J., A novel QKD approach to enhance IIOT privacy and computational knacks. *Sensors*, 22, 18, 20226741.
17. Anand, R. and Sindhwani, N., Cognitive Internet of Things, Its Applications, and Its Challenges: A Survey, in: *Harnessing the Internet of Things (IoT) for a Hyper-Connected Smart World*, pp. 91–113, 2022.
18. Dhiman, G., Viriyasitavat, W., Mohafez, H., Hadizadeh, M., Islam, M.A., Gulati, K., A novel machine-learning-based hybrid CNN model for tumor identification in medical image processing. *Sustainability*, 14, 3, 20221447.
19. Aggarwal, S., Gupta, S., Gupta, D., Gulzar, Y., Alwan, A.A., Nauman, A., An artificial intelligence-based stacked ensemble approach for prediction of protein subcellular localization in confocal microscopy images. *Sustainability*, 15, 2, 20231695.

20. Jain, V. and (Eds.), *Handbook of Machine Learning for Computational Optimization: Applications and Case Studies*, CRC Press, 2021.
21. Mishra, R. and Sharma, D.A., PDF Based Scale-Free Topology Construction Model for Wireless Sensor Networks. *Wireless Pers. Commun.*, 131, 2371–2397, 2023. https://doi.org/10.1007/s11277-023-10418-z.
22. Tulshyan, V., Sharma, D., Mittal, M., An Eye on the Future of COVID-19: Prediction of Likely Positive Cases and Fatality in India over a 30-Day Horizon Using the Prophet Model. *Disaster Med. Public Health Preparedness.*, 16, 3, 980–986, 2022. doi:10.1017/dmp.2020.444.

14

Case Study on AI-Based Ethical Decision-Making for Smart Transportation

S. Muthu Lakshmi[1]*, K. Mythili[2], Malathy Sathyamoorthy[1], Rajesh Kumar Dhanaraj[3] and Aanjan Kumar S.[4]

[1]*Department of Information Technology, KPR Institute of Engineering and Technology, Coimbatore, India*
[2]*Department of Information Technology, Sri Krishna College of Technology, Coimbatore, India*
[3]*Symbiosis Institute of Computer Studies and Research, Symbiosis International (Deemed University), Pune, India*
[4]*School of Computing Science and Engineering, VIT Bhopal University, Bhopal-Indore Highway, Kothrikalan, Sehore, Madhya Pradesh, India*

Abstract

Artificial Intelligence (AI) in transportation plays a vital role in addressing challenges such as traffic congestion, safety, and sustainability. The integration of AI and smart transportation brings about various advantages such as route optimization, decision-making, reducing congestion, and accessibility. Even though it has numerous advantages, AI smart transportation has ethical implications and equitable outcomes. This chapter takes a look at AI transportation and ethics in smart transportation, discussing and observing the key dimensions such as safety, fairness, privacy, transparency, and environmental impact. This literature review and case studies consider the ethical considerations inherent in autonomous vehicles, route optimization, route prediction, vehicle-to-vehicle (V2V) communication, traffic signal management, and data confidentiality and security measures. It also discusses the challenges and opportunities accompanying ethical deployment of AI transportation and how to improve the performance of mobility, safety, and sustainability in the future directions. Finally, the research emphasizes incorporating the ethical values of AI-driven transportation system to promote trust, social responsibility, and accountability.

**Corresponding author*: muthunjanu@gmail.com

Sapna Juneja, Rajesh Kumar Dhanaraj, Abhinav Juneja, Malathy Sathyamoorthy and Asadullah Shaikh (eds.) Ethical Decision-Making Using Artificial Intelligence: Challenges, Solutions and Applications, (343–366) © 2025 Scrivener Publishing LLC

Keywords: Decision making process, artificial intelligence, smart transportation, ethics, data confidentiality, data sharing, autonomous vehicles, data privacy and security

14.1 Introduction

With the rapid development of technology, different sectors such as healthcare, finance, transportation, banking, and other areas are gradually moving towards AI. The AI transition streamlines operations and offers less complexity and low cost, and also expands productivity. Nowadays, many industries use AI to automate their systems, which helps to reduce human intervention and increases productivity. Notably, traffic congestion and route optimization addressed by the implementation of AI tools provide better results.

Society faces significant challenges while integrating AI systems that confirm the ethical standards governing decisions made by intelligent systems. AI systems hold the ability to autonomously influence individuals, possibly mingled with positive and negatively with the responses. The autonomous vehicles try to repeat human behavior in the domain of AI smart transportation. While driving autonomous vehicles, the system may face failures or meet accidents, based on current situations, the decisions can be made by the system on time. This decision-making process focuses on justice and equity that ensure the road users' safety on AI systems. Utilizing unmatchable speed and power for examining vast amounts of data that make it a powerful force. This procedure cannot be done just with experts in the AI field. The AI systems should obey lawful principles and societal norms. The collection of data, data usage and transparency of decisions supports privacy standards.

The transport ecosystem contributes safer, more equitable and socially responsible decision-making algorithms by integrating ethical principles in AI smart transportation with decision-making algorithms. Maintaining the deployment of these sophisticated AI technologies benefits the society ethically. Accordingly, AI endeavors to transform transportation and other sectors; building trust is essential in prioritize ethical considerations, fairness and durability in our increasingly programmed world. The AI used to analyze the ethical issues that are close to the society has two dimensions.

1. Artificial intelligence is ruled by ethical principles, so existing transportation infrastructure necessitates revamping the decisions made by the system.

2. In specific situations where people are directly affected by the AI decisions, the moral behaviour of AI involves programming AVs to prioritize passenger safety and also consider pedestrians and other vehicle drivers on the road.

14.2 Artificial Intelligence

The AI system development and utilization are designed to replicate human intelligence in various aspects. The process includes collecting and learning data from the machines, solving the problem automatically, decisions made by the systems based on the available information, and rectifying the error or refining their approaches without any involvement of human beings. An AI system tackles a wide range of challenges across various domains such as natural language processing, image recognition, robotics and autonomous driving. The system focuses on learning, perception, the decision-making process, and solving problems. Through the continuous development and refinement of an AI technology, it grasps the promise of revolutionizing numerous industries and has an overwhelming impact on our daily lives. Figure 14.1 shows the process flowchart of an AI system.

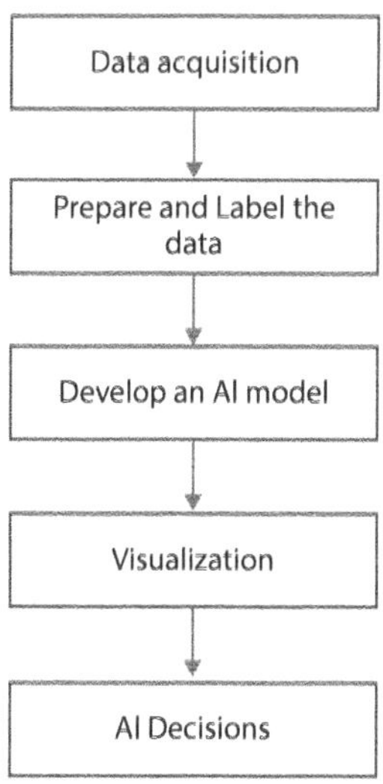

Figure 14.1 AI decision-making process flowchart.

Data Acquisition: This ethical process collects the relevant data from the machines and prioritizes privacy and agreement. It offers a piece of clear information about the utilization of the data and compromises transparent communication with individuals whose data is being collected. Additionally, the data acquisition method tries to ensure diverse representation across demographic groups and geographic regions. The collection of data leads to taking necessary decisions guided by ethical considerations and associated with principles of fairness and concern about individual rights and respect.

Prepare and Label the Data: It is important to label the data by explaining and preparing the data ethically. Human interpretation should be required to recognize or to prevent and reduce the negative decision on labeling. The quality of data label should assure in place to validate the accuracy of annotations. Moreover, the complex data should be handled more carefully and anonymized data or aggregate data should be taken care of with privacy protection. The preparation and labeling of data for AI training should follow the ethical guidelines and best practices should be informed to take necessary decisions based on the current situation.

Develop an AI Model: Development of AI should be prepared transparently, with model architecture, training procedure, and evaluation of the metrics of the AI model. In the AI model, fairness-aware algorithms are used, and conducting testing and validation should be needed to identify and reduce bias. Making decisions about model deployment must prioritize safety, equality, and societal protection, while deliberating on the potential impact on all stakeholders. This model ethically involves transparency, accountability, and impartiality.

Visualization: To visualize AI outputs that confirm the information provided the visual presentation should be clear, balanced, and understandable based on ethical considerations. Ethical information is considered and provided to visualize the AI model. Visualization techniques are carefully chosen to eliminate misunderstanding or misrepresentation of data. Through the use of visualization approaches, the AI model's decision-making processes become more accurate, providing more exact direction for interpreting its results. It is necessary to ensure the visualization tools are available to all shareholders, regardless of their level of technical knowledge or experience.

AI Decision: AI smart transportation is used to make ethical decision making, which is essential to implementation in real-world applications. The various aspects such as prioritizing safety, fairness, and societal well-being, with careful consideration of the potential risks and benefits, are carefully measured while making decisions in AI transportation. Stakeholders' inputs and suggestions are important to ensure the decisions taken reflects the values and inclinations of the communities exaggerated by AI systems. Ensuring the decisions continue to operate safely and ethically in dynamic transportation environments requires regular monitoring and evaluation of AI systems. Transparent, liable, fairness principles, justice and respect for human rights should be processed by the decision-making process ethically.

14.3 Role of Artificial Intelligence in Transportation

As the population increases in global urbanization, traffic congestion, procedural obstacles, and transportation problems are also increased. As a result, cities are facing extraordinary pressure on the transportation system. Transportation systems integrated with AI technology to tackle these problems efficiently. An AI smart transportation system uses huge amounts of data from various sources, such as traffic signal systems, autonomous vehicles, V2V communicated data, and vehicle management systems. The authorized transportation authorities can extract valuable insights and make better decisions from the information provided by the system. The AI transportation data includes traffic analysis, improved system efficiency, and optimized route prediction [1].

By analyzing a wide range of data including traffic patterns, route prediction and real-time sensor information, employing sophisticated procedures and machine learning techniques, AI systems take a better decision-making process. For example, traffic congestion prediction and enhancing traffic signal timing based on traffic congestion. Similarly, AI depends on real-time sensor data to cross traffic signals and make decisions on speed and route planning on autonomous vehicles [2].

AI systems permit continuous learning, algorithm enhancements based on the requirements, and ensure the accuracy in the decision-making process. Identifying the travel pattern becomes more difficult in advanced AI systems due to inconsistent user travel behavior, infrastructure limitations and unpredictable weather conditions. AI solutions to address the complexities such as collaboration and innovation are crucial to mounting robust urban transport systems.

14.4 Literature Review

This literature review is arranged into three main sections. Section 14.4.1 observes AV analyzed in a real-world scenario, Section 14.4.2 discovers message passing between vehicles, and Section 14.4.3 focuses on GPS technology used for tracking the devices.

14.4.1 Autonomous Vehicle

In this literature review [3], self-driving vehicles (SDVs) transform transportation by improving efficacy, reducing traffic mortalities, and increasing throughput while reducing social impact. The study services a policy scenario methodology to construct a future scenario that focuses on challenges and opportunities by 2025. Some of the highlighted key factors include societal impacts, such as autonomy, privacy, liability, security, data protection, and economic considerations, which are influencing SDV adoption. Ethical principles, legal laws, and social impacts are also examined. Finally, it concludes with an endorsement for proactive measures to address risks and optimize SDV deployment.

In the rapid development of AI, the study found that 74% of participants used automated driving vehicles. Many other countries strongly disagree with implementing smart AI transport networks. The Bosch research revealed that only 33% of Germans favored self-driving cars, and only 31% of Americans supported autonomous vehicles [4].

This study [5] delivers an exhaustive analysis of the key wireless technologies that are essential for Intelligent Transportation Systems (ITS), significantly increasing the state of information currently available. The research not only summaries the vital elements of network architecture, it also supports AVs and closely observed the technological progress, hindrances, and boundaries that AVs must overcome to achieve widespread use. This paper aims to integrate abstract technological paradigms with their concrete consequences on human mobility, transport systems, and infrastructure, in contrast to previous literature that frequently explores discrete aspects like technological innovations, adoption, or regulatory challenges. It explains important architectural ideas and summarises the results of current research on Vehicular Ad-Hoc Network (VANET) technologies, including their uses, benefits, and drawbacks. It does this by connecting theoretical frameworks with practical issues.

For the improvement of AVs, decision-making datasets are important, which were carried out in this literature review [6]. This research focuses on four main areas: vehicles-related data, environments, drivers, and specific applications. According to features, observations, and data categories, researchers and developers, classification of datasets are provided and resources accessible for AV decision-making algorithms are discussed and summaries are provided. Dataset limitations and possible applications in decision-making contexts are discussed. Comparison and feature analysis are also performed in the research study. A clear examination was done on which datasets are used in this section. In the future, the research clearly provides how to gather the data from the vehicles and important tools to develop AV decision-making technology.

14.4.2 Communication Between Vehicles

In their study [7], the authors introduced ensuring a safe inter-vehicular distance, a trusted framework on both vehicles' consigned sensors, and V2V communication that accurately identifies the longitudinal and lateral motion. The proposed system was tested with two distinct scenarios: first, Curved Road Driving: At different velocities of 12 m/s and 21 m/s, the driving involved in the curved road scenario. Second, Double Lane-Change Maneuver: At varying velocities of 12 m/s and 20 m/s, implementing in the double lane-change maneuver scenario. Determining both longitudinal and lateral vehicle motion, demonstrated the consistency of the system, and gained accurate test results. Utilization of a low-cost on-board millimeter-wave radar sensor is accomplished through V2V communications, which are achieved exclusively. Overall, the research study highlighted the controlled framework for the proposed system; detecting the vehicle movement, guaranteeing safety, and changes in speed and direction are the main scenarios included.

The authors [8] suggested using a multi-protocol gateway to enable smooth data sharing between organizations with different technology backgrounds. They assessed the compatibility and real-time responsiveness of multiple Internet of Things Ethernet-based communication protocols, including DDS, eCAL middleware, and SOME/IP. The authors also looked into the hardware architecture that they used for their simulation. This configuration consisted of microprocessors with native POSIX-based operating systems for most nodes, and general-purpose computers with virtualized Linux operating systems to simulate connection with an Internet of Things supervisor node.

In this literature review [9], the authors ensure the secure transmission and protection of data in V2V communication networks is crucial for maintaining the integrity, privacy, and reliability of exchanged information. For vehicular communication safety and categorizing key challenges, the paper observes the latest solutions. Security protocols advancement and backgrounds discussing vulnerabilities incorporating with V2X networks are emphasized. Asymmetric key infrastructure and elliptic curve cryptography play a major role in securing V2V communications. It utilizes cryptographic techniques that provide the vigorous foundation for communication between vehicles [10, 11]. Enhanced Secure Ad hoc On-Demand Distance Vector (ES-AODV) routing protocol, and data transmission security development enhanced the integrity of data. Moreover, a Software-Defined Networking (SDN)-based security classical model enhances V2V communication proficiency and safety. Additionally, to promote eco-friendly security Internet of Connected Vehicles (IoCV) architecture are proposed.

14.4.3 Tracking Using GPS

The authors [12] discussed the hazards incorporated with Geographic Information Systems (GIS) for investigation and possible misuse of data by the external members. Even if sensitive data is encrypted, weaknesses may be exploited by hackers, for-profit telecommunications companies, or cloud storage providers. There have been cases reported when encryption failed to prevent access to personal data. Computer viruses or malware may also make use of encryption flaws in order to access data for nefarious purposes, like ransomware scams. In addition, aside from security lapses, there exists a possibility that the data may be produced under subpoena in court, endangering the confidentiality of those involved. These indicate the gaps that exist now with regard to data accessibility.

In this literature [13], GPS data provides digital representations of travel behaviour, including distance travelled, speed, and duration of trip, in real time in both geographical and temporal dimensions. This feature lessens the workload associated with reporting by streamlining information reporting. There are two types of GPS data: logging GPS and real-time tracking GPS. Every second, GPS sensors for real-time tracking record the coordinates of a vehicle. But there are disadvantages to using GPS information. First, because of selection criteria, statistics might not always be representative. Results accuracy may be impacted by unclear criteria. For each participant, assigning GPS devices will effect insufficient device and does not respond to the data gathered by the system. The high amount spent on data collection procedure returns a worst-case scenario and it becomes more complicated, and other related expenses such as recruiting a person to collect data, and decision makers are also increased.

14.5 Challenges

Several important challenges must be focused on to ensure their implementation and broader application in AI-motivated smart transportation systems.

Safety and Regulations: To manage the design, testing, organizing, and developing of AVs robust regulations and standards are needed. These regulations are essential to reducing the risks of accidents and confirming public trust in the AI smart transportation systems.
Data Privacy and Security: Protecting the data against cyber threats is essential while the huge amount of data is received from various systems such as vehicles, organization, and travelers. Integrity of AI transportation systems includes avoiding misuse of data, maintaining trust and creating more confidence in the public, which ensures the privacy protections.
Equity and Accessibility: The risk increases in AI-driven transportation systems, which worsen existing inequities, especially while accessing transportation services. The technologies must be available and easily accessible by all members of society, particularly in underserved communities and individuals with incapacities.
Ethical Dilemmas: It is difficult to address ethical considerations concerning decisions taken in passenger safety prioritization, handling emergencies in pedestrian safety and so on. To address these dilemmas requires critical thought and transparency in algorithm design and decision-making processes.
Infrastructure Integration: Compatibility issues, cost adaption and stakeholder coordination are required to address these problems, while Integrating AI technologies into existing transportation structure. The integration of AI technologies and transportation systems is essential to realize the maximum potential and reveal the benefits for society.

14.6 AI Ethics

The use of AI technologies in transportation systems refers to the ethics in smart transportation, integrities, and strategies to govern their development and deployment. Modern transportation incorporating AI is increased with ethical considerations becoming dominant. While integrating technologies, societal values and concerns are taken into consideration. Figure 14.2 illustrates the key terms of AI transport ethics.

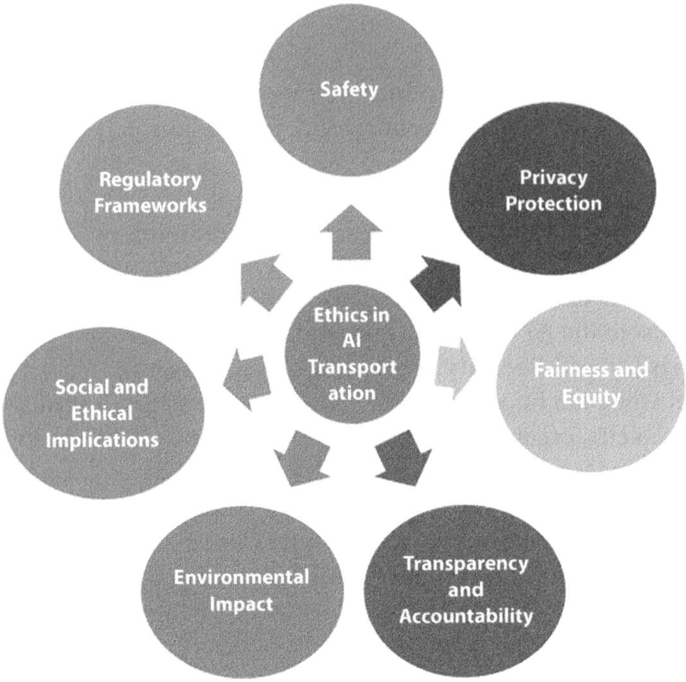

Figure 14.2 Ethics in AI transport.

Safety: While the vehicle is being driven, the AI system should authorize the passengers' safety, pedestrians, traffic congestion, route prediction, and other aspects of driver security. AI systems are mainly constructed with the goal of reducing the risk of accidents or failures in the system. This includes safety regulations, handling failure mechanisms, and observance of safety standards.

Fairness and Equity: AI algorithms used in transportation must be fair and unbiased, avoiding discrimination against certain demographic groups or communities. It is mandatory to ensure the equitable access to transportation services to avoid deteriorating existing inequalities, and highly exposed groups are considered.

Privacy Protection: AI smart transportation systems often collect and analyze large amounts of data, including personal data from travelers and drivers. Data protection law is essential to safeguard the individuals' privacy rights and compliance testing. It is important to approve the necessity of data collection, availability of data and accessing data.

Transparency and Accountability: With perfect accountability, AI-based transportation systems are recognized. The AI system may face failures, accidents, or opposing outcomes; tasks have been clearly elucidated. Transparent decision-making processes and clear understanding of the requirements of AI systems build confidence and trust among end users.

Environmental Impact: To reduce the environmental impact, AI-enabled smart transportation systems prioritize sustainability. This involves energy efficiency improvisation, emission minimization and approving an eco-friendly transportation system.

Social and Ethical Implications: Apart from security and efficiency, social and ethical significance are important for an AI-enabled smart transportation system. This includes unemployment, adaptable community, urban enlargement and life quality in urban cities. Shareholder commitment and ethical effect assessments help to recognize and address these concerns.

Regulatory Frameworks: To govern the growth, deployment, and transportation usage in AI, regulatory frameworks are essential. These frameworks are balanced between endorsing improvement and securing public safety, confidentiality and other ethical deliberations.

14.6.1 AI Smart Transportation Use Cases

The new innovative solutions are redesigning the traditional traveling experiences in the field of AI-driven smart transportation. The modern devices operate with route optimization and safety enhancement, which improve the overall performance of the AI transportation system. AI smart transportation has entered into a new era of flexibility and convenience for travelers across the world. Figure 14.3 shows some of the use cases of AI smart transportation. These use cases include the detection of objects, monitoring the driver's activities, predicting optimized route, and traffic signal management during vehicle congestion. It also includes other use cases such as predictive maintenance, live route suggestion, and autonomous vehicles. Additionally, it also explains how the AI industries drastically alter the transportation industry.

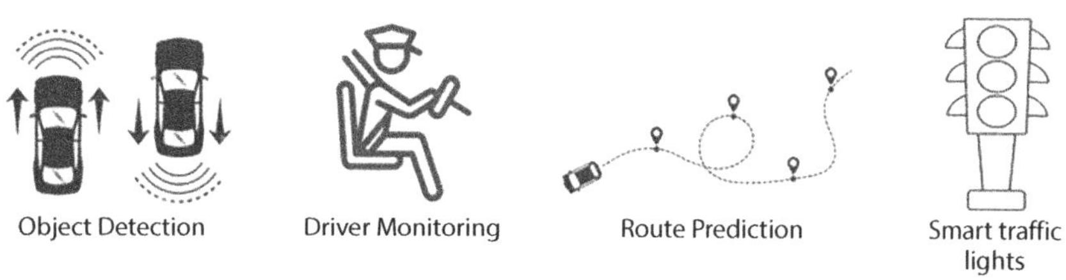

Figure 14.3 Example of use cases of AI smart transportation.

14.6.1.1 *Object Detection*

AI-enabled object detection is crucial in smart transportation to enhance safety and efficiency. The AI-enabled system recognizes foot travelers, automobiles, and hindrances, allowing autonomous navigation and traffic controlling management. Ethical considerations such as privacy and prejudice must monitor its alignment. Monitoring the surroundings, and safety measures on the roads or railways are supported by object detection. The system warns/alerts the end users and optimizes traffic signals based on the real-time data available on the system and should make necessary decisions based on the current situation. Handling real-time data and making decisions is essential to provide transparency and accountability. Generally, detection of object adds a safer and more efficient mobility.

14.6.1.2 *Driver Monitoring*

To reduce the risk of accidents caused by driver tiredness, the systems identify the signs of drowsiness and tiredness and advise the drivers to take breaks. Moreover, the system alerts the driver to focus on driving by using AI algorithms to recognize the interruptions of mobile usage. Real-time analysis of driving behavior permits feedback and training to improve driver performance and adherence to safety protocols. Facial recognition technology must confirm driver identification and confirmation, enhancing fleet safety. During emergencies, the driver monitoring system provides critical information to support fast and synchronized emergency responses. Additionally, monitoring driver behavior and encouraging safer practices can be determined more correctly by the insurance premiums. Efficient resource allocation and schedule maintenance are enabled in fleet management based on the understanding of driver behavior. Another way to ensure regulatory compliance is tracking and authenticating safety guidelines. Finally, smooth transitions between physical and autonomous vehicles driving modes are required to maintain safety measure.

14.6.1.3 *Route Prediction*

Based on the input of real-time traffic analysis, user travel pattern history, and other terms such as conditions of weather and events, the AI algorithm exactly calculates the optimal route for users or maps. This process is analyzed to reduce traffic congestion and travel time, and that obviously improves the traffic flow. Based on individual preferences and traffic conditions, personalized route suggestions are offered. Personalized navigation facilities are provided to the users with the experience of user movement. By optimizing schedules and capacity, the system will improve service consistency and minimize waiting time. During emergencies or natural disasters, coordination is also improved through route prediction, navigating efficiently by enabling responders and giving priority to critical tasks. In fleet management, analytical maintenance consumes recommended routes in route prediction that reduces wear and tear on vehicles, and reduces maintenance costs and downtime. Optimizing routes and schedules improves efficiency, and minimizes distribution times; these are some of the key advantages in supply chain logistics. To reduce fuel consumption and emissions by optimizing vehicle routing is accomplished in environmental impact reduction.

14.6.1.4 Smart Traffic Lights

AI knowledge-assisted smart traffic lights modernized traffic management, and road safety. These smart lights automatically adjust signal timings based on the data available in real time to enhance the traffic flow. This process reduces congestion and avoids traffic jams on the road. Additionally, pedestrian safety is also improved, with smart lights identifying approaching pedestrians and adjusting traffic signals accordingly. Adjustable signal control, learned by AI algorithms, frequently learns from traffic patterns to further optimize efficacy. Vehicles are integrated with smart traffic lights that provide real-time traffic data and deliver route optimization. Contribution towards environmental sustainability is important, as they help minimize fuel consumption and emissions by reducing congestion. During an emergency period, they enable smooth clearing routes through coordinated traffic administration. Smart traffic lights produce data that supports well-versed decision-making by transportation experts and urban planners. Finally, they create the potential for future mobility to be integrated, assuring that new technologies are efficiently combined into transportation systems.

14.6.2 Ethics in Autonomous Vehicles

In transportation, AI creates a new set of ethical issues, especially when it comes to AVs. The self-driving cars raise significant questions about public trust, decision-making algorithms, and safety measures. In smart transportation, software errors and hardware failure in AVs can have important repercussions for safety and reliability. These vehicles trust AI procedures to distinguish their environment, make decisions, and control their movements [14].

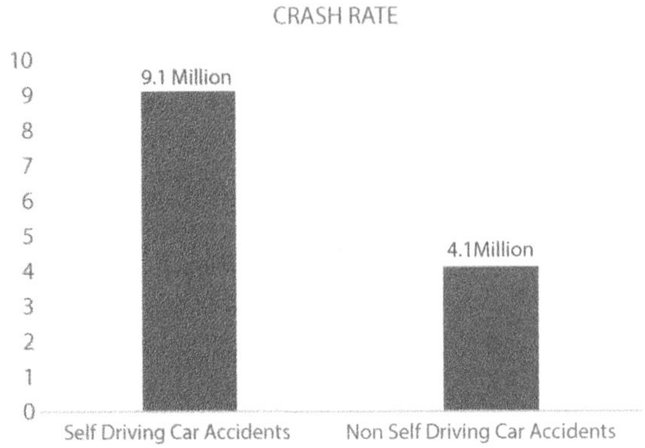

Figure 14.4 Comparing accident rates between self-driving and non-self-driving cars.

Any faults or miscalculations in these algorithms could possibly lead to accidents or crashes, emphasizing the critical importance of robust software development and testing observations. If a single component or system faces failure unexpectedly, redundancies confirm that the vehicle can operate safely. The prominence of severe testing supports the values of safety authentication in AI smart transportation. Under various testing conditions, the testing validation includes simulation-based testing, real-world driving tests, and scenario-based validation to ensure the performance of autonomous systems. Before positioning vehicles on public roads, this approach supports identifying and addressing potential issues [15].

Based on the data from the Gitnux Marketdata Report, self-driving cars are involved in accidents at a rate of 9.1 crashes per million miles driven. This means that for every million miles these AV travel, there are approximately 9.1 accidents reported. In comparison, non-self-driving cars have an average crash rate of 4.1 crashes per million miles driven. This suggests that traditional, human-driven vehicles experience fewer accidents per million miles traveled compared to self-driving cars. In Figure 14.4 the statistics highlight the need for ongoing evaluation and improvement in the safety features and technology of self-driving cars to reduce accident rates and enhance overall safety on the roads [16].

14.6.3 Managing Traffic and Congestion Prediction

AI-enabled traffic managing systems trust a vast data source, including sensors devices, cameras, connected vehicles, and social media sentiment analysis, to uninterruptedly monitor and examine traffic circumstances [17]. By processing this information using AI algorithms, these systems can forecast traffic patterns, identify congestion places, and improve traffic signal controls in real time. The system automatically adjusts lane usage based on current claim and analyzes and responds to incidents like accidents or road closures [18]. This approach reduces congestion, enhances travel pattern and reduces fuel consumption and emissions. Moreover, V2V communication systems provide real-time updated data and recommended optimal routes, facilitating improved urban mobility and added efficient traffic flow. Generally, AI-enabled traffic management systems play a major role in creating more effective and maintainable transportation networks in smart cities [19].

14.6.4 Decision-Making Process in Smart Transportation Systems

The decision-making algorithm is an essential component of AVs technology that governs how the vehicle responds to various circumstances on the road. To make decisions in a split-second, AVs trust sophisticated algorithms. With AVs systems, the decisions can be made in various situations, such as turning left or right, parking, braking, and more. These decisions depend upon various algorithms that exploit detecting objects, classification and nearby objects movement identification. Additionally, these algorithms must be intentionally focused with ethical considerations, reducing accidents, adhering to traffic laws and avoid risky situations. An AI transportation system uses route optimization, vehicle routing and users travel pattern to make decisions on various situations based on decision-making algorithms.

a) Decision-Making Process on Route Optimization

In route optimization, the process goes beyond simple logistical competence to integrate a broader range of ethical deliberations. A significant goal in AI transportation is to decrease the time limit of route identification on the system, and resource application remains the core objective; proper decision-making requires a more fine-tuned approach. The primary objective focuses on vindicating the environmental effect in an AI transportation system. The finest paths are selected not only for fuel efficiency but also to avoid intricate environmental areas and reduce overall carbon emission. By selecting eco-friendly paths that steer clear of jammed regions and idling traffic, route optimization algorithms contribute to environmental sustainability. Ethical route optimization takes into account the well-being of communities along the chosen paths [20, 21]. Noise pollution, traffic congestion, and potential disruptions to local businesses are some of the factors involved. The AI algorithm inspires a harmonious synchronicity between a network of transportation and the communities it passes that reduces the opposite effects on urban areas and ecosystems.

AI transportation systems focus on another important term, "Safety". The optimal routes are stored in the system that can be accessed by the pedestrian and drivers. Earlier prediction of road damage reduces accidents and ensures the safety of all road users by means of AI algorithms. In route optimization, equity is another concern that safeguards everyone who is involved in accessing the road journey. During heavy traffic on the road, the AI system resources are sharable, which provides opportunities to the drivers to take an alternate path to reach their destination without any further delay. The accessibility of these sharable resources ensures ethical regulations.

Data privacy is another concern in an AI-enabled transportation system. While making/taking decisions on route optimization algorithm, the AI system must adhere to the ethical standards to safeguard the personal information of the user. While communicating between vehicles, AI algorithms temporarily entrust responsibility to their operations and also consider the individuals' privacy. By combining the ethical consideration on transport and route optimization techniques, the decision-making process must ensure the safety, equity and data privacy of the road users such as drivers, pedestrians and cyclists.

b) Decision-Making Process on Travel Patterns

Decision-making and ethical considerations are two different terms that interconnect with each other in AI-driven transportation to figure the mobility in the future. Autonomous vehicles and AI-enabled transportation systems employ safety protocols and confirm every decision taken by passengers and also pedestrians. Another critical characteristic of AI transportation systems is protecting user data privacy. By ethically collecting and maintaining users' personal data, trust and transparency is developed. An AI smart transport system must confirm that equitable access interruptions are removed and that the system guarantees that everyone, including individuals with disabilities and members of other communities, is accessing the systems in a well-defined manner. Implementing an unfairness algorithm ensures that services are delivered in an equitable and inclusive manner. This process indicates the algorithmic unfairness are taken out and it is verified that the services are delivered in an equitable and inclusive manner. In the decision-making procedure, environmental effect is another key term that leads to the development of an eco-friendly infrastructure. These environmental effects provide high priority to energy-efficient operations.

The introduction of an AI transportation system will worry the workers because of job displacement. This framework supports the workers with reorientation and help in any required transition. To endorse accountability, transparency, and justice in the decision-making process, AI algorithms face critical issues in the aspect of ethics. Building trust and acceptance entails proactive engagement and transparent communication, focusing the concerns associated with safety, privacy, equity, and environmental impact. AI-enabled transportation delivers the potential of a future where flexibility is not just proficient but also sustainable, equitable, and all-encompassing because it embraces ethical values at each and every stage.

c) Decision-Making Process on Self-Driving Cars

In self-driving cars, decision-making and ethics are complicatedly connected, given the impact AVs can have in enhancing road safety and on societal values. Another dominant concern in designing an algorithm to safeguard self-driving cars is the main focus on reducing the risk of accidents and assigning actions in situations that will reduce harm to all road users, including passengers, pedestrians, drivers, and cyclists. Ethical considerations extend to another scenario that self-driving cars face, such as the classic "Trolley Problem," requiring algorithms that align the situations with societal values and legal frameworks [21].

Additionally, self-driving cars must prioritize the well-being of every individual, regardless of socioeconomic situation or demographic features, without discrimination due to necessary ethical concerns. There must be a specific mechanism for holding individuals accountable for their actions, particularly in the event of accidents or failures of systems, and a developed algorithm to explain their choices. Privacy protection is another ethical concern that arises from the vast volumes of data that self-driving cars gather and estimate. Strict privacy regulations are essential to ensure that people's right to privacy is safeguarded. Data anonymization, knowledgeable approval for data collection, and loyalty to privacy laws are some of these precautions.

d) Decision-Making Process Traffic Signal

AI-enabled traffic signal control gives priority to safety by analyzing factors like the speed of the vehicle, traffic volume, and pedestrian movement. This ethical concern is to minimize the accident risk and offer safeguards to all road users. It allows adequate time for pedestrians to cross the road safely and decreases the possibility of collisions at connections. Another important term is efficiency. The aim is to minimize congestion, and doing dynamic alteration on signal timings will enhance traffic control on the road. Enhancing the control of traffic leads to reduced travel times, fuel consumptions, and emissions, and ethical deliberations necessitate consistent efficiency such as pedestrian safety and equitable access to transportation resources [22].

Another critical deliberation in traffic signal decision-making is fairness and equity. AI algorithms are available to all communities to ensure that they have equitable access to the resources in transportation systems. Traffic signals are programmed that provide fair treatment to all the users on the road [10]. This procedure ensures the access and mobility of the transportation system by considering the needs of underserved communities.

e) Decision-Making Process on V2V Communication

V2V communication is another important aspect in the recent transportation system in terms of convergence of technological innovation and safety development. In V2V communication, real-time data is collected from the vehicles and a collaborative environment is implemented on the roads. This transformation of data enables safety features such as collision avoidance, vehicle emergency warnings and cooperative driving tactics. This V2V communication considers various consideration of needs in order to realize the full potential. Developing high technological standards that ensure connectivity among vehicles is another critical part. Whether attaching Dedicated Short Range Communications (DSRC) or Cellular Vehicle-to-Everything (C-V2X) tools, selecting the right standard is essential for scalability and efficacy. In the successful implementation of V2V communication, public alertness and acceptance plays a vital role.

Infrastructure deployment requires measurable investments on roadside units, communication towers, and network infrastructure that support better implementation. Association and partnerships among government supports, industry users, academia, and advocacy groups are essential for driving improvement in V2V communication. Deployment and effectiveness of V2V communication by supporting efforts, shared resources, and development innovation for all stakeholders ultimately improve road safety and transportation effectiveness for all.

14.7 Data Confidentiality and Security

AI transportation systems will obtain different kinds of data like vehicle position, route projection, and trip pattern analysis, which are important for the effective functioning of transportation services including route optimization, traffic flow management, and safety enhancement. There will be security and privacy issues with the huge volume of data obtained by AI transportation systems. Unauthorized access to those data may result in identity theft, privacy violations, or improper use of personal data, so it is very critical to use a strong protection to safeguard the data's integrity and confidentiality.

Encryption is one of the security techniques that encrypts data. The authorized users must have the correct decryption code to decrypt the data. During data transmission between the vehicles and computer server, the AV transportation system must have low probability of interference and intruder influence. While transferring data between smart vehicles, encryption techniques must ensure safety and privacy. Adding additional enhancement of implementing AI smart transport systems such as user rights, verification procedures and security verification protects the sensitive data from cyberattacks. Authentication techniques verify the user credentials and then the system will allow the user to access the shared data. This authorized access ensures confidentiality and enhances the integrity between the users and the AI system. Illegal user entries are restricted by doing frequent security audits and vulnerabilities can be identified quickly, and more security can therefore be provided to the smart transportation system. Doing these types of activities reduces the risk of data breaches in transportation. This procedure creates confidence among the users, securing dynamic data, improving the confidentiality and integrity of an AI-enabled system.

14.8 Vision from Data: Smart Decision-Making in Transportation

An AI-enabled smart transport refines the performance of the system and efficiency. In a real-time environment, the transport system collects a variety of data such as traffic congestion, emergency situation, accidents and so on from various sources. AI algorithms have the ability to process all these types of data and approve the enhancement in a smart transport system. While gathering data from pattern of traffic, route prediction, and vehicle communications, AI algorithms analyze the complex datasets. AI algorithms focus on infrastructure, allocating resources, i.e., dynamic traffic signal changes based on the traffic congestion, ambulance vehicle arrival, etc. AI algorithm analyzes the regular traffic patterns and identifies traffic jams, inefficiencies and worsening road conditions and thus enhances the overall performance of the system. Traffic operations are required to improve, which is another important application in the AI transportation systems.

Traffic signal timing adjustment based on traffic congestion, rerouting vehicles and managing congestion in real time is a crucial task for the system. AI-enabled systems control these traffic congestions effectively and they also reduce travel times. AI algorithms are implemented to predict traffic patterns and events, allowing real-world interferences to alleviate disruptions and improve overall system efficiency. Proposing AI-enabled data-driven recommendations for infrastructure planning for the design and development of transportation networks is essential. With AI algorithms enhancing infrastructure development, mobilization needs to ensure alignment, and urban development goals are performed through predictive analytics and simulation modeling. While doing construction on roads, bridges, and public transit systems, the transportation authorities can make better decisions.

Transportation resources such as public transit vehicles, rideshare fleets, and parking spaces are effectively utilized in AI-enabled transportation. Based on the demands and users' choices, service facilities, improved accessibility, and decreased operational charges are optimized by AI algorithms. While exploiting resource usage and reducing environmental impact, the system should confirm the transportation services are personalized to meet the emerging needs of various communities. The decision-making process makes the user take appropriate decisions in the transportation domain by applying data analytics on data that improve system efficiency as well as user experience and drive sustainable mobility solutions. AI-enabled smart transportation systems appear resilient, responsive, and effective by accessing the data and AI technologies that meet the requirements of future transportation. An AI-enabled smart transportation system faces the challenges posed by ethical challenges and regulatory complexities; substantial chances exist for leveraging to create more sustainable, efficient, and inclusive systems. In future, mobility is ethical and intellectual, and may be achieved by embracing transparency, accountability and stakeholder involvement to consider these issues and connect the transformative potential of AI. To foster collaboration and develop robust ethical frameworks to develop AI transportation, it is important to continue future research. Building trust and smart mobility advantages can be accessed by all people in the society, which integrates ethical principles into AI-driven transportation systems. In the future, a more ethical and sustainable transportation future can be developed.

14.9 Conclusions

When AI is integrated with the transportation system, AI can increase transportation, improve safety, and advance sustainability. The transition must assure accountable and reasonable results by ethical standards. AI-enabled transportation systems have been observed carefully in this topic to ensure the ethics issues surrounding self-driven cars, traffic management systems, route optimization algorithms, vehicle-to-vehicle (V2V) communication, data privacy and security protocols.

Studies have examined the importance of safety, fairness, privacy, transparency, and environmental impact by addressing those issues needed to evaluate the practical actions. In ethical consideration, AI transportation systems enhance the fairness and accessibility of route prediction algorithm to safeguard the system while making decision-making processes on AVs.

14.10 Future Directions

Smart transportation in AI systems is implemented with harmless, structured and user-friendly transport. The origin of the AV developments points to revolutionizing traffic that perfectly directs the complex environments. During V2V communication, these AV-enabled vehicles gradually reduce accidents and ensure the safety of drivers, and overall performance of the transportation system is improved. AI-enabled infrastructure is associated with the implementation of AVs. The development of AI-enabled traffic lights, street lights and road surrounds by sensors will optimize control of the lights and reduce traffic congestion. Through dynamic or lively communication with vehicles, systems help to reduce travel times and enhance overall performance, improving the quality of urban life. In addition, AI algorithms can transform transportation services by providing unprecedented customization. Based on individual demands to on-demand ride-sharing stages, optimized routes are refined based on passenger requirements for personalized transportation solutions; this improvisation promises to reevaluate the user's access and knowledge of transportation services.

References

1. Bostrom, N. and Yudkowsky, E., The Ethics of Artificial Intelligence, in: *Cambridge Handbook of Artificial Intelligence*, Cambridge University Press, 2013.
2. Sommer, C., German, R., Dressler, F., Bidirectionally Coupled Network and Road Traffic Simulation for Improved IVC Analysis. *IEEE Trans. Mob. Comput. (TMC)*, 10, 3–15, 2011.
3. Ryan, M., The Future of Transportation: Ethical, Legal, Social and Economic Impacts of Self-driving Vehicles in the Year 2025. *Sci. Eng. Ethics*, 26, 3, 1185–1208, 2020 Jun. doi: 10.1007/s11948-019-00130-2. Epub 2019 Sep 3. PMID: 31482471; PMCID: PMC7286843.
4. *Bosch launches its automated driving initiative in China*, 2017, April 19, Retrieved from https://www.bosch-presse.de/pressportal/de/en/bosch-launches-itsautomated-driving-initiative-in-china-101056.html.
5. Baras, S., Saeed, I., Tabaza, H.A., Elhadef, M., VANETs-Based Intelligent Transportation Systems: An Overview, in: *Advances in Computer Science and Ubiquitous Computing*, pp. 265–273, 2017.
6. Wang, Y., Han, Z., Xing, Y., Xu, S., Wang, J., A Survey on Datasets for the Decision Making of Autonomous Vehicles. *IEEE Intell. Transp. Syst. Mag.*, 16, 2, 23–40, 2024.
7. Wei, S., Zou, Y., Zhang, X., Zhang, T., Li, X., An Integrated Longitudinal and Lateral Vehicle Following Control System with Radar and Vehicle-to-Vehicle Communication. *IEEE Trans. Veh. Technol.*, 68, 2, 1116–1127, Feb. 2019. doi: 10.1109/TVT.2018.2890418.
8. He, K. and Li, B., Automotive V2X Communication Security Key Technology and Test Method Research, in: *Proceedings of the 2022 7th International Conference on Cyber Security and Information Engineering (ICCSIE)*, Brisbane, QLD, Australia, 23–25 September 2022, IEEE, Piscataway, NJ, USA, 2022.
9. Muslam, M.M.A., Enhancing Security in Vehicle-to-Vehicle Communication: A Comprehensive Review of Protocols and Techniques. *Vehicles*, 6, 450–467, 2024. https://doi.org/10.3390/vehicles6010020.
10. Petrov, T., Sevcik, L., Pocta, P., Dado, M., A Performance Benchmark for Dedicated Short-Range Communications and LTE-Based Cellular-V2X in the Context of Vehicle-to-Infrastructure Communication and Urban Scenarios. *Sensors*, 21, 5095, 2021. https://doi.org/10.3390/s21155095.
11. Chang, J.-J., Li, Y.-H., Liao, W., Chang, I.-C., Intersection-based routing for urban vehicular communications with traffic-light considerations. *IEEE Wireless Commun.*, 19 1, 82–88, 2012.
12. Apte, A., Ingole, V., Lele, P., Marsh, A., Bhattacharjee, T., Hirve, S., Campbell, H., Nair, H., Chan, S., Juvekar, S., Ethical considerations in the use of GPS-based movement tracking in health research - lessons from a care-seeking

study in rural west India. *J. Glob. Health.*, 9, 1, 010323, 2019 Jun. doi: 10.7189/jogh.09.010323.

13. Huang, A. and Levinson, D., Axis of travel: Modeling non-work destination choice with GPS data. *Transp. Res. Part C Emerging Technol.*, 58, Part B, 208–223, 2015. ISSN 0968-090X, https://doi.org/10.1016/j.trc.2015.03.022.
14. Evans, K., de Moura, N., Chauvier, S., Chatila, R., Dogan, E., Ethical decision making in autonomous vehicles: The AV ethics project. *Sci. Eng. Ethics*, 26, 3285–312, 2020 Dec.
15. Finn, A. and Scheding, S., *Developments and Challenges for Autonomous Unmanned Vehicles: A Compendium*, Springer, Berlin, 2010.
16. https://gitnux.org/self-driving-cars-accident-statistics/#:~:text=GM's%20Cruise%20self%2Ddriving%20car,per%2011%2C017%20miles%20in%202018.
17. Goodall, N.J., Ethical Decision Making during Automated Vehicle Crashes. *Transp. Res. Record J. Transp. Res. Board*, 2424, 1, 58–65, 2014.
18. Lai, W.K., Lin, M.-T., Yang, Y.-H., A Machine Learning System for Routing Decision-Making in Urban Vehicular Ad Hoc Networks. *Int. J. Distrib. Sens. Netw.*, 11, 3, 2015. doi:10.1155/2015/374391.
19. American Association of State Highway and Transportation Officials, *A Policy on Geometric Design of Highways and Streets*, AASHTO, Washington, DC, 2011.
20. Akhtar, M. and Moridpou, S., A Review of Traffic Congestion Prediction Using Artificial Intelligence. *J. Adv. Transp.*, 2021, 8878011. https://doi.org/10.1155/2021/8878011.
21. Chen, Z., Jiang, Y., Sun, D., Liu, X., Discrimination and prediction of traffic congestion states of urban road network based on spatio-temporal correlation. *IEEE Access*, 8, 3330–3342, 2020.
22. Cunneen, M., Mullins, M., Murphy, F., Shannon, D., Furxhi, I., Ryan, C., Autonomous vehicles and avoiding the trolley (dilemma): vehicle perception, classification, and the challenges of framing decision ethics. *Cybern. Syst.*, 51, 1, 59–80, 2020 Jan 2.

15

Case Study on AI-Based Decision-Making in E-Commerce: Exploring Location-Based Insights for Analysis of Geospatial Data

Ashima Arya[1]*, Daksh Rampal[1], Ekagra[1], Kashish Varshney[1], Rohit Vashisht[1] and Yonis Gulzar[2]

[1]KIET Group of Institution, Ghaziabad, India
[2]Department of Management Information Systems, College of Business Administration, King Faisal University, Eastern Province - Al Ahsa, Saudi Arabia

Abstract
Exploratory analysis of geolocational data refers to the process of analyzing geospatial data obtained from different sources such as GPS coordinates, satellite images, and street addresses, among others. The purpose of this analysis is to extract useful insights and patterns that can be used to make informed decisions about places and regional human behavior. The analysis may involve applying various statistical methods such as clustering, regression, and data visualization techniques to identify trends and relationships within the data. In addition, the exploratory analysis of geolocational data may be used to classify accommodation based on student preferences and rank migrant shelters based on their amenities, budget, and proximity preferences. In the fast-paced, demanding world that most individuals live in, it is common for everyone to be limited to homemade meals, each person having specific preferences, tastes, and budgets. Furthermore, if individuals can consistently enjoy affordable homemade meals and find accommodations that match their specific preferences, there is no need to incur additional expenses by going out for social or recreational purposes. Regardless of location, cuisine, or budget, it is widely recognized that the food one consumes plays a significant role in shaping one's lifestyle. The goal and the objective of this project is to predict or find a suitable place for the people according to their preferences, taste, budget, etc.

**Corresponding author*: ashima.arya@kiet.edu

Sapna Juneja, Rajesh Kumar Dhanaraj, Abhinav Juneja, Malathy Sathyamoorthy and Asadullah Shaikh (eds.) Ethical Decision-Making Using Artificial Intelligence: Challenges, Solutions and Applications, (367–392) © 2025 Scrivener Publishing LLC

***Keywords*:** Prediction, machine learning, supervised learning, data mining, k-means clustering, foursquare API

15.1 Introduction

Geospatial data analysis (GDA) is type of data analysis that deals with the components of geographical information. Geographical features are represented as population, cities, landmarks, water bodies, temperature, elevation, technological presence and connectivity, imaging, traffic patterns, and others. In this analysis data are collected and visualized to retrieve information for the extractor. The extractor can belong to any industry dealing with research, manufacturing, healthcare, agriculture, business setup, and others. Simply we can say that, with the help of geospatial data analysis, find hidden patterns, opportunities and risk mitigation for growth and development.

The geospatial information represents in the form of coordinates, maps, or Geographic Information Systems in different area of sectors as shown in Figure 15.1:

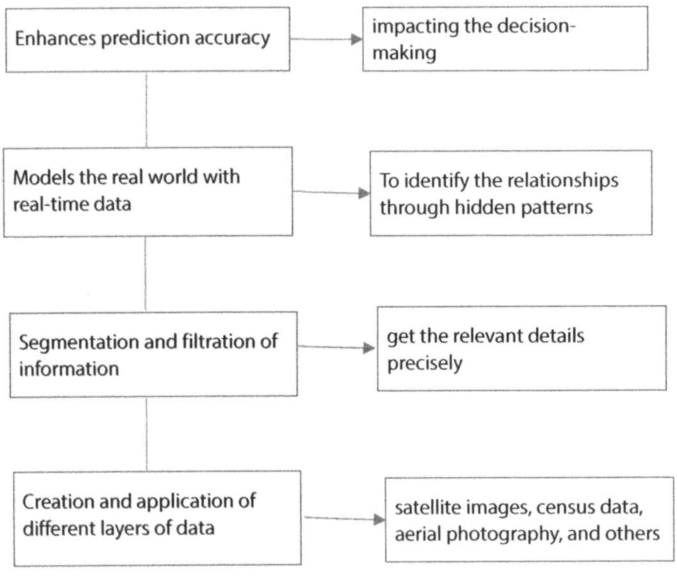

Figure 15.1 Geolocation data sectors.

15.1.1 Method of Geospatial Data Analysis

The steps of the process for geospatial data analysis are representing in Figure 15.2:

1. Reading/writing spatial data:
    - loads datasets into the analysis environment
    - exploring and manipulation of the data
    - save modified datasets and sharing results
2. Retrieving data
    - used data source
    - updated and detailed information for analysis
3. Reprojection
    - Reprojected into common CRS for accuracy
4. Spatial Join
    - Combine the information or attributes from different datasets
    - overlay analysis and data linking

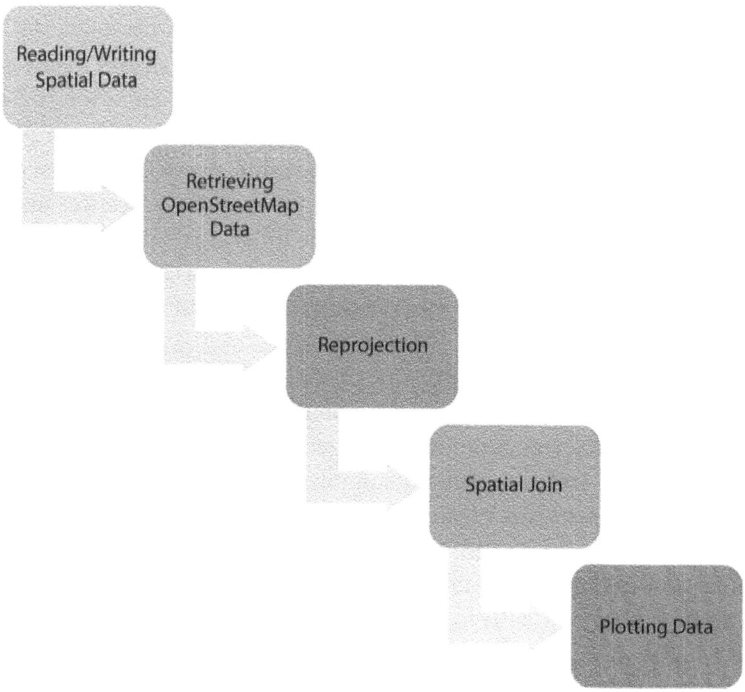

Figure 15.2 Method of geospatial data analysis.

5. Plotting data
    - Visualization and interpretation
    - creation of maps

Moving to a new city is always exciting. However, with excitement comes difficulties. Sometimes essentials like food, transportation, water, shelter, etc., need more attention and planning. Young college students and working professionals have to move to different cities for studies, jobs and many other purposes. Discovering a fitting place to reside, considering personal preferences for amenities and budget, can be a challenging endeavor, particularly when the company or college does not offer arranged accommodation, hostel, or mess facilities. First, food can be a significant concern. Within the rapid and busy lifestyle of the average person, it frequently occurs that one becomes too fatigued to cook a home-cooked meal after a typical 9 to 5 job. Similarly, for college students who live on their own, not having the knowledge or skills to prepare their own meals can pose an inconvenience [5, 8].

With the help of geographic coordinate system, positions can be defined on Earth which rely on geolocation data such as the GPS (Global Positioning System). These data can be used for analysis of routes, vehicles and drivers. The most common example is data-driven transportation systems [6].

Inevitably, even when we have the luxury of home-cooked meals every day, it's natural to seek out a delightful dining experience for social or entertainment purposes from time to time. Recognizing the impact of food on our lifestyle regardless of where we reside, now envision a scenario where someone has recently relocated. With unique preferences and distinct tastes, it would greatly benefit both the individual and food providers if the person could conveniently access their preferred eateries nearby. This harmony of convenience not only maximizes sales but also saves valuable time for the customers [7].

Our project aims to simplify the process of finding ideal accommodations for students, working professionals, and others. By considering factors such as preferred amenities, budget, and proximity to desired locations, we classify and recommend suitable options. Using advanced techniques like data retrieval, cleaning, analysis, and K-Means Clustering on geolocational data, we ensure accurate and optimal accommodation suggestions for immigrants in a city. The appealing part in our innovation is to use MI algorithm and APIs to fetch the user's choice data and to make our project highly user friendly and easy to use [16, 17].

The information that is particular to a specific location and can be retrieved from a mobile device or other location-aware devices is referred to as geolocational data. Healthcare organizations use geolocational data for various services such as to improve patient care and treatment outcomes [9, 10].

With analysis of data it has been found that geolocational data may help healthcare professionals in several ways. Figure 15.3 shows the applications of Geolocation data and Figure 15.4 the evidence of application of healthcare.

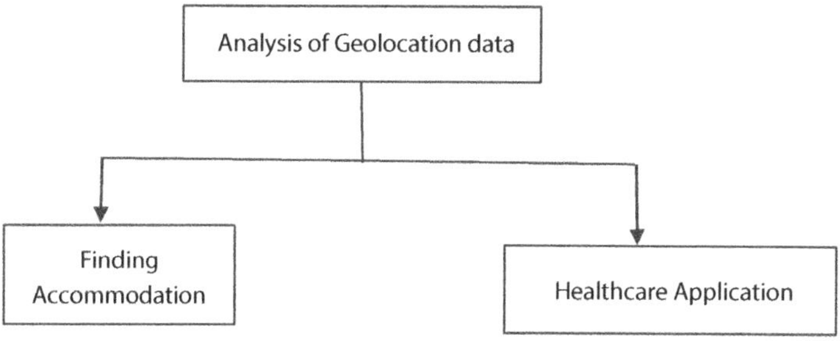

Figure 15.3 Application of geolocation data.

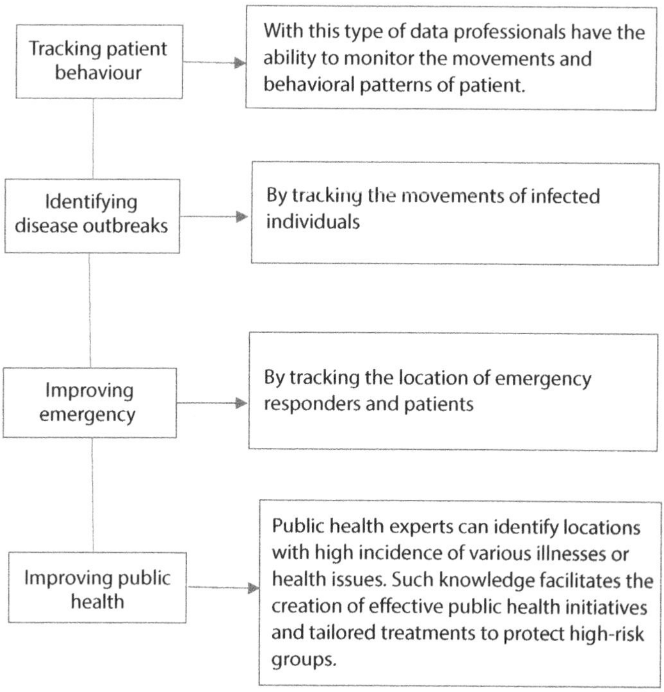

Figure 15.4 Geolocation data in healthcare.

15.2 Objective

The project's objective is to suggest the best and optimal accommodations for the user. We are using the K-means cluster algorithm that helps to find the best and optimal results of your choice. It offers a platform where users can have a variety of accommodations according to their preferences, taste, budget, etc. Our service will be highly beneficial and accepted in all small-scale places like rural areas. Since the user interface and user experience are simple and easy to use, most people will find it easy to use our software. We will provide different plans of service so that customers can have a choice and choose what may seem better for them.

15.3 Background Knowledge

a) Python

Python is a versatile programming language suitable for a wide range of applications. It offers a gentle learning curve with a straightforward syntax and excellent readability. Python supports both object-oriented and procedure-oriented programming paradigms. Being an open-source language, it is backed by a vast array of libraries, providing abundant resources for diverse implementations.

b) Jupyter Notebook

The Jupyter Notebook is a web-based open-source application that enables the creation and sharing of documents comprising live code, equations, visualizations, and text narratives. Its versatile applications encompass data cleaning and transformation, numerical simulation, statistical modeling, data visualization, machine learning, and numerous other functionalities.

c) K-Means Clustering

Clustering in simple words is nothing but creating different groups. Those groups consist of similar elements. Clustering is a system of dividing the similar detail or records units into organizations consisting of comparable facts; it points the point inside one cluster as similar as possible while the points belonging to other clusters are completely specific from the points in the first cluster. And clustering is regularly known as an unmonitored studying technique. Now coming to where it's often used—organizing dinners in a restaurant, and gadgets organized in a mall are examples of K-means clustering. Suppose there are two tables in a restaurant, table 1 and 2. The group of people sitting on desk T1 might be related to each other or they may be a collection of individuals or anything. The same applies to the people sitting at desk T2. When we evaluate the people sitting on Table T1 and the people sitting on Table T2 we observe that they're entirely unique. They are not in any component associated with every different [11]. Clustering is also achieved in the identical manner that the facts point inside one cluster are completely specific from the information factors of the opposite cluster and all of the factors in a cluster are both equal and linked. When you visit Walmart, a retail store, you will note that similar objects are grouped together for you. It's not like the items are just positioned everywhere; the vegetable sections, for example, are not mixed collectively. You wouldn't be able to locate the oranges if they were mixed with potatoes, so what they do is create clusters of items so that you can without difficulty shop and find your items with no trouble [18].

Customer segmentation is a common practice in marketing, often utilizing unsupervised clustering methods like K-means Clustering. By grouping individuals based on similarities such as preferences and purchasing power, clustering provides valuable insights to enhance the customer base and target specific areas. This technique aids in identifying groups of homes with similar characteristics, including value, type, and geographic location. Figure 15.5 represents different K-means clustering example. Client architecture is representing in Figure 15.6.

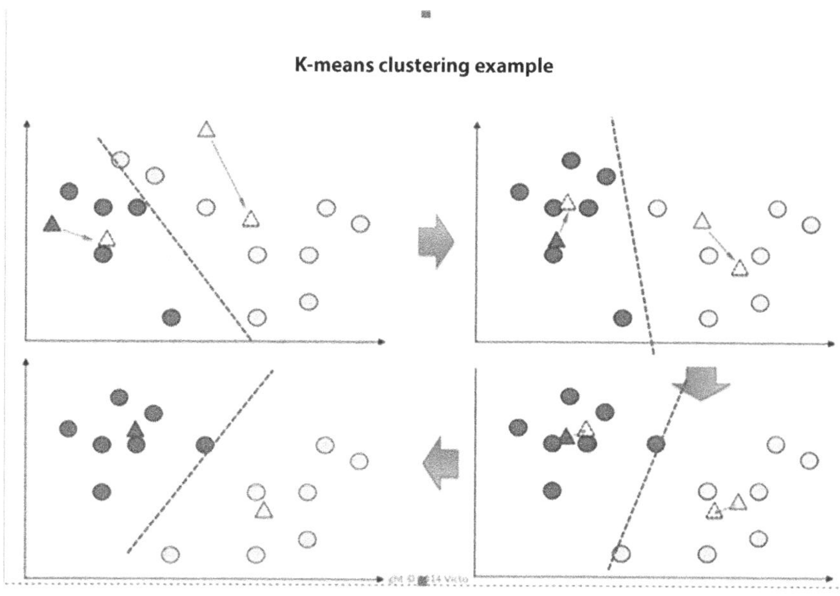

Figure 15.5 Means clustering.

Figure 15.6 Client server architecture.

With the help of K-means Clustering, clusters are organised according to the locations with similar food preferences. Each cluster has a defined centre. These cluster centres are pointed out as potential locations for opening restaurants or food outlets. This software will also point out the accommodations to individuals who share these food preferences. These cluster centres, also known as centroids, are located at the shortest distance possible from all sites inside a certain cluster, ensuring that food outlets are close to the intended clients in each cluster [19, 20].

d) REST API

Representational State Transfer (REST) is an architectural style that provides a set of principles for creating web services. REST API allows for accessing web services in a straightforward and adaptable manner, without any additional processing required.

Working: Web services rely on clients sending requests to servers using various HTTP request methods such as GET, POST, PUT, or DELETE. These requests are typically in the form of web URLs. In response, servers provide resources, which can take the form of HTML, XML, images, or JSON. JSON has become the prevalent format for web services in recent times [21, 22].

15.4 Related Work

Housing can be difficult when we move to a completely new city. Aside from the fact that we won't be physically on site to review all the properties, we generally have to guess which neighborhood is best for us and what reasonable rental rates may be in the area. Fortunately, the Internet exists, but the research work of going through all the housing options based on one's budget and preferences and doing all the legal work is still an intimidating task for someone who is just a college student or a working professional. Therefore, at present, in most situations, ideally people prefer to contact a real estate agent (or broker). A real estate agent assists home buyers and sellers by providing buyers with options based on their desired location, wish list, budget, and move-in date. Rental agents are great resources, especially when one is having trouble narrowing down their options or are just completely lost and not sure where to start. But when it comes to students, along with budget, food preferences of the individual become an important factor while suggesting/providing housing options. As most of them don't know how to cook, they rely on food outlets for their meals on almost a regular basis. Although a rental agent has a list of all the sellers and the renters residing in that city in different locations, it is quite common that he might not know all the food outlet options available in the neighborhood of the property according to the preference of the students. Now coming to another scenario, there are many things to consider when starting a restaurant or food outlet and choosing a property, but some basic principles can help restaurant chain owners better understand what makes a good restaurant location. Location analysis is a method of finding the best location for your new food outlet. Apart from analyzing accessibility, parking, visibility, and potential competitors around that area, one very important factor is Target Demographics. A target market or demographic is a specific group of consumers to whom you market your products. Demographics in this case are defined by certain characteristics such as age, gender, income level, and food preferences of people residing near the potential location [23].

A combination of all of these factors provides the best demographic picture to determine how a particular location would affect your business. To determine the population base of a given area [5] a location study is performed. However, these cost a good amount of money. Most people starting their first restaurant don't have enough money to complete a professional survey. Depending on the size of the business, the initial financial outlay, and associated risk, professional demographic research and location analysis is appropriate.

The researcher examines the Brazilian states' COVID-19 distribution patterns using millions of anonymised mobile visitation data. This study also explores the prospective of mobile geolocation data which may be used as a gauge of population mobility and to assist public managers in creating action plans for allocating resources [1].

In this article, the author recommends a methodology for estimating the sale prices of homes. To complete this study various algorithms, such as feature correlation analysis, elimination of variables with low correlation, and a method to handle missing data are incorporated. The study also reveals that the K-nearest neighbor algorithm is utilized for focusing on KNN-MCF feature in large datasets for handling missing values [2].

In this work, the researchers demonstrate the portable commercial components and cost-effective real-time kinematic (RTK) geolocation services.

The technology achieves centimetre-level precision within a 15-kilometer radius of the mobile base station and rover. The usage of open source and free software facilitates the distribution of corrected data *via* internet access. In remote and distant locales small Design RTK base station and rover enable diverse can be used [3].

Using an online survey that gathered 112 responses from parents of kids between the ages of 5 and 18, this article investigates parental views and practises regarding this contentious practise. Several parents admitted to employing tracking devices. Parents' opinions on the practise were occasionally conflicting and equivocal. Different viewpoints were presented, such as those that supported geotracking as beneficial for children's well-being as well as family management and logistics, disputed the usage of the word "surveillance" to characterise it, and opposed the use of such technology as being inimical to children's autonomy and choice [4].

Sudhir Singh and Nasib Singh Gill have released a research paper discussing the analysis Clustering Algorithm (K-means). This study sheds light on the functionality of k-means clustering as well as its shortcomings, particularly its lengthy runtime when applied to large datasets. Consequently, we integrated the concept of clustering with the k-means algorithm to achieve faster and more efficient results [5].

Shi Na, Liu Xumin, and Guan Yong delve into the K-means Clustering Algorithm, highlighting its significance in data mining analytics. This paper provides us with a comprehensive and in-depth comprehension of the clustering algorithm. This study explores the use of clustering for extracting valuable insights from the dataset and visualizing it effectively on a map [27].

A blog by Karan Bhanot titled "Exploring venues in Chandigarh, India using Foursquare and Zomato API", in 2019 focused mainly on the data plotting using APIs like Foursquare and Zomato. This paper represents the working of API which is required and important for data plotting.

In 2019, Enago Academy posted an article, "Report Research Data Using Box Plots and Bar Charts", that contained detailed information of box plots that are helpful for us to visualize out dataset. This paper consists the working of the box plotting. Box plotting is the major component of our project as it helps in better visualizing and understanding of the data of our dataset. We came to know about terms like outlier, maximum, upper quartile, median, lower quartile, minimum that are required for understanding the data plotted using the boxplots. It gives us detailed understanding of the difference between the box plots and bar charts. Table 15.1 shows the survey that includes algorithm that were used for the problem.

Table 15.1 Literature review.

Reference	Year	Technology/ algorithm	Description
[24]	2022	Agglomerative Hierarchical Clustering	For finding the best accommodation - Foursquare API (Application programming Interface) URL (Uniform Resource Locator).
[26]	2024	Origin-Destinations maps, spatial nesting technique	Proposed an abstraction framework "GRIDIFY - and an interactive open-source tool" implementing this framework using several levels of nested maps.
[25]	2021	Clustering and overlapping techniques	Analysing geolocation data for data driven transportation system.
[28]	2020	Mining techniques	Inferring process states from geolocation data.
[29]	2018	Geolocation Prediction (Content-based and User-profiling)	Hybrid approach is used that combines both prediction category to overcome the problem of geotagged data limitations on Location-distribution Analysis.
[30]	2016	mining popular geolocation region (MPGR), mining personal trajectory (MPT)	Emerging mobility big data (MBD).

15.5 Data Analysis of Geolocation Data

- **Data collection**

Google Colab or Jupyter Notebook platform are used by the author to retrieve the necessary data and configure the environment. Data frame is prepared by Pandas library for obtaining the required data.

- **Data Cleaning *via* Pandas**

With the help of Pandas library, the author has handled values such as NaN values, referred to as data cleaning.

- **Data Exploration and Visualization**

Now the dataset has been obtained, visualization through graphs is an excellent method for comprehending the dataset. A box plot graph is used to read numerous rows of data and for examining distributed groups.

	cook	eating_out	employment	ethnic_food	exercise	fruit_day	income	on_off_campus	pay_meal_out	sports	veggies_day
0	2.0	3	3.0	1	1.0	5	5.0	1.0	2	1.0	5
1	3.0	2	2.0	4	1.0	4	4.0	1.0	4	1.0	4
2	1.0	2	3.0	5	2.0	5	6.0	2.0	3	2.0	5
3	2.0	2	3.0	5	3.0	4	6.0	1.0	2	2.0	3
4	1.0	2	2.0	4	1.0	4	6.0	1.0	4	1.0	4

Figure 15.7 Result after data cleaning.

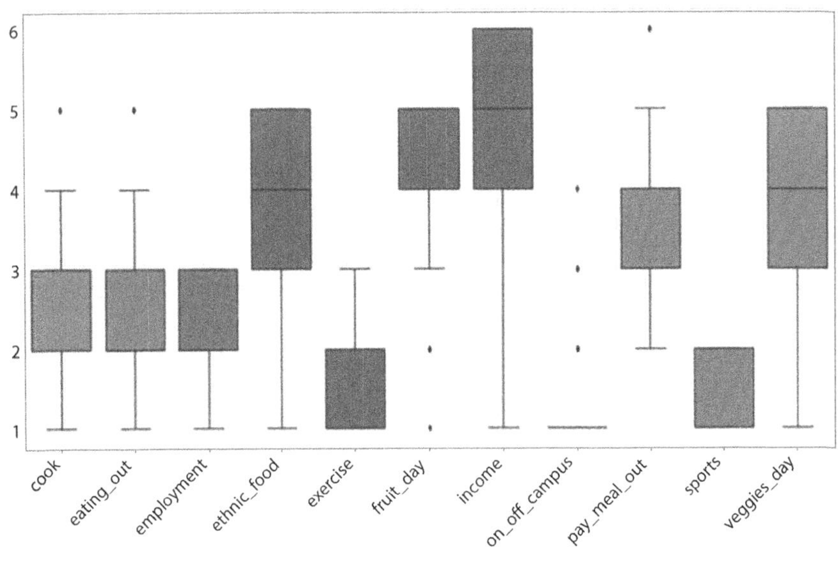

Figure 15.8 Data exploration and visualization.

This graph provides a snapshot of the concentration of residents and allows us to compare outliers to the average within the group [15]. Figure 15.7 describes the datset after cleaning. Figure 15.8 represents visualization of data set.

- **Run K-Means Clustering on the Data**

The K-Means Clustering algorithm is used to assist in categorizing locations based on the amenities. Similar locations together are grouped together and labeled as either "Amenity Rich" if they have a large number of nearby shops or "Amenity Poor" if they have fewer amenities. Initially, this algorithm is applied to the dataset for organizing the population into

	categories	hasPerk	id	location.address	location.cc	location.city	location.country	location.cross Street	locat
0	[{'id': '4d954b06a24385684965b473', 'name': 'R...	False	4db7040e0437fa536a641766	Banaswadi Main Rd	IN	Bangalore	India	hight street	
1	[{'id': '4d954b06a24385684965b473", 'name': 'R...	False	594f23a82be42528bc56a739	NaN	IN	Bangalore	India	NaN	
2	[{'id': '4d954b06a24385684965b473', 'name': 'R...	False	51319d59e4b04a7c6799abe4	Ananthapura Road	IN	Bangalore	India	Yelahanka New Town	
3	[{'id': '4d954b06a24385684965b473', 'name': 'R...	False	56133261498e95c619c830f8	NaN	IN	Bangalore	India	NaN	
4	[{'id': '4bf58dd8d48988d12b951735' 'name': 'B...	False	52dd2fd2498ebd1fc2edf286	NaN	IN	NaN	India	NaN	

Figure 15.9 Fetch geolocational data.

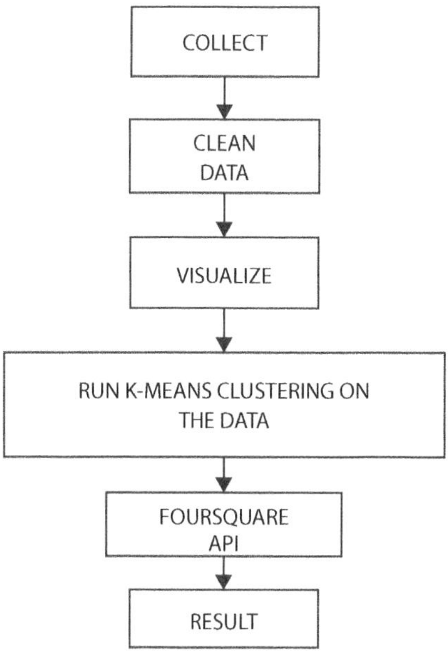

Figure 15.10 Flow chart of whole process.

distinct groups. Then, the value of K is identified by analysing the resulting clusters and considering the parameters used to differentiate them.

- **Fetch Geolocational data from Foursquare API (REST API):**

After determining the optimal K value for the population, the next step is to retrieve geolocation data from the Foursquare API. This will allow the author to identify suitable locations for accommodating the immigrants. IT will then create a data frame containing the latitude and longitude coordinates of each location, as well as a count of the total number of amenities in the vicinity of each location. Figure 15.9 showing the fetching location according to the category.

- **Visualized Clustered locations on a Map:**

In the output, we should have a map centred on the location (city) of our choice, with the locations differentiated by different colour schemes [14]. The following description flow diagram summarises all the steps mentioned above. The flow chart for the complete process is elborated by Figure 15.10.

15.6 Proposed Methodology

In our project we have used the K-Means clustering algorithm to find the best and optimal results according to the user's requirements.

K-means clustering algorithm is an unsupervised algorithm and there is no such term as accuracy. However, we have to find the best value of K, where K is the number of clusters where the distance between two clusters should be maximum and the distance between data points inside a cluster should be minimum. To find the best value of K for our data set we can go for two methods:

- Elbow method
- Silhouette analysis

K-means clustering is an unsupervised algorithm. Before you know what K-means clustering does and how you can solve the subproblems with K-means algorithm, let's just understand the unsupervised and supervised. The unsupervised is simple, which is that you will be given a labelled data. A labelled data is given in the example below. So here in the K-nearest neighbour algorithm the datasets and the class are given; if the point is 4.2 and 2.8, that class belongs to 1. The result is always 1 or 0. Either it belongs to class 1 or it belongs to class 0. So, there is a label given but in case of K-means you won't be given class 1 or 0. This is a labelled data. K-means clustering is unsupervised because there is no labelled data like the K neighbour algorithm. So, this is the main difference between supervised algorithms and unsupervised algorithms.

The K-means algorithm is based on clustering, which involves grouping data points together. Each cluster has its own centroid, represented by μ1, μ2, μ3 for three different clusters. By determining the closest centroid, we can assign test data points (x, y) to the corresponding cluster. To achieve this, we calculate the distance between the test data and the centroids μ1, μ2, μ3.

The Elbow method is used to determine the optimal number of clusters. It aims to minimize the distance between points within a cluster and maximize the gap between clusters. In K-means, the Within Clusters Sum of Squares (WCSS) is used to assess the clustering solution. Just as SST, SSR, and SSE are metrics in regression analysis, WCSS measures distances within clusters. Minimizing WCSS leads to the most appropriate clustering result. However, having too few or too many clusters is not beneficial.

If all countries are considered separate clusters or if all observations are included within a single cluster, the WCSS value becomes irrelevant. Ideally, we want WCSS to be as low as possible while having a reasonable number of clusters. Plotting WCSS against the number of clusters helps visualize this relationship [13].

It appears to resemble the shape of an elbow. Therefore, the key point is that the within cluster sum of squares (WCSS) exhibits a decreasing trend, meaning it decreases as the number of clusters increases. Here's an important finding: the initial WCSS decreases rapidly until it reaches a point that resembles an elbow. Beyond this point, increasing the number of clusters does not lead to significant improvement in terms of WCSS. Rather, the optimal number of clusters is identified as three, as it represents the highest number of clusters where a substantial decrease in WCSS is still observed. After this point, the improvement is minimal. To obtain the required information, we need two pieces of data: the number of clusters (K) which we determine at the start of the process, and the WCSS for a specific number of clusters. While K is chosen by us, there is a sklearn method available that provides us with the WCSS, for example, to obtain the WCSS for our final example.

To plot the elbow in the k-means clustering algorithm, we need to calculate the within-cluster sum of squares (WCSS) for different values of k (number of clusters). We can achieve this by iterating through different values of k (from 1 to 6 in this case) and computing the WCSS for each iteration.

First, we initialize an empty list called WCSS. Then, using a loop, we iterate over each value of k. Within each iteration, we fit the input data X to the k-means algorithm using k-means.fit(X). Next, we calculate the WCSS for the iteration by accessing the inertia_ attribute of the k-means object (WCSS_iter = k-means.inertia). Finally, we append the WCSS_iter value to the WCSS list using the append () method. The implementation is done with K means algorithm that show in Figure 15.11.

After running the code, the WCSS list will contain the WCSS values for one cluster, two clusters, and so on until six clusters. By plotting the WCSS values against the corresponding number of clusters, we can visualize the elbow curve. The elbow method helps us determine the optimal number of clusters by identifying the point on the curve where the rate of decrease in WCSS significantly slows down.

To plot the elbow curve, we can assign the values of k to a list called number_clusters (number_clusters = range(1, 7)). Then, using conventional plotting code, we can plot the number_clusters on the x-axis and the WCSS values on the y-axis [12].

Finally, we will use the elbow method to decide the optimal number of clusters. There can be two points which can be the elbow. A three-cluster solution is definitely the better one as after it there's not much to gain. A two-cluster solution in this case would be suboptimal as the leap from two to three is very big in terms of WCSS. Since K-means clustering is an unsupervised learning, there is no direct way of measuring the accuracy. Figure 15.12 shows the elbow method for clustering. There is a defined coefficient that is known as

```
In [12]:  kmeans.inertia_

Out[12]:  13208.95812

In [13]:  wcss=[]

          for i in range(1,7):
              kmeans = KMeans(i)
              kmeans.fit(x)
              wcss_iter = kmeans.inertia_
              wcss.append(wcss_iter)

In [14]:  wcss

Out[14]:  [42605.41356666667,
           13208.95812,
           290.10523333333333,
           113.91233333333332,
           39.00624999999998,
           0.0]
```

Figure 15.11 Implementation of WCSS.

The Elbow Method

```
In [15]: number_clusters = range(1,7)
         plt.plot(number_clusters,wcss)
         plt.title('The Elbow Method')
         plt.xlabel('Number of clusters')
         plt.ylabel('Within-cluster Sum of Squares')

Out[15]: Text(0,0.5,'Within-cluster Sum of Squares')
```

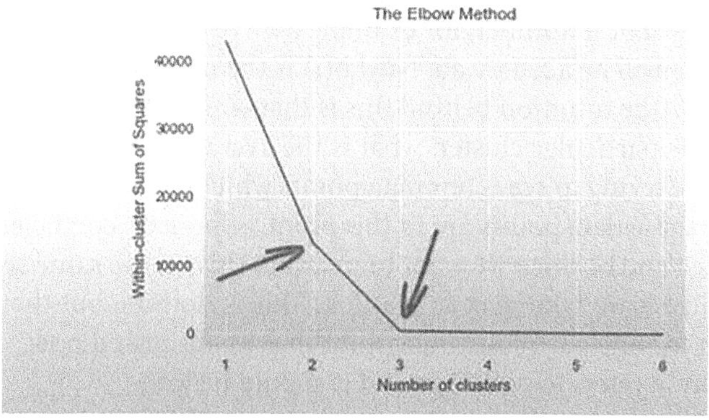

Figure 15.12 Implementation of elbow method.

silhouette coefficient or silhouette distance which ranges from +1 to -1 based on which we can get to know how good our clusters are formed. Two purposes of K-means Clustering are Cohesion, i.e., items in a cluster should be similar to each other, and Separation, i.e., items in one cluster should be different from the items in another cluster. Using this silhouette coefficient, we measure these two things together and in the end we say that how good our clusters are formed. So, there are two numbers associated to measure these two. To understand it very simply we will take only one data point. Let's say there are two clusters, cluster A and cluster B. Let us take this data point. There are two variables defined to compute the silhouette coefficient for this data point and in the end the silhouette coefficient of your entire cluster is nothing but the mean of all your silhouette coefficients [31–33].

So, let's see how to compute silhouette coefficient for this data point. In our observation we have six data points and all of these will have one – one Silhouette coefficient each. Now we have to take the mean; whatever that number comes that is your silhouette coefficient of the entire cluster. Let us understand how to compute for one data point. There is a variable 'a', which is nothing but the mean of all the distances within cluster from this point. So, compute the distance of this point to other points in the cluster and let these distances be d1.d2.d3… and so on [34–36].

Distance means Euclidean or Manhattan distance (typically Euclidean distance). There is d1 and there is d2. We take the average of d1 and d2 that becomes a for this particular data point. Now this is to measure the cohesion, how closely this cluster is associated with its neighboring points. And to measure separation we have something known as 'b'. So, b for a data point is nothing but the distance of this point from all the points in another cluster. Let's say those are d3, d4 and d5, now take the mean of all these. This mean will be a number, for example a1. We have 6 clusters so for each cluster there will be a2, a3...a6. Now b(i) is the minimum of these average a1, a2.... a6. The intuition behind this is that whichever is the nearest cluster from this particular cluster, what is the average distance for this point. What we are trying to see is few data points which is not part of this cluster, how close these data points are to this point. Silhouette coefficient is nothing but b - a and12 since we want to measure this on the same scale, hence to normalize it we take max of b and a. This is nothing but the silhouette coefficient for one particular data point that we discussed now.

Typically, a refers to cohesion and it should be low.

Let's take two cases:

<u>Case 1:</u> a = 0.2, b = 0.8
<u>Case 2:</u> a = 0.8, b = 0.2

Let us calculate the silhouette coefficient for both these cases. In the first case, the numerator will be 0.6 and the denominator will be max of these two which means 0.8, i.e., 3/4. Similarly for the second case the silhouette coefficient become -3/4. So, for silhouette coefficient, the closer it is to +1 is better. So, as you can see when b becomes small and a becomes large it is becoming negative, and other way around it is becoming positive. That is why this measures cohesion and b measures separation. b should be always large and a should be as small as possible [37–40, 47–49].

15.7 Results

We have obtained a Pandas dataframe with the relevant parameters which we will analyze in a Colab notebook as shown in Figure 15.13.

Now we have visualized our clean dataset using box plot model.

We have also found the suitable value of K (K = 6) for our dataset, and also, the features which will differentiate the clusters. We have filtered

	cook	eating_out	employment	ethnic_food	exercise	fruit_day	income	on_off_campus	pay_meal_out	sports	veggies_day
0	2.0	3	3.0	1	1.0	5	5.0	1.0	2	1.0	5
1	3.0	2	2.0	4	1.0	4	4.0	1.0	4	1.0	4
2	1.0	2	3.0	5	2.0	5	6.0	2.0	3	2.0	5
3	2.0	2	3.0	5	3.0	4	6.0	1.0	2	2.0	3
4	1.0	2	2.0	4	1.0	4	6.0	1.0	4	1.0	4
...	...	...	...	...	...	...	...	...	...	...	...
120	3.0	2	1.0	4	2.0	5	4.0	3.0	4	1.0	5
121	3.0	4	3.0	3	2.0	4	2.0	1.0	4	NaN	5
122	3.0	3	3.0	5	2.0	4	2.0	1.0	4	2.0	4
123	3.0	5	2.0	2	1.0	5	4.0	1.0	3	2.0	3
124	NaN	1	2.0	3	2.0	3	5.0	1.0	3	2.0	4

Figure 15.13 Dataset.

the locations by distance and only selected the locations which have the required amenities in their proximity. We have obtained a dataframe with the locations (in latitude, longitude format). The count of amenities like Restaurants, Fruits, Vegetables, Grocery stores present around each location are also displayed in the dataframe. Figure 15.14 displays result after applying box plot.

Finally, we have got a map centered on our target location (Bangalore City) with different clusters differentiated by different colors. Figures 15.15 and 15.16 show the final output as result 1 and result 2, respectively.

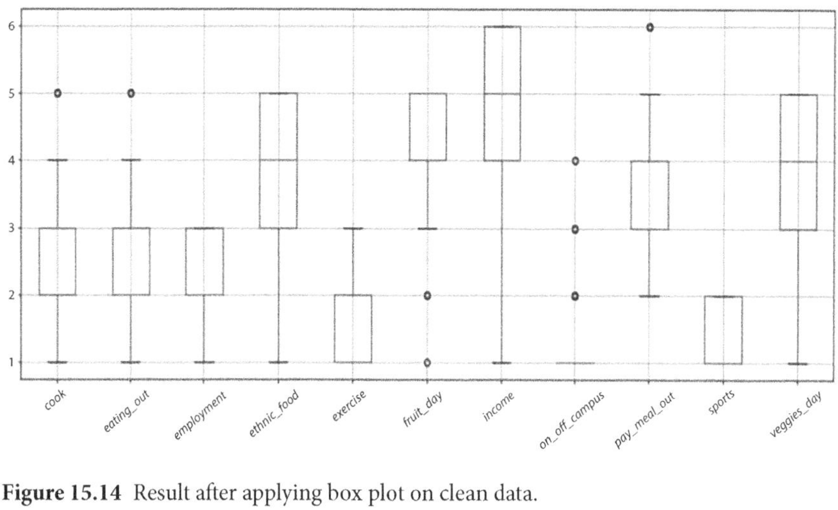

Figure 15.14 Result after applying box plot on clean data.

	lat	long	venue.location.formattedAddress	restaurant	others
0	17.435868	78.457443	[Ground Floor, Lifestyle Building, Greenlands ...	28	19
1	17.483180	78.552104	[HP Petrol Bunk, Kushaiguda, Secunderabad, And...	7	3
2	17.423612	78.462541	[The park, Hyderabad, Telangana, India]	23	18
3	17.400678	78.488575	[Himayatnagar (Narayanguda-himayat Nagar X Roa...	23	14
4	17.432374	78.457585	[Greenlands Flyover, Greenlands, Punjagutta, H...	39	28
...	...	...	...	...	...
95	17.301213	78.475706	[Barakas, India]	5	1
96	17.260920	78.386497	[India]	4	1
97	17.236604	78.429977	[Rajiv Gandhi International Airport, Opp KFC (...	15	14
98	17.236599	78.429579	[Rajiv Gandhi International Airport, Hyderabad...	15	14
99	17.309767	78.475790	[India]	4	0

Figure 15.15 Result 1 after applying methodology.

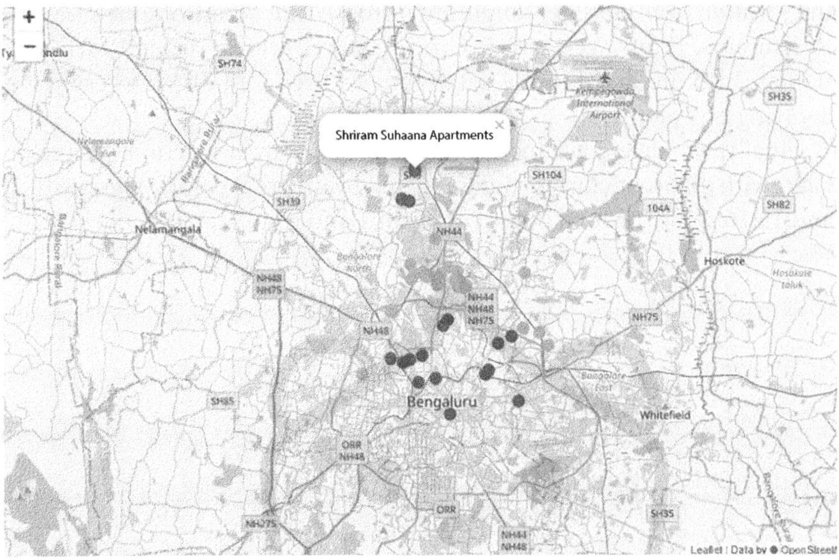

Figure 15.16 Result 2 after applying methodology.

15.8 Conclusion

It was a very insightful and a great learning journey through entire project creation. We were able to build a view of the project. In the entire process we learned about many new methods that are used in Exploratory Data Analysis, for example, K-Means clustering, methods for finding optimum value of K (Elbow Method, Silhouette Analysis) and plotting the results on a map using Folium. We also got exact locations of all the restaurants, groceries, and gyms using Foursquare API.

15.9 Future

An emerging technology or science in which big data technology **extracts meaning**, **patterns**, and **insights** from complex geospatial datasets. By finding hidden patterns from different sources of datasets, this technology **scales the analysis of big data**. Figure 15.17 show the application of geo analytics [41–46].

☐ **Crime Incidents:** location of crimes with time stamps
proximity of the nearest police stations
☐ **Environmental Monitoring:** Monitoring carbon monoxide creating space-time cubes
☐ **Traffic Accidents:** analysing traffic accidents at blind intersections
☐ **Service Vehicles:** locations of service vehicles
☐ **Trade Areas:** market area and potential customer

☐ **Crime Incidents:** location of crimes with time stamps
proximity of the nearest police stations
☐ **Environmental Monitoring:** Monitoring carbon monoxide
☐ creating space-time cubes
Traffic Accidents: analysing traffic accidents at blind intersections
☐ **Service Vehicles:** locations of service vehicles
☐ **Trade Areas:** market area and potential customer

Figure 15.17 Applications of geo analytics.

Acknowledgment

This work was supported by the Deanship of Scientific Research, the Vice Presidency for Graduate Studies and Scientific Research, King Faisal University, Saudi Arabia (GrantA121).

References

1. Sanjar, K., Bekhzod, O., Kim, J., Paul, A., Kim, J., Missing data imputation for geolocation-based price prediction using KNN–MCF method. *ISPRS Int. J. Geo-Inf.*, *9*, 4, 227, 2020.
2. Rakhimberdiev, E., Senner, N. R., Verhoeven, M. A., Winkler, D. W., Bouten, W., Piersma, T., Comparing inferences of solar geolocation data against high-precision GPS data: annual movements of a double-tagged black-tailed godwit. *J. Avian Biol.*, 47, 4, 589–596, 2016.
3. Broekman, A. and Gräbe, P.J., A low-cost, mobile real-time kinematic geolocation service for engineering and research applications. *HardwareX*, *10*, e00203, 2021.
4. Sehgal, M., Arya, A., Gaba, S., Nagpal, S., AI for Tourism: Pioneering New Frontiers in the Industry, in: *2024 International Conference on Computational Intelligence and Computing Applications (ICCICA)*, vol. 1, pp. 280–285, IEEE, May, 2024.
5. Singh, S. and Gill, N.S., Analysis and Study of K-Means Clustering Algorithm, in: *IJERT*, Dept of Computer Science & Applications, M. D. University, Rohtak, Haryana, 2013.
6. Sreelatha, G., Dachepalli, V., Sahiti, G., Data Analysis for Students Based on Geolocation Approach. *IInt. J. Interpr. Enigma Eng.*, 1, 3, 33–41, 2024.
7. Mavoa, J., Coghlan, S., Nansen, B., "It's About Safety Not Snooping": Parental Attitudes to Child Tracking Technologies and Geolocation Data. *Surveillance Soc.*, *21*, 1, 45–60, 2023.
8. Bähr, S., Haas, G.C., Keusch, F., Kreuter, F., Trappmann, M., Missing data and other measurement quality issues in mobile geolocation sensor data. *Soc. Sci. Comput. Rev.*, *40*, 1, 212–235, 2022.
9. Ochoa Gomez, C., Willingness to participate in geolocation-based research. *PLoS One*, *17*, 12, e0278416, 2022.
10. Yin, B. and Leurent, F., Exploring individual activity-travel patterns based on geolocation data from mobile phones. *Transp. Res. Rec.*, *2675*, 12, 771–783, 2021.
11. Cui, M., Introduction to the k-means clustering algorithm based on the elbow method. *Accounting Auditing Finance*, *1*, 1, 5–8, 2020.
12. Humaira, H. and Rasyidah, R., Determining the appropiate cluster number using Elbow method for K-Means algorithm, in: *Proceedings of the 2nd*

Workshop on Multidisciplinary and Applications (WMA) 2018, Padang, Indonesia, 24-25 January 2018, 2020, February.

13. Sammouda, R. and El-Zaart, A., An optimized approach for prostate image segmentation using K-means clustering algorithm with elbow method. *Comput. Intell. Neurosci., 2021*, 2021.
14. Syakur, M.A., Khotimah, B.K., Rochman, E.M.S., Satoto, B.D., Integration k-means clustering method and elbow method for identification of the best customer profile cluster, in: *IOP Conference Series: Materials Science and Engineering*, vol. 336, IOP Publishing, p. 012017, 2018, April.
15. Lester, J.N., Cho, Y., Lochmiller, C.R., Learning to do qualitative data analysis: A starting point. *Hum. Resour. Dev. Rev., 19*, 1, 94–106, 2020.
16. Hariri, R.H., Fredericks, E.M., Bowers, K.M., Uncertainty in big data analytics: survey, opportunities, and challenges. *J. Big Data, 6*, 1, 1–16, 2019.
17. El-Hasnony, I.M., Barakat, S.I., Elhoseny, M., Mostafa, R.R., Improved feature selection model for big data analytics. *IEEE Access, 8*, 66989–67004, 2020.
18. Sinaga, K.P. and Yang, M.S., Unsupervised K-means clustering algorithm. *IEEE Access, 8*, 80716–80727, 2020.
19. Juneja, A., Juneja, S., Bali, V., Jain, V., Upadhyay, H., Artificial intelligence and cybersecurity: current trends and future prospects, in: *The Smart Cyber Ecosystem for Sustainable Development*, pp. 431–441, 2021.
20. Dutta, M., Gupta, D., Juneja, S., Shah, A., Shaikh, A., Shukla, V., Kumar, M., Boosting of fruit choices using machine learning-based pomological recommendation system. *SN Appl. Sci., 5*, 9, 241, 2023.
21. Arya, A., Malik, S.K., Software Fault Prediction using K-Mean-Based Machine Learning Approach. *IInt. J. Perform. Eng.*, 19, 2, 133, 2023.
22. Hammad, R., Irfan, P., Mukti, M.T.P., Geolocation data incorporation in Mapbox for comprehensive mapping of tourism areas on Lombok Island. *Matrix: Jurnal Manajemen Teknologi dan Informatika*, 14, 1, 33–42, 2024.
23. Nauman, A., Uppal, M., Gupta, D., Alroobaea, R., Muminov, B., Tao, Y., Machine learning-based defect prediction model using multilayer perceptron algorithm for escalating the reliability of the software. *J. Supercomputing*, 1–26, 2023.
24. Kishan, S.R., Kakunuri, K.S., Raj Parasa, A., Patlolla, V., Gamini, P., Exploratory Analysis on Geo-Locational Data, in: *2022 International Conference on Automation, Computing and Renewable Systems (ICACRS)*, Pudukkottai, India, pp. 1–4, 2022, doi: 10.1109/ICACRS55517.2022.10029164.
25. Tavares, J., Ribeiro, J., Fontes, T., Detection of vehicle-based operations from geolocation data. *Transp. Res. Procedia*, 2022.
26. Whalley, W.B., Enhancing the Digital Earth *via* Digital Decimal Geolocation and the FAIR Data Principles. *Earth Sci. Syst. Soc., 4*, 10110, 2024.
27. Wu, C., Ye, X., Ren, F., Wan, Y., Ning, P., Du, Q., Spatial and social media data analytics of housing prices in Shenzhen, China. *PLoS One*, 11, e0164553, 2016.

28. Mohta, Y., Singh, U., Arya, A., NLP-Enabled Bot for Managing Third-Party Risk, in: *2024 International Conference on Computational Intelligence and Computing Applications (ICCICA)*, vol. 1, pp. 131–135, IEEE, May 2024.
29. Utomo, M.N.Y., Adji, T.B., Ardiyanto, I., Geolocation prediction in social media data using text analysis: A review, in: *2018 International Conference on Information and Communications Technology (ICOIACT)*, IEEE, pp. 84–89, 2018, March.
30. Xu, G., Gao, S., Daneshmand, M., Wang, C., Liu, Y., A survey for mobility big data analytics for geolocation prediction. *IEEE Wireless Commun.*, *24*, 1, 111–119, 2016.
31. Vanitha, C.N., Sathyamoorthy, M., Dhanaraj, R.K., Rai, P., V, G., Manikantan, M., Exploration of Ripe Raw and Defective Tomatoes with Deep Learning Techniques, in: *2023 Second International Conference on Augmented Intelligence and Sustainable Systems (ICAISS)*, vol. 2023, IEEE, 2023.
32. Gondree, M. and Peterson, Z.N., Geolocation of data in the cloud, in: *Proceedings of the Third ACM Conference on Data and Application Security and Privacy*, pp. 25–36, 2013, February.
33. Han, B., Cook, P., Baldwin, T., Geolocation prediction in social media data by finding location indicative words, in: *Proceedings of COLING 2012*, pp. 1045–1062, 2012, December.
34. Singh, A., Ajmera, G., Singh, J.N., Data Analysis using ML on Geolocational Data, in: *2022 4th International Conference on Advances in Computing, Communication Control and Networking (ICAC3N)*, IEEE, pp. 6–10, 2022, December.
35. Pérez-Arnal, R., Conesa, D., Alvarez-Napagao, S., Suzumura, T., Català, M., Alvarez-Lacalle, E., Garcia-Gasulla, D., Comparative analysis of geolocation information through mobile-devices under different COVID-19 mobility restriction patterns in Spain. *ISPRS Int. J. Geo-Inf.*, *10*, 2, 73, 2021.
36. Lee, S.J., Liu, H., Ward, M.D., Lost in space: Geolocation in event data. *Political Sci. Res. Methods*, *7*, 4, 871–888, 2019.
37. George, S., Seles, J.K.S., Brindha, D., Jebaseeli, T.J., Vemulapalli, L., Geopositional Data Analysis Using Clustering Techniques to Assist Occupants in a Specific City. *Eng. Proc.*, *59*, 1, 8, 2023.
38. McKitrick, M.K., Schuurman, N., Crooks, V.A., Collecting, analyzing, and visualizing location-based social media data: review of methods in GIS-social media analysis. *GeoJournal*, *88*, 1, 1035–1057, 2023.
39. Kumar, S.A., Muchahari, M.K., Poonkuntran, S., Kumar, L.S., Dhanaraj, R.K., Karthikeyan, P., Application of hybrid capsule network model for malaria parasite detection on microscopic blood smear images, in: *Multimedia Tools and Applications*, Springer Science and Business Media LLC, 2024, https://doi.org/10.1007/s11042-024-19062-6.
40. Peixoto, P.S., Marcondes, D., Peixoto, C., Oliva, S.M., Modeling future spread of infections *via* mobile geolocation data and population dynamics. An application to COVID-19 in Brazil. *PLoS One*, *15*, 7, e0235732, 2020.

41. Laki, S., Mátray, P., Hága, P., Sebők, T., Csabai, I., Vattay, G., Spotter: A model based active geolocation service, in: *2011 Proceedings IEEE INFOCOM*, IEEE, pp. 3173–3181, 2011, April.
42. Arya, A. and Gupta, S., A cognitive model of navigation and path finding using cellular automata agent, in: *2015 International Conference on Advances in Computer Engineering and Applications*, IEEE, pp. 512–516, 2015, March.
43. Chawla, P., *et al.*, Artificial intelligent systems in smart medical healthcare: Current trends. *Int. J. Adv. Sci. Technol.*, 29.10, 1476–1484, 2020.
44. Juneja, A., *et al.*, Artificial intelligence and cybersecurity: current trends and future prospects. *Smart Cyber Ecosyst. Sustain. Dev.*, 431–441, 2021.
45. Monga, C., *et al.*, Sustainable network by enhancing attribute-based selection mechanism using Lagrange interpolation. *Sustainability*, 14, 10, 20226082.
46. Zhang, Y., *et al.*, Improving college ideological and political education based on deep learning. *Int. J. Inf. Commun. Technol.*, 24, 42024, 431–447.
47. Soni, T., *et al.*, Explicability of artificial intelligence in healthcare 5.0, in: *2023 International Conference on Artificial Intelligence and Smart Communication (AISC)*, IEEE, 2023.
48. Arya, A., *et al.*, Heart disease prediction with machine learning and virtual reality: from future perspective, in: *Extended Reality for Healthcare Systems*, pp. 209–228, Academic Press, 2023.
49. Dhall, A., *et al.*, Machine Learning Algorithms for Industry Using Image Sensing, in: *Healthcare Solutions Using Machine Learning and Informatics*, pp. 75–97, Auerbach Publications, 2022.

Index

Also of Interest

Check out these other related titles from Scrivener Publishing

Artificial Intelligence Enabled Businesses: How to Develop Strategies for Innovation, Edited by Sweta Dixit, Mohit Maurya, Vishal Jain and Geetha Subramaniam, ISBN: 9781394233977. This book has a multidimensional perspective on AI solutions for business innovation and real-life case studies to achieve competitive advantage and drive growth in the evolving digital landscape.

Artificial Intelligence-Based System Models in Healthcare, Edited by A. Jose Anand, K. Kalaiselvi and Jyotir Moy Chatterjee, ISBN: 9781394242498. *Artificial Intelligence-Based System Models in Healthcare* provides a comprehensive and insightful guide to the transformative applications of AI in the healthcare system.

Quantum Computing and Artificial Intelligence: The Industry Use Cases, Edited by Pethuru Raj, B. Sundaravadivazhagan, Mariya Ouaissa, V. Kavitha and K. Shantha Kumari, ISBN: 9781394242368. This groundbreaking volume provides a comprehensive understanding of the synergistic relationship between quantum computing and artificial intelligence and their transformative potential across various industries.

Internet of Medicine for Smart Healthcare, Edited by Abhishek Kumar, Narayan Vyas, Pramod Singh Rathore, Abhineet Anand, and Pooja Dixit, ISBN: 9781394272235. This book provides in-depth explanations and discussions of the latest applications of AI, machine learning, and the Internet of Medicine, offering readers the cutting edge on this rapidly growing technology that has the potential to transform healthcare and improve patient outcomes.

Artificial Intelligence and Cybersecurity in Healthcare, Edited by Rashmi Agrawal, Pramod Singh Rathore, Ganesh Gopal Devarajan, and Rajiva Ranjan Divivedi, ISBN: 9781394229796. *Artificial Intelligence and Cybersecurity in Healthcare* offers a vital exploration of the intersection of artificial intelligence and cybersecurity within healthcare Cyber Physical Systems, equipping readers with knowledge on how to navigate the transformative yet complex technological landscape shaping modern patient care and data protection.

Explainable Artificial Intelligence in the Healthcare Industry, Edited by Abhishek Kumar, T. Ananth Kumar, Prasenjit Das, Chetan Sharma, and Ashutosh Kumar Dubey, ISBN: 9781394249268. Discover the essential insights and practical applications of explainable AI in healthcare that will empower professionals and enhance patient trust with Explainable AI in Healthcare, a must-have resource for anyone looking to navigate the future of medical practices with confidence.

Printed and bound by CPI Group (UK) Ltd, Croydon, CR0 4YY
17/09/2026
14964262-0004